John Mounteney Lely

The Law of Municipal Corporations

Containing the Municipal Corporations Act, 1882, and the Enactments Incorporated

therewith

John Mounteney Lely

The Law of Municipal Corporations
Containing the Municipal Corporations Act, 1882, and the Enactments Incorporated therewith

ISBN/EAN: 9783337251284

Printed in Europe, USA, Canada, Australia, Japan

Cover: Foto ©Suzi / pixelio.de

More available books at **www.hansebooks.com**

THE LAW OF MUNICIPAL CORPORATIONS.

THE

LAW OF

PAL CORPORATIO

CONTAINING THE

AL CORPORATIO

AND THE

TMENTS INCORPORATED,

ECTION OF SUPPLEM

INCLUDING THEREI

CTRIC LIGHTIN

WITH NOTE

By J. M. LEL

BARRISTER-AT-LAW,

itor of " Chitty's Statutes of P

LONDON:

S AND SONS, 119, CHANCER

RY SWEET, 3, CHANCERY LAN

Law Publishers and Booksellers.

1882.

LONDON :
PRINTED BY C. F. ROWORTH, BREAM'S BUILDINGS,

PREFACE.

————◆————

THE Municipal Corporations Act, 1882, is a consolidation of some forty Statutes, or parts of Statutes, "with some amendments," and it incorporates by reference such portions of the Parliamentary and Municipal Registration Act, the Ballot Act, and the Corrupt Practices Act, as are applicable to Municipal Corporations.

In the present book care has been taken to trace the various sources of each section, to point out the amendments effected where they could be discovered, and to give references to cases under the repealed Acts where applicable or likely to be useful. Special attention has also been given to facilitating reference, the marginal notes in particular (which have no legal value for the purposes of construction) being occasionally altered and frequently added to. Such parts of the incorporated enactments as are applicable to Municipal Corporations are printed separately, and the parts of such enactments which are not so applicable are wholly omitted, the omissions being marked by asterisks.

It has also been deemed adv█ selection from the numerous e█ specially affect Municipal Corpo█ which will be found Leeman's Act█ the consolidation as being appl█ governing bodies besides Town █ the Electric Lighting Act, 188█ other such enactments is given in█

The short history and summ█ hoped, be found useful not only█ may be approaching the subject fo█ but also to other readers.

THE TEMPLE,
   November, 1882.

TABLE OF CONTENTS.

—◆—

* *Detailed Tables of Contents are prefixed to each Statute.*

—◆—

APPENDIX.

TABLE OF CASES.

Law of Municipal Corporations.

HISTORY AND SUMMARY.

A MUNICIPAL corporation is a body of persons inhabiting the same town, having by law the powers of acting as one person, of holding and perpetually transmitting the corporate property, and of regulating the internal government of the town.

From very early times the principal towns in England were governed by such corporations, deriving their authority in every case from infinitely varying charters, granted by the Crown, at various dates, in order that they might " be well and quietly governed," becoming in many cases possessed of much land and money, and large charitable funds. They generally exercised their authority through smaller bodies, called "town councils," presided over by a mayor, and having superior officers called "aldermen." The jurisdiction of the county justices was in many cases excluded by a clause commonly called the " non-intromittant " clause of the charter, and separate commissions of the peace were issued and confirmed to persons having no qualification by landed estate. From these borough justices an appeal lay to the recorder, who was constituted by the charter a court of quarter sessions for the borough, and in many cases also judge of a borough civil court having a limited local jurisdiction.

The town councils being either self elected or owing their election in great measure to improper means, and diverting their revenues from their legitimate uses, and even misappropriating to themselves their charitable funds, there gradually came to prevail amongst the inhabitants

of a great majority of the incorporated towns a general
dissatisfaction with their municipal institutions. Shortly
after the passing of the Reform Bill of 1832, therefore,
a royal commission was appointed to examine into these
grievances; and the report of the commissioners, which
concluded with the representation—founded on a series of
local inquiries—that "the existing municipal corporations
of England and Wales neither possessed nor deserved the
confidence or respect of her Majesty's subjects, and that a
thorough reform must be effected before they could
become useful and efficient instruments of local government," quickly led to the passing of the Municipal Corporation Act of 1835 (5 & 6 Will. 4, c. 76).

This Act dealt with 178 of the 282 corporations visited
by the commissioners, and established therein one uniform government and one uniform franchise applicable
to all. The main provisions of the Act were these :—
All existing charters and rights thereunder which were
inconsistent with the Act were annulled, with savings for
certain special rights of property only. The qualification
for the franchise was fixed at three years' occupation of a
house or shop within the borough, or seven miles of it,
provided that the occupier had been rated to the poor
rate and paid the rate, and been "enrolled" on the
burgess roll, to be made up from burgess lists by the
overseers of each parish, and revised in open court by the
mayor with the assistance of two assessors to be chosen
by the burgesses. An annual election of councillors by
the burgesses was appointed to be held by open voting,
the number of councillors for each borough being fixed
by the schedule to the Act. The councillors elected the
mayor and aldermen, the mayor holding office for one
year, the aldermen for six years, and the councillors themselves for three years, one third-part of the council going
out of office annually. The larger boroughs were divided
into "wards," as specified in the schedule to the Act, and
an election of councillors was appointed for each ward by
the burgesses qualified in that ward. Power was given

to the Crown, on petition of the council, to grant to a borough a separate commission of the peace, and a separate Court of Quarter Sessions.

It was also enacted that, on petition of the inhabitants to the Sovereign, any other towns besides those scheduled to the Act might receive a charter, and become subject to the provisions of the Act upon consideration of the petition by the Privy Council, and it may be here remarked that Manchester, Birmingham, and many other towns of importance, became subject to the Act by this procedure, and that the Corporation of London has always been exempt from the provisions of the Municipal Corporations Acts.

Such was the Act of 1835, the main provisions of which have remained unaltered. Its general arrangement was by no means good, its phraseology very cumbrous, its sections lengthy and ill put together, and it was defective in many points of detail. Of the numerous amending Acts which were passed from time to time, the only ones worth mentioning here are as follows :—

In 1836, it was enacted by 6 & 7 Will. 4, c. 104, that any person elected to a corporate office might resign it on payment of a fine, and by 6 & 7 Will. 4, c. 105, the powers of justices of the peace under local Acts of Parliament were transferred to the council, and the recorder was constituted judge of the borough civil court.

In 1841, the corporations became rateable to the poor rate by 4 & 5 Vict. c. 48.

In 1869, by 32 & 33 Vict. c. 55, the term of occupation requisite for the franchise was shortened from three years to one, and women were admitted to the franchise.

In 1872, secret voting by ballot was established by the Ballot Act, 1872 (35 & 36 Vict. c. 33), and provision was made for the better prevention of corrupt practices at elections, and for establishing a tribunal for the trial of the validity of such elections, by "The Corrupt Practices (Municipal Elections) Act, 1872" (35 & 36 Vict. c. 60).

In 1872, also, "Leeman's Act" (35 & 36 Vict. c. 91) authorized town councils to apply the borough revenues to

the promoting or opposing parliamentary and other proceedings for the benefit of the inhabitants; subject, however, to the important condition precedent that no expense
should be incurred after the deposit of a bill until the promotion or opposition should have had the consent of the
owners and ratepayers in the borough.

In 1875, the Municipal Elections Act, 1875 (38 & 39
Vict. c. 40), assimilated the procedure on nomination of
candidates for municipal offices to that in use at parliamentary elections, repeating, however, *mutatis mutandis*,
and not incorporating, by reference, the provisions of the
Ballot Act.

In 1877, the Municipal Corporations (New Charters)
Act, 1877 (40 & 41 Vict. c. 69), substituted more detailed
provisions for the single section of the Act of 1835, which
empowered the sovereign to apply that Act to newly-
incorporated towns.

In 1878, the Parliamentary and Municipal Registration
Act, 1878 (41 & 42 Vict. c. 26), provided for the concurrent revision, under the Parliamentary Registration Acts,
of the municipal burgess lists and the lists of parliamentary voters. This Act applies to parliamentary boroughs
only.

The Municipal Corporations Act, 1882 (45 & 46
Vict. c. 50), which had been originally introduced by
Lord Cairns in the House of Lords in 1878, was introduced in the House of Commons by Mr. Hibbert, the
President of the Local Government Board, and passed
after but little discussion in either House of Parliament.
Prepared in pursuance of the recommendation of the
Statute Law Committee, this is almost entirely a Consolidation Act, wholly repealing the Act of 1835 and the
greater portion of the amending Acts, and replacing them
by a well drawn and symmetrical statute of 260 sections
and 9 schedules. Notwithstanding its length and general
excellence of arrangement, however, the Act is very far
from being a " code." It follows the old law in incorporating by reference the Parliamentary Registration

Acts in respect of the revision of the burgess lists in parliamentary boroughs, and the Ballot Act and Corrupt Practices Acts (which are only temporary statutes, so that provision has to be made for the expiration of the Ballot Act) in respect of elections generally. Neither does the Act contain any list of the towns subject to its provisions, or of the numbers of councillors, aldermen, and wards in each borough; information on these heads must be gathered from the schedules to the Act of 1835 and other sources. "Leeman's Act," too, is omitted from the consolidation, and the large body of local government law must be sought for in the Public Health Act, the Towns Improvement Clauses Act, the Towns Police Clauses Act, or in the varying "local Acts" applicable in most boroughs of importance.

The amendments effected by the Act of 1882 are comparatively few and unimportant. Generally speaking, the same substantive law reappears in altered phraseology and arrangement—although it may often turn out to be difficult to say whether a different legal meaning is intended by the altered phraseology—and the legislature has taken occasion to affirm many judicial interpretations of the old Acts. The preamble, however, expressly referring to "amendments," it may be well to state in this place that the principal alterations effected are these :—

The power of the town clerk to appoint a deputy (sect. 17).

The requirement of a *written* resignation of a corporate office (sect. 36).

The power of the clerk of the peace to appoint a deputy (sect. 164).

The dispensing with the necessity of a new appointment on increase of salary of the recorder (sect. 163).

The power of a deputy recorder to form a second court of quarter sessions (sect. 168, sub-s. 9).

The restriction of the number of the watch committee to one-third of the number of the council (sect. 190).

The power of the Privy Council to amend a scheme of incorporation (sect. 218).

The power of borough constables to take bail by day (sect. 227).

The enactment that councillors present at a meeting and not voting cannot be counted in a majority (Sched. II., Rule 10).

Such is the Municipal Corporations Act, 1882. It is now proposed to set out shortly the effect of the Act and the Acts which it incorporates, making some little mention also of the principal statutes from which municipal corporations derive special powers.

SUMMARY.

Places to which the Act of 1882 applies.

The Act of 1882 applies to the following 246 towns and no others:—

178 boroughs named in the schedules to the Act of 1835.

68 boroughs subsequently incorporated under section 141 of that Act and the Act of 1877.

All towns which may hereafter be incorporated under section 210 of the Act of 1882.

Act of 1882, s. 6, p. 2, post; Appendix, p. 343, post.

The Municipal Corporation.

A place to which the Act applies is governed by a municipal corporation, consisting of the burgesses, acting through the council, and styled a borough.

Act of 1882, s. 8, p. 4, post.

The Wards.

Larger boroughs, as mentioned in Schedule A. to the Act of 1835, or as divided upon petition of two-thirds of the council, are divided into wards for the purposes of elections.

Act of 1882, s. 30, p. 18, post; Appendix, p. 343, post.

The Burgesses.

The burgesses are all qualified persons enrolled as such and no other persons. Qualified persons are all persons, except aliens, infants, married women, recipients of parochial relief, and felons, who—

For twelve months prior to any 15th day of July have occupied a house or part of a house, a warehouse, counting house, shop, or other building in the borough, *and* have resided in the borough, or within seven miles of it, *and* have been rated to the poor rates in respect of such qualifying property, *and* have on or before the 20th day of the same July, " paid all such rates, including borough rates (if any) as have become payable by him in respect of such qualifying property up to the last preceding 5th of January."

Act of 1882, s. 9, p. 4, post.

THE ENROLMENT OF THE BURGESSES.

The burgess roll is a printed copy of the revised parish burgess lists, made out by the overseers of each parish situate wholly or partly within the borough.

Burgess roll.

Act of 1882, s. 48, p. 29, post.

Where the whole or part of the area of a borough is co-extensive with or included in the area of a parliamentary borough, the parish burgess lists are made out and revised under the Parliamentary and Municipal Registration Act, 1878, as follows:—

Parliamentary boroughs

On or before the 31st July the overseers are bound to make out lists of the persons entitled to be enrolled as burgesses. The lists are to state the name of each such person, his place of abode, the nature of his qualification, and the situation and description of the qualifying property. They are to be signed by the overseers, and copies of them are to be kept for sale and gratuitous inspection, and are also to be posted up at telegraph, post, and municipal offices. On or before the 25th August any person omitted from the lists, and claiming to be named therein, and any person named therein and objecting to any other person being named therein, must send notice of such claim or objection, as the case may be, to the overseers, who must, on or before the 1st of September, publish lists of the claimants and the persons objected to. On or before the 12th October the lists are to be revised by the same revising barrister who revises the lists of parliamentary voters.

Act of 1882, s. 44, p. 26, post; Registration Act, 1843, p. 170, post; Registration Act, 1878, p. 201, post.

Non-Parliamentary boroughs. Where no part of the area of a borough is co-extensive with or included in the area of a parliamentary borough, the parish burgess lists are made out as follows:—

On or before the 1st of September in every year the overseers are bound to make out a list of all persons entitled to be enrolled. Copies of the list are to be printed and published. On or before the 15th September any person omitted from the list and claiming to be named therein, and any person named therein objecting to any other person being named therein, must give notice in writing of such claim or objection, as the case may be, to the town clerk, who must during the last seven days of September publish lists of the claimants and the persons objected to.

The lists are revised by the mayor and two revising assessors (elected by the burgesses), on one of the first fifteen days of October, in open Court.

Act of 1882, sched. iii., part 1, p. 145, post.

The Council.

The councillors are elected by the enrolled burgesses on the 1st of November in every year.

Act of 1882, s. 52, p. 30, post.

Qualification. Persons qualified to be councillors are:—all fit persons, except officers of the council, revising assessors, ministers of religion, and persons interested in contracts with the council not relating to land, loans of money, or newspaper advertisements, or made by companies in which they are shareholders, who—

Are enrolled and entitled to be enrolled as burgesses, or reside within fifteen miles of the borough and possess a certain property qualification, or, except in respect of residence, would be entitled to be enrolled as burgesses.

Act of 1882, ss. 11, 12, pp. 7, 8, post.

Persons elected councillors must, unless specially exempted by reason of infirmity of body or other causes, serve the office or pay a fine not exceeding 50*l.*

Act of 1882, s. 34, p. 21, post.

The office of councillor is avoided by six months' absence or bankruptcy.

Act of 1882, s. 39, p. 24, post.

The number of councillors in each borough is that fixed **Number of councillors.** by Schedules A. and B. to the Act of 1835, or by charter in the case of a borough incorporated after the passing of that Act.

Act of 1882, s. 212, p. 113, post; Appendix, p. 346, post.

ELECTION OF COUNCIL.

At least nine days' public notice of the election must be **Notice.** given.

Act of 1882, s. 54, p. 30, post.

The nomination must be in writing subscribed by two **Nomination.** burgesses as proposer and seconder, and by eight as assenting. A candidate may be nominated in his absence and without his consent, unless he be absent from the United Kingdom, in which case the nomination is void, "unless his written consent, given within one month before the day of his nomination in the presence of two witnesses, is produced at the time of his nomination." The nomination papers must be delivered seven days at least before the day of election. On the day next after the last day for the delivery of nomination papers objections are considered by the mayor, whose decision is final if disallowing an objection, but "if allowing an objection, shall be subject to reversal on petition questioning the election or return." At least four days before the day of election the names of all persons duly nominated are to be printed and fixed on the town hall.

Act of 1882, sched. iii., part 2, p. 148, post.

Uncontested election.

If there are as many persons nominated as there are vacancies, the persons nominated are elected.

If the number of persons nominated is less than that of the vacancies, the persons nominated shall be deemed to be elected, and such of the retiring councillors as were highest on the poll at their election, or if the poll was equal or there was no poll, as are selected by the mayor, are re-elected. If there is no nomination, the retiring councillors are re-elected.

Act of 1882, s. 56, p. 31, post.

Contested election.

A contested election is, with certain unimportant modifications, conducted in the same manner as a contested parliamentary election, i.e. by secret voting in accordance with the provisions of the Ballot Act, 1872. Every person enrolled, and no other person, may vote. A voter may vote for any number of candidates not exceeding the number of vacancies, but may not give more than one vote for any one candidate. The poll is open for one day, from 9 A.M. to 4 P.M. (Greenwich time), the returning officer having power to close it earlier if one hour elapses during which no vote is tendered. A non-compliance with the rules of the Ballot Act does not necessarily avoid the election.

Act of 1882, s. 58, p. 31, post; Ballot Act, 1872, p. 236, post.

QUESTIONING OF ELECTION.

Grounds for questioning of election and limit of time.

An election may be questioned on the ground of corrupt practices, or disqualification of the person whose election was questioned, or false return, by petition presented within twenty-one days after the day on which the election was held, or within twenty-eight days after a corrupt payment specifically alleged to have been made by, or for, the person elected since the election.

Act of 1882, ss. 87, 88, pp. 43, 44, post.

An election petition is tried by a barrister of not less than fifteen years' standing, not being a member of the House of Commons, or holding any office under the Crown other than that of recorder.

Act of 1882, ss. 92, 93, pp. 45, 46, post.

Trial of election petition.

QUO WARRANTO.

If an election petition lies, an election cannot be questioned by *quo warranto*. But if a person elected becomes disqualified after election, his office may be declared void by means of an information in the nature of a *quo warranto*, to be applied for within twelve months from the time when he became disqualified.

Act of 1882, s. 87, sub-s. (2), p. 43, post; s. 225, p. 120, post.

Where quo warranto lies and limit of time for it.

THE MAYOR.

"The mayor shall be a fit person elected by the council from among the aldermen or councillors or persons qualified to be such." He is elected on the 9th of November; his election being the first business transacted by the council. He receives little, if any, remuneration. He is bound to serve or pay a fine not exceeding 100*l.*

Act of 1882, ss. 15, 34, 61, pp. 11, 21, 34, post.

Election of mayor.

The term of office of mayor is one year, but he continues in office until his successor has accepted office. He may appoint a "deputy mayor" during illness or absence, but if (except in case of illness) he is continuously absent from the borough for more than two months, he becomes disqualified for office, and also liable to the same fine as for non-acceptance of office.

Act of 1882, ss. 15, 16, 39, pp. 10, 11, 24, post.

Term of office of mayor— Effect of absence.

Principal
duties of
mayor.

The principal duties of the mayor are to preside at the meetings of the council, to revise the parish burgess lists in non-parliamentary boroughs, and to act as returning officer in parliamentary and municipal elections.

THE ALDERMEN.

Election of
aldermen.

The aldermen are fit persons, not necessarily councillors, but qualified so to be, in number one-third of the number of councillors, elected by the council on the 9th of November by signed voting-papers. Their term of office is six years, and one-half of the whole number go out of office in every third year. They receive no salary. They are obliged to accept the office or pay a fine not exceeding 50*l.*

Act of 1882, ss. 14, 34, 61, pp. 9, 21, 61, post.

Principal
duties of
aldermen.

The principal duties of an alderman are to preside at the meetings of the council in the absence of the mayor and deputy-mayor (if any), to act as returning officer at an election for a ward, and, in the absence or incapacity of the mayor, at the election of the whole borough.

MEETINGS OF THE COUNCIL.

Time for
meetings,
quorum, &c.

There are four quarterly meetings for general business. The mayor or any five councillors may at any time call a meeting for special business. Questions are decided by a majority of the members present and voting, one-third of the number of the whole council forming a quorum for ordinary purposes, and two-thirds for the passing of a bye-law.

Committees.

The council may appoint committees, "but the acts of every committee shall be submitted to the council for their approval."

Act of 1882, ss. 22, 23, and sched. 2, pp. 13, 15, 143, post.

OFFICERS OF THE COUNCIL.

Enumeration
of officers
under the
Municipal
Corporations
Act.

The officers of the council under the Municipal Corporations Act are the town clerk and treasurer, who hold office during the pleasure of the council, and may not be the same person, and "the council shall from time to time appoint such other officers as have been usually appointed in the borough, or as the council think necessary, and may at any time discontinue the appointment of any officer appearing to them not necessary to be appointed." Security must be required from, and reasonable remuneration allowed to, these officers.

Act of 1882, ss. 17—21, pp. 11—13, post.

The principal officers of the council under statutes other than the Municipal Corporations Act are the borough surveyor, the public analyst, the inspector of nuisances, the medical officer of health, and the clerk of the burial board. *Officers under statutes other than the Municipal Corporations Act.*

Public Health Act, 1875, s. 189; Sale of Food and Drugs Act, 1875, s. 10.

OFFICERS OF THE CROWN IN CERTAIN BOROUGHS.

The mayor and ex-mayor are borough justices *ex officio;* and, upon petition of the council, the Crown may grant to a borough a "separate commission of the peace," and thereupon appoint borough justices from time to time, having in a borough the same jurisdiction as county justices have in a county. They must reside in or within seven miles of the borough, or occupy a house or other property within it, but they need not be burgesses. *Borough justices.*

Act of 1882, ss. 156—158, pp. 86, 87, post.

"The justices for a borough shall, from time to time, appoint a fit person to be their clerk, to be removeable at their pleasure," and not to be interested in prosecutions. *Clerk to borough justices.*

Act of 1882, s. 159, p. 87, post.

On petition by the council to a Secretary of State the Crown may appoint as stipendiary magistrate in any borough, at a salary not exceeding that mentioned in the petition, and holding office during the pleasure of the Crown, a barrister of seven years' standing. On vacancy, a new application must be made. *Stipendiary magistrate.*

Act of 1882, s. 161, p. 88, post.

Recorder.

On petition by the council to the sovereign in council, the sovereign may grant that a separate court of quarter sessions may be held in any borough, and thereupon, and from time to time, may appoint as recorder in such borough, at a salary not exceeding that mentioned in the petition, and holding office during good behaviour, a barrister of five years' standing.

The recorder has cognizance of all matters cognizable by court of quarter sessions for counties; except that he may not allow a rate or grant a licence for the sale of intoxicating liquors. He is also judge of the "borough civil court," if there is one.

Act of 1882, ss. 162, 163, p. 89, post.

Sheriff.

It is the duty of the council of every borough, which is a county of itself, on the 9th of November in every year, to " appoint a fit person to execute the office of sheriff."

Act of 1882, s. 170, p. 94, post.

Coroner.

It is the duty of the council of a borough having a separate court of quarter sessions, to appoint from time to time a fit person, not an alderman or councillor, to be coroner of the borough. He is entitled to 1*l.* 6*s.* 8*d.* for every inquest taken. He is usually either a solicitor or a medical practitioner. He may appoint a deputy, who must be either a barrister or solicitor.

Act of 1882, s. 171, p. 95, post.

POWERS AND DUTIES OF THE COUNCIL.

Powers of the council under the Municipal Corporations Act.

Under the Municipal Corporations Act the council are the general agents of the corporation, and " shall exercise all powers vested in the corporation " by that Act or otherwise. Their special powers under the Act are:—to make bye-laws; to appoint officers; to manage the corporate property; to levy a borough rate; and, by a watch committee not exceeding one-third of their number, to levy a watch rate; and to manage the borough police.

The powers of the council under Acts other than the Municipal Corporations Act are very many and various. Their power to make bye-laws for the suppression of nuisances is limited to cases where the nuisances are " not already punishable in a summary manner by virtue of any Act in force throughout the borough."

The most important duties and powers arise under the Public Health Act, 1875 (38 & 39 Vict. c. 55), by sect. 4 of which they are constituted " urban sanitary authority " under that Act, having as such the control of sewers within the borough, and the duty of keeping them in repair ; the power, and, if required by the Local Government Board, the duty, of cleansing the streets ; the power of supplying water ; the duty of registering and superintending common lodging houses ; the duty of inspecting the borough for the detection of nuisances, and of abating and prosecuting nuisances ; the duty to take provisions against the spread of infectious diseases, and the power to establish hospitals and mortuaries ; the general control of the streets ; the power to take lands ; and the power to levy general district, private improvement, and highway rates.

If they make default in enforcing any of the provisions of the Public Health Act, which it is their duty to enforce, complaint may be made to the Local Government Board, which board, " if satisfied, after due inquiry, that the council has been guilty of the alleged default, shall make an order limiting a time for the performance of their duty in the matter of such complaint."

The council may also be appointed a burial board by Order in Council, under 20 & 21 Vict. c. 81 ; may make bye-laws as to the conveyance and storage of explosives, under sect. 67 of the Explosives Act, 1875 ; have the duty of protecting gardens and ornamental grounds, under 26 & 27 Vict. c. 13 ; may undertake the powers and duties of visiting justices of lunatic asylums ; and have the duty of

Powers of the council under Acts other than the Municipal Corporations Act.

appointing inspectors under and otherwise administering the Weights and Measures Act, 1878.

Further, they have the duty of administering the Baths and Washhouses Acts, the Labourers' Dwellings Acts, and the Public Libraries Acts, in the event of those Acts being in force within the borough.

See Appendix, p. 346, post.

MANAGEMENT OF THE BOROUGH REVENUES.

The borough fund. The income of the corporation is called the borough fund. Out of it are paid the salaries of the salaried officers, whether appointed by the Crown or by the council, the expenses of election petitions, the expenses of the revision of the burgess lists, and the expenses of providing corporate buildings, the fees of the coroner, the expenses of the borough police, and special constables, all sums payable to the county treasurer, and other necessary expenses. If there is any surplus it "shall be applied under the direction of the council for the public benefit of the inhabitants and improvement of the borough," and may also, together with the proceeds of a rate, be applied, in pursuance of a resolution of an absolute majority of the council, and, by the consent of a Secretary of State, in promoting or opposing bills in Parliament, or in prosecuting or defending any legal proceedings necessary for the promotion or protection of the interests of the inhabitants of the borough; but no further expense in promoting a bill may be incurred after the deposit of it, and no expense whatever may be incurred in opposing a bill until the promotion or opposition has had the consent of the whole body of owners and ratepayers of the borough.

Act of 1882, s. 140, and sched 5, pp. 76, 153; 35 & 36 Vict. c. 91, p. 298, post.

Order for payment out of borough fund. Payments out of the borough fund cannot, with few exceptions, be made without an order of the council,

signed by three councillors, and countersigned by the
town clerk; and any such order may be removed by certiorari into the High Court, which may discharge or confirm the order at discretion.

Act of 1882, s. 141, p. 77, post.

BOROUGH RATE.

If the borough fund is insufficient for the purposes to
which it is applicable, the council is bound to make up the
deficiency by levying a borough rate.

The borough rate is levied by the council assessing
contributions thereto on the several parishes within the
borough in proportion to the total annual value of the
hereditaments in each parish which are rateable to the poor
rate, and by ordering the overseers of the parish either to
pay or collect the amount to be contributed. The overseers may appeal to the recorder against the amount of a
contribution.

Act of 1882, ss. 144, 145, pp. 78—80, post.

WATCH RATE.

" Where at the commencement of this Act [of 1882] any
rate might be levied in a borough or in any part of a borough
for the purpose of watching solely by day or by night, or
for the purpose of watching by day or by night conjointly
with any other purpose, the council may from time to time
make and levy a watch rate on the occupiers of all hereditaments within such parts of the borough as are watched
by day and by night, and as are, from time to time, by
order of the council, declared liable to watch rate."

The rate is not to exceed eightpence in the pound on
the net annual value of the hereditaments rated thereto.

Act of 1882, s. 197, p. 106, post.

GOVERNMENT CONTROL.

The town council is subject to the control of the
Treasury in respect of certain dealings with corporate

land (*a*), of the Local Government Board in respect of accounts (*b*), of the Privy Council and Local Government Board in respect of bye-laws (*c*), and of a Secretary of State in respect of police (*d*).

GRANT OF NEW CHARTER.

A charter of incorporation may be granted by the sovereign to any town on the petition of the inhabitant householders thereof.

Act of 1882, s. 210, p. 112, post.

(*a*) Act of 1882, s. 105 et seq., post, p. 55.
(*b*) Ib. s. 28, p. 17, post.
c) Ib. s. 23, p. 15, post.
(*d*) Ib. s. 192, p. 104.

MUNICIPAL CORPORATIONS ACT, 1882.

CONTENTS:

MUNICIPAL CORPORATIONS ACT, 1882.

(45 & 46 Vict. c. 50.)

*An Act for consolidating, with Amendments, enactments re-
lating to Municipal Corporations in England and Wales.*

[18th August, 1882.

Whereas divers bodies corporate at sundry times have been
constituted in the cities, towns, and boroughs of England and
Wales, to the intent that the same might for ever be and
remain well and quietly governed:

And whereas the Act of the session of the fifth and sixth
years of the reign of King William the Fourth, chapter
seventy-six, "to provide for the regulation of Municipal
Corporations in England and Wales" (a), applies to most
of those bodies constituted before the passing of that Act,
and to every of those bodies constituted after the passing
of that Act; and that Act having been from time to time
much altered and added to by other Acts (b), it is expedient
that all the Acts aforesaid be reduced into one Act, with some
amendments (c):

Be it therefore enacted by the Queen's most excellent
Majesty, by and with the advice and consent of the lords
spiritual and temporal, and commons, in this present

(a) "The Municipal Corporations Act, 1835," which applied 'to
178 out of 282 of the bodies constituted before that Act, and to
68 bodies constituted after that Act.
(b) See these "other Acts," post, p. 139.
(c) See *e. g.*, sects. 17, 36, 163, 190, 218, 227, 237, Sched. ii.
rule 10, and Sched. iii. part 2, and notes thereto; but the amendments effected by these and other provisions of the Act are comparatively minute, although the whole phraseology and arrangement
of the law are frequently much changed.

Act of 1882
s. 1.

Parliament assembled, and by the authority of the same, as follows :—

PART I.—PRELIMINARY.

Short title.

1. This Act may be cited as the Municipal Corporations Act, 1882.

Division of
Act into
Parts.

2. This Act is divided into Parts, as follows :
PART I.—Preliminary.
PART II.—Constitution and government of borough.
PART III.—Preparations for and procedure at elections.
PART IV.—Corrupt practices and election petitions.
PART V.—Corporate property and liabilities.
PART VI.—Charitable and other trusts and powers.
PART VII.—Borough fund : borough rate : county rate.
PART VIII.—Administration of justice.
PART IX.—Police.
PART X.—Freemen.
PART XI.—Grant of charters.
PART XII.—Legal proceedings.
PART XIII.—General.

Extent.

3. This Act shall not extend to Scotland or Ireland.

The principal Scotch Acts are :—3 & 4 Will. 4, c. 76, and 39 & 40 Vict. c. 12 ; and the principal Irish Acts, 3 & 4 Vict. c. 108, and 6 & 7 Vict. c. 93.

Commence-
ment.

4. This Act shall commence and have effect from and immediately after the 31st of December, 1882.

Repeals.
* Page 139.
† Page 137.

5. The enactments described in the First Schedule * are hereby repealed, subject to the exceptions and qualifications in this Act mentioned.†

Application.

‡ Page 112.

6. This Act shall apply to every city and town to which the Municipal Corporations Act, 1835, applies at the commencement of this Act, and to any town, district, or place whereof the inhabitants are incorporated after the commencement of this Act, and whereto the provisions of the Municipal Corporation Acts are under this Act extended by charter,‡ but to no other place.

Interpreta-
tion and con-
struction.

7.—(1.) In this Act—

" Borough " means, unless a contrary intention appears, a city or town to which this Act applies :

" Municipal corporation " means the body corporate constituted by the incorporation of the inhabitants of a borough :

"Municipal Corporations Act, 1835," means the recited Act of King William the Fourth, the date of the passing whereof is the 9th of September, 1835 :

Act of 1882 s. 7.

"Municipal Corporations Acts" means this Act and any Act to be passed amending this Act :

"Burgess" includes citizen :

"Corporate seal" means the common seal of a municipal corporation :

"Corporate office" means the office of mayor, alderman, councillor, elective auditor, or revising assessor :

"Corporate office."

"Corporate land" means land belonging to or held in trust for a municipal corporation :

"Municipal election" means an election to a corporate office :

"Parliamentary borough" means any borough, city, county of a city, county of a town, place, or combination of places, returning a member to serve in parliament, and not being a county at large, or a riding, parts, or division of a county at large :

"Parliamentary borough."

"Parliamentary election" means an election of a member to serve in Parliament :

"Parish" means any place for which a separate poor rate is or can be made :

"Parish."

"Overseers" means overseers of the poor of a parish, township, or place, and includes all persons who execute the duties of overseers :

"County" does not include a county of a city or county of a town, but includes a riding, parts, division, or liberty of a county :

"Trustees" means trustees, commissioners, or directors, or the persons charged with the execution of a trust or public duty, however designated :

"Person" includes a body of persons corporate or unincorporate :

"Treasury" means the Commissioners of her Majesty's Treasury :

"The Secretary of State" means one of her Majesty's principal secretaries of state :

"High Court" means her Majesty's High Court of Justice :

"Justice" means one of her Majesty's justices of the peace :

"Borough civil court" means an inferior court of record for the trial of civil actions which by charter, custom, or otherwise, is or ought to be holden in a borough, but does not include a county court:

"Bank of England" means the governor and company of the Bank of England:

"Schedule" means schedule to this Act, and "part" means part of this Act:

"Writing" includes print, and "written" includes printed.

(2.) Words in this Act referring to a borough, municipal corporation, authority, officer, or office, shall be construed distributively, as referring to each borough, corporation, authority, officer, or office to which or to whom the provision is applicable.

(3.) Words in this Act referring to a parish shall be construed, unless a contrary intention appears, as referring to every parish situate wholly or in part in a borough.

(4.) The schedules shall be read and have effect as if they were part of this Act.

PART II.—Constitution and Government of Borough.

Corporate Name.

8. The municipal corporation of a borough shall bear the name of the mayor, aldermen, and burgesses of the borough, or, in the case of a city, the mayor, aldermen, and citizens of the city.

This re-enacts a part of sect. 6 of the Act of 1835; for the various styles of the corporate bodies before that Act, see Schedule A. to that Act.

Burgesses.

9.—(1.) A person shall not be deemed a burgess for any purpose of this Act unless he is enrolled as a burgess.

(2.) A person shall not be entitled to be enrolled as a burgess unless he is qualified as follows:

(a.) Is of full age (¹); and

(b.) Is on the 15th of July in any year, and has been during the whole of the then last preceding twelve months, in occupation, [joint or several (*d*)], of any

---

(*d*) Words in brackets new; they affirm *R.* v. *Mayor of Exeter*, L. R., 4 Q. B. 114.

Act of 1882
s. 9.

house, warehouse, counting-house, shop, or other building (*e*) (in this Act referred to as qualifying property) in the borough; and

(c.) Has during the whole ([2]) of those twelve months re-sided ([3]) in the borough, or within seven miles (*f*) thereof; and

(d.) Has been rated ([4]) in respect of the qualifying property to all poor rates made during those twelve months for the parish wherein the property is situate; and

(e.) Has on or before the 20th of the same July paid ([5]) all such rates, including borough rates (if any), as have become payable by him in respect of the qualifying property up to the then last preceding 5th of January.

(3.) Every person so qualified shall be entitled to be enrolled as a burgess, unless he (*g*)—

Disqualifications.

(a.) Is an alien ([6]); or

(b.) Has within the twelve months aforesaid received union or parochial relief or other alms ([7]); or

(c.) Is disentitled under any Act of Parliament ([8]).

This section reproduces in effect, but in terms more expressly exhaustive, sect. 1 of the Act of 1869, 32 & 33 Vict. c. 55 (which, repealing sect. 9 of the Act of 1835, amended the law by, *inter alia*, shortening the required period of occupation from three years to one, and admitting women to the franchise), as amended by sect. 7 of the Act of 1878 (which merely substituted " 15th " for " last day " of July).

The section is very similar to sect. 3 of the Representation of the People Act, 1867 (30 & 31 Vict. c. 102), so that decisions on that section will be, in most cases, applicable to this. Upon sect. 1 of the Act of 1869 there are no reported decisions. Upon sect. 9 of the Act of 1835 there were many, and some of them may perhaps be still applicable.

([1]) *Infants.*]—A question might be raised in parliamentary boroughs whether *Hargreaves*, app., *Hopper*, resp. (1 C. P. D. 195), applies, so as to require the party to have been of full age on the 15th day of July in the qualifying year. It is submitted that the case does not apply, on the ground that the Legislature could not have intended to work a disfranchisement by the Act of 1878, much less a partial disfranchisement.

([2]) *Successive Occupation, &c.*]—As to successive occupation and

---

(*e*)　Or part of a house.　See sect. 31, post.

(*f*)　As to measuring distance, see sect. 231, post.

(*g*)　Or she.　See sect. 63, p. 35, post.

**Act of 1882
s. 9.** rating, and power of occupier to claim to be rated instead of owner, see sects. 32, 33, post.

(³) *Break of Residence.*]—A break of residence is constituted by the party quitting, by himself, his family, and his servants, without the power or intention of returning (see *Ford* v. *Pye*, L. R., 9 C. P. 269; 43 L. J., C. P. 21; 29 L. T. 684; 22 W. R. 159; *Whithorn*, app., *Thomas*, resp., 7 M. & G. 1); as *e. g.* if he should let the whole of his house furnished for ever so short a time, or if he be a clerk serving under articles to a solicitor outside the borough. (See *Ford* v. *Drew*, 5 C. P. D. 59; 49 L. J., C. P. 172.)

(⁴) *" Has been rated."*]—The rate must have been both signed by the parish officers and allowed by the justices during the twelve months. (See *Jones* v. *Butt*, L. R., 4 C. P. 468.)

(⁵) *Payment of Rates.*]—Payment by the party's own act is essential; payment by another for and by way of gift to him is no payment within the statute (*Reg.* v. *Mayor of Bridgnorth*, 10 A. & E. 66); and is, moreover, a "corrupt practice" by 30 & 31 Vict. c. 102, s. 49 (post, p. 269). The rate must be a legal one for the disqualification by nonpayment to operate. (*Reg.* v. *Mayor of New Windsor*, 7 Q. B. 908.)

(⁶) *Alien.*]—An alien is a person born out of the dominions of the Crown to an alien father. As to naturalization and certificate thereof, which would seem to confer the municipal franchise amongst other privileges, see Naturalization Act, 1870 (33 Vict. c. 14), s. 7.

(⁷) *Receipt of Alms.*]—For modifications as to medical relief, &c., see sect. 33, sub-sect. 4, post. Relief to a man's father is not relief to himself within this provision. (See *Reg.* v. *Ireland*, L. R., 3 Q. B. 130; 37 L. J., Q. B. 73.) The "other alms" must be strictly parochial. (See *Reg.* v. *Mayor of Lichfield*, 2 Q. B. 693.)

(⁸) *Statutory Disqualifications.*]—By 33 & 34 Vict. c. 23, s. 2, a conviction for any felony, if followed by a sentence of penal servitude or imprisonment with hard labour, or for more than twelve months, works a disqualification until the party shall have served his time or been pardoned. A conviction of a corrupt practice at a school board election works a disqualification for six years, by sect. 91 of the Education Act, 1870 (33 & 34 Vict. c. 75).

Council; Mayor, Aldermen, and Councillors.

Constitution of council. **10.**—(1.) The municipal corporation of a borough shall be capable of acting by the council of the borough, and the council shall exercise all powers vested in the corporation by this Act or otherwise.

(2.) The council shall consist of the mayor, aldermen, and councillors.

This section is taken from sect. 6 of the Act of 1835, which seems to have given (as the present section seems to give) the right of suing and being sued in the name of the council. It has been the general practice, however, since the Act of 1835, for a corporation

to sue or be sued as "The Mayor, Aldermen, and Burgesses of
 ," and, it is presumed, that this practice will still be ad-
hered to.

11.—(1.) The councillors shall be fit persons (¹) elected by
the burgesses.

(2.) A person shall not be qualified to be elected or to be
a councillor, unless he—

(a.) Is enrolled and entitled (*g*) to be enrolled as a burgess; or

(b.) Being entitled to be so enrolled in all respects except
that of residence, is resident beyond seven miles but
within fifteen miles (*h*) of the borough, and is entered
in the separate non-resident list directed by this Act
to be made; * and

(c.) In either of those cases, is seised or possessed of real
or personal property or both, to the value or amount,
in the case of a borough having four or more wards,
of one thousand pounds, and in the case of any
other borough, of five hundred pounds, or is rated
to the poor rate in the borough, in the case of a
borough having four or more wards, on the annual
value of thirty pounds, and in the case of any other
borough of fifteen pounds.

* Sect. 49.

(3.) Provided, that every person shall be qualified to be
elected and to be a councillor, who is, at the time of election,
qualified to elect to the office of councillor; which last-
mentioned qualification for being elected shall be alternative
for and shall not repeal or take away any other qualification (²).

(4.) But if a person qualified under the last foregoing proviso ceases for six months to reside in the borough, he shall
cease to be qualified under that proviso, and his office shall
become vacant, unless he was at the time of his election and
continues to be qualified in some other manner.

This section is taken from sects. 25 and 28 of the Act of 1835, as
amended by sect. 3 of the Act of 1869 and by sect. 1 of the Town
Councils and Local Boards Act, 1880 (43 Vict. c. 17).

(¹) "*Fit Persons.*"]—There is no decided case, so far as the Editor
is aware, in which the power of the burgesses to select whom they
please, not being expressly disqualified by statute, has been contested. A woman would seem to be ineligible at common law,

(*g*) This affirms *Middleton* v. *Simpson*, 5 C. P. D. 183.
(*h*) As to measuring distance, see sect. 231, post.

and perhaps a quo warranto would lie under this section to remove a person grossly unfit. As to amotion by the council, see note to next section.

(²) *The alternative Qualification.*]—The alternative qualification consists in being qualified to elect, whether the party be enrolled in any burgess list or not.

Disqualifications for councillor.

12.—(1.) A person shall be disqualified for being elected and for being a councillor, if and while he—

Officer of council.

(a.) Is an elective auditor or a revising assessor, or holds any office or place of profit, other than that of mayor or sheriff, in the gift or disposal of the council; or

Minister.

(b.) Is in holy orders (¹), or the regular minister of a dissenting congregation (²); or

Interested in contract with council.

(c.) Has directly or indirectly, by himself or his partner, any share or interest in any contract or employment with, by, or on behalf of the council (³):

(2.) But a person shall not be so disqualified, or be deemed to have any share or interest in such a contract or employment, by reason only of his having any share or interest in—

(a.) Any lease, sale, or purchase of land, or any agreement for the same; or

(b.) Any agreement for the loan of money, or any security for the payment of money only; or

(c.) Any newspaper in which any advertisement relating to the affairs of the borough or council is inserted; or

(d.) Any company which contracts with the council for lighting or supplying with water or insuring against fire any part of the borough; or

(e.) Any railway company, or any company incorporated by Act of Parliament or royal charter, or under the Companies Act, 1862.

This section is taken from sect. 28 of the Act of 1835, sect. 15 of the Act of 1837, sects. 1, 7 and 8 of the Act of 1842, sects. 1 and 6 of the Act of 1852, and sect. 5 of the Act of 1869.

For penalty on unqualified person acting, see sect. 41 and note; for exemptions, see sect. 34, and for avoidance of office, sect. 39.

Petition and Quo Warranto.]—If a disqualified person be elected, the mode of displacing him is by election petition, as to which see Part IV., sects. 87 et seq. post. If a party become disqualified after election, the mode of displacing him is by quo warranto, as to which see sect. 225, post.

Amotion.]—As to "amotion," or the removal of a corporate officer by his fellow officers, it appears, upon general grounds, from the use of the word "amotion" in the repealed 6 & 7 Vict.

c. 89, and from the preservation of old usages by the 1st section of the Act of 1835, so far as not inconsistent with that Act, that the power of "amotion," or the removal of the holder of a corporate office by the council, upon which this Act, like the Act of 1835, still exists in undiminished force; but since the Act of 1835, the power of amotion has, it is believed, been very rarely exercised or called for, and the alternative course of pressing for a resignation, but remitting the fine, would seem to be preferable to its exercise in many cases which possibly might call for it.

Should, however, the council determine to exercise the power, the many cases decided before the Act of 1835 will apply, as well as the charters and usages. See the cases up to 1796, collected in 2 Kyd on Corporations, pp. 50 et seq., where it is said that the offences justifying the amotion of a corporate officer must be either—(1) committed in his official character; or (2) infamous; or (3) indictable. Habitual drunkenness was held a sufficient cause in *R.* v. *Taylor*, 3 Salk. 231.

A bye-law giving power to amove for just cause was held good in *R.* v. *Richardson*, 1 Burr. 539.

(¹) *Holy Orders.*]—If the party, being in Anglican Holy Orders, execute a deed of relinquishment under the Clerical Disabilities Act, 1870 (33 & 34 Vict. c. 91), the disqualification ceases. See sect. 242, sub-s. 2, and sched. 9, Part II. post.

(²) *Dissenting Minister.*]—A Baptist deacon in a borough who preached for an Independent chapel every Sunday for three months in a village ten miles off, and agreed to preach for six months more, was held not disqualified in *Reg.* v. *Oldham*, L. R., 4 Q. B. 290.

(³) *Interest in Contract.*]—See further sect. 22, sub-s. 3. A similar disqualification attaches in the case of poor law guardians, &c., under 4 & 5 Will. 4, c. 76, s. 77, as to which see *Davies* v. *Harvey* (L. R., 9 Q. B. 433), and in the case of members of local boards under rule 64 of sched. 2 of the Public Health Act, 1875. The disqualification attaches, although the contract is void in law. (*Reg.* v. *Francis*, 18 Q. B. 526.)

13.—(1.) The term of office of a councillor shall be three years. Term of office and rotation of councillors.

(2.) On the ordinary day of election of councillors in every year one-third of the whole number of councillors for the borough or for the ward, as the case may be, shall go out of office, and their places shall be filled by election.

(3.) The third to go out shall be the councillors who have been longest in office without re-election.

This is taken from sects. 30, 31 and 43 of the Act of 1835.

14.—(1.) The aldermen shall be fit persons elected by the council. Number, term of office, and rotation of aldermen.

(2.) The number of aldermen shall be one-third of the number of councillors.

(3.) A person shall not be qualified to be elected or to be an

Act of 1882 s. 14.

Aldermen— continued.

alderman unless he is a councillor, or qualified to be a councillor.

(4.) If a councillor is elected to, and accepts, the office of alderman he vacates his office of councillor.

(5.) The term of office of an alderman shall be six years.

(6.) On the ordinary day of election of aldermen in every third year one-half of the whole number of aldermen shall go out of office, and their places shall be filled by election.

(7.) The half to go out shall be those who have been aldermen for the longest time without re-election.

This is taken from sects. 25 and 27 of the Act of 1835.

As to time and mode of election, see sect. 61, post; and as to meaning of "fit" person, see note to sect. 11, ante.

It will be observed that the term of an alderman's office is double that of a councillor's, and that an alderman need not necessarily be a councillor elected by the burgesses, but need only be qualified to be so elected. It has been suggested that this retention of the principle of co-optation was intended to introduce into the councils a "superior class of men, free from the influence of popular prejudice and party spirit;" but that, as a matter of fact, "in the majority of cases, in the selection of members, the only qualification required is thorough political partizanship." See an article in the "Contemporary Review" for March, 1879, by Mr. J. A. Picton. On the other hand, it may be pointed out that as a councillor, on being elected alderman, vacates his office as councillor, the election of non-councillors saves the borough from the possible disquiet and expense of a fresh election of councillors.

Qualification, term of office, salary, precedence, and powers of mayor.

15.—(1.) The mayor shall be a fit person elected by the council from among the aldermen or councillors or persons qualified to be such.

(2.) An outgoing alderman is eligible.

(3.) The term of office of the mayor shall be one year, but he shall continue in office until his successor has accepted office and made and subscribed the required declaration.

(4.) He may receive such remuneration as the council think reasonable.

(5.) He shall, subject to the provisions of this Act respecting justices, have precedence in all places in the borough.

(6.) The mayor of a borough named in the schedules to the Municipal Corporations Act, 1835, shall be capable in law to do and suffer all acts which the chief officer of the borough might at the passing of that Act lawfully do or suffer, as far as the same were not altered or annulled by that

Act, or have not been altered or annulled by any subsequent Act.

Act of 1882 s. 15.

This is taken from sects. 6, 25, 49, 57 and 58 of the Act of 1835.

As to time and mode of election of mayor, see sect. 61, post; as to fine for non-acceptance of office, see sect. 34, post.

Remuneration of Mayor.]—It is believed that in many boroughs the mayor serves gratuitously (and a gratuitous service is pointed at by the words "remuneration, *if any*, of the mayor," in Part I. of schedule 5, p. 143, post); and that where a remuneration is paid, it is in most cases very small.

16.—(1.) The mayor may from time to time appoint an alderman or councillor to act as deputy mayor during the illness or absence of the mayor.

Power of mayor to appoint deputy.

(2.) The appointment shall be signified to the council in writing, and be recorded in their minutes.

(3.) A deputy mayor may, while acting as such, do all acts which the mayor as such might do, except that he shall not take the chair at a meeting of the council unless specially appointed by the meeting to do so, and shall not, unless he is a justice, act as a justice or in any judicial capacity.

This is taken from sects. 7 and 8 of the Act of 1835.

See further as to deputy mayor, sect. 237, and rule 9 of schedule 2.

Officers of Council.

17.—(1.) The council shall from time to time appoint a fit person, not a member of the council, to be the town clerk of the borough.

The town clerk and deputy.

(2.) The town clerk shall hold office during the pleasure of the council.

(3.) He shall have the charge and custody of, and be responsible for, the charters, deeds, records, and documents of the borough, and they shall be kept as the council direct.

(4.) A vacancy in the office shall be filled within twenty-one days after its occurrence.

(5.) In case of the illness or absence of the town clerk, the council may appoint a deputy town clerk, to hold office during their pleasure.

(6.) All things required or authorized by law to be done by or to the town clerk may be done by or to the deputy town clerk.

This is taken from sects. 58 and 65 of the Act of 1835, the power to appoint a deputy being new. Sect. 58 provided in terms that

Act of 1882
s. 17.

the town clerk might be a solicitor, " any law, statute or charter to
the contrary notwithstanding," which repeal is kept up by sect. 260,
sub-s. 2, post. As to remuneration, see sect. 20, infra. The appointment ought to be under the seal of the corporation. See
Arnold v. *Mayor, &c. of Poole,* 4 M. & G. 860.

The treasurer.

18.—(1.) The council shall from time to time appoint a fit
person, not a member of the council, to be the treasurer of
the borough.

(2.) The treasurer shall hold office during the pleasure of
the council.

(3.) A vacancy in the office shall be filled within twenty-one
days after its occurrence.

(4.) The offices of town clerk and treasurer shall not be
held by the same person.

This section is taken from sect. 58 of the Act of 1835—under
which the appointment was made annually—as amended by sect. 6
of the Act of 1843, which described the office as being "one of
great trust," to which an annual appointment was "inconvenient
and unnecessary."

Other
borough
officers.

19. The council shall from time to time appoint such other
officers as have been usually appointed in the borough, or as
the council think necessary, and may at any time discontinue
the appointment of any officer appearing to them not necessary to be re-appointed.

It seems clear that an appointment may be discontinued without
compensation, and it is conceived further that any payment of
compensation for abolition of office would be illegal.

Security
by and
remuneration
of officers.

20. The council shall require every officer appointed by
them to give such security as they think proper for the due
execution of his office, and shall allow him such remuneration
as they think reasonable.

This reproduces a part of sect. 58 of the Act of 1835. As to
remuneration of town clerk for extra services, see *Thomas* v. *Mayor,
&c. of Swansea,* 2 Dowl., N. S. 470; *Steavenson* v. *Mayor, &c. of
Berwick,* 1 Q. B. 154; and *R.* v. *Prest,* 16 Q. B. 32; in which latter
case it was held that the absence of a retainer under seal was no
ground, after payment, for quashing an order to pay for extra
services out of the borough fund.

Accounta-
bility of
officers.

21.—(1.) Every officer appointed by the council shall at
such times during the continuance of his office, or within
three months after his ceasing to hold it, and in such manner

as the council direct, deliver to the council, or as they direct, Act of 1882 s. 21. a true account in writing of all matters committed to his charge, and of his receipts and payments, with vouchers, and a list of persons from whom money is due for purposes of this Act in connexion with his office, showing the amount due from each.

(2.) Every such officer shall pay all money due from him to the treasurer, or as the council direct.

(3.) If any such officer—

(a.) Refuses or wilfully neglects to deliver any account or list which he ought to deliver, or any voucher relating thereto, or to make any payment which he ought to make; or Penalty for refusing to deliver accounts, books, &c.

(b.) After three days' notice in writing, signed by the town clerk or by three members of the council, given or left at his usual or last known place of abode, refuses or wilfully neglects to deliver to the council, or as they direct, any book or document which he ought so to deliver, or to give satisfaction respecting it to the council or as they direct;

a court of summary jurisdiction having jurisdiction where the officer is or resides may, by summary order, require him to make such delivery or payment, or to give such satisfaction.

(4.) But nothing in this section shall affect any remedy by action against any such officer or his surety, except that the officer shall not be both sued by action and proceeded against summarily for the same cause.

This is taken from sect. 60 of the Act of 1835.

Jurisdiction of County Justices.]—Under sect. 60 of the Act of 1835, it appears to have been held (the words being "justice of the peace for the county or other jurisdiction," wherein, &c.) that the county and borough justices had a concurrent jurisdiction. See *Re Gateshead*, 6 A. & E. 550, n. (a). It is conceived that under this section and sect. 158 the jurisdiction, in quarter-sessions boroughs having a charter with a non-intromittant clause, is vested in the borough justices only.

Meetings and Proceedings of Council; Committees.

22.—(1.) The rules in the Second Schedule* shall be observed. Meetings of council; appointment of committees, &c.

(2.) The council may from time to time appoint out of their own body such and so many committees, either of a general * Page 143.

Act of 1882
s. 22.

Meetings of
council—
continued.

or special nature, and consisting of such number of persons, as they think fit, for any purposes which, in the opinion of the council, would be better regulated and managed by means of such committees; but the acts of every such committee shall be submitted to the council for their approval.

(3.) A member of the council shall not vote or take part in the discussion of any matter before the council, or a committee, in which he has, directly or indirectly, by himself or by his partner, any pecuniary interest.

(4.) No act or proceeding of the council, or of a committee, shall be questioned on account of any vacancy in their body.

(5.) A minute of proceedings at a meeting of the council, or of a committee, signed at the same or the next ensuing meeting, by the mayor, or by a member of the council, or of the committee, describing himself as, or appearing to be, chairman of the meeting at which the minute is signed, shall be received in evidence without further proof.

(6.) Until the contrary is proved, every meeting of the council, or of a committee, in respect of the proceedings whereof a minute has been so made, shall be deemed to have been duly convened and held, and all the members of the meeting shall be deemed to have been duly qualified; and where the proceedings are proceedings of a committee, the committee shall be deemed to have been duly constituted, and to have had power to deal with the matters referred to in the minutes.

This section, together with the rules in the second schedule, is taken from sects. 69 and 70 of the Act of 1835, sect. 22 of the Act of 1837, sect. 2 of the Act of 1842, and sect. 3 of the Act of 1873.

As to disqualification for election on ground of interest, see sect. 12, ante.

Bye-laws.

Power of
council to
make bye-
laws.

23.—(1.) The council may, from time to time, make such bye-laws as to them seem meet for the good rule and government of the borough, and for prevention and suppression of nuisances not already punishable in a summary manner by virtue of any Act in force throughout the borough ([1]), and may thereby appoint such fines, not exceeding in any case five pounds, as they deem necessary for the prevention and suppression of offences against the same.

(2.) Such a bye-law shall not be made unless at least two-thirds of the whole number of the council are present.

Act of 1882 s. 23.

(3.) Such a bye-law shall not come into force until the expiration of forty days after a copy thereof has been fixed on the town hall.

(4.) Such a bye-law shall not come into force until the expiration of forty days after a copy thereof, sealed with the corporate seal, has been sent to the Secretary of State; and if within those forty days the Queen, with the advice of her Privy Council, disallows the bye-law or part thereof, the bye-law or part disallowed shall not come into force; but it shall be lawful for the Queen, at any time within those forty days, to enlarge the time within which the bye-law shall not come into force, and in that case the bye-law shall not come into force until after the expiration of that enlarged time.

Submission of bye-laws to Secretary of State.

(5.) Any offence against such a bye-law may be prosecuted summarily.

(6.) Nothing in this section shall interfere with the operation of section one hundred and eighty-seven of the Public Health Act, 1875 (*a*); and that section shall have effect as if this section were therein referred to, instead of section ninety of the Municipal Corporations Act, 1835; but nothing in the Public Health Act, 1875, shall be construed as having restricted the meaning or scope of the Municipal Corporations Act, 1835, or as restricting the meaning or scope of this section, with respect to prevention or suppression of nuisances.

Submission of bye-laws to Local Government Board.

This section is taken from sects. 90 and 91 of the Act of 1835.
As to bye-laws imposing a fine for non-acceptance of office, see sect. 34, p. 21, post. A bye-law giving the council power to amove a councillor for just cause was held good, long before the Act of 1835, in *R.* v. *Richardson*, 1 Burr. 539. Since the Act of 1835 bye-laws for the regulation of a trade (*Everett* v. *Grapes*, 3 L. T. 669), and for the suppression of the sale of unsound meat, &c. (*Shillito* v. *Thomson*, 1 Q. B. D. 12; 45 L. J., M. C. 18; 33 L. T. 506; 24 W. R. 57), have been held good; but in *Elwood* v. *Bullock* (6 Q. B. 383) a bye-law restricting the erection of booths was held bad.

(¹) *Suppression of Nuisances under Public Health Act, &c.*]—The words "not already punishable in a summary manner," &c., have the effect of very much restricting the power of the council to make bye-laws against nuisances. See especially the Public Health Act, 1875 (38 & 39 Vict. c. 55), ss. 47, 80 and 91—111, which provides for

(*a*) See post, p. 310, tit. "*Supplementary Enactments.*"

Act of 1882 s. 23.

the summary punishment of nuisances from animals, manure, smoke, &c.; and sect. 171, incorporating certain sections of the Towns Police Clauses Act, 1847 (10 & 11 Vict. c. 89), as to nuisances in the streets. See post, tit. "*Supplementary Enactments.*" In many boroughs, also, there is in force some local Act applicable to the case. See *e. g.* the Birmingham Improvement Act, 1851.

The Public Health Act, 1875, gives power also to make bye-laws as to offensive trades, sect. 113; and as to houses let in lodgings, sect. 90.

Evidence of bye-laws.

24. The production of a written copy of a bye-law made by the council under this Act, or under any former or present or future general or local Act of Parliament, if authenticated by the corporate seal shall, until the contrary is proved, be sufficient evidence of the due making and existence of the bye-law, and, if it is so stated in the copy, of the bye-law having been approved and confirmed by the authority whose approval or confirmation is required to the making or before the enforcing of the bye-law.

This is a re-enactment of sect. 3 of the Act of 1873.

Accounts and Audit.

The borough auditors.

25.—(1.) There shall be three borough auditors, two elected by the burgesses, called elective auditors, and one appointed by the mayor, called mayor's auditor.

(2.) An elective auditor must be qualified to be a councillor, but may not be a member of the council or the town clerk or the treasurer.

(3.) The mayor's auditor must be a member of the council.

(4.) The term of office of each auditor shall be one year.

(5.) The appointment of the mayor's auditor shall be made on the ordinary day of election of the elective auditors.

(6.) On a casual vacancy in his office an appointment to fill it shall be made within ten days after the occurrence of the vacancy.

This section is taken from sects. 37 and 93 of the Act of 1835.

Half-yearly accounts of treasurer.

26. The treasurer shall make up his accounts half-yearly to such dates as the council, with the approval of the Local Government Board, from time to time appoint; and, subject to any such appointment, to the dates in use at the commencement of this Act.

This and the next section are taken from sect. 93 of the Act of 1835.

27.—(1.) The treasurer shall within one month from the date to which he is required to make up his accounts in each half year, submit them, with the necessary vouchers and papers, to the borough auditors, and they shall audit them.

(2.) After the audit of the accounts for the second half of each financial year the treasurer shall print a full abstract of his accounts for that year.

Act of 1882 s. 27.

Audit and publication of treasurer's accounts.

28.—(1.) The town clerk shall make a return to the Local Government Board of the receipts and expenditure of the municipal corporation for each financial year.

(2.) The return shall be made for the financial year ending on the 25th of March, or on such other day as the Local Government Board, on the application of the council, from time to time prescribe.

(3.) The return shall be in such form and contain such particulars as the Local Government Board from time to time direct.

(4.) The return shall be sent to the Local Government Board within one month after the completion of the audit for the second half of each financial year.

(5.) If the town clerk fails to make any return required under this section, he shall for each offence be liable to a fine not exceeding twenty pounds to be recovered by action on behalf of the Crown in the High Court.

(6.) The Local Government Board shall in each year prepare an abstract of the returns made in pursuance of this section, under general heads, and it shall be laid before both Houses of Parliament.

Returns to Local Government Board by town clerk.

Abstract of returns for Parliament.

This section in effect reproduces the corresponding enactments of the Local Taxation Returns Act, 1877 (40 & 41 Vict. c. 66), repealed as to boroughs within this Act by sect. 5 and Sched. 1, Part II.

Revising Assessors.

29.—(1.) In every borough whereof no part of the area is co-extensive with or included in the area of a parliamentary borough, there shall be two revising assessors elected by the burgesses.

(2.) Every person shall be eligible who is qualified to be a councillor and is not a member of the council or the town clerk or treasurer.

Revising assessors in non-parliamentary boroughs.

Act of 1882
s. 29.
────────
Revising
assessors—
continued.

(3.) The term of office of each revising assessor shall be one year.

(4.) Every revising assessor shall, as soon as conveniently may be after his election, and from time to time as occasion requires, appoint, by writing signed by him, a person eligible to the office of revising assessor, to be his deputy, to act for him in case of his illness or incapacity to act.

(5.) The appointment shall be signified to the council, in writing signed by the assessor, and be recorded in their minutes.

This section is taken from sect. 37 of the Act of 1835, as amended by sects. 4 and 17 of the Act of 1837, and sect. 20 of the Parliamentary and Municipal Registration Act, 1878 (40 & 41 Vict. c. 26), which latter enactment abolished revising assessors in parliamentary boroughs.

As to time and mode of election, see sect. 62, post; as to duties, see sect. 44, sub-s. 2, and Part I. of Sched. 3.

Division of Borough into Wards, or alteration of Wards.

Proceedings
for division
of borough
into wards
or alteration
of wards.

30.—(1.) If two-thirds of the council of a borough agree to petition, and the council thereupon petition, the Queen for the division of the borough into wards, or for the alteration of the number and boundaries of its wards, it shall be lawful for her Majesty from time to time, by Order in Council, to fix the number of wards into which the borough shall be divided; and the borough shall be divided into that number of wards.

(2.) Notice of the petition, and of the time when it pleases her Majesty to order that the same be taken into consideration by her Privy Council, shall be published in the London Gazette one month at least before the petition is so considered.

(3.) Where an Order in Council has been so made, the Secretary of State shall appoint a commissioner to prepare a scheme for determining the boundaries of the wards and apportioning the councillors among them.

(4.) In case of division into wards, the commissioner shall apportion all the councillors among the wards.

(5.) In case of alteration of wards, he shall so apportion among the altered wards the councillors for those wards as to provide for their continuing to represent as large a number as possible of their former constituents.

(6.) In either case, each councillor shall hold his office in the ward to which he is assigned for the same time that he would have held it had the borough remained undivided or the wards unaltered.

(7.) In case of division into wards the returning officer at the first election for each ward held after the division shall, notwithstanding anything in this Act, be the mayor or a person appointed by the mayor.

(8.) If by reason of any division or alteration under this section any doubt arises as to which councillor should go out of office, the doubt may be determined by the council.

(9.) The division of a borough into a greater number of wards shall not affect the qualification of aldermen or councillors.

(10.) The number of councillors assigned to each ward shall be a number divisible by three; and in fixing their number the commissioner shall, as far as he deems it practicable, have regard as well to the number of persons rated in the ward as to the aggregate rating of the ward.

Number of councillors in each ward to be divisible by three.

(11.) The commissioner shall make the scheme in duplicate, and shall deliver one of the duplicates to the town clerk, and shall send the other to the Secretary of State, to be submitted by him to her Majesty in council for approval.

(12.) The scheme shall be published in the London Gazette, and shall come into operation at the date of that publication, and thenceforth the boundaries of wards and apportionment of councillors determined and made by the scheme shall be observed and be in force.

(13.) If her Majesty in council does not approve the scheme, as originally prepared by the commissioner, it shall nevertheless be published in the London Gazette, and shall be in force for the purposes of any municipal election until her Majesty in council, on further information and report from the commissioner, definitively approves a scheme in that behalf.

(14.) The commissioner may administer oaths, and may require any person having the custody of any book containing a poor rate made for a parish to produce the book for his inspection; and every person required by the commissioner to answer any question put to him for the purposes of this section shall answer it.

Powers of commissioner.

Act of 1882
s. 30.

* Page 152.

(15.) The commissioner shall have remuneration as appearing by the fourth and fifth schedules.*

This section is taken from sects. 39, 40, 42 and 43 of the Act of 1835, as amended by sect. 10 of the Act of 1837, and extended by sects. 1—3 of the Act of 1859, under which, however, the commissioner had to be a barrister—a qualification not required by this Act.

Supplemental and Exceptional Provisions.

Occupation
of part of
house.

31. In and for the purposes of this Act—

(a.) The terms house, warehouse, counting house, shop, or other building include any part of a house, where that part is separately occupied for the purposes of any trade, business, or profession; and any such part may, for the purpose of describing the qualification, be described as office, chambers, studio, or by any like term applicable to the case.

(b.) Where an occupier is entitled to the sole and exclusive use of any part of a house, that part shall not be deemed to be occupied otherwise than separately by reason only that the occupier is entitled to the joint use of some other part.

This section is substantially identical with part of sect. 5 of the Parliamentary and Municipal Registration Act, 1878, 41 & 42 Vict. c. 26, which see post, "*Incorporated Enactments—Registration.*"

Claim by
occupier to
be rated.

32.—(1.) If an occupier of any qualifying property, whether the landlord is or is not liable to be rated to the poor rate in respect thereof, claims to be rated to the poor rate in respect thereof, and pays or tenders to the overseers of the parish where the property is situate the full amount of the poor rate last made in respect of the property, the overseers shall put the occupier's name on the rate book in respect of that rate.

(2.) If they fail to do so, he shall nevertheless for the purposes of this Act be deemed rated to that rate.

This section in effect reproduces sect. 11 of the Act of 1835, with the exception of a proviso repealed by the Statute Law Revision Act, 1874.

As to rating owner instead of occupier of small tenements by order of vestry, see 59 Geo. 3, c. 12, s. 19, and 32 & 33 Vict. c. 41, by sect. 19 of which the overseers must enter in the occupier's column of the rate book the name of the occupier of every rateable hereditament; but it is provided that "any occupier whose name has been omitted shall, notwithstanding such omission and that no claim to be rated has been made by him, be entitled to every qualification and franchise depending upon rating, in the same manner as if his name had not been so omitted,"—which proviso will, by the effect of sect. 9 of the present Act, ensure the party a right to vote at an election under this Act only if he be enrolled.

33.—(1.) Where a person succeeds to qualifying property by descent, marriage, marriage settlement, devise, or promotion to a benefice or office, then, for the purpose of qualification, the occupancy of the property by a predecessor in title, and the rating of the predecessor in respect thereof, shall be equivalent to the occupancy and rating of the successor; and rating in the name of the predecessor shall, until a new rate is made after the date of succession, be equivalent to rating in the name of the successor; and the successor shall not be required to prove his own residence, occupancy, or rating before the succession.

Rules as to qualification of burgess on succession, &c.

(2.) The qualifying property need not be throughout the twelve months constituting the period of qualification the same property or in the same parish.

(3.) Where by law a borough rate is payable by instalments, payment by any person of any such instalment shall, as regards his qualification to be enrolled as a burgess, be deemed a payment of the borough rate in respect of the period to which the instalment applies.

(4.) A person shall not be disentitled to be enrolled as a burgess by reason only—

No disqualification by—

(a.) That he has received medical or surgical assistance from the trustees of the municipal charities, or has been removed, by order of a justice, to a hospital or place for reception of the sick, at the cost of any local authority; or ·

Medical aid:

(b.) That his child has been admitted to and taught in any public or endowed school.

School aid.

This section is taken from sects. 10 and 12 of the Act of 1835, as amended by sects. 8 and 9 of the Act of 1837, and from sect. 1 of the Act of 1869.

34.—(1.) Every qualified person elected([1]) to a corporate office,* unless exempt under this section or otherwise by law([2]), either shall accept the office by making and subscribing the declaration required by this Act within five days after notice of election, or shall, in lieu thereof, be liable to pay to the council a fine of such amount not exceeding, in case of an

Obligation to accept office or pay fine.
* Page 3.

alderman, councillor, elective auditor, or revising assessor, fifty pounds, and in case of a mayor one hundred pounds, as the council by bye-law determine.

(2.) If there is no bye-law determining fines, the fine, in case of an alderman, councillor, elective auditor, or revising assessor, shall be twenty-five pounds, and in case of a mayor fifty pounds.

Exemptions
from office.

(3.) The persons exempt under this section are—

(a.) Any person disabled by lunacy or imbecility of mind, or by deafness, blindness, or other permanent infirmity of body ([3]); and

(b.) Any person who, being above the age of sixty-five years, or having within five years before the day of his election either served the office or paid the fine for non-acceptance thereof, claims exemption within five days after notice of his election.

(4.) A fine payable under this section shall be recoverable summarily.

This section in effect reproduces sect. 51 of the Act of 1835.

For disqualifications by this Act itself, see sect. 12, ante.

Unless absent from the United Kingdom (Sched. III., Part 2, Rule 15), a party may be nominated without his consent.

([1]) *Elected, &c.*]—See sect. 7 for definition of corporate office. The word "elected" will include the case of an alderman, although he is not elected by the burgesses, but by the council.

([2]) *Exemptions.*]—Persons exempt "otherwise by law" are:—commissioned officers in the army on full pay, by the Army Act, 1881 (44 & 45 Vict. c. 58), s. 146, who are incapable of serving; also employés of the Post Office, by 7 Will. 4 & 1 Vict. c. 33, s. 12; of the Inland Revenue Office, by 16 & 17 Vict. c. 59, s. 17; and of the customs, by the Customs Consolidation Act, 1876 (39 & 40 Vict. c. 36), s. 9, who cannot be compelled to serve; also inspectors of factories, by the Factory and Workshop Act, 1878 (41 Vict. c. 16), s. 67, and members of the reserve force, by the Reserve Force Act, 1882 (45 & 46 Vict. c. 48), s. 7, who are not liable to serve; also medical practitioners (if registered), by the Medical Act, 1858 (21 & 22 Vict. c. 90), s. 35, and dentists, by the Dentists' Act, 1878 (41 & 42 Vict. c. 33), s. 30, who are exempt "if they so desire."

Convicted felons are also disqualified by 33 & 34 Vict. c. 23, s. 2, if suffering a sentence of penal servitude or imprisonment not yet expired.

([3]) *Lunacy.*]—Paragraph (3) (a) is clearly taken from sect. 10 of the County Juries Act, 1825 (6 Geo. 4, c. 50), which disqualifies for the office of juror the same persons by the same words.

Declaration
on acceptance
of office.

35. A person elected to a corporate office shall not, until he has made and subscribed before two members of the council, or the town clerk, a declaration as in the eighth schedule,* act in the office except in administering that declaration.

Act of 1882 s. 35.

* Page 157.

This section reproduces sect. 50 of the Act of 1835, with the exception of a proviso repealed by the Promissory Oaths Act, 1871 (34 & 35 Vict. c. 48).

By sect. 14 the qualification for the office of alderman is the same as that for the office of councillor; but the obligation to make the declaration was no doubt imposed upon aldermen only on account of their six years' term of office.

36.—(1.) A person elected to a corporate office may at any time, by writing signed by him and delivered to the town clerk, resign the office, on payment of the fine provided* for non-acceptance thereof.

Resignation of office.

* Sect. 34.

(2.) In any such case the council shall forthwith declare the office to be vacant, and signify the same by notice in writing, signed by three members of the council and countersigned by the town clerk, and fixed on the town hall, and the office shall thereupon become vacant.

(3.) No person enabled by law to make an affirmation instead of taking an oath, shall be liable to any fine for non-acceptance of office, by reason of his refusal on conscientious grounds to take any oath or make any declaration required by this Act, or to take on himself the duties of the office (¹).

Conscientious refusal to take office.

This is taken from sect. 8 of the Act of 1836 (6 & 7 Will. 4, c. 104), the requirement of a *written* resignation being new.

(¹) *Conscientious Refusal.*]—The persons enabled, as in the third paragraph mentioned, at the time of the passing of the Act of 1836, were Quakers and Moravians (by 3 & 4 Will. 4, c. 49), and Separatists (by 3 & 4 Will. 4, c. 82), both of which Acts applied to oaths of all kinds. Afterwards, by the Common Law Procedure Act, 1854 (17 & 18 Vict. c. 125), s. 20, and by the Evidence Further Amendment Act, 1869 (32 & 33 Vict. c. 68), s. 4, similar relief was given to conscientious objectors and to Atheists respectively, but in such terms as to restrict the relief to oaths for the taking of evidence. It is submitted that this paragraph includes the persons relieved by the Acts of 1854 and 1869, as well as those relieved by the earlier Acts in force in 1836; but the point is not quite free from doubt. At any rate, a party seeking relief under the present paragraph from the duties of office must not only bring himself within the Acts enabling him to affirm, but must also show a conscientious ground for refusal.

37. A person ceasing to hold a corporate office shall, unless disqualified to hold the office, be re-eligible.

Re-eligibility of office-holders.

This is taken from sects. 25 and 31 of the Act of 1835.

Act of 1882
s. 38.

Mayor and
aldermen to
continue
members of
council.

38. The mayor and aldermen shall, during their respective offices, continue to be members of the council, notwithstanding anything in this Act as to councillors going out of office at the end of three years.

This is taken from sect. 26 of the Act of 1835.

Avoidance of
office by
bankruptcy—

By absence.

39.—(1.) If the mayor, or an alderman or councillor—

(a.) Is declared bankrupt, or compounds by deed with his creditors, or makes an arrangement or composition with his creditors, under the Bankruptcy Act, 1869, by deed or otherwise; or

(b.) Is (except in case of illness) continuously absent from the borough, being mayor, for more than two months, or, being alderman or councillor, for more than six months:

he shall thereupon immediately become disqualified, and shall cease to hold the office.

(2.) In any such event the council shall forthwith declare the office to be vacant, and signify the same by notice signed by three members of the council, and countersigned by the town clerk, and fixed on the town hall, and the office shall thereupon become vacant.

(3.) Where a person becomes so disqualified by being declared bankrupt, or compounding, or making an arrangement or composition, as aforesaid, the disqualification, as regards subsequent elections, shall, in case of bankruptcy, cease on his obtaining his order of discharge, and shall, in case of a compounding or composition as aforesaid, cease on payment of his debts in full, and shall, in case of an arrangement as aforesaid, cease on his obtaining his certificate of discharge.

* Sect. 34.

(4.) Where a person becomes so disqualified by absence, he shall be liable to the same fine as for non-acceptance of office,* recoverable summarily, but the disqualification shall, as regards subsequent elections, cease on his return.

This section is taken from sect. 52 of the Act of 1835, as extended by 32 & 33 Vict. c. 62, s. 21.
Hardwick v. *Brown* (L. R., 8 C. P. 406; 28 L. T. 502), in which it was held that compounding with creditors did not of itself render the office void, would seem to be still law.
In *Aslatt* v. *Southampton Corporation*, 16 Ch. D. 143; 50 L. J. Ch. 31; 43 L. T. 464; 29 W. R. 117; Jessel, M. R., restrained the defendants from declaring vacant the office of an alderman who had compounded with his creditors, but executed no composition deed.

40.—(1.) On a casual vacancy in a corporate office, an election shall be held by the same persons and in the same manner as an election to fill an ordinary vacancy; and the person elected shall hold the office until the time when the person in whose place he is elected would regularly have gone out of office, and he shall then go out of office.

Act of 1882 s. 40.

Filling of casual vacancies.

(2.) In case of more than one casual vacancy in the office of councillor being filled at the same election, the councillor elected by the smallest number of votes shall be deemed to be elected in the place of him who would regularly have first gone out of office, and the councillor elected by the next smallest number of votes shall be deemed to be elected in the place of him who would regularly have next gone out of office, and so with respect to the others; and if there has not been a contested election, or if any doubt arises, the order of rotation shall be determined by the council.

(3.) Non-acceptance of office by a person elected creates a casual vacancy.

Non-accept-ance of office.

This is principally taken from sects. 27 and 47 of the Act of 1835, substituting the term " casual " for " extraordinary."

41.—(1.) If any person acts in a corporate office without having made the declaration by this Act required, or without being qualified at the time of making the declaration, or after ceasing to be qualified, or after becoming disqualified, he shall for each offence be liable to a fine not exceeding fifty pounds, recoverable by action.

Penalty on unqualified person acting in office.

(2.) A person being in fact enrolled in the burgess roll shall not be liable to a fine for acting in a corporate office on the ground only that he was not entitled to be enrolled therein.

The first paragraph of this section is taken from sect. 53 of the Act of 1835. It was held upon that section, in *Lewis* v. *Curr* (1 Ex. D. 484; 46 L. J., Ex. 314; 36 L. T. 44; 24 W. R. 940, C. A.), that there was no forfeiture for acting after a contract with the council (see sect. 12 of this Act) had ceased, and that decision would seem to apply to a similar case under the present section. The second paragraph is taken from sect. 7 of the Act of 1836 (6 & 7 Will. 4, c. 104).

As to notice of action and other restrictions, see sect. 224, post. The forfeit was a full 50*l*. under sect. 53 of the Act of 1835, and the effect of substituting the words " not exceeding " seems to be to allow the plaintiff to claim less than the 50l. if he pleases, but not to allow the court to give judgment for less if the whole is claimed by the plaintiff.

Validity of acts done notwithstanding disqualification, &c.

42.—(1.) The acts and proceedings of a person in possession of a corporate office, and acting therein, shall, notwithstanding his disqualification or want of qualification, be as valid and effectual as if he had been qualified.

(2.) An election of a person to a corporate office shall not be liable to be questioned by reason of a defect in the title, or want of title, of the person before whom the election was had, if that person was then in actual possession of, or acting in, the office giving the right to preside at the election.

(3.) A burgess roll shall not be liable to be questioned by reason of a defect in the title, or want of title, of the mayor or any revising authority by whom it is revised, if he was then in actual possession and exercise of the office of mayor or revising authority.

The first paragraph is taken from sect. 53 of the Act of 1835, and the second and third from sects. 1 and 5 of the Act of 1837.

Duties of town clerk, deputy, and treasurer, during vacancy or incapacity.

43. If there is no town clerk, and no deputy town clerk, or there is no treasurer, or the town clerk, deputy town clerk, or treasurer (as the case may be) is incapable of acting, all acts by law authorized or required to be done by or with respect to the town clerk or the treasurer (as the case may be) may, subject to the provisions of any other Act, be done by or with respect to a person appointed in that behalf by the mayor.

This, with small additions, is taken from sect. 16 of the Act of 1835. Parliamentary registration duties, by 6 Vict. c. 8, s. 101, p. 194, post, are to be performed by the returning officer or his appointee if there is no town clerk.

PART III.—PREPARATIONS FOR AND PROCEDURE AT ELECTIONS.

Parish Burgess Lists; Burgess Rolls; Ward Rolls.

Preparation and revision of parish burgess lists in parliamentary borough.

44.—(1.) Where the whole or part of the area of a borough is co-extensive with or included in the area of a parliamentary borough, the lists of burgesses are to be made out and revised, and claims and objections relating thereto are to be made, in accordance with the provisions of the Parliamentary and Municipal Registration Act, 1878.

(2.) Where no part of the area of a borough is co-extensive with or included in the area of a parliamentary borough, the lists of burgesses shall be made out and revised, and claims and objections relating thereto may be made, in accordance, as nearly as may be, with the provisions of Part I. of the Third Schedule.*

(3.) In either case the lists shall be styled the parish burgess lists.

The first paragraph of this section is a repetition of the first paragraph of sect. 18 of the Parliamentary and Municipal Registration Act, 1878 (41 & 42 Vict. c. 26), prior to which Act the revision of the municipal lists proceeded independently in all boroughs.

For such sections of the Act of 1878 as are applicable to a municipal revision, see "*Incorporated Enactments (Registration Acts)*," p. 201, post.

45.—(1.) When the parish burgess lists have been revised and signed, the revising authority shall deliver them to the town clerk, and a printed copy thereof, examined by him and signed by him, shall be the burgess roll of the borough.

(2.) The burgess roll shall be completed on or before the 20th of October in each year, and shall come into operation on the 1st of November in that year, and shall continue in operation for the twelve months beginning on that day.

(3.) The names in the burgess roll shall be numbered by wards or by polling districts, unless in any case the council direct that the same be numbered consecutively without reference to wards or polling districts.

(4.) Where the borough has no wards, the burgess roll shall be made in one general roll for the whole borough.

(5.) Where the borough has wards, the burgess roll shall be made in separate rolls, called ward rolls, one for each ward, containing the names of the persons entitled to vote in that ward, and the ward rolls collectively shall constitute the burgess roll.

(6.) A burgess shall not be enrolled in more than one ward roll.

(7.) Where a duplicate of a burgess list is made under section thirty-one of the Parliamentary and Municipal Regis-

Act of 1882
s. 45.

* Page 220.

Effect of
enrolment
and non-
enrolment.

tration Act, 1878,* it shall have the same effect as the original, and may be delivered instead thereof.

(8.) Every person enrolled in the burgess roll shall be deemed to be enrolled as a burgess, and every person not enrolled in the burgess roll shall be deemed to be not enrolled as a burgess.

(9.) No stamp duty shall be payable in respect of the enrolment of a burgess.

This is taken from sects. 22, 44 and 45 of the Act of 1835.

Arrangement
of lists and
rolls.

46.—(1.) If and as far as the council so direct, the parish burgess lists, and the burgess roll, and the ward rolls (if any), and the lists of claimants and respondents, or any of those documents, shall be arranged in the same order in which the qualifying properties appear in the rate book for the parish in which they are situate, or otherwise in such order as will cause those lists and rolls to record the qualifying properties in successive order in the street or other place in which they are situate.

* Sect. 64.

(2.) Subject to any such direction, and to the provisions of this Act as to polling districts,* the arrangement of the lists and rolls shall be alphabetical.

This is chiefly taken from sect. 21 of the Parliamentary and Municipal Registration Act, 1878.

Correction of
burgess roll
by High
Court.

* Page 220.

47.—(1.) Where the parish burgess lists are revised under the Parliamentary and Municipal Registration Act, 1878, the burgess roll is subject to alteration or correction in manner provided by section thirty-five of that Act.*

(2.) Where the parish burgess lists are revised under this Act, any person whose claim has been rejected or name expunged at the revision of the lists may apply, within two months after the last sitting of the revision court, to the High Court in the Queen's Bench Division for a mandamus to the mayor to insert his name in the burgess roll ; and thereupon the court shall (a) inquire into the title of the applicant to be enrolled.

(a) [Shall]. This affirms *R.* v. *Mayor of Harwich* (8 Ad. & E. 919), in which the words " it shall be lawful for," &c. were held imperative.

(3.) If the court grants a mandamus, the mayor shall insert the name in the burgess roll, and shall add thereto the words " by order of Her Majesty's High Court of Justice," and shall subscribe his name to those words.

Act of 1882 s. 47.

The 35th section of the Act of 1878 incorporates certain provisions of 6 Vict. c. 18, as to appeal from decision of the revising barrister and alteration of the lists, in pursuance of the judgment of the High Court. See the sections in question, together with sect. 35 and other sections of the Act of 1878, post, tit. " *Incorporated Enactments (Registration)*," p. 201, post.

Paragraph (2) is taken from sect. 24 of the Act of 1837 (7 Will. 4 & 1 Vict. c. 78).

48.—(1.) The town clerk shall cause the parish burgess lists, the lists of claimants and respondents, and the burgess roll, to be printed, and shall deliver printed copies to any person on payment of a reasonable price for each copy.

Printing and sale of burgess roll and other documents.

(2.) Subject to section thirty of the Parliamentary and Municipal Registration Act, 1878,* the proceeds of sale shall go to the borough fund.

* Page 219.

This is taken from sects. 15, 17 and 23 of the Act of 1835, substituting, however, "reasonable price" for "one shilling" in the case of the lists of claimants and respondents.

By sect. 30 of the Act of 1878 (which see post), the proceeds of sale in parliamentary boroughs are charged with certain expenses, after payment of which half the surplus is to be dealt with as therein mentioned, and half is to be paid to the borough fund.

49.—(1.) The overseers of each parish shall at the same time that they make the parish burgess list make a list of the persons entitled in respect of the occupation of property in that parish to be elected councillors, as being resident within fifteen miles although beyond seven miles from the borough.

Separate list of persons qualified to be councillors, but not to be burgesses.

(2.) The provisions of this Act as to the parish burgess lists, and claims and objections relating thereto, and the revision of those lists, shall, as nearly as circumstances admit, apply to the lists made under this section.

(3.) The town clerk shall arrange the names entered in these lists, when revised, in alphabetical order as a separate list (in this Act called the separate non-resident list), with an appropriate heading, at the end of the burgess roll.

This is taken from sect. 3 of the Act of 1869, as amended (respecting parliamentary boroughs) by sect. 19 of the Act of 1878.

Election of Councillors.

**Borough
and ward
elections.**

50.—(1.) Where a borough has no wards, there shall be one election of councillors for the whole borough.

(2.) Where a borough has wards, there shall be a separate election of councillors for each ward.

This is taken from sects. 43 and 44 of the Act of 1835.

Title to vote.

51.—(1.) At an election of councillors a person shall be entitled to subscribe a nomination paper, and to demand and receive a voting paper, and to vote, if he is enrolled in the burgess roll, or, in the case of a ward election, the ward roll, and not otherwise.

(2.) No person shall subscribe a nomination paper in or for more than one ward, or vote in more than one ward.

(3.) Nothing in this section shall entitle any person to do any act therein mentioned who is prohibited by law from doing it, or relieve him from any penalty to which he may be liable for doing it.

The first two paragraphs of this section are taken from sects. 29 and 44 of the Act of 1835; but the continuing power of a burgess to select a ward where he has qualifications in more wards than one, which was given by sect. 44 (see *Reg.* v. *Harrald*, L. R., 8 Q. B. 418), is, failing a choice by himself at the revision, now transferred to the revision court by Sched. 3, Part I., Rule 18, in non-parliamentary boroughs, and by sect. 28, sub-s. 14 of the Parliamentary and Municipal Registration Act, 1878, in parliamentary boroughs.

**Day of
election.**

52. The ordinary day of election of councillors shall be the 1st of November.

This is taken from sect. 30 of the Act of 1835. If the first be on a Sunday, the election will be on the second. Sect. 230, post.

**Returning
officer at
election.**

53.—(1.) At an election of councillors for a whole borough the returning officer shall be the mayor.

(2.) At an election for a ward the returning officer shall be an alderman assigned for that purpose by the council at the meeting of the 9th of November.

This is taken from sects. 32 and 43 of the Act of 1835.

**Notice of
election.**

54. Nine days at least before the day for the election of a councillor, the town clerk shall prepare and sign a notice thereof, and publish it by fixing it on the town hall, and, in the case of a ward election, in some conspicuous place in the ward.

Act of 1882 s. 54.

This is taken from paragraph 1 of sect. 1 of the Municipal Corporations Elections Act, 1875. For form of notice, see Form (H), Sched. 8, Part II.

55. The nomination of candidates for the office of councillor shall be conducted in accordance with the rules in Part II. of the Third Schedule.*

Nomination of candidates.

* Page 148.

56.—(1.) If the number of valid nominations exceeds that of the vacancies, the councillors shall be elected from among the persons nominated.

Relation of nomination to election.

(2.) If the number of valid nominations is the same as that of the vacancies, the persons nominated shall be deemed to be elected.

(3.) If the number of valid nominations is less than that of the vacancies, the persons nominated shall be deemed to be elected, and such of the retiring councillors for the borough or ward as were highest on the poll at their election, or, if the poll was equal, or there was no poll, as are selected for that purpose by the mayor, shall be deemed to be re-elected to make up the required number.

(4.) If there is no valid nomination, the retiring councillors shall be deemed to be re-elected.

This and sect. 57 are taken from sect. 8 of the Municipal Elections Act, 1859 (22 Vict. c. 35).

57. If an election of councillors is not contested, the returning officer shall publish a list of the persons elected not later than eleven o'clock in the morning (*a*) on the day of election.

Publication of uncontested election.

58.—(1.) If an election of councillors is contested, the poll shall, as far as circumstances admit, be conducted as the poll at a contested parliamentary election is by the Ballot Act, 1872,† directed to be conducted, and, subject to the modifications expressed in Part III. of the Third Schedule,‡ and to the other provisions of this Act, the provisions of the Ballot Act, 1872, relating to a poll at a parliamentary election (including the provisions relating to the duties of the returning officer after the close of the poll), shall apply to a poll at an election of councillors.

Mode of conducting poll at contested election.

† Page 236.

‡ Page 150.

(*a*) Greenwich time: Statutes (Definition of Time) Act, 1880, 43 & 44 Vict. c. 9.

Act of 1882 s. 59.

Poll at election— continued.

(2.) Every person entitled to vote may vote for any number of candidates not exceeding the number of vacancies.

(3.) The poll shall commence at nine o'clock in the forenoon and close at four o'clock in the afternoon of the same day (a).

(4.) But if one hour elapses during which no vote is tendered, and the returning officer has not received notice that any person has within that hour been prevented from coming to the poll by any riot, violence, or other unlawful means, the returning officer may, if he thinks fit, close the poll at any time before four o'clock.

(5.) Where an equality of votes is found to exist between any candidates, and the addition of a vote would entitle any of those candidates to be declared elected, the returning officer, whether entitled or not to vote in the first instance, may give such additional vote by word of mouth or in writing.

(6.) Nothing in the Ballot Act, 1872, as applied by this Act, shall be deemed to authorize the appointment of any agents of a candidate at a municipal election; but if, in the case of a municipal election, an agent of a candidate is appointed, and notice in writing of the appointment is given to the returning officer, one clear day before the polling day, then the provisions of the Ballot Act, 1872, with respect to agents of candidates, shall, as far as regards that agent, apply in the case of that election.

The first and last paragraphs of this section are in substitution for, but a substantial re-enactment of, sect. 20 of the Ballot Act, 1872, repealed by the present Act. The remaining paragraphs are taken from sects. 32 and 35 of the Act of 1835.

For such portions of the Ballot Act, 1872, as apply to municipal elections, see "*Incorporated Enactments (Ballot Act, 1872)*," p. 236, post.

Questions which may be put to voters.

59.—(1.) At an election of councillors, the presiding officer shall, if required by two burgesses, or by a candidate or his agent, put to any person offering to vote, at the time of his presenting himself to vote, but not afterwards, the following questions, or either of them :

(a.) Are you the person enrolled in the burgess [*or* ward] roll now in force for this borough [*or* ward] as follows [*read the whole entry from the roll*]?

(a) Greenwich time: Statutes (Definition of Time) Act, 1880, 43 & 44 Vict. c. 9.

(b.) Have you already voted at the present election [*add, in case of an election for several wards*, in this or any other ward]?

Act of 1882 s. 59.

(2.) The vote of a person required to answer either of these questions shall not be received until he has answered it.

(3.) If any person wilfully makes a false answer thereto he shall be guilty of a misdemeanour.

(4.) Save as by this Act authorized, no inquiry shall be permitted at an election as to the right of any person to vote.

This is taken from sect. 34 of the Act of 1835, as amended by the Ballot Act.

Election of Aldermen.

60.—(1.) The ordinary day of election of aldermen shall be the 9th of November, and the election shall be held at the quarterly meeting of the council.

Time and mode of election of aldermen.

(2.) The election shall be held immediately after the election of the mayor, or, if there is a sheriff, the appointment of the sheriff.

(3.) An outgoing alderman, although mayor elect, shall not vote.

(4.) Every person entitled to vote may vote for any number of persons not exceeding the number of vacancies, by signing and personally delivering at the meeting to the chairman a voting paper containing the surnames and other names and places of abode and descriptions of the persons for whom he votes.

Signed voting papers.

(5.) The chairman, as soon as all the voting papers have been delivered to him, shall openly produce and read them, or cause them to be read, and then deliver them to the town clerk to be kept for twelve months.

(6.) In case of equality of votes the chairman, although as an outgoing alderman or otherwise not entitled to vote in the first instance, shall have the casting vote.

Casting vote.

(7.) The persons, not exceeding the number of vacancies, who have the greatest number of votes, shall be declared by the chairman to be, and thereupon shall be, elected.

This is taken from sect. 25 of the Act of 1835, sect. 14 of the Act of 1837, and sect. 13 of the Act of 1853. The voting papers do not require a stamp, *Reg.* v. *Strachan*, L. R., 7 Q. B. 463; 41 L. J., Q. B. 210.

Election of Mayor.

Time and
mode of
election of
mayor.

61.—(1.) The ordinary day of election of mayor shall be the 9th of November.

(2.) The election of mayor shall be the first business transacted at the quarterly meeting of the council on the day of election.

(3.) An outgoing alderman may vote although the person for whom he votes is an alderman.

(4.) In case of equality of votes, the chairman, although not entitled to vote in the first instance, shall have the casting vote.

This is taken from sects. 49 and 69 of the Act of 1835.

Election of Auditors and Assessors.

Time and
mode of
election of
auditors and
assessors.

62.—(1.) The ordinary day of election of elective auditors shall be the 1st of March, or such other day as the council, with the approval of the Local Government Board, from time to time appoint.

(2.) The ordinary day of election of revising assessors shall be the 1st of March.

(3.) If the election of elective auditors and that of revising assessors are held at the same time, then at the poll one voting paper only shall be used by any person voting. The names of the candidates for the respective offices shall be therein separate, and distinguished so as to show the office for which each is a candidate, and the provisions of the Ballot Act, 1872, shall be varied accordingly; but in the counting of the votes every voting paper shall be deemed to be a separate voting paper in respect of each office, and any objections thereto shall be considered and dealt with accordingly.

(4.) An elector shall not vote for more than one person to be elective auditor or revising assessor.

(5.) Elections of elective auditors and of revising assessors shall be held at the town hall or some one other convenient place appointed by the mayor.

(6.) Save as in this section provided, all the provisions of this Act with respect to the nomination and election of councillors for a borough not having wards shall apply to the nomination and election of elective auditors and revising assessors.

Act of 1882 s. 62.

This is taken from sect. 37 of the Act of 1835, sect. 4 of the Act of 1837, and sect. 6 of the Act of 1875.

For form of ballot paper, see Form K. of Sched. VIII., Part 2, p. 161.

Supplemental and Exceptional Provisions.

63. For all purposes connected with and having reference to the right to vote * at municipal elections words in this Act importing the masculine gender include women.

Right of women to vote.

[* Sects. 9, 51.]

This is a substantial reproduction of sect. 9 of the Act of 1869 (32 & 33 Vict. c. 55), under which it was held by Cockburn, C. J., and Mellor and Hannen, JJ., in *Reg.* v. *Harrald* (L. R., 7 Q. B. 361; 41 L. J., Q. B. 173; 26 L. T. 616; 28 W. R. 328), in making absolute a rule for a quo warranto against a councillor elected by a majority of one, that a married woman, although living apart from her husband, and paying rates as if she were single, was not entitled to vote; and the court (Hannen, J., dub.) also intimated, though it did not decide, that a woman, enrolled when single, lost her right to vote by marrying before an election. The court proceeded on the first point on the ground that by the common law the political rights of a married woman are merged in those of her husband; and although it is hard to see how this afforded ground for introducing an exception, which the legislature might have introduced if it had chosen, it is conceived also that the legislature, by repeating the words of the Act of 1869 without change, intended the judicial interpretation of them to prevail.

Reg. v. *Harrald* would probably be followed by a divisional court on the first point, but might be dissented from on the second. On either point there is an appeal to the Court of Appeal under sect. 19 of the Judicature Act of 1873, and a further appeal to the House of Lords under sect. 3 of the Appellate Jurisdiction Act, 1876, if the question should arise upon a quo warranto; but if it should arise upon a case stated by a revising barrister, there would be an appeal to the Court of Appeal by leave only, and no further appeal to the House of Lords. Judicature Act, 1881 (44 & 45 Vict. c. 68), s. 14.

The Married Women's Property Act, 1882 (which received the royal assent on the same day as this Act), if the reasoning in *Reg.* v. *Harrald* be correct, does not seem to carry the political rights of married women any further.

The exclusion of women from the parliamentary franchise, which had never been doubted, was formally settled in *Chorlton* v. *Lings*, L. R., 4 C. P. 374.

64. The council may divide the borough or any ward into polling districts, and thereupon the overseers shall, as far as practicable, make out the parish burgess list so as to divide the names in conformity with the polling districts.

Polling districts.

This and sect. 65 are taken from sects. 10 and 8 of the Act of 1875 respectively,

Notices as
to elections.

65. Any notice required to be given in connexion with a municipal election may, as to elective auditors and revising assessors, be comprised in one notice, and may, as to ward elections, comprise matter necessary for several wards.

Time for
filling casual
vacancies.

66.—(1.) On a casual vacancy in a corporate office, the election shall be held within fourteen days after notice in writing of the vacancy has been given to the mayor or town clerk by two burgesses.

(2.) Where the office vacant is that of mayor, the notice of the meeting for the election shall be signed by the town clerk.

(3.) In other cases the day of election shall be fixed by the mayor.

This is taken from sects. 27, 47 and 49 of the Act of 1835, and sects. 9 and 11 of the Act of 1853.

Death,
absence, &c.,
of mayor or
returning
officer.

67.—(1.) If the mayor is dead, or is absent or otherwise incapable of acting in the execution of his powers and duties as to elections under this Act, the council shall forthwith choose an alderman to execute those powers and duties in the place of the mayor.

(2.) In case of the illness, absence, or incapacity to act of the alderman assigned to be returning officer at a ward election, the mayor may appoint to act in his stead another alderman, or, if the number of aldermen does not exceed the number of wards, a councillor not being a councillor for that ward, and not being enrolled in the ward roll for that ward.

This is taken from sect. 36 of the Act of 1835, sect. 16 of the Act of 1837, and sect. 10 of the Act of 1853.

Election of
councillor in
more than
one ward.

68. If a person is elected councillor in more than one ward, he shall, within three days after notice thereof, choose, by writing signed by him and delivered to the town clerk, or in his default the mayor shall, within three days after the time for choice has expired, declare, for which of those wards he shall serve, and the choice or declaration shall be conclusive.

This is taken from sect. 46 of the Act of 1835.

Elections not
in churches.

69. A municipal election shall not be held in any church, chapel, or other place of public worship.

This reproduces the concluding proviso of sect. 33 of the Act of 1835.

70.—(1.) If a municipal election is not held on the appointed day or within the appointed time, it may be held on the day next after that day or the expiration of that time.

Act of 1882 s. 70.

Omission to hold election, or election void.

(2.) If a municipal election is not held on the appointed day or within the appointed time, or on the day next after that day or the expiration of that time, or becomes void, the municipal corporation shall not thereby be dissolved or be disabled from electing, but the High Court may, on motion, grant a mandamus for the election to be held on a day appointed by the court.

(3.) Thereupon public notice of the election shall, by such person as the court directs, be fixed on the town hall, and shall be kept so fixed for at least six days before the day appointed for the election; and in all other respects the election shall be conducted as directed by this Act respecting ordinary elections.

This is taken from sects. 25 and 26 of the Act of 1837 (7 Will. 4 & 1 Vict. c. 78), incorporating 11 Geo. 1, c. 4, repealed as to boroughs within this Act by sect. 5 and Sched. 1, Part II.

The case of Sunday, &c. is provided for by sect. 230, post.

71.—(1.) If a parish burgess list is not made or revised in due time, the corresponding part of the burgess roll in operation before the time appointed for the revision shall be the parish burgess list until a burgess list for the parish has been revised and become part of the burgess roll.

Burgess roll to be in operation until revision of new burgess roll.

(2.) If a burgess roll is not made in due time, the burgess roll in force before the time appointed for the revision shall continue in force until the new burgess roll is made.

This is taken from sect. 6 of the Act of 1837 (7 Will. 4 & 1 Vict. c. 78), as amended by sect. 6 of the Act of 1857 (20 & 21 Vict. c. 50).

72. An election shall not be invalidated by non-compliance with the rules in the Third Schedule,* or mistake in the use of the forms in the Eighth Schedule,† if it appears to the court having cognizance of the question that the election was conducted in accordance with the principles laid down in the body of this Act.

Non-compliance with rules.

* Page 145.
† Page 158.

This section in part repeats sect. 13 of the Ballot Act, 1872, post p. 241, under which an election of a candidate doubly nominated and doubly voted for was held good in *Northcote* v. *Pulsford*, L. R., 10 C. P. 476; 44 L. J., C. P. 217; 32 L. T. 602; 23 W. R. 700

Election
valid unless
questioned
within twelve
months.

73. Every municipal election not called in question within twelve months after the election, either by election petition or by information in the nature of a quo warranto, shall be deemed to have been to all intents a good and valid election.

This is taken, as to quo warranto, from sect. 1 of the Act of 1843 (6 & 7 Vict. c. 89). For the limit in case of an election petition, see sect. 88, sub-s. (4), post.

Offences in
relation to
nomination
papers.

74.—(1.) If any person forges or fraudulently defaces or fraudulently destroys any nomination paper, or delivers to the town clerk any forged nomination paper, knowing it to be forged, he shall be guilty of a misdemeanour, and shall be liable to imprisonment for any term not exceeding six months, with or without hard labour.

(2.) An attempt to commit any such offence shall be punishable as the offence is punishable.

This is taken from sect. 3 of the Ballot Act, 1872, applied to municipal nomination papers by sect. 1, sub-s. (4) of the Municipal Elections Act, 1875 (38 & 39 Vict. c. 40).

Offences in
relation to
lists and
elections.

75.—(1.) If a mayor or revising assessor neglects or refuses to revise a parish burgess list, or a mayor or alderman neglects or refuses to conduct or declare an election, as required by this Act, he shall for every such offence be liable to a fine not exceeding one hundred pounds, recoverable by action.

(2.) If—

(a.) An overseer neglects or refuses to make, sign, or deliver a parish burgess list, as required by this Act; or

(b.) A town clerk neglects or refuses to receive, print, and publish, a parish burgess list or list of claimants or respondents, as required by this Act; or

(c.) An overseer or town clerk refuses to allow any such list to be inspected by a person having a right thereto;

he shall for every such neglect or refusal be liable to a fine not exceeding fifty pounds, recoverable by action.

(3.) An action under this section shall not lie after three months from the neglect or refusal. A moiety of any fine recovered therein shall, after payment of the costs of action, be paid to the plaintiff.

This is a substantial reproduction of sect. 48 of the Act of 1835, under which it was held in *King* v. *Burrell* (12 Ad. & E. 460), that an overseer neglecting to sign, &c. was liable to the penalty, although the neglect was not wilful or corrupt; and to the same effect was *Hunt* v. *Hibbs*, 29 L. J., Ex. 222.

This section overrides Order LV. of the Rules of the Supreme Court, and gives the plaintiff a right to his costs.

By sect. 140 the other moiety of the fine goes to the borough fund. As to recovery thereof from a successful plaintiff, see *Mayor of Harwich* v. *Grant*, 5 E. & B. 182.

No notice of action appears to be necessary.

76.—(1.) If the Ballot Act, 1872, ceases to be in force, so much of this Act as directs that the poll at a contested election of councillors shall be conducted as the poll at a contested parliamentary election is by the Ballot Act, 1872, directed to be conducted, and as applies provisions of the Ballot Act, 1872, to a poll at a contested election of councillors, shall forthwith cease to be in force, and thereupon the enactments in Part IV. of the Third Schedule* shall revive and be in force.

Revival of former law on expiration of Ballot Act.

* Page 151.

(2.) But this cesser and revivor shall not affect any act done, right acquired, or liability or fine incurred, or the institution or prosecution to its termination of any proceeding in respect of any such right, liability, or fine.

The Ballot Act, 1872—originally directed to continue till 31st December, 1880, by sect. 33 of that Act, and afterwards continued by successive Expiring Laws Continuance Acts—is by the Expiring Laws Continuance Act, 1882 (45 & 46 Vict. c. 64), continued till the 31st December, 1883.

PART IV.—Corrupt Practices and Election Petitions.

Corrupt Practices.

77. In this Part—

"Bribery," "treating," "undue influence," and "personation," include respectively anything done before, at, after, or with respect to a municipal election, which if done before, at, after, or with respect to a parliamentary election would make the person doing the same liable to any penalty, punishment, or disqualification for bribery, treating (¹), undue influence, or personation, as the case may be, under any Act for the time being in force with respect to parliamentary elections (²):

Definitions.

"Bribery," "treating," "undue influence," "personation."

Act of 1882
s. 77.
" Corrupt
practice."
"Corrupt practice" means bribery, treating, undue influence, or personation :

"Candidate" means a person elected, or having been nominated, or having declared himself a candidate for election, to a corporate office :

"Canvasser" means any person who solicits or persuades, or attempts to persuade, any person to vote or to abstain from voting at a municipal election, or to vote or to abstain from voting for a candidate at a municipal election:

"Voter" means a burgess or a person who votes or claims to vote at a municipal election :

" Election
court."
[* Sect. 92.]
"Election court" means a court constituted under this Part* for the trial of an election petition :

"Municipal election petition" or "election petition" means a petition under this Part complaining of an undue municipal election :

"Parliamentary election petition" means a petition under the Parliamentary Elections Act, 1868 :

"Prescribed" means prescribed by general rules made under this Part:

"Borough" and "election" when used with reference to a petition mean the borough and election to which the petition relates.

Part IV. of this Act is a substantial reproduction of the Corrupt Practices (Municipal Elections) Act, 1872 (35 & 36 Vict. c. 60).

(1) *Treating.*]—Sect. 23 of the Corrupt Practices Act, 1854, is applicable. *Hargreaves* v. *Simpson*, 4 Q. B. D. 403 ; 48 L. J., Q. B. 607 ; 41 L. T. 216 ; 27 W. R. 885.

(2) *Corrupt Practices Acts.*]—See the Corrupt Practices Act, 1854, and other Acts now (October, 1882) in force with respect to parliamentary elections, post, tit. "*Incorporated Enactments (Corrupt Practices Acts).*"

General
penalties
for corrupt
practices.
78. A person guilty of a corrupt practice at a municipal election shall be liable to the like actions, prosecutions, penalties, forfeitures, and punishments as if the corrupt practice had been committed at a parliamentary election.

A separate penalty is recoverable for each of many acts of bribery at one election. *Milnes* v. *Bale*, L. R., 10 C. P. 591 ; 44 L. J., C. P. 336 ; 33 L. T. 174 ; 23 W. R. 660.

79.—(1.) Where it is found by the report of an election court that a corrupt practice has been committed by or with the knowledge and consent of a candidate at a municipal election, that candidate shall be deemed to have been personally guilty of a corrupt practice at the election, and his election, if he has been elected, shall be void ; and he shall (whether elected or not) during seven years from the date of the report be subject to the following disqualifications :

Act of 1882 s. 79.

Disqualifications and avoidance of election for corrupt practices by candidates.

He shall be incapable of—

(a.) Holding or exercising any corporate office or municipal franchise, or being enrolled or voting as a burgess :

(b.) Acting as a justice or holding any judicial office :

(c.) Being elected to or sitting or voting in Parliament :

(d.) Being registered or voting as a parliamentary voter :

(e.) Being employed by a candidate in a parliamentary or municipal election :

(f.) Acting as overseer or as guardian of the poor.

(2.) If any person is on indictment or information found guilty of a corrupt practice at a municipal election, or is in any action or proceeding adjudged to pay a penalty or forfeiture for a corrupt practice at a municipal election, he shall, whether he was a candidate at the election or not, be subject during seven years from the date of the conviction or judgment to all the disqualifications mentioned in this section.

(3.) If after a person has become disqualified under this Part any witness on whose testimony he has become disqualified is, on his prosecution, convicted of perjury in respect of that testimony, the High Court may, on motion, and on proof that the disqualification was procured by means of that perjury, order that the disqualification shall cease.

80. If it is found by an election court that a candidate has by an agent been guilty of a corrupt practice at a municipal election, or that any offence against this Part has been committed at a municipal election by a candidate, or by an agent for a candidate with the candidate's knowledge and consent, the candidate shall during the period for which he was elected to serve, or for which, if elected, he might have served, be disqualified for being elected to and for holding any corporate office in the borough, and if he was elected his election shall be void.

Act of 1882
s. 81.

Avoidance of
election for
general
corruption.

81. A municipal election shall be wholly avoided by such general corruption, bribery, treating, or intimidation at the election as would by the common law of Parliament avoid a parliamentary election.

Paid agents
and can-
vassers.

82.—(1.) A burgess of a borough shall not be retained or employed for payment or reward by or on behalf of a candidate at a municipal election for that borough or any ward thereof as a canvasser for the purposes of the election.

(2.) If any person is retained or employed in contravention of this prohibition, that person and also the person by whom he is retained or employed shall be guilty of an offence against this Part, and shall be liable on summary conviction to a fine not exceeding ten pounds.

(3.) An agent or canvasser retained or employed for payment or reward for any of the purposes of a municipal election shall not vote at the election, and if he votes he shall be guilty of an offence against this Part, and shall be liable on summary conviction to a fine not exceeding ten pounds.

The slight variation of sect. 7 of the Act of 1872, effected by paragraph (1), will prevent a burgess registered in one ward from canvassing in another. This was formerly doubtful. See *Maude* v. *Lowley*, L. R., 9 C. P. 165.

Payment for
conveyance
of voters.

83. If a candidate or an agent for a candidate pays or agrees to pay any money on account of the conveyance of a voter to or from the poll, he shall be guilty of an offence against this Part, and shall be liable on summary conviction to a fine not exceeding five pounds.

Prosecutions
for corrupt
practices.

84.—(1.) The costs and expenses of a prosecutor and his witnesses in the prosecution of any person for bribery, undue influence, or personation at a municipal election, with compensation for trouble and loss of time, shall, unless the court otherwise directs, be allowed, paid, and borne as in cases of felony (¹).

(2.) The clerk of the peace of the borough, or, if there is none, of the county in which the borough is situate, shall, if so directed by an election court, prosecute any person for bribery, undue influence, or personation at the election in respect of which the court acts, or sue or proceed against any person for penalties for bribery, treating, undue influence, or any offence against this Part at the election.

As in cases of Felony.]—The reference appears to be to 7 Geo. 4, c. 64, ss. 22, 25, and 14 & 15 Vict. c. 55, ss. 5, 6, by which, under regulations of a Secretary of State, these costs are payable out of the borough rate. By 33 & 34 Vict. c. 23, s. 3, persons convicted of felony may be themselves ordered to pay the costs. See these statutes, Chit. Stat. vol. ii. tit. "*Criminal Law.*"

Act of 1882 s. 84.

85. The votes of persons in respect of whom any corrupt practice is proved to have been committed at a municipal election shall be struck off on a scrutiny.

Striking off votes.

86. The enactments for the time being in force for the detection of personation and for the apprehension of persons charged with personation at a parliamentary election shall apply in the case of a municipal election.

Personation.

The enactments now (October, 1882) in force are 6 Vict. c. 18, ss. 85—89 (Registration Act, 1843); and 35 & 36 Vict. c. 33 (Ballot Act, 1872), s. 24, which see, p. 257, post, tit. "*Incorporated Enactments (Personation).*"

Election Petitions.

87.—(1.) A municipal election may be questioned by an election petition on the ground—

Ground for questioning municipal election by petition.

> (a.) That the election was as to the borough or ward wholly avoided by general bribery, treating, undue influence, or personation; or
>
> (b.) That the election was avoided by corrupt practices or offences against this Part committed at the election; or
>
> (c.) That the person whose election is questioned was at the time of the election disqualified; or
>
> (d.) That he was not duly elected by a majority of lawful votes.

(2.) A municipal election shall not be questioned on any of those grounds except by an election petition.

88.—(1.) An election petition may be presented either by four or more persons who voted or had a right to vote at the election or by a person alleging himself to have been a candidate at the election.

Presentation of petition.

(2.) Any person whose election is questioned by the petition (¹), and any returning officer of whose conduct a petition complains, may be made a respondent to the petition.

Respondent.

(3.) The petition shall be in the prescribed form and shall be signed by the petitioner, and shall be presented in the

Act of 1882
s. 88.
Presentation
of election
petition—
continued.

prescribed manner to the High Court in the Queen's Bench Division, and the prescribed officer shall send a copy thereof to the town clerk, who shall forthwith publish it in the borough.

(4.) It shall be presented within twenty-one days after the day on which the election was held, except that if it complains of the election on the ground of corrupt practices, and specifically alleges that a payment of money or other reward has been made or promised since the election by a person elected at the election, or on his account or with his privity, in pursuance or furtherance of such corrupt practices, it may be presented at any time within twenty-eight days after the date of the alleged payment or promise, whether or not any other petition against that person has been previously presented or tried.

(¹) *Questioned by the Petition.*]—These words include a person assuming to be, though not in fact, elected (*Yates* v. *Leach*, L. R., 9 C. P. 605; 43 L. J., C. P. 377); but an unsuccessful candidate cannot be made respondent to a petition against the return of successful candidates with whom he coalesced for purposes of canvassing. (*Lovering* v. *Dawson*, L. R., 10 C. P. 711; 44 L. J., C. P. 321; 32 L. T. 819.)

89.—(1.) At the time of presenting an election petition or within three days afterwards, the petitioner shall give security for all costs, charges, and expenses which may become payable by him to any witness summoned on his behalf, or to any respondent.

(2.) The security shall be to such amount, not exceeding five hundred pounds, as the High Court, or a judge thereof, on summons, directs, and shall be given in the prescribed manner, either by a deposit of money, or by recognizance entered into by not more than four sureties, or partly in one way and partly in the other.

(3.) Within five days after the presentation of the petition the petitioner shall in the prescribed manner serve on the respondent a notice of the presentation of the petition, and of the nature of the proposed security, and a copy of the petition.

(4.) Within five days after service of the notice the respondent may object in writing to any recognizance on the ground than any surety is insufficient or is dead, or cannot be found or ascertained for want of a sufficient description in the recognizance, or that a person named in the recognizance has not duly acknowledged the same.

(5.) An objection to a recognizance shall be decided in the prescribed manner.

(6.) If the objection is allowed, the petitioner may, within a further prescribed time not exceeding five days, remove it by a deposit in the prescribed manner of such sum of money as will, in the opinion of the court or officer having cognizance of the matter, make the security sufficient.

(7.) If no security is given, as prescribed, or any objection is allowed and is not removed, as aforesaid, no further proceedings shall be had on the petition.

90. On the expiration of the time limited for making objections, or, after objection made, on the objection being disallowed or removed, whichever last happens, the petition shall be at issue.

Petition at issue.

91.—(1.) The prescribed officer shall as soon as may be make a list, in this Act referred to as the municipal election list, of all election petitions at issue, placing them in the order in which they were presented, and shall keep at his office a copy of this list, open to inspection in the prescribed manner.

Municipal election list.

(2.) The petitions shall, as far as conveniently may be, be tried in the order in which they stand in the list.

(3.) Two or more candidates may be made respondents to the same petition, and their cases may be tried at the same time, but for the purposes of this Part the petition shall be deemed to be a separate petition against each respondent.

(4.) Where more petitions than one are presented relating to the same election, or to elections held at the same time for different wards of the same borough, they shall be bracketed together in the list as one petition, but shall, unless the High Court otherwise directs, stand in the list in the place where the last of them would have stood if it had been the only petition relating to that election.

92.—(1.) An election petition shall be tried by an election court consisting of a barrister qualified and appointed as in this section provided, without a jury.

Constitution of election court.

(2.) A barrister shall not be qualified to constitute an election court if he is of less than fifteen years' standing, or is a member of the Commons House of Parliament, or holds any office or place of profit under the Crown, other than that of recorder.

(3.) A barrister shall not be qualified to constitute an election court for trial of an election petition relating to any borough for which he is recorder, or in which he resides, or which is included in a circuit of her Majesty's judges on which he practises as a barrister.

(4.) As soon as may be after a municipal election list is made out the prescribed officer shall send a copy thereof to each of the judges for the time being on the rota for the trial of parliamentary election petitions; and those judges or two of them shall forthwith determine the number of barristers, not exceeding five at any one time, necessary to be appointed for the trial of the election petitions at issue, and shall appoint that number accordingly as commissioners under this Part, and shall assign the petitions to be tried by each.

(5.) If a commissioner to whom the trial of a petition is assigned, dies, or declines or becomes incapable to act, the said judges or two of them may assign the trial to be conducted or continued by any other of the commissioners appointed under this section.

(6.) The election court shall for the purposes of the trial have the same powers and privileges as a judge on the trial of a parliamentary election petition, except that any fine or order of committal by the court may on motion by the person aggrieved be discharged or varied by the High Court, or in vacation by a judge thereof, on such terms, if any, as the High Court or judge thinks fit.

93.—(1.) An election petition shall be tried in open court, and notice of the time and place of trial shall be given in the prescribed manner not less than seven days before the day of trial.

(2.) The place of trial shall be within the borough, except that the High Court may, on being satisfied that special circumstances exist rendering it desirable that the petition should be tried elsewhere, appoint some other convenient place for the trial.

(3.) The election court may in its discretion adjourn the trial from time to time, and from any one place to any other place within the borough or place where it is held.

(4.) At the conclusion of the trial the election court shall determine whether the person whose election is complained of, or any and what other person, was duly elected, or whether the election was void, and shall forthwith certify in writing the determination to the High Court, and the determination so certified shall be final to all intents as to the matters at issue on the petition.

(5.) Where a charge is made in a petition of any corrupt practice or offence against this Part having been committed at the election the court shall, in addition to the certificate, and at the same time, report in writing to the High Court as follows:

(a.) Whether any corrupt practice or offence against this Part has or has not been proved to have been committed by or with the knowledge and consent of any candidate at the election, and the nature of the corrupt practice or offence;

(b.) The names of all persons (if any) proved at the trial to have been guilty of any corrupt practice or offence against this Part;

(c.) Whether any corrupt practices have, or whether there is reason to believe that any corrupt practices have, extensively prevailed at the election in the borough or in any ward thereof.

(6.) The election court may at the same time make a special report to the High Court as to any matters arising in the course of the trial, an account of which ought, in the judgment of the election court, to be submitted to the High Court.

(7.) If, on the application of any party to a petition made in the prescribed manner to the High Court, it appears to the High Court that the case raised by the petition can be conveniently stated as a special case, the High Court may direct the same to be stated accordingly, and any such special case shall be heard before the High Court, and the decision of the High Court shall be final (¹).

(8.) If it appears to the election court on the trial of a petition that any question of law as to the admissibility of

Side notes:

Act of 1882 s. 93.

Report as to corrupt practices.

Special case.

Act of 1882
s. 93.

Trial of
election
petition—
continued.

evidence, or otherwise, requires further consideration by the High Court, the election court may postpone the granting of a certificate until the question has been determined by the High Court, and for this purpose may reserve any such question, as questions may be reserved by a judge on a trial at nisi prius.

(9.) On the trial of a petition, unless the election court otherwise directs, any charge of a corrupt practice or offence against this Part may be gone into, and evidence in relation thereto received before any proof has been given of agency on behalf of any candidate in respect of the corrupt practice or offence.

(10.) On the trial of a petition complaining of an undue election and claiming the office for some person, the respondent may give evidence to prove that that person was not duly elected, in the same manner as if he had presented a petition against the election of that person.

(11.) The trial of a petition shall be proceeded with notwithstanding that the respondent has ceased to hold the office his election to which is questioned by the petition.

(12.) A copy of any certificate or report made to the High Court on the trial of a petition, and, in the case of a decision by the High Court on a special case, a statement of the decision, shall be sent by the High Court to the Secretary of State.

(13.) A copy of any such certificate and a statement of any such decision shall also be certified by the High Court, under the hands of two or more judges thereof, to the town clerk of the borough.

This section appears substantially to re-enact sect. 15 of the Corrupt Practices (Municipal Elections) Act, 1872 (35 & 36 Vict. c. 50).

(¹) *Finality of Decision of High Court.*]—It was held in *Harmon v. Park* (6 Q. B. D. 323, C. A.), that an appeal lies to the Court of Appeal from an order of the High Court upon an interlocutory matter in a municipal election petition; but it was afterwards enacted by sect. 14 of the Judicature Act, 1881 (44 & 45 Vict. c. 68), that "the jurisdiction of the High Court to decide questions of law upon appeal or otherwise, under" the Parliamentary Registration Acts, the Corrupt Practices (Municipal Elections) Act, 1872, "or any Act amending the same respectively," should "henceforth be final and conclusive, unless in any case it shall seem fit to the said High Court to give special leave to appeal therefrom to her Majesty's

Act of 1882 s. 93.

Court of Appeal, whose decision in such case shall be final and conclusive."

It would seem that these special words of the Judicature Act, 1881, override the general words of sub-section 7 of this section, on the analogy of *Crush* v. *Turner* (3 Ex. D. 303), and because the present Act is an Act "amending" the Corrupt Practices Act, 1872, within the meaning of sect. 14 of the Judicature Act, 1881; and that therefore there will be an appeal, *by leave*, to the Court of Appeal.

94.—(1.) Witnesses at the trial of an election petition shall be summoned and sworn in the same manner, as nearly as circumstances admit, as witnesses at a trial at nisi prius, and shall be liable to the same penalties for perjury. Witnesses.

(2.) On the trial the election court may, by order in writing, require any person who appears to the court to have been concerned in the election to attend as a witness, and any person refusing to obey the order shall be guilty of contempt of court.

(3.) The court may examine any person so required to attend or being in court although he is not called and examined by any party to the petition.

(4.) A witness may, after his examination by the court, be cross-examined by or on behalf of the petitioner and respondent or either of them.

(5.) A witness on an election petition shall not be excused from answering any question relating to a corrupt practice or offence against this Part committed at or connected with the election on the ground that the answer thereto may criminate or tend to criminate him; but if he answers it he shall be entitled to receive from the court a certificate stating that he was on his examination required by the court to answer questions the answers whereto criminated or tended to criminate him, and that he answered all such questions. Witness compelled to answer criminating questions.

(6.) If any information, indictment, or action is at any time thereafter pending against the witness in any court for any corrupt practice or offence against this Part committed at or in relation to the election before the time of his giving his evidence, that court shall, on production and proof of the certificate, stay the proceedings, and may, in its discretion, award to him such costs as he has been put to therein. Certificate of court indemnifying witness.

(7.) The giving of or refusal to give any such certificate by the election court shall be final and conclusive.

L.C.   E

Act of 1882
s. 94.

(8.) A statement made by any person in answer to a question put to him by or before an election court shall not, except in cases of indictment for perjury, be admissible in evidence in any proceeding, civil or criminal.

(9.) The reasonable expenses incurred by any person in appearing to give evidence at the trial of an election petition, according to the scale allowed to witnesses on the trial of civil actions at the assizes, may be allowed to him by a certificate of the election court or of the prescribed officer, and if the witness was called and examined by the court, shall be deemed part of the expenses of providing a court, but otherwise shall be deemed costs of the petition.

Withdrawal
of petition.

95.—(1.) A petitioner shall not withdraw an election petition without the leave of the election court or High Court on special application, made in the prescribed manner, and at the prescribed time and place.

(2.) The application shall not be made until the prescribed notice of the intention to make it has been given in the borough.

(3.) On the hearing of the application any person who might have been a petitioner in respect of the election may apply to the court to be substituted as a petitioner, and the court may, if it thinks fit, substitute him accordingly.

(4.) If the proposed withdrawal is in the opinion of the court induced by any corrupt bargain or consideration, the court may by order direct that the security given on behalf of the original petitioner shall remain as security for any costs that may be incurred by the substituted petitioner, and that to the extent of the sum named in the security, the original petitioner and his sureties shall be liable to pay the costs of the substituted petitioner.

(5.) If the court does not so direct, then security to the same amount as would be required in the case of a new petition, and subject to the like conditions, shall be given on behalf of the substituted petitioner before he proceeds with his petition and within the prescribed time after the order of substitution.

(6.) Subject as aforesaid, a substituted petitioner shall, as nearly as may be, stand in the same position and be subject to the same liabilities as the original petitioner.

(7.) If a petition is withdrawn, the petitioner shall be liable to pay the costs of the respondent.

(8.) Where there are more petitioners than one, an application to withdraw a petition shall not be made except with the consent of all the petitioners.

96.—(1.) An election petition shall be abated by the death of a sole petitioner or of the survivor of several petitioners.

(2.) The abatement of a petition shall not affect the liability of the petitioner or of any other person to the payment of costs previously incurred.

(3.) On the abatement of a petition the prescribed notice thereof shall be given in the borough, and, within the prescribed time after the notice is given, any person who might have been a petitioner in respect of the election may apply to the election court or High Court in the prescribed manner and at the prescribed time and place to be substituted as a petitioner; and the court may, if it thinks fit, substitute him accordingly.

(4.) Security shall be given on behalf of a petitioner so substituted, as in the case of a new petition.

97.—(1.) If before the trial of an election petition a respondent other than a returning officer—

(a.) Dies, resigns, or otherwise ceases to hold the office to which the petition relates; or

(b.) Gives the prescribed notice that he does not intend to oppose the petition;

the prescribed notice thereof shall be given in the borough, and within the prescribed time after the notice is given any person who might have been a petitioner in respect of the election may apply to the election court or High Court to be admitted as a respondent to oppose the petition, and shall be admitted accordingly, except that the number of persons so admitted shall not exceed three.

(2.) A respondent who has given the prescribed notice that he does not intend to oppose the petition shall not be allowed to appear or act as a party against the petition in any proceedings thereon.

98.—(1.) All costs, charges, and expenses of and incidental to the presentation of an election petition, and the proceedings consequent thereon, except such as are by this Act otherwise provided for, shall be defrayed by the parties to the petition in such manner and proportions as the election court determines; and in particular any costs, charges, or expenses which in the opinion of the court have been caused by vexatious conduct, unfounded allegations, or unfounded objections on the part either of the petitioner or of the respondent, and any needless expense incurred or caused on the part of petitioner or respondent, may be ordered to be defrayed by the parties by whom it has been incurred or caused, whether they are or not on the whole successful.

Taxation of costs.

(2). The costs may be taxed in the prescribed manner, but according to the same principles as costs between solicitor and client in an action in the High Court, and may be recovered as the costs of such an action, or as otherwise prescribed.

(3.) If a petitioner neglects or refuses for three months after demand to pay to any person summoned as a witness on his behalf, or to the respondent, any sum certified to be due to him for his costs, charges, and expenses, and the neglect or refusal is, within one year after the demand, proved to the satisfaction of the High Court, every person who has under this Act entered into a recognizance relating to the petition shall be held to have made default in the recognizance, and the prescribed officer shall thereon certify the recognizance to be forfeited, and it shall be dealt with as a forfeited recognizance relating to a parliamentary election petition.

Reception of and attendance on the election court.

99.—(1.) The town clerk shall provide proper accommodation for holding the election court; and any expenses incurred by him for the purposes of this section shall be paid out of the borough fund or borough rate.

(2.) All chief and head constables, superintendents of police, head-boroughs, gaolers, constables, and bailiffs shall give their assistance to the election court in the execution of its duties, and if any gaoler or officer of a prison makes default in receiving or detaining a prisoner committed thereto in pursuance of this Part, he shall be liable to a fine not exceeding five pounds for every day during which the default continues.

(3.) The election court may employ officers and clerks as prescribed.

Act of 1882 s. 99.

(4.) A shorthand writer shall attend at the trial of an election petition, and shall be sworn by the election court faithfully and truly to take down the evidence given at the trial. He shall take down the evidence at length. A transcript of the notes of the evidence taken by him shall, if the election court so directs, accompany the certificate of the election court. His expenses, according to a prescribed scale, shall be treated as part of the expenses incurred in receiving the court.

Shorthand writer.

100.—(1.) The judges for the time being on the rota for the trial of parliamentary election petitions, may from time to time make, revoke, and alter general rules for the effectual execution of this Part, and of the intention and object thereof, and the regulation of the practice, procedure, and costs of municipal election petitions, and the trial thereof, and the certifying and reporting thereon.

Rules of procedure and jurisdiction.

(2.) All such rules shall be laid before both Houses of Parliament within three weeks after they are made, if Parliament is then sitting, and if not, within three weeks after the beginning of the then next session of Parliament, and shall, while in force, have effect as if enacted in this Act.

(3.) Subject to the provisions of this Act, and of the rules made under it, the principles, practice, and rules for the time being observed in the case of parlimentary election petitions(¹), and in particular the principles and rules with regard to agency and evidence, and to a scrutiny, and to the declaring any person elected in the room of any other person declared to have been not duly elected, shall be observed, as far as may be, in the case of a municipal election petition.

(4.) The High Court shall, subject to this Act, have the same powers, jurisdiction, and authority with respect to a municipal election petition and the proceedings thereon as if the petition were an ordinary action within its jurisdiction.

(5.) The duties to be performed by the prescribed officer under this Part shall be performed by the prescribed officer of the High Court.

(6.) The general rules in force(²) at the commencement of

this Act with respect to matters within this Part shall, until superseded by rules made under this section, and subject to any amendment thereof by rules so made, have effect, with the necessary modifications, as if made under this section.

(¹) *Rules in the case of Parliamentary Election Petitions.*]—See these rules, Rogers on Elections.

(²) *General Rules in force.*]—The Act commences on the 1st January, 1883. Three sets of Rules are now (October, 1882) in force, bearing date respectively 20th November, 1872, 10th December, 1872, and 27th January, 1875. See these rules, Rawlinson's Municipal Corporation Acts, 7th ed., by Geary, pp. 628 et seq.

In view of a probable new issue with modifications, as required by the Judicature Acts and this Act, it is not deemed expedient to print these old rules in this book.

Expenses of election court.

101.—(1.) The remuneration and allowances to be paid to a commissioner for his services in respect of the trial of an election petition, and to any officers, clerks, or shorthand writers employed under this Part, shall be fixed by a scale made and varied by the election judges on the rota for the trial of parliamentary election petitions, with the approval of the Treasury. The remuneration and allowances shall be paid in the first instance by the Treasury, and shall be repaid to the Treasury, on their certificate, out of the borough fund or borough rate.

(2.) But the election court may in its discretion order that such remuneration and allowances, or the expenses incurred by a town clerk for receiving the election court, shall be repaid, wholly or in part to the Treasury or the town clerk, as the case may be, in the cases, by the persons, and in the manner following (namely):

(a.) When in the opinion of the election court a petition is frivolous and vexatious, by the petitioner;

(b.) When in the opinion of the election court a respondent has been personally guilty of corrupt practices at the election, by that respondent.

(3.) An order so made for the repayment of any sum by a petitioner or respondent may be enforced as an order for payment of costs; but a deposit made or security given under this Part shall not be applied for any such repayment until all costs and expenses payable by the petitioner or respondent to any party to the petition have been satisfied.

102. Where a candidate who has been elected to a corporate office is, by a certificate of an election court or a decision of the High Court, declared not to have been duly elected, acts done by him in execution of the office, before the time when the certificate or decision is certified to the town clerk, shall not be invalidated by reason of that declaration.

Act of 1882 s. 102.

Acts done pending a petition not invalidated.

103. Where on an election petition the election of any person to a corporate office has been declared void, and no other person has been declared elected in his room, a new election shall be held to supply the vacancy in the same manner as on a casual vacancy; and for the purposes of the election any duties to be performed by a mayor, alderman, or other officer, shall, if he has been declared not elected, be performed by a deputy, or other person who might have acted for him if he had been incapacitated by illness.

Provisions as to elections in the room of persons unseated on petition.

104. A person who has voted at a municipal election by ballot shall not in any proceeding to question the election be required to state for whom he has voted.

Prohibition of disclosure of vote.

PART V.—Corporate Property and Liabilities.

Corporate Land.

105. A municipal corporation may contract for the purchase of and hold any land not exceeding in the whole five acres, either in or out of the borough, and thereon, or on any land belonging to or held in trust for the corporation, may build a town hall, council house, justices' room, with or without a police station and cells, or lock-ups, or a quarter and petty sessions-house, or an assize court-house, with or without judges' lodgings, or a polling station, or any other building necessary or proper for any purpose of the borough.

Power to purchase land for town hall, &c.

This is taken from sect. 40 of the Act of 1837 (7 Will. 4 & 1 Vict. c. 78).

Except as authorized by this or the following sections, or by licence from the Crown under 7 & 8 Will. 3, c. 37, the corporation may not hold land for general purposes; but the Public Health Act, 1875 (38 & 39 Vict. c. 55), ss. 175 et seq., and some other Acts, give power to hold land for special purposes.

106. The council may, with the approval of the Treasury, borrow at interest on the security of any corporate land, or of any land proposed to be purchased by the council under this

Power to borrow with approval of Treasury.

Act of 1882 s. 106.

Act, or of the borough fund or borough rate, or of all or any of those securities, such sums as the council from time to time think requisite for the purchase of land, or for the building of any building which the council are by this Act authorized to build.

This and the next section are taken from sect. 8 of the Act of 1860 (23 & 24 Vict. c. 16).

Power to acquire land with the approval of the Treasury.

107.—(1.) Where a municipal corporation has not power to purchase or acquire land, or to hold land in mortmain, the council may, with the approval of the Treasury, purchase or acquire any land in such manner and on such terms and conditions as the Treasury approve, and the same may be conveyed to and held by the corporation accordingly.

Incorporation of part of Lands Clauses Acts.

(2.) The provisions of the Lands Clauses Consolidation Acts, 1845, 1860, and 1869, relating to the purchase of land by agreement, and to agreements for sale, and conveyances, sales, and releases of any lands or hereditaments, or any estate or interest therein by persons under disability, shall extend to all purchases of land under this section.

The second paragraph of this section substantially re-enacts sect. 6 of the Lands Clauses Consolidation Act, 1860 (23 & 24 Vict. c. 106), repealed by this Act.

The provisions of the Lands Clauses Act, 1845, which relate to purchase by agreement, are sects. 6—15, which sections also relate to purchases from parties under disability.

The Public Health Act, 1875 (38 & 39 Vict. c. 55), s. 176, incorporates, for the purposes of that Act, the *compulsory* powers of the Lands Clauses Act, subject to special provisions in that section mentioned.

Restrictions on alienation.

108.—(1.) The council shall not, unless authorized by Act of Parliament, sell, mortgage, or alienate any corporate land without the approval of the Treasury.

Leases.

(2.) The council shall not, unless authorized by Act of Parliament, lease or agree to lease any corporate land without the approval of the Treasury, except as follows :

    (a.) They may make a lease or agreement for a lease for a term not exceeding thirty-one years from the date of the lease or agreement, so that there be reserved and made payable during the whole of the term such clear yearly rent as to the council appears reasonable, without any fine.

(b.) They may make a lease or agreement for a lease for a term not exceeding seventy-five years from the date of the lease or agreement, and either at a reserved rent or on a fine, or both, as the council think fit,—

Building leases.

(i.) Of tenements or hereditaments, the greater part of the yearly value of which, at the date of the lease or agreement, consists of any building or buildings; or

(ii.) Of land proper for the erection of any houses or other buildings thereon, with or without gardens, yards, curtilages, or other appurtenances to be used therewith; or

(iii.) Where the lessee or intended lessee agrees to erect a building or buildings thereon of greater yearly value than the land,—of land proper for gardens, yards, curtilages or other appurtenances to be used with any other house or other building erected or to be erected on any such land, belonging either to the corporation or to any other proprietor, or proper for any other purpose calculated to afford convenience or accommodation to the occupiers of any such house or building.

This and the two next sections are taken from sects. 94—96 of the Act of 1835, as amended by sect. 2 of the Act of 1836 (6 & 7 Will. 4, c. 104).

109. The council may, with the approval of the Treasury, dispose of any corporate land either by way of absolute sale, or by way of exchange, mortgage, charge, demise, lease, or otherwise, in such manner and on such terms and conditions as the Treasury approve.

Power to dispose of land with approval of Treasury.

110. In the following cases,—

Renewal of leases in pursuance of covenant, &c. in force in 1835.

(a.) Where a body corporate of a borough was on the 5th of June, 1835, bound or engaged by any covenant or agreement, expressed or implied, or was enjoined by any deed, will, or other document, or was sanctioned or warranted by ancient usage, or by custom or practice, to make any renewal of any lease for years, or for life or lives, or for years determinable with any life or lives at any fixed or determinate or known or accustomed period, or after the lapse of any number of years, or on the dropping of any life or lives, and years determinable after the lapse of any number of years, at a fine certain, or under any special or specific terms or conditions :

(b.) Where a body corporate of a borough theretofore ordinarily made renewal of any lease for years, or for life or lives, or for years determinable with any life or lives at any fixed or determinate or known or accustomed period, or after the lapse of any number of years, or on the dropping of any life or lives, on the payment of an arbitrary fine,—

Then, notwithstanding anything in this Act, the council of the borough may renew the lease for such term or number of years, either absolutely or determinable with any life or lives, or for such life or lives, and at such rent, and on the payment of such fine or premium, either certain or arbitrary, and with or without any covenant for the future renewal thereof, as the council could or might have done if this Act had not been passed.

Working Men's Dwellings.

111.—(1.) If a municipal corporation determines to convert any corporate land into sites for working men's dwellings, and obtains the approval of the Treasury for so doing, the corporation may, for that purpose, make grants or leases for terms of nine hundred and ninety-nine years, or any shorter term, of any parts of the corporate land.

(2.) The corporation may make on the land any roads, drains, walls, fences, or other works requisite for converting the same into building land, at an expense not exceeding such sum as the Treasury approve.

(3.) The corporation may insert in any grant or lease of any part of the land (in this section referred to as the site) provisions binding the grantee or lessee to build thereon as in the grant or lease prescribed, and to maintain and repair the building, and prohibiting the division of the site or building, and any addition to or alteration of the character of the building, without the consent of the corporation, and for the re-vesting of the site in the corporation, or its re-entry thereon, on breach of any provision in the grant or lease (¹).

(4.) Every such provision shall be valid in law to all intents, and binding on the parties ([2]).

(5.) All costs and expenses incurred or authorized by a corporation in carrying into execution or otherwise in pursuance of this section, shall be paid out of the borough fund and borough rate, or by money borrowed by the corporation under this Part.

(6.) In this section the term working men's dwellings means buildings suitable for the habitation of persons employed in manual labour and their families; but the use of part of a building for purposes of retail trade or other purposes, approved by the council, shall not prevent the building from being deemed a dwelling.

This section reproduces the Working Men's Dwellings Act, 1874 (37 & 38 Vict. c. 59), the preamble of which recites that "it is expedient to encourage the erection of dwelling-houses suitable for persons employed in manual labour, and to afford increased facilities for the acquisition of sites for such dwelling-houses."

([1]) For Forms of Lease, &c., see Part III. of Schedule 8, Forms (L)—(O), p. 162, post.

([2]) It is conceived that without trenching on the rule that an Act of Parliament cannot bind a future Parliament, the 4th subsection of this section will be subject to the restrictions upon and relief against forfeiture provided by the 14th section of the Conveyancing and Law of Property Act, 1881.

Repayment of Loans.

112.—(1.) Where the Treasury approve a mortgage or charge under this Part they may, as a condition of their approval, require that the money borrowed on the security of the mortgage or charge be repaid, with all interest thereon, in thirty years, or any less period, and either by instalments or by means of a sinking fund, or both.

Power for Treasury to impose conditions as to repayment of money borrowed.

(2.) In that case the sums required for providing for the repayment of the principal and interest of the money borrowed shall be by virtue of this Act a charge on all or any of the following securities, namely, the land comprised in the mortgage (without prejudice to the security thereby created), or any other corporate land, or the borough fund, or the borough or other rates legally applicable to payment of the money borrowed or of the expenses which the money is borrowed to defray, as the Treasury direct.

This and the four next sections substantially reproduce corresponding enactments of the Act of 1860 (23 & 24 Vict. c. 16).

Act of 1882
s. 113.

Provisions as to sinking fund.

113.—(1.) Where money borrowed under this Part is directed to be repaid by means of a sinking fund, the council shall, out of the rents and profits of the land on which, or out of the borough fund or rates on which, the sums required for the sinking fund are charged under this Act, invest such sums, at such times, and in such government annuities, as the Treasury direct, and shall also from time to time invest in like manner all dividends of those annuities.

(2.) The annuities shall, in the books of the Bank of England, be placed to the account of the corporation, and in the matter of this Act, or of any previous Act under which the investment is made.

(3.) The dividends of the annuities shall be received and invested by such persons as the council by power of attorney under the corporate seal from time to time appoint.

(4.) No transfer shall be made of the annuities, or of any part thereof, without the consent in writing of the Treasury addressed to the chief accountant of the Bank of England.

(5.) The direction in writing of the council by power of attorney under the corporate seal, with the consent in writing of the Treasury, shall be sufficient authority to the bank for permitting any such transfer.

Purchase or Compensation Money.

Provision for replacing purchase or compensation money paid to treasurer.

114.—(1.) Where purchase-money or compensation has been paid to the Bank of England under an Act of Parliament in respect of land or any interest therein purchased or taken from a municipal corporation, or in respect of permanent damage to land of a municipal corporation, and the Treasury approve of the payment of the money or compensation, or of any money to arise from the sale of any Government securities in which the same has been invested, to the corporation or the treasurer, the Treasury may, as a condition of their approval, require provision to be made for raising and for investing in Government annuities a sum equivalent to the amount of money so paid.

(2.) The foregoing provisions of this Part applicable in the case of a sinking fund, as regards the mode of investing, payment of dividends, and transfer of annuities, shall be applicable in the case of investments under this section.

(3.) The Treasury shall, when it appears to them that an amount of annuities equivalent to the amount so paid has been raised by investment, direct that the accumulation shall cease; and the annuities and the dividends thereof shall thenceforth be applicable as if the annuities had arisen from investment under the Act of Parliament under which the purchase-money or compensation became payable.

(4.) But this section shall not apply to money payable to a municipal corporation when provision for the application of the money, or of the price or compensation from which the money is derived, is contained in any local Act of Parliament relating thereto, and the money is to be paid to the corporation to be applied in conformity with that provision.

115.— (1.) Where the Treasury approve of the sale or exchange of any corporate land or of any interest therein, their approval may be subject to such conditions as they think fit in relation to the investment for the benefit of the corporation of the money arising from the sale or exchange.

(2.) If the Treasury direct the money to be invested in Government annuities, the foregoing provisions of this part respecting the mode of investing, payment of dividends, and transfer of annuities shall be applicable, but not so as to make any accumulation necessary.

(3.) If the Treasury consent to the application of the money or of any part thereof for the benefit of the inhabitants of the borough, they may, as a condition of their consent, require the like provision to be made as they are authorized to require in the case of their approval of payment to a municipal corporation or the treasurer.

116. The Treasury may at any time approve of the application of any annuities arising from investments under either of the two last preceding sections, or of the money to arise from the sale thereof, or any part thereof respectively, for the benefit of the inhabitants of the borough ; and, as a condition of their approval, may require the like provision to be made as they are authorized to require in the case of their approval of payment to a municipal corporation or the treasurer, and so from time to time, and the provisions of this Part shall be applicable accordingly: but it shall not be imperative on the

Side notes:

Act of 1882 s. 114.

Investment of proceeds of sale or exchange authorized by Treasury.

Power for Treasury to authorize application of certain investments for benefit of borough.

Act of 1882
s. 116.

Treasury to impose the condition aforesaid where by reason of the application of the annuities or money to improvement of the property of the corporation or for the permanent benefit of the borough, or otherwise, under the special circumstances of the case, the Treasury in their discretion think fit to dispense with the condition.

Misappropriation.

Penalty for misappropriation of moneys.

117. If any person authorized to receive money to arise from the sale of any annuities or securities purchased or transferred under the foregoing provisions of this Part, or under any Act repealed by this Act, or any dividends thereon, or any other such money as aforesaid, appropriates the same otherwise than as directed by this Act, or by the Treasury in pursuance thereof, he shall be guilty of a misdemeanour, and shall be subject in respect thereof to the provisions of the Larceny Act, 1861 (^{1}), applicable to a person guilty of a misdemeanour under section seventy-five of that Act, or to the provisions of any enactment for the time being substituted for that section.

This substantially reproduces sect. 7 of the Act of 1860 (23 & 24 Vict. c. 16).

(^{1}) " *The Larceny Act.*"]—Sect. 75 of the Larceny Act, 1861 (24 & 25 Vict. c. 96), provides that any agent, &c. embezzling money or selling securities entrusted to him " shall be guilty of a misdemeanour, and being convicted thereof shall be liable, at the discretion of the court, to be kept in penal servitude for any term not exceeding seven years [altered to five by the Penal Servitude Act, 1864 (27 & 28 Vict. c. 47), s. 2] years, or to be imprisoned not exceeding two years, with or without hard labour, and with or without solitary confinement."

Corporate Stock.

Transfer of and other dealings with corporate stock.

118.—(1.) Any stocks, funds, or public securities (in this section referred to as stock) standing in the books of the Bank of England or of any other public company or society in the name of a municipal corporation, under any style or title of incorporation, and the dividends and interest thereof and all bonuses and accretions thereto, belonging to the municipal corporation, without being subject to any trust for charitable purposes, may be transferred by and paid to such persons as the council appoint by an instrument under the corporate seal, signed and sealed also by the clerk to the trustees of the municipal charities, who shall on request sign and seal it.

(2.) Any stock and money so standing belonging to the trustees of the municipal charities solely on charitable trusts may be transferred by and paid to persons appointed under the hands and seals of the greater part of the trustees, the appointment being attested under the hand and seal of their clerk, and being also sealed with the corporate seal, which seal the mayor shall on request cause to be affixed thereto.

(3.) The dividends and interest of any stock and money so standing, belonging partly to the municipal corporation but subject to charitable trusts, may be paid to persons authorized to have the same paid to them by an instrument in writing under the corporate seal, and appointed under the hands and seals of the greater part of the trustees, the appointment being attested under the hand and seal of their clerk.

(4.) In every case the receipt of the persons authorized to give a receipt to the company or society by an instrument under the corporate seal, and signed and sealed by the clerk to the trustees of the municipal charities, shall be an effectual discharge to the company or society.

(5.) So much of the money so paid as is held on charitable trusts shall be paid over to the trustees of the municipal charities, and so much as the municipal corporation is entitled to beneficially shall go to the borough fund.

(6.) But the company or society shall not be bound to see to the application of that money, or to the validity of the appointment of the clerk to the trustees of the municipal charities, or to the execution of any instrument by any of them, or to inquire whether or not the stock or money is charged with or held on any charitable trust.

(7.) Every person authorized to so receive any money shall account to the council and to the trustees of the municipal charities for all money received by him, and on his failure so to account a court of summary jurisdiction may, on complaint either of the council or of the trustees, by summary order require him to do so.

This section substantially reproduces sects. 45—48 of the Act of 1837 (7 Will. 4 & 1 Vict. c. 78).

Borough Bridges.

Maintenance
of borough
bridges.

119.—(1.) Every bridge which is either wholly or in part in a borough and which the borough and not the county wherein the borough is situate is legally bound to maintain or repair shall, as to the whole of the bridge if it is wholly in the borough, or as to such part only as is in the borough, be maintained, altered, widened, repaired, improved, or rebuilt under the sole management and control of the council.

(2.) For that purpose the council shall have all the powers which the justices of a county have with respect to a county bridge, but the notices required in the case of a county bridge shall not be required in the case of a borough bridge.

(3.) All expenses incurred for the purposes of this section shall be paid out of the borough fund or borough rate, or out of money borrowed on the security thereof.

(4.) The council, with the consent of the Treasury, may from time to time borrow on that security such sums as they deem requisite for any of those purposes, and may mortgage the borough fund and borough rate for the purpose of securing the repayment, with interest, of any money so borrowed.

This section substantially reproduces the Municipal Corporations (Bridges) Act, 1860 (13 & 14 Vict. c. 64), repealed by this Act as to boroughs within the Act.

For the powers of county justices in relation to county bridges, see Chit. Stat. 4th ed. tits. " *County Rate*" and " *Highways (Bridges).*"

Loans for Municipal Buildings.

Power to
borrow for
buildings.

* Sect. 105.

120. The council of a borough may borrow money from the Public Works Loan Commissioners for the purpose of building, enlarging, repairing, improving, and fitting up any building which they are by this Act authorized to build,* and may levy a rate or an increase of the borough rate for the purpose of paying the principal and interest of the loan, and may mortgage the rate or borough rate to the Commissioners in accordance with the Public Works Loans Act, 1875, or any amendment thereof, in such manner and form as the Commissioners direct.

This section reproduces the second paragraph (repealed by this Act) of sect. 40 of the Public Works Loans Act, 1875 (38 & 39 Vict. c. 89). See that Act and the amending Acts of 1878 and 1879 (41 Vict. c. 18, and 42 & 43 Vict. c. 77), Chit. Stat. vol. iv. tit. " *Loans.*"

Advowsons and similar Rights.

Act of 1882
s. 121.

121.—(1.) Notwithstanding any sale by a municipal corporation of any advowson, or of any right of nomination or presentation to a benefice, ecclesiastical preferment, or office of priest, curate, preacher, or minister, whether the sale is made before or after the commencement of this Act, the corporation and its property shall continue liable to the same obligation (if any) of providing for and maintaining or contributing to the maintenance of any priest, curate, preacher, or minister, as if the sale had not been made; and that liability may be enforced by the same means, at the instance of the Crown or otherwise, as if this Act had not been passed, and the advowson or right had remained vested in the corporation.

(2.) Where a municipal corporation holds land subject to an obligation to provide a priest, curate, preacher, or minister, nothing in this Act shall preclude the corporation from augmenting or endowing his office, either by assigning to him and his successors in office a competent portion of the land, or by charging thereon an annual stipend, either in money or in kind, for his and their use and benefit, except that no such augmentation or endowment shall be valid without the approval of the Treasury.

(3.) Where a municipal corporation sells a right of nomination to an ecclesiastical preferment, not being a benefice or perpetual curacy, that preferment shall, from and after the sale, be a benefice presentative, and the holder thereof and his successors shall be a body corporate, having perpetual succession and capable of taking and holding in perpetuity all property granted to or purchased for them by the Governors of the Bounty of Queen Anne, or by other persons contributing with those governors as benefactors.

Obligations and powers in respect of advowsons, &c.

This and the next section are taken from sect. 139 of the Act of 1835, as amended by sects. 2—4 of the Act of 1838 (1 & 2 Vict. c. 31).

122.—(1.) Where at the passing of the Municipal Corporations Act, 1835, a body corporate, or any particular class, number, or description of members thereof, or the governing body thereof, were in their corporate capacity, and not as trustees of a charity, seised or possessed of any manor or

Regulations as to sale of ecclesiastical patronage belonging to municipal corporation.

Act of 1882 s. 122.

land whereto any advowson, or right of nomination or presentation to any benefice or ecclesiastical preferment was appendant or appurtenant, or of any advowson in gross, or of any right of nomination or presentation to a benefice, ecclesiastical preferment, or office of priest, curate, preacher, or minister, the advowson or right, if not sold before the commencement of this Act, shall be sold at such time and in such manner as the Ecclesiastical Commissioners for England direct, so that the best price be obtained for the same.

(2.) Upon any such sale the council shall, with the consent in writing of those Commissioners, signed by any three or more of them, convey, under the corporate seal, the advowson or right to the purchaser, or as he directs, and the advowson or right shall vest accordingly.

(3.) The proceeds of sale shall be paid to the treasurer and invested in Government securities, and the income thereof shall go to the borough fund; or those proceeds, or any part thereof, may be applied towards the liquidation of any debt contracted by the body corporate before the passing of the Municipal Corporations Act, 1835.

(4.) Any vacancy arising before the sale shall be supplied by the presentation or nomination of the bishop or ordinary of the diocese in which the benefice or preferment is situate.

Special Rates.

Power to continue rates for special purposes.

123. Where before the passing of the Municipal Corporations Act, 1835, a rate might be levied in a borough for the purpose of watching conjointly with any other purpose, nothing in this Act shall prevent the levying and collecting of such a rate for that other purpose solely, or affect the powers given in any Act anterior to the Municipal Corporations Act, 1835, as far as they relate to that other purpose; but where the amount of that rate might not before the passing of the Municipal Corporations Act, 1835, exceed a given rate in the pound on the value of property rateable thereto, the rate to be levied for the other purpose solely shall not exceed such proportion of that given rate as appears to have been expended for that other purpose by an account of the average yearly expenditure during the last seven years before the passing of the Municipal Corporations Act, 1835,

or during those of the same seven years during which the rate was levied.

This is a substantial reproduction of the proviso of sect. 84 of the Act of 1835.

Misapplication of Corporate Property.

124.—(1.) It shall not be lawful for a municipal corporation, or the council of a borough, or a corporate officer, or a trustee, or other person acting for a municipal corporation, to pay or apply any money, stocks, funds, securities, or personal property, of or held in trust for the corporation, in payment of any expenses occasioned by a parliamentary election or incurred by any person offering himself as a candidate at or before a parliamentary election.

Prohibition of expenditure of corporate funds on parliamentary elections.

(2.) Any bond, covenant, recognizance, or judgment given by a corporation, council, officer, trustee, or person as aforesaid, for securing payment of such expenses, shall be void.

(3.) Any payment, application, bond, covenant, recognizance, or judgment made or given by a corporation, council, officer, trustee, or person as aforesaid, for inducing any person to labour in a parliamentary election at a future time, or to pay or incur expenses as aforesaid at a future time, shall be deemed to be forbidden and declared void by this section, although colourably made or given for any other cause or consideration.

(4.) Any mortgage or other disposition of corporate land for securing or satisfying any expenses or engagements incurred or to be incurred as aforesaid, and any estate or charge thereby created, shall be void.

(5.) Any resolution, bye-law, or other proceeding of a council, purporting to direct or authorize any payment or thing forbidden by this section, or made or adopted for evading the provisions thereof, shall be void.

(6.) If any member of a municipal corporation authorizes or directs any payment or application forbidden by this section, or assents to, or concurs or participates in, any affirmative vote or proceeding relating thereto, or signs or seals in his individual capacity, or affixes the corporate seal to, any instrument by this section declared void, he shall be guilty of a misdemeanour, and, on conviction thereof in the

Act of 1882
s. 124.

High Court, shall, in addition to such punishment as the court awards, be for ever disabled to take, hold, or exercise any office in the same corporation.

(7.) If any corporate officer, trustee, or other person as aforesaid, makes, or concurs in making, any payment or application of money or property as aforesaid, he shall be deemed to have done so in his own wrong, and he shall be individually liable to repay and make good the amount or value thereof to the corporation, notwithstanding any release or pretended indemnity given to him in the name or on behalf of the corporation.

(8.) Any two or more burgesses may bring and prosecute any action in the name of the corporation against any officer, trustee, or person making any illegal payment or application as aforesaid, as if they, their executors and administrators, were jointly and severally appointed the irrevocable attorneys of the corporation for that purpose; but the plaintiffs shall, on the application of the defendant, give reasonable security, as the court directs, for costs, as between solicitor and client.

(9.) Nothing in this section shall affect the provisions of the Ballot Act, 1872, or of any other Act for the time being in force regulating the payment by the returning officer or otherwise of expenses relating to parliamentary elections.

This re-enacts 2 & 3 Will. 4, c. 69, repealed by this Act as to boroughs within it, sub-s. 9 being new.

Transitory Provisions.

Transfer of investments made before 1860 in names of trustees.

125.—(1.) In the several cases following:

(a.) Where before the 15th of May, 1860, the Treasury on approving of a mortgage of corporate land had required a sinking fund in names of trustees;

(b.) Where before the same day the Treasury, on approving of the payment to a corporation or their treasurer of purchase money for or compensation in respect of corporate land, or of money arising from sale of Government securities in which the same had been invested, had required provision for raising by investments in names of trustees an amount equivalent to the amount so paid;

(c.) Where before the same day the Treasury, on approving of a sale or alienation of corporate land, had required the investment of the proceeds in names of trustees;

The Treasury, if they have not so done before the commencement of this Act, may require any securities in which any such investments had been made to be transferred into the name of the corporation in the matter of this Act, or may require any money applicable for the purposes of such sinking fund to be invested in the purchase of Government annuities in the name of the corporation and in the matter of this Act.

(2.) The order in writing of the Treasury for that purpose shall be a sufficient discharge to the trustees from all claims in respect of the transfer of the securities in pursuance of the order.

(3.) The Treasury may, in the cases aforesaid, give such directions as they might give in the analogous cases in this Part provided for, arising after the commencement of this Act, or as near thereto as circumstances require, and the provisions of this Part shall apply accordingly.

(4.) Where any such transfer as aforesaid has before the commencement of this Act been made into the name of the corporation in the matter of any Act repealed by this Act, this Act shall, if the Treasury so direct, be substituted in the title of the account for that Act.

This and the two next sections re-enact sects. 6, 10 and 11 of the Act of 1860 (23 & 24 Vict. c. 16), which received the Royal Assent on the 15th May, 1860.

126. Where in a borough any mortgage debt had been before the 15th of May, 1860, incurred, for discharge of which no adequate provision then existed, the council, if they have not so done before the commencement of this Act, may submit to the Treasury any scheme for the discharge thereof by instalments, or a sinking fund, or both, extending over any term of years, and if the Treasury approve of the scheme, the sums required for discharge of the debt as proposed therein shall by virtue of this Act become charged on all or any part of the corporate land, or the borough fund, or borough rate, or any other rate applicable to discharge of the debt, or on all or any of those securities, as the Treasury direct, and the provisions of this Part applicable for repayment of money borrowed on mortgage by a sinking fund, or instalments, or both, except the limitation to a period of thirty years, shall apply for discharge of the debt.

Act of 1882 s. 127.

Consolidation of debts incurred before 1860.

127. Where in a borough debts had from time to time, before the 15th of May, 1860, been incurred under Acts of Parliament, with different periods assigned for discharge thereof, the council, if they have not so done before the commencement of this Act, may, with the consent of the Treasury, and with the previous consent in writing of the persons or bodies corporate to whom the debts are owing, consolidate the debts into one, and provide for discharge of the consolidated debt by annual instalments, or a sinking fund or both, extending over a period not exceeding thirty years, and make the instalments or payments a charge on the borough fund, or borough rate, or any other rate applicable to the discharge of the debts, or on all or any of those securities, as the Treasury direct.

Saving for sales, &c. in pursuance of past contracts and resolutions.

128. Nothing in this Act shall affect any power to sell, mortgage, alienate, or lease corporate lands in pursuance of an agreement made on or before the 5th day of June, 1835, or of a resolution entered in the books of a body corporate on or before that date.

This reproduces a part of sect. 94 of the Act of 1835.

Saving for rates in respect of past debts.

129. Nothing in this Act shall prevent the levying or collection of any rate for the purpose of paying any debt contracted before the commencement of this Act or any interest thereon.

Saving for rights of creditors in respect of tolls or dues.

130. It shall not be lawful for the council of a borough of which the body corporate had before the passing of the Municipal Corporations Act, 1835, contracted any lawful debt chargeable on any tolls or dues belonging or payable to that body corporate, or to any member or officer thereof in his corporate capacity, or towards the satisfaction whereof such tolls or dues or any part thereof were or was applicable before the passing of that Act, to alter or reduce the amount to be levied and payable of such tolls or dues, or to grant for any consideration any remission thereof or exemption therefrom or of or from any part thereof, except with the consent in writing, under the hands of a majority in number and amount, of the creditors to whom the debt is due, until after the debt and all arrears of interest due thereon have been fully paid and satisfied.

This and the two next sections reproduce part of sect. 92 of the Act of 1835, as amended by sect. 1 of the Act of 1836 and sect. 28 of the Act of 1837.

131.—(1.) Notwithstanding anything in this Act, the application of the borough fund to the several payments specified in the Fifth Schedule or otherwise authorized by this Act shall be subject to the payment of any lawful debt due from the municipal corporation to any person which was contracted before the passing of the Municipal Corporations Act, 1835, and is unredeemed, or of so much thereof as the council from time to time are required or deem it expedient to redeem, and to the payment from time to time of the interest on so much thereof as remains unredeemed.

(2.) The council may from time to time execute under the corporate seal any deed or obligation in the name of the corporation for securing repayment and satisfaction of any such debt or obligation contracted by or on behalf of the corporation before the passing of the Municipal Corporations Act, 1835.

(3.) Money borrowed by a council for the purpose of being applied, and applied, in or towards satisfaction and discharge of any such pre-existing debt or obligation, shall be deemed to be a debt contracted by or on behalf of the corporation before the passing of the Municipal Corporations Act, 1835.

132. Nothing in this Act shall make liable to the payment of any debt contracted by any body corporate of a borough before the passing of the Municipal Corporations Act, 1835, any part of the real or personal estate of that body corporate which before the passing of that Act was not liable thereto or authorize the levy of any rate within any part of any borough for the purpose of paying any debt contracted before the passing of that Act, which before the passing of that Act could not lawfully be levied therein towards payment of the same.

PART VI.—CHARITABLE AND OTHER TRUSTS AND POWERS.

Charitable Trusts.

Administration of charitable trusts and vesting of legal estate.

133.—(1.) Where at the passing of the Municipal Corporations Act, 1835, the body corporate of a borough, or any one or more of the members thereof, in his or their corporate capacity, stood solely, or together with any person or persons elected solely by that body corporate, or solely by any particular number, class, or description of members thereof, seised or possessed, for any estate or interest, of land, in whole or in part in trust or for the benefit of any charitable uses or trusts, and the legal estate in that land was, at the passing of the Municipal Corporations Act, 1835, vested in the body corporate or persons so seised or possessed thereof, and was by the Charitable Trusts Acts, 1853 ([1]), vested in the trustees appointed by the Lord Chancellor under the Municipal Corporations Act, 1835, or such of them as should be surviving and continuing trustees under that appointment, according to the respective estates and interests therein, and subject to such and the same charges and incumbrances, and on such and the same trusts, as the same were subject to before such vesting, then, in every case, on the death, resignation, or removal of any trustee, and on any appointment of a new trustee, the legal estate in that land and in all other lands subject to any such charitable uses or trusts for the time being vested in the trustees or any of them, or in any persons or the heirs or devisees of any person deceased, resigned or removed, shall vest in the persons who after such death, resignation, or removal, and such appointment of a new trustee, continue or are the trustees for the time being, without any conveyance or assurance.

(2.) Nothing in this section shall take away, abridge, or prejudicially affect any power, authority, or jurisdiction of the Charity Commissioners for England and Wales.

This section is taken from sect. 71 of the Act of 1835. As to boroughs within it, see for the application of sect. 71 of the Act of 1835, *R.* v. *Sankey,* 5 A. & E. 423; *In re Oxford Charities,* 3 My. & C. 239; and see also *Doe* v. *Bristol Hospital,* 11 M. & W. 913; *Attorney-General* v. *Newberry,* 3 My. & Cr. 647; *Attorney-General* v. *Phillimore,* 9 L. J., Ch. 338; *In re Newark Charities,* 6 L. J., Ch. 216.

([1]) Charitable Trusts Act, 1853 (16 & 17 Vict. c. 137), s. 65.

Special Trusts and Powers.

134. The municipal corporation of a borough shall be trustees for executing by the council the powers and provisions of all Acts of Parliament made before the passing of the Municipal Corporations Act, 1835 (other than Acts made for securing charitable uses and trusts), and of all trusts (other than charitable uses and trusts) of which the body corporate of the borough, or any of the members thereof in their corporate capacity, was or were sole trustees before the first election of councillors in the borough under the Municipal Corporations Act, 1835.

Corporation to be trustee where corporators trustees.

This and the next section substantially reproduce sects. 72 and 73 of the Act of 1835. As to the application of sect. 72, see *Reg.* v. *Mayor of Poole*, 7 A. & E. 730; and *Staniland* v. *Hopkins*, 9 M. & W. 178.

135.—(1.) In every borough in which the body corporate, or a particular or limited number, class, or description of members thereof, or of persons appointed by the body corporate, was or were before the passing of the Municipal Corporations Act, 1835, trustees jointly with other trustees for the execution of any Act of Parliament, or of any trust, or in which the body corporate, or any particular or limited number, class, or description of members or nominees thereof, by any statute, charter, bye-law, or custom, before the passing of the Municipal Corporations Act, 1835, was or were, lawfully appointed to or exercised any powers, duties, or functions, not otherwise in the Municipal Corporations Act, 1835, or this Act, provided for, and the continuance of which is not inconsistent with the provisions of the Municipal Corporations Act, 1835, or this Act, the council, on the day prescribed in any Act of Parliament as aforesaid, or in the deed or will by which the trust is created, for a new election, nomination, or appointment of trustees, or on which a new election, nomination, or appointment has usually been made, (and if there is no day prescribed or usually observed, then on or within ten days after the 1st of January in every year), shall appoint the like number of members of the council, or as near as may be to the like number of members of the council, as there were theretofore members or nominees of the body corporate of the borough who in right of their office were

Appointment of members of council to be trustees in cases of joint trusts and other cases.

such trustees, or charged with the execution of such powers, duties, and functions, in room of the members or nominees of the body corporate ceasing to be trustees, or ceasing to exercise such powers, duties, and functions by virtue of the Municipal Corporations Act, 1835.

(2.) In every case of extraordinary vacancy among the trustees or persons so appointed, the council shall forthwith appoint one other member of the council in the room of the person by whom the vacancy has been made, to hold his trust or office for such time as that person would regularly have held it.

Local Acts.

136.—(1.) The trustees appointed or acting by or under any local (a) Act of Parliament for the time being in force, for paving, lighting, supplying with water or gas, cleansing, watching, regulating, or improving, a borough, or any part thereof, or for providing or maintaining a cemetery or market in or for a borough, or any part thereof, whether in any such case their powers under the local Act do or do not extend beyond the borough, may, if they think fit, at a meeting called for this purpose, transfer to the municipal corporation of the borough, with the consent of the council but not otherwise, all the rights, powers, estates, property, and liabilities for the time being vested in or imposed on the trustees under the local Act.

(2.) The transfer shall be made in writing under the common seal of the trustees if they are a corporation, and if not, then by deed executed by the trustees, or by any two of them acting by their authority and on their behalf.

(3.) On the transfer being made, the municipal corporation shall become and be the trustees for executing by the council the powers and provisions of the local Act; and all the rights, powers, estates, and property vested in the transferring trustees shall vest in the corporation; and all the liabilities and obligations of the transferring trustees shall be transferred to and borne by the corporation, and the transferring trustees shall be discharged therefrom.

This is taken from sects. 2 and 3 of the Act of 1857 (20 & 21 Vict. c. 50).

(a) The word "local" is now, so as to affirm *Stanford* v. *Keble*, L. R., 9 Q. B. 549.

For power of corporation to acquire tramways by compulsory purchase, see Tramways Act, 1870 (33 & 34 Vict. c. 78), s. 43; and for similar power as to electric light undertakings, see Electric Lighting Act, 1882 (45 & 46 Vict. c. 56), s. 27, p. 330, post.

Act of 1882 s. 136.

137.—(1.) Where at the passing of the Municipal Corporations Act, 1835, there was a local Act of Parliament for lighting part of a borough then incorporated, the council may, if they think fit, make an order that any specified part of the borough not within the provisions of any such local Act shall, after a day fixed in the order, be within those provisions; and after that day the part so specified shall be within those provisions; as far as relates to lighting, or to any rate authorized to be levied for lighting.

Power for council to extend local lighting Act.

(2.) But the part so specified shall be lighted in like manner as those parts of the borough which before the making of the order were within those provisions; and any rate raised for the purpose of defraying the expenses of lighting the part so specified shall not exceed the average expense in the pound of lighting the other parts of the borough.

This is taken from sect. 87 of the Act of 1835.

138. Everything provided under any local Act of Parliament in force on the 20th of August, 1836, to be done exclusively by a particular or limited number, class, or description of the members of any body corporate named in the Schedules to the Municipal Corporations Act, 1835, the continuance of which was not inconsistent with the provisions of that Act, and everything provided in any such local Act to be done by the justices, or by some particular class or description, or members of such body corporate, being justices, at a court of quarter sessions, which did not relate to the business of a court of criminal or civil judicature, if the same respectively has been lawfully continued to be done up to the commencement of this Act by the council, or a committee thereof, shall be continued thereafter to be done by the council at a quarterly meeting, or by any three of a committee of the council appointed at such a meeting.

Exercise of powers under local Acts.

This is taken from sect. 8 of the Act of 1836 (6 & 7 Will. 4, c. 105).

PART VII.—BOROUGH FUND : BOROUGH RATE : COUNTY RATE.

Borough Fund.

Payments to
borough fund.

139. The rents and profits of all corporate land, and the interest, dividends, and annual proceeds (¹) of all money, dues, chattels, and valuable securities belonging or payable to a municipal corporation, or to any member or officer thereof in his corporate capacity, and every fine or penalty for any offence against this Act (except where and as far as the application thereof is otherwise provided for) shall go to the borough fund.

This section reproduces the opening paragraph of the 92nd section of the Act of 1835.

(¹) *Proceeds.*]—The use of the term " proceeds" prevents a corporation from expending capital. *Ex parte Hythe Corporation,* 4 Y. & C. 55.

Application
of borough
fund.
* Page 153.

140.—(1.) The borough fund shall be applicable to and charged with the several payments specified in the Fifth Schedule.*

(2.) The payments specified in Part I. of that schedule may be made without order of the council; those specified in Part II. may not be made without such order.

(3.) No other payment shall be made out of the borough fund, except—

(a.) Under the authority of an Act of Parliament (*a*); or

(b.) By order of the council; or

(c.) By order of the court of quarter sessions for the borough; or

(d.) By order of a justice in pursuance of this Act; or

(e.) In cases in which the court of quarter sessions for a county, or a justice acting in and for a county in the discharge of his judicial duty, might make an order for the payment of money on the treasurer of the county.

(4.) Saving, nevertheless, in relation to the application of the borough fund as authorized by this section, or otherwise by this Act, all rights, interests, and demands of all persons in or on the real or personal estate of the municipal corpora-

(*a*) See *e. g.* sect. 30 of the Parliamentary and Municipal Registration Act, 1878, post, p. 218.

tion, by virtue of any legal proceeding, or of any mortgage, Act of 1882
s. 140. or otherwise (*b*).

This section, as supplemented by Schedule 5, is taken from sects. 59 and 92 of the Act of 1835. As to signing and countersigning of orders and removal of orders by certiorari, see sect. 141, infra. As to application of borough fund *or borough rate* to promoting or opposing bills, or prosecuting or defending proceedings in the interest of the borough, see 35 & 36 Vict. c. 91 ("Leeman's Act"). post, tit. "*Supplementary Enactments.*"

141.—(1.) An order of the council for payment of money Orders for
payment of
money. out of the borough fund shall be signed by three members of the council, and countersigned by the town clerk.

(2.) Any such order may be removed into the Queen's Bench Division of the High Court by writ of certiorari (¹), and may be wholly or partly disallowed or confirmed on motion and hearing, with or without costs, according to the judgment and discretion of the court (²).

The first paragraph of this section is taken from sect. 59 of the Act of 1835, and the second from sect. 44 of the Act of 1847 (7 Will. 4 & 1 Vict. c. 78), which section recited that "it is expedient to give all persons interested in the borough fund a more direct and easy remedy for any misapplication of such fund" than that before existing.

(¹) *Certiorari.*]—The Chancery Division of the High Court appears to have a concurrent jurisdiction to restrain a payment by injunction. See *Attorney-General* v. *Mayor of Brecon*, 10 Ch. D. 204; 48 L. J., Ch. 153, and the cases there cited, in none of which, however, was the jurisdiction disputed, and in all of which the Attorney-General instituted proceedings at the relation of ratepayers.

There is no statutory limit of time within which to apply, the six months' limit of 13 Geo. 2, c. 18, s. 5, applying only to the removal of proceedings before justices (*R.* v. *Mayor, &c. of Sheffield*, L. R., 6 Q. B. 652; 40 L. J., Q. B. 247); but there should be no unreasonable delay.

(²) *Discretion of Court.*]—The discretionary powers are very wide, and would seem even to allow the court to sanction a payment for which no express legal authority can be found, in cases where it is equitable and for the good of the borough to sanction such a payment. The court has refused to disallow a payment not legally enforceable. *R.* v. *Prest*, 16 Q. B. 32.

There is an appeal to the Court of Appeal under sect. 19 of the Judicature Act, 1873; and a further appeal to the House of Lords under sect. 3 of the Appellate Jurisdiction Act, 1876.

142.—(1.) All payments to and out of the borough fund Payments
to and by
treasurer. shall be made to and by the treasurer.

(*b*) This saving affirms *Arnold* v. *Mayor of Gravesend*, 2 K. & J. 574.

Act of 1882
s. 142.

(2.) All payments to the treasurer shall go to the borough fund.

Application of surplus of borough fund.

143.—(1.) If the borough fund is more than sufficient for the purposes to which it is applicable under this Act [or otherwise by law,] the surplus thereof shall be applied under the direction of the council for the public benefit of the inhabitants and improvement of the borough (¹).

(2.) If the surplus arises from the rents and profits of the property of the municipal corporation, and not from a borough rate, and the borough is a sanitary district under the Public Health Act, 1875, then the municipal corporation, as the sanitary authority for the borough, may apply the surplus in payment of any expenses incurred by them as such sanitary authority, before or after the commencement of this Act, in improving the borough, or any part thereof, by drainage, enlargement of streets, or otherwise, under the Public Health Act, 1875, or any Act thereby repealed.

The first paragraph re-enacts (with the addition of the words in brackets) a part of sect. 92 of the Act of 1835; the second is taken from sect. 12 of the Act of 1860, which gave similar powers under the then in force Public Health Act, 1848 (11 & 12 Vict. c. 63), and Local Government Act, 1858 (21 & 22 Vict. c. 98), repealed by the Public Health Act, 1875 (38 & 39 Vict. c. 55).

(¹) *Application of Surplus Borough Fund.*]—Only the surplus arising from rents, &c., and not any surplus arising from rates, &c., can be applied for the public benefit of the inhabitants, &c. (*Reg.* v. *Mayor of Sheffield*, L. R., 6 Q. B. 652; 40 L. J., Q. B. 247; 24 L. T. 659; 19 W. R. 1159); but it seems that whether there be a surplus or not, the corporation has the right, under the general law applicable to trustees, to defray out of the corporate funds the expenses of opposing any bill in Parliament which attacks the existence, property or privileges of the corporation; and further, that that right is not affected by 35 & 36 Vict. c. 91, (p. 298, post). *Attorney-General* v. *Mayor of Brecon*, 10 Ch. D. 204; 48 L. J., Ch. 153; 40 L. T. 52; 27 W. R. 332; per Jessel, M. R.: see too, *Attorney-General* v. *Mayor of Wigan*, Kay, 268; 5 De G., M. & G. 52.

There have been many other decisions as to the legality of payments out of the borough fund; but as they chiefly turned upon the question whether the payments were incurred "in carrying into effect the provisions" of the Act of 1835, they are collected in a note to Schedule V., part 2, post, p. 155.

Power for council to make borough rate and assess contribution thereto.

Borough Rate.

144.—(1.) If the borough fund is insufficient for the purposes to which it is applicable under this Act or otherwise by law, the council shall from time to time estimate, as correctly as may be, what amount, in addition to the borough fund, will be sufficient for those purposes.

Act of 1882 s. 144.

(2.) In order to raise that amount, the council shall, subject to the provisions of this Act, from time to time order a rate, called a borough rate, to be made in the borough.

(3.) A borough rate may be made retrospectively, in order to raise money for the payment of charges and expenses incurred, or which have come in course of payment, at any time within six months before the making of the rate.

(4.) The council shall assess the contributions to the borough rate on the several parishes and parts of parishes in the borough in proportion to the total annual value of the hereditaments in each parish or part which are rateable to the poor, or in respect of which a contribution is made to the poor rate.

Assessment of contributions on parishes.

(5.) That value shall be estimated according to the valuation list (if any) in force for the time being, and if there is none, according to the last poor rate.

(6.) But if for any reason the council think that the valuation list or poor rate is not a fair criterion of value they may cause an independent valuation to be made.

(7.) For the purpose of assessing a borough rate, or for the purpose of an independent valuation, the council from time to time may cause any of the books of assessment of any rates or taxes, parliamentary or parochial, on any property, and the valuation by which the assessment is made, in the hands of the overseers, to be brought before them, and may take copies thereof or extracts therefrom, or may direct any person to take copies of or extracts from such books being in his hands, without having the same brought before the council, or may call before them any overseer to give evidence respecting the same ; and may cause copies of the total amount assessed in each parish in respect of any tax payable to the Crown, and the total amount of the valuation of the property on which that assessment was made in any past year, to be made out by the clerk to the commissioners of each district.

(8.) The overseers and such persons as they select, by warrant of the council, signed by the mayor and sealed with the corporate seal, may enter on, view, and examine any

Act of 1882
s. 144.

Borough rate
—continued.

land chargeable to the borough rate, in order to ascertain the annual value at which it ought to be charged; but no such entry shall in any case be made unless fourteen days' previous notice in writing, signed by the mayor and sealed with the corporate seal, of the intention to make the entry, has been given to the overseers and to the persons on whose land the entry is to be made.

Appeal by
parish to
quarter
sessions.

(9.) If on any occasion the overseers of a parish think that their parish is aggrieved by a borough rate, on account of the proportions assessed as the contributions of the respective parishes being unequal, or on account of some parish being without sufficient cause omitted, or on account of any other just cause of complaint, they may appeal to the recorder at the next quarter sessions for the borough, or if there is none, to the next quarter sessions for the county wherein the borough is situate, or whereto it is adjacent, against such part of the rate only as affects their parish.

(10.) The recorder or quarter sessions shall hear and finally determine the appeal, and either confirm such parts of the rate as are appealed against, or correct any inequalities, disproportions, or omissions proved to exist therein, as to him or them appears just.

(11.) The expenses of the appeal shall be paid by such parishes or persons and in such proportions as the recorder or court having cognizance of the appeal directs.

Failure of
custodian to
produce book.

(12.) If any person having custody of any book for which the council call under this section, fails to produce it to the council, or to permit any copy thereof or extract therefrom to be made or taken, or to give such evidence as the council require, he shall, on summary conviction, be liable to a fine not exceeding ten pounds.

Failure of
clerk to
make copy.

(13.) If any clerk to the commissioners of a district fails to make any copy, which he is required to make under this section, within a reasonable time after his receipt of the order to make it, he shall, on summary conviction, be liable to a fine not exceeding twenty pounds.

This section is taken from part of sect. 92 of the Act of 1835, which incorporated by reference the repealed 55 Geo. 3, c. 51, as to collection of county rates; and from 15 & 16 Vict. c. 81, substituted for that Act.

145.—(1.) Where a parish is wholly in a borough, the council may from time to time, if they think fit, order the overseers to pay the contribution of the parish to the borough rate out of the poor rate made or to be made for the parish.

(2.) The overseers shall pay the contribution to the council or as they order.

(3.) If the overseers fail to pay as ordered, the amount may be levied off the goods of them or any of them, by distress, by virtue of a warrant signed by the mayor and sealed with the corporate seal, or signed by two justices in and for the borough.

Act of 1882 s. 145.

Collection of borough rate in undivided parish.

This section re-enacts 7 Will. 4 & 1 Vict. c. 81, repealed by this Act, as to which see *Jones* v. *Johnson* (5 Ex. 862) and *Reg.* v. *Hunslet Overseers* (1 E. & B. 775), in which latter case a mandamus commanding the overseers to levy the rate was refused, on the ground that the statutory remedy by distress ought to be pursued.

146.—(1.) Where a parish is partly in and partly out of a borough, the overseers, on receipt of an order for payment of money for the contribution of the part in the borough towards a borough rate, which order the council may make as if the whole parish was in the borough, shall assess on and levy from the occupiers of hereditaments rateable to the poor rate in that part of the parish the amount necessary for the contribution, either as a separate rate, for which the overseers shall have all the powers which belong to them for levying a poor rate, or with and as part of the poor rate to which occupiers in that part of the parish are liable in common with occupiers in the other part.

Collection of borough rate in divided parish.

(2.) Any person rated under this section may appeal against the rate in like manner and with the like consequences, and subject to the like provisions and regulations, as in appeals against a poor rate (¹).

Appeal against rate.

(3.) The overseers shall pay the amount of the contribution to the council, or as they order, and in default thereof shall be subject to all provisions and penalties provided by law concerning nonpayment of contribution to a borough rate.

(4.) Every overseer and collector shall account for the money collected and expended under this section to the auditor of the district comprising the parish in the like manner, and with the like incidents, consequences, liabilities, and power of appeal as in the case of the poor rate; and the Local Government Board shall have the like power to make orders to regulate the mode of accounting as they have in regard to other local rates.

(5.) If any balance is found in the hands of any such overseer or collector he shall apply it towards the next rate required under this section, or pay it to his successor in office.

(6.) In default of his so applying it while in office, or making payment to his successor within seven days after the balance is found, the auditor shall proceed to recover it.

(7.) The officers ordinarily employed in the collection of the poor rate shall, if required by the overseers, collect the rate under this section, and shall receive thereout such remuneration for the additional duty as the overseers with the consent of the vestry, determine.

(8.) The collector or other person appointed shall, for the purposes of this section, have all the powers of overseers.

(9.) The overseers in estimating the amount of their assessment under this section, may include a sum for costs of assessment and collection, and a reasonable sum for rates excused or irrecoverable.

This section is taken from sect. 2 of 12 & 13 Vict. c. 65, and sect. 10 of 13 & 14 Vict. c. 101, repealed by this Act.

(¹) *Appeals against a Rate.*]—The enactments regulating appeals against a poor rate are 17 Geo. 2, c. 38 ; 6 & 7 Will. 4, c. 96, ss. 6, 7 ; and the Union Assessment Committee Acts, 1862 and 1864 (25 & 25 Vict. c. 103, and 27 & 28 Vict. c. 34). See Glen's Poor Law Acts ; Chit. Stat. vol. v. tit. "*Poor (Rating)*."

Rating of
owners
instead of
occupiers for
borough rate
in certain
cases.

147. Where the vestry of a parish has made or makes, before or after the commencement of this Act, under section four of The Poor Rate Assessment and Collection Act, 1869, an order, as in that section provided, to the effect that the owners, instead of the occupiers, of such rateable hereditaments, as therein mentioned, shall be rated to the poor rate in respect thereof, every such order, while in force after the commencement of this Act, shall be deemed to apply to and include rating to the borough rate, with the same incidents, conditions, powers, liabilities, and remedies as if the borough rate were a poor rate.

Sect. 4 of the Poor Rate Assessment and Collection Act, 1869 (32 & 33 Vict. c. 41), provides for the rating (by order of the vestry) of owners instead of occupiers of hereditaments, the rateable value of which does not exceed 13*l.* in Liverpool, 10*l.* in Manchester, or 8*l.* elsewhere.

148. Any warrant required for the levy or collection of a borough rate may be issued by the mayor, signed by him, and sealed with the corporate seal.

Warrants for levy of borough rate.

This section is taken from sect. 5 of the Act of 1836 (6 & 7 Will. 4, c. 104).

149. All sums levied in pursuance of the borough rate shall go to the borough fund ; and, subject to the foregoing provisions of this part, the same shall be applied to all purposes to which the borough fund is applicable under this Act, or otherwise by law ; and, as regards a borough named in the schedules to the Municipal Corporations Act, 1835, to all purposes to which, before the passing of that Act, a borough rate was by law applicable in the borough, or a county rate was applicable in a county.

Borough rate to go to borough fund; and its application.

This section is taken from part of sect. 92 of the Act of 1835.
For purposes of county rate both before and after 1835 see 12 Geo. 2, c. 29.

County Rate.

150.—(1.) Where a borough has a separate court of quarter sessions, the justices of a county wherein the borough or any part thereof is situate shall not assess any hereditaments in the borough to any county rate ; and, except as is expressly by this Act provided, every part of the borough shall be wholly free from contributing to any rate or assessment of any kind of and for that county.

General exemption of quarter sessions boroughs from county rate.

(2.) But nothing in this section shall prevent the levy or collection of arrears of any county rate made before the grant of a separate court of quarter session.

This and the next section are taken from sects. 112 and 114 of the Act of 1835 respectively.

151. The municipal corporation of a borough having a separate court of quarter sessions shall be liable to pay such sums, if any, as are expended out of the county rate of the county in which the borough is situate, and as are not otherwise paid or chargeable, in respect of the costs arising out of the prosecution, maintenance, conveyance, transport, or punishment of all offenders committed for trial from the borough to the assizes for the county.

Liability of quarter sessions borough for prosecution expenses of county.

Act of 1882
s. 152.

Liability of
certain quar-
ter sessions
boroughs to
other county
expenses.

152.—(1.) If the whole or any part of the area for the time being comprised in a borough having a separate court of quarter sessions was, before the 11th of July (a), 1832, chargeable with or liable to contribute to the county rate of the county in which it is situate, the municipal corporation shall, in addition to its liability to pay for the purposes mentioned in the last foregoing section, continue liable to contribute to the county rate for other purposes (in this Act referred to as general county purposes), as if this Act had not been passed.

(2.) General county purposes shall not include the costs arising out of coroners' inquests, or the expenses incurred under the Sale of Food and Drugs Act, 1875, in respect of the county, or, in the case of a borough having its own inspector of weights and measures, the expenses relating to the inspection of weights and measures for the county, or payments to or in respect of special constables.

This section is taken from sect. 117 of the Act of 1835, the word " area" being inserted in the first line in affirmance of *Reg.* v. *Monck*, 2 Q. B. D. 544.

By the Weights and Measures Act, 1878 (41 & 42 Vict. c. 49), ss. 43, 50, boroughs having a separate commission of the peace appoint their own inspectors of weights and measures.

Mode of
accounting
by quarter
sessions
borough to
county.

153.—(1.) The treasurer of each county shall, not more than twice in every year, send to the council of each borough situate in the county and having a separate court of quarter sessions an account showing separately—

(a.) The sums, if any, expended out of the county rate in respect of the costs arising out of the prosecution, maintenance, conveyance, transport, or punishment of offenders committed for trial from the borough to the assizes for the county; and

(b.) If the borough is liable to contribute to the county rate for general county purposes, all sums expended out of the county rate for general county purposes, and all sums received in aid or on account of the county rate, and the proportion chargeable on the borough of the sums so expended after deduction of the sums so received;

(a) 11th July, 1832, is the date of the passing of the Boundary Act (2 & 3 Will. 4, c. 64).

and shall make an order on the council for the payment of the Act of 1882 s. 153. sum appearing by this account to be due from the municipal corporation of the borough.

(2.) The council shall thereupon forthwith order the sum so appearing to be due, with all reasonable charges of making and sending the account, to be paid to the treasurer of the county out of the borough fund.

(3.) If the order is not complied with, two justices for the county may, on the complaint of the treasurer of the county, made within one month after the issue of the order, issue and send to the treasurer of the borough a warrant requiring him to pay to the treasurer of the county, besides the sum mentioned in the order, the additional sum mentioned in the warrant, the same being calculated in the proportion of one shilling to every ten on the sum mentioned in the order; and until payment thereof the treasurer of the county shall have, in respect of the warrant, all the powers for the recovery thereof which are given against a guardian or overseer for the recovery of county rates and surcharges.

(4.) If any difference arises concerning the account, it shall be decided by the arbitration of a barrister, named, on the application either of the treasurer of the county or of the treasurer of the borough, by the Secretary of State. The arbitrator may, if he thinks fit, adjourn the hearing from time to time, and may require all such information to be afforded by either party as he thinks fit. He shall by his award in writing determine the amount to be paid by the council to the treasurer of the county, and his award shall be final and conclusive. He shall also assess the costs of the arbitration and determine by whom and out of what fund they shall be paid.

The first two paragraphs of this section are taken from sect. 117 of the Act of 1835, the third from 15 & 16 Vict. c. 36, repealed by this Act, and the fourth from 5 Geo. 4, c. 85, s. 2.

PART VIII.—Administration of Justice.

County Justices.

154.—(1.) Where a borough has not a separate court of quarter sessions, the justices of the county in which the borough is situate shall exercise the jurisdiction of justices in and for the borough as fully as they can or ought in and for the county. Jurisdiction of county justices in borough.

Act of 1882
s. 154.

(2.) No part of a borough having a separate court of quarter sessions shall be within the jurisdiction, [exerciseable out of quarter sessions,] of the justices of a county, where the borough was exempt therefrom before the passing of the Municipal Corporations Act, 1835.

This section reproduces sect. 111 of the Act of 1835, the words of the second paragraph within brackets being new, and affirming *Reg.* v. *Deane*, 2 Q. B. 96.

For list distinguishing boroughs which have separate quarter sessions, see Appendix, p. 343, post.

Borough Justices.

Mayor and last mayor to be borough justices.

155.—(1.) The mayor shall, by virtue of his office, be a justice for the borough, and shall, unless disqualified to be mayor, continue to be such a justice during the year next after he ceases to be mayor.

(2.) The mayor shall have precedence over all other justices acting in and for the borough, and be entitled to take the chair at all meetings of justices held in the borough at which he is present by virtue of his office of mayor; except that he shall not by virtue of this section have precedence over the justices acting in and for the county in which the borough or any part thereof is situate, unless when acting in relation to the business of the borough, or over any stipendiary magistrate engaged in administering justice.

This section reproduces sect. 57 of the Act of 1835, as amended by sect. 2 of the Act of 1861.

Separate commission of peace.

156. It shall be lawful for the Queen, on the petition of the council of a borough, to grant to the borough a separate commission of the peace.

This section is taken from sect. 98 of the Act of 1835.

Qualification of borough justice.

157.—(1.) It shall be lawful for the Queen, from time to time, to assign to any persons her Majesty's commission to act as justices in and for each borough having a separate commission of the peace.

Oaths.

(2.) A justice for a borough shall not be capable ([1]) of acting as such until he has taken the oaths required to be taken by justices ([2]), except the oath as to qualification by estate, and made before the mayor or two other members of the council a declaration as in the Eighth Schedule.*

* Page 158.

(3.) He must, while acting as such, reside in or within seven miles* of the borough, or occupy a house, warehouse, or other property in the borough.

* Sect. 231.

(4.) He need not be a burgess or have such qualification by estate as is required for a justice of a county.

Act of 1882 s. 157.

This section substantially re-enacts sects. 98, 101 and 104 of the Act of 1835, as amended by sect. 3 of the Act of 1836 (6 & 7 Will. 4, c. 105), and sect. 3 of the Act of 1861.

(¹) *Not be capable.*]—Similar words have been held to have the effect only of making the acting unlawful, and not of making the acts invalid (*Margate Pier Co.* v. *Hannam*, 3 B. & Ald. 266); but that case is perhaps distinguishable on the ground that the statute on which it is turned imposed a pecuniary penalty.

(²) *Oaths.*]—The oaths required are the oath of allegiance and judicial oath, which are required by the Promissory Oaths Act, 1868 (31 & 32 Vict. c. 72), s. 5, and Part II. of the schedule, to be taken by "justices of the peace for counties and boroughs," sect. 7 enacting that declining or refusing to take such oaths when "duly tendered" shall cause vacation of office if entered upon, or disqualification from entering on it if not already entered on. The Promissory Oaths Act, 1871 (34 & 35 Vict. c. 48), s. 2, provides for the taking of these oaths "in open court at the general or quarter sessions of the peace for the county, borough, or place in which the person taking the oaths acts as justice."

158.—(1.) A justice for a borough shall, with respect to offences committed and matters arising within the borough, have the same jurisdiction and authority as a justice for a county has under any local or general Act with respect to offences committed and matters arising within the county; except that he shall not, by virtue of his being a justice for the borough, act as a justice at any court of goal delivery or quarter sessions, or in making or levying any county or borough rate.

Jurisdiction of borough justices.

(2.) A justice shall not be disabled from acting in the execution of this Act by reason of his being liable to the borough rate (¹).

This section is taken from sects. 101 and 128 of the Act of 1835, sect. 31 of the Act of 1837 (7 Will. 4 & 1 Vict. c. 78), and sect. 9 of the Act of 1850 (13 & 14 Vict. c. 91).

(¹) *Removal of Disability.*]—For removals of disability on other similar grounds, see as to rates and taxes generally, 16 Geo. 2, c. 18; and as to offences arising under Acts to be put in execution by municipal corporations, &c., Justices of the Peace Act, 1867 (30 & 31 Vict. c. 115).

159.—(1.) The justices for a borough shall from time to time appoint a fit person to be their clerk, to be removeable at their pleasure.

Clerk to borough justices.

(2.) They shall not appoint or continue as their clerk an alderman or councillor of the borough, or the clerk of the peace of the borough, or of the county in which the borough is situate, or the partner of any such clerk of the peace.

(3.) The clerk to the justices shall not, by himself or his partner or otherwise, be directly or indirectly employed or interested in the prosecution of any offender committed for trial by those justices, or any of them, at any court of gaol delivery or quarter sessions.

(4.) If any person acts in contravention of the last fore-going provision of this section, he shall for every offence be liable to a fine not exceeding one hundred pounds, recoverable by action.

(5.) One moiety of any fine so recovered shall, with costs, be paid to the person bringing the action to recover it.

(6.) Nothing in this Act shall prevent the justices for a borough from re-appointing as their clerk any person being clerk of the peace of the borough or of the county in which the borough is situate, or partner of any such clerk of the peace, if the person re-appointed was, on the 6th of August, 1861, or has not ceased to be at the time of re-appointment, the clerk of those justices.

This section is taken from sect. 101 of the Act of 1835, as amended by sect. 5 of the Act of 1861, the date of the passing of which fixes the date in the last paragraph of this section.

Justices' room.

160.—(1.) The council of a borough having a separate com-mission of the peace shall provide and furnish a suitable justices room, with offices, for the business of the borough justices.

(2.) No room in a house licensed for the sale of intoxicating liquors may be used for this purpose.

This is taken from sect. 100 of the Act of 1835, but the second paragraph applies to a house licensed for the sale of liquor to be drunk either on or off the premises, whereas the corresponding words of that section applied to a sale for drinking on the premises only.

As to purchase of land for justices' room, see sect. 105, ante.

Stipendiary Magistrate.

Appointment of stipendiary magistrate.

161.—(1.) If the council desire the appointment of a sti-pendiary magistrate for the borough, they may present a petition for the appointment to the Secretary of State, and thereupon it shall be lawful for the Queen to appoint to that office a barrister of seven years' standing.

(2.) He shall hold office during her Majesty's pleasure.

(3.) He shall, by virtue of his office, be a justice for the borough.

(4.) There shall be paid to him such yearly salary, not exceeding, except with the consent of the council, that mentioned in the petition, as her Majesty from time to time directs.

Act of 1882
s. 161.

(5.) It shall be paid by four equal quarterly payments, and in the same proportion up to the time of his death or ceasing to act.

(6.) On a vacancy, a new appointment shall not be made until the council again make application as before the first appointment.

(7.) More than one stipendiary magistrate may be appointed for a borough.

This is taken from sect. 99 of the Act of 1835. A stipendiary has, in some cases, been appointed under special Act of Parliament. See e. g. 7 & 8 Vict. c. 30, as to borough of Manchester. The Stipendiary Magistrates Act, 1863 (26 & 27 Vict. c. 97), under which towns having a population of at least 25,000 may apply for the appointment of a stipendiary, does not apply to municipal corporations. By 21 & 22 Vict. c. 73, a stipendiary may do alone acts authorized to be done by two justices; and by sect. 39 of the Licensing Act, 1872 (35 & 36 Vict. c. 94), he may act in granting or confirming licences for the sale of intoxicating liquors.

Borough Quarter Sessions: Recorder: Clerk of the Peace.

162.—(1.) It shall be lawful for the Queen, on the petition to her Majesty in council of the council of a borough, to grant that a separate court of quarter sessions be holden in and for the borough.

Grant of separate court of quarter sessions.

(2.) The petition shall set forth the grounds of the application and the salary which the council are willing to pay to the recorder.

(3.) The grant may be made on and subject to such terms and conditions, if any, as to her Majesty in council seem fit.

(4.) Within ten days after receipt of the grant the council shall send a copy thereof, sealed with the corporate seal, to the clerk of the peace of the county, or each county if more than one, in which the borough or any part thereof is situate.

This is taken from sects. 103 and 112 of the Act of 1835, sub-s. 3 being new. For list of present "quarter-sessions boroughs," see Appendix, post.

163.—(1.) It shall be lawful for the Queen from time to time to appoint for a borough having a separate court of quarter sessions a barrister of five years' standing to be recorder of the borough.

The recorder.

Act of 1882
s. 163.

The recorder
—*contd.*

(2.) He shall hold office during good behaviour.

(3.) He shall, by virtue of his office, be a justice for the borough.

* Sect. 157.
* Page 158.

(4.) He shall not act as recorder, or as a justice, until he has taken the oaths required to be taken by a borough justice,* and made before the mayor or two other members of the council a declaration as in the Eighth Schedule.*

(5.) He shall have precedence in all places within the borough next after the mayor.

Seat in
Parliament.

(6.) He shall not, during his office, be eligible to serve in Parliament for the borough, or be an alderman, councillor, or stipendiary magistrate of the borough; but he may be appointed revising barrister for the borough, and shall be eligible to serve in Parliament except for the borough.

Salary.

(7.) There shall be paid to him such yearly salary, net exceeding that stated in the petition on which the grant of a separate court of quarter sessions was made, as her Majesty directs; but the same may at any time be increased by resolution of the council, approved by the Secretary of State, without the resignation and re-appointment of the recorder being necessary.

Appointment
for more
boroughs
than one.

(8.) A person may be appointed recorder of two or more boroughs conjointly.

This is taken from sects. 103 and 104 of the Act of 1835, as amended by sect. 3 of the Act of 1836 (6 & 7 Will. 4, c. 105). As to the oaths, see sect. 157, and note thereto, ante, p. 87.

The paragraph of sub-s. 7, as to increase of salary, is new, and was inserted in committee, on the motion of Mr. Bulwer, Q.C. The old law was that increase of salary necessitated a new appointment, the acceptance of which by members of Parliament vacated their seats.

The clerk of
the peace.

164.—(1.) The council of a borough having a separate court of quarter sessions shall from time to time appoint a fit person to be the clerk of the peace for the borough.

(2.) The clerk of the peace shall hold office during good behaviour.

Deputy.

(3.) The clerk of the peace may from time to time, by writing signed by him, appoint a fit person to act as deputy for him, in case of his illness, incapacity, or absence.

(4.) The appointment of the deputy shall be signified in

writing, signed by the clerk of the peace, to the council, and **Act of 1882 c. 164.**
shall be recorded in their minutes.

(5.) Where a table of the fees to be taken by the clerk of **Fees of clerk of the peace.**
the peace has been made by the council and confirmed by the
Secretary of State, and is for the time being in force, the
clerk of the peace, if paid by fees, may take the fees to which
he appears by that table to be entitled.

(6.) The council may from time to time make a new table
of the fees to be taken by the clerk of the peace, but shall
submit every such table to the Secretary of State for confirmation, and he may confirm and allow the same, either as
submitted, or with such alterations, additions, or abatements
as he thinks proper, and any such table shall be of no validity
until it is so confirmed.

The first two paragraphs reproduce a paragraph of sect. 103 of
the Act of 1835, under which it was held that the clerk of the peace
might be removed by the recorder for misconduct in his office under
1 W. & M. sess. 1, c. 21, s. 6 (*Reg.* v. *Hayward*, 31 L. J., M. C.
177). The power of removal for misconduct not in the office would
seem to be vested in two of the borough justices by the Clerks of
the Peace Removal Act, 1864 (27 & 28 Vict. c. 65).

The third and fourth paragraphs, as to a deputy, are new; the
fifth and sixth are taken from sect. 124 of the Act of 1835.

165.—(1.) The recorder shall hold, once in every quarter **Recorder to hold court of quarter sessions.**
of a year, or oftener, if and as he thinks fit, or the Secretary
of State directs, a court of quarter sessions in and for the
borough.

(2.) He shall sit as sole judge of the court.

(3.) The court shall be a court of record, and shall have **Jurisdiction of recorder.**
cognizance of all crimes, offences, and matters cognisable by
courts of quarter sessions for counties in England (¹) and the
recorder shall, notwithstanding his being sole judge, have
power to do all things necessary for exercising that jurisdiction as fully as those courts.

(4.) But the recorder shall not, by virtue of his office, have
power

(a.) To allow, apportion, make, or levy any borough rate; or

(b.) Subject to the provisions of this Act respecting appeals
from a rate, to do any act in relation to the allowance, apportionment, making, or levying of any rate
whatsoever; or

(c.) To grant any licence or authority to any person to keep an inn, alehouse, or victualling house to sell exciseable liquors by retail; or

(d.) To exercise any power by this Act specially vested in the council.

This is taken from sect. 105 of the Act of 1835; and as to jurisdiction in rating, from the proviso of sect. 8 of the Act of 1836 (6 & 7 Will. 4, c. 105).

(¹) *Jurisdiction.*]—The general jurisdiction of justices to hear and determine all manner of felonies—which is conferred by this section upon a recorder, unless an exception can be shown—given by 34 Edw. 3, c. 1, has been much cut down by particular statutes; and by 5 & 6 Vict. c. 38, they cannot try any person for treason, murder, or capital felony, or any felony which, when committed by a person not previously convicted of felony, is punishable by penal servitude for life; or for eighteen offences particularized therein, of which the principal are perjury, forgery and bigamy. Jurisdiction in respect of offences of " fraudulent debtors " is given by the Debtors Act, 1869 (32 & 33 Vict. c. 62), s. 20. As to appeal against summary convictions, see generally the Summary Jurisdiction Act, 1879, ss. 32, 33.

Paragraph 4 (c) deprives the recorder of any power to hear an appeal from a refusal to grant or renew a licence (*Reg.* v. *Deane*, 2 Q. B. 96).

The recorder may reserve a point of law for the Court of Criminal Appeal, under 11 & 12 Vict. c. 78 (*Reg.* v. *Masters*, 1 Den. C. C. 332); and may hold sessions during the assizes (*Smith* v. *Regina*, 13 Q. B. 738).

166.—(1.) The recorder may, in case of sickness or unavoidable absence, appoint, by writing signed by him, a barrister of five years' standing to act as deputy recorder at the quarter sessions then next ensuing or then being held, and not longer or otherwise.

(2.) But the sessions shall not be illegal, nor shall the acts of a deputy recorder be invalid, by reason of the cause of the absence of the recorder not being unavoidable.

This reproduces sect. 8 of the Act of 1843 (6 & 7 Vict. c. 89).

Powers of
mayor in
absence of
recorder and
deputy
recorder.

167.—(1.) In the absence of the recorder and deputy recorder, the mayor shall, at the times for the holding of the court of quarter sessions, open the court, and adjourn the holding thereof, and respite all recognisances conditioned for appearing thereat, until such day as he then and there, and so from time to time, causes to be proclaimed.

(2.) But nothing in this section shall authorize the mayor

to sit as a judge of the court for the trial of offenders, or, save as aforesaid, to do any other act in the character of a judge of the court.

Act of 1882 s. 167.

This reproduces sect. 106 of the Act of 1835.

168.—(1.) If at any time it appears to the recorder that the quarter sessions are likely to last more than three days, including the day of assembling, he may in his discretion, but subject to the provisions of this section, order a second court to be formed, and appoint, by writing signed by him, a barrister of five years' standing to preside therein, and try such felonies and misdemeanours as shall be referred to him therein.

Power for recorder to form a second court.

(2.) The barrister so appointed shall be styled assistant recorder, and shall have and exercise the same powers, subject to the same regulations (save as regards the making of a declaration as in the Eighth Schedule*) as the recorder; and the proceedings had by and before the assistant recorder shall be as effectual as if had by or before the recorder, and shall be enrolled and recorded accordingly.

"Assistant recorder."

* Page 158.

(3.) But the assistant recorder shall not have any power or jurisdiction except while the recorder is sitting in quarter sessions; save that the assistant recorder may finish any case in which the prisoner has pleaded, and in the trial whereof the assistant recorder is actually engaged at the time when the recorder ceases to sit, and may sentence any prisoner tried before him, but not then sentenced.

(4.) If at any time during the sitting of the second court the recorder is of opinion that it is no longer required, he may direct the assistant recorder at a proper opportunity to adjourn it.

Adjournment.

(5.) Where a second court is so formed, the clerk of the peace shall, on the request of the recorder, appoint an assistant, and the recorder shall appoint an additional crier for the second court.

(6.) The recorder shall not exercise the powers given by this section unless—

Certificate for appointment of assistant recorder.

(a.) It has been before each quarter sessions certified to him in writing, signed by the mayor or two aldermen or the town clerk, that the council have resolved that it

Assistant
recorder—
contd.

will be expedient that those powers be exercised; and

(b.) The name of the barrister to be appointed has at some previous time been approved by the Secretary of State as that of a fit person to be from time to time so appointed.

(7.) Where a resolution of the council is so certified, the resolution and certificate shall, if the resolution so provides, continue in force during twelve months from the date of the resolution, and during such continuance no fresh resolution or certificate shall be necessary.

(8.) An assistant recorder, assistant clerk of the peace, and additional crier shall have remuneration, as appearing by the

* Page 152.

Fourth and Fifth Schedules.*

(9.) The powers given to the recorder by this section may be exercised by the deputy recorder.

(10.) Appointments made and certificates given under this section shall not be subject to any stamp duty or other tax.

This reproduces sects. 1—3 of 7 Will. 4 & 1 Vict. c. 19, as amended by 40 & 41 Vict. c. 17; but sub-sects. 3 and 9 are new.

Liability of
borough
having
quarter
sessions for
prosecutors'
expenses.

169. A municipal corporation of a borough having a separate court of quarter sessions, shall be liable to pay the costs and expenses attending the prosecution of any felony committed or supposed to have been committed in the borough, and of any other offence committed or supposed to have been committed in the borough, the costs and expenses attending the prosecution whereof are by law payable as in the case of a felony. The amount of those costs and expenses shall be ascertained as directed by law, and the order of the court for the payment thereof shall be directed to the treasurer of the borough.

This is taken from sect. 113 of the Act of 1835.

Sheriff.

Appointment
of sheriff
in counties
of cities
and counties
of towns.

170.—(1.) The council of every borough being a county of itself, and of the city of Oxford, shall, on the 9th of November in every year, appoint a fit person to execute the office of sheriff.

(2.) The appointment shall be made at the quarterly meeting of the council immediately after the election of the mayor.

(3.) The sheriff shall hold office until the appointment of his successor.

Act of 1882 s. 170.

(4.) He shall have the same duties and powers as the sheriff or the person filling the office of sheriff in the respective borough or city would have had if this Act had not been passed.

This is taken from sect. 61 of the Act of 1835, which expressly named the places comprised therein,—being Oxford, Berwick, Bristol, Canterbury, Chester, Coventry, Exeter, Gloucester, Lichfield, Lincoln, Norwich, Worcester, York, Caermarthen, Haverfordwest, Kingston-upon-Hull, Newcastle-upon-Tyne, Nottingham, Poole, and Southampton.

As to duties and powers of sheriffs, see Atkinson's Sheriff Law and Churchill's Sheriff Law, and Chit. Stat. vol. v. p. 1340, tit. "*Sheriff.*"

Coroner.

171.—(1.) The council of a borough having a separate court of quarter sessions shall, within ten days next after receipt of the grant thereof by the council, and thenceforward from time to time, appoint a fit person, not an alderman or councillor of the borough, to be coroner of the borough; and thereafter no person other than the coroner so appointed shall take in the borough any inquisition belonging to the office of coroner.

Appointment, fees, &c. of borough coroner in boroughs having separate quarter sessions.

(2.) The coroner shall hold office during good behaviour.

(3.) A vacancy in the office shall be filled up within ten days after it occurs.

(4.) The coroner shall have, by order of the recorder, remuneration as appearing in the Fourth and Fifth Schedules*.

* Pages 153, 154.

This is taken from sect. 62 of the Act of 1835. As to the duties of the coroner, see Jervis on Coroner; Chit. Stat. vol. i. tit. "*Coroner.*"

172.—(1.) In case of illness or unavoidable absence, the coroner shall appoint by writing signed by him a fit person, being a barrister or solicitor, and not an alderman or councillor of the borough, to act for him as deputy coroner during his illness or unavoidable absence, but not longer or otherwise.

Power of borough coroner to appoint a deputy.

(2.) The mayor or two justices for the borough shall on each occasion certify by writing signed by him or them the necessity for the appointment of a deputy coroner. This

Act of 1882
s. 172.

certificate shall state the cause of absence of the coroner, and shall be openly read to every inquest jury summoned by the deputy coroner.

This reproduces sect. 6 of the Act of 1836 (6 & 7 Will. 4, c. 105). By sect. 235 the acts of a deputy are not invalidated by any defect in his appointment; and see *Reg.* v. *Perkin,* 7 Q. B. 165.

Returns by borough coroners.

173. On or before the 1st of February in every year the coroner shall send to the Secretary of State a return in writing, in such form as the Secretary of State directs, of the particulars of each case in which the coroner or his deputy was called upon to hold an inquest during the year ending on the then last 31st of December.

This and the next section reproduce sects. 63 and 64 of the Act of 1835.

Acting of county coroner in borough.

174.—(1.) Where a borough has not a separate court of quarter sessions no person other than the coroner for the county or district in which the borough is situate shall take in the borough any inquisition belonging to the office of coroner.

(2.) That coroner shall, for every inquisition duly taken by him within the borough, be entitled to such rateable fees and salary as would be allowed and due to him, and to be allowed and paid in like manner, as for any other inquisition taken by him within the county or district.

The fees of county coroners are regulated by 7 Will. 4 & 1 Vict. c. 68, Chit. Stat. vol. i. tit. "*Coroner.*"

Borough Civil Court.

Judge of borough civil court where there is a recorder.

175.—(1.) The recorder, if there is one, shall continue to be the judge of the borough civil court, except in the following cases, that is to say, where the court is regulated by a local Act of Parliament, or where a barrister of five years' standing acted at the passing of the Municipal Corporations Act, 1835, as judge or assessor of the court.

(2.) The recorder, if judge, may, in case of his illness or unavoidable absence, appoint by writing signed by him a barrister of five years' standing to act for him as deputy judge of the court at the court or courts then next to be holden, or then being holden, and not longer or otherwise.

(3.) The recorder on every occasion of his appointing a

deputy judge shall forthwith send to the Secretary of State a statement of his reason for so doing.

(4.) A court shall not be illegal, nor shall the acts of the deputy judge be invalid, by reason of the absence of the recorder not being unavoidable.

(5.) The recorder, where judge, and the deputy judge, shall have such remuneration as the council fix by bye-law.

(6.) Where the recorder is judge, the court may in his absence be holden for all purposes within the competency of the court, except the trial of issues of fact or of law, before any person, being a barrister of five years' standing or a solicitor of five years' practice, from time to time appointed for that purpose by the recorder by writing signed by him.

(7.) Where the recorder or his deputy is judge, all orders, affidavits, and matters, except the trial of issues in law or in fact, relating to the business of the court, if not regulated by a local Act, may be made, sworn, or done in or out of court in the absence of the recorder and his deputy by or before the registrar or such other person, being a barrister of five years' standing, or a solicitor of five years' practice, as the recorder appoints by writing signed by him.

This section is taken from sect. 118 of the Act of 1835, as amended by sect. 9 of the Act of 1836 (6 & 7 Will. 4, c. 105), and sects. 32 and 33 of the Act of 1837 (7 Will. 4 & 1 Vict. c. 78).

176. Where there is a borough civil court, but no recorder, such officer of the borough as by the charter constituting the court, or by custom, is the judge of the court, shall continue to be and act as such judge; and the council, whether the court is regulated by a local Act or not, shall have power for that purpose to appoint the necessary officer.

> Judge of borough civil court where there is no recorder.

This and the next section are taken from sect. 118 of the Act of 1835.

177. Every judge or assessor of a borough civil court, other than the mayor, shall hold his office during good behaviour.

> Tenure of judge.

178.—(1.) Except where the town clerk acts as registrar, the council shall from time to time appoint a registrar of the borough civil court.

> Registrar and other officers and fees.

(2.) The council shall from time to time appoint other requisite officers and servants of the court.

Act of 1882
s. 178.

(3.) The fees to be taken by the registrar and other officers of the court shall be from time to time fixed by the council, subject to the approval of the Secretary of State.

(4.) If and as far as the fees are not so fixed, they shall be those usually taken before the passing of the Municipal Corporations Act, 1835.

This and the next section are taken from sects. 119 and 124 of the Act of 1835.

Solicitors.

179.—(1.) The registrar of a borough civil court, or any other officer of the court, shall not himself, or by any partner or clerk, practise as a solicitor or attorney, in the court ; nor shall any partner or clerk of the registrar act as agent for any other solicitor or attorney in the court.

(2.) Unless so disqualified, every solicitor of the Supreme Court of Judicature may practise as solicitor in the court.

Time of holding court.

180.—(1.) Each borough civil court shall be holden for trial of issues of fact and of law four times at least in each year, and with no greater interval than four months between two successive courts.

(2.) Subject as aforesaid, where the recorder is judge, the court shall be holden at such times as the recorder thinks fit, or as the Secretary of State from time to time directs.

This section is taken from sect. 9 of the Act of 1836 (6 & 7 Will. 4, c. 105), and sect. 2 of the Act of 1839 (2 & 3 Vict. c. 27), sect. 2 of which is re-enacted by the next section.

Procedure.

181. Every personal action brought in a borough civil court shall be commenced by writ of summons.

Power for judge to make rules of procedure.

182.—(1.) Subject to the provisions of this Act, the judge of a borough civil court may from time to time make rules for regulating the times of holding the court and the procedure, practice, and pleadings therein, and the fees of solicitors therein, and may by any rule revoke or alter any former rule.

(2.) But where there is a recorder and he is not the judge of the court, every rule made by the judge shall be subject to the approval of the recorder in writing signed by him ; save that this provision shall not apply where the recorder acts as deputy of the judge.

(3.) In every case (whether the recorder is judge or not)

---

rules made by the judge under this section shall be subject to the approval of three judges of the High Court.

Act of 1882 s. 182.

This is taken from sect. 118 of the Act of 1835, sect. 9 of the Act of 1837 (6 & 7 Will. 4, c. 105), and sect. 1 of the Act of 1839 (2 & 3 Vict. c. 27).

183.—(1.) Where by the Municipal Corporations Act, 1835, jurisdiction was conferred on a borough civil court whereof the recorder is judge, or wherein a barrister of five years' standing acts as judge or assessor, to try personal actions wherein the sum sought to be recovered does not exceed twenty pounds, and actions of ejectment between landowner and tenant wherein the annual rent of the property whereof possession is sought to be recovered does not exceed twenty pounds, no fine having been reserved or made payable, then that court shall continue to have that jurisdiction.

Jurisdiction of borough civil court.

(2.) Any action wherein the title to land of any tenure, or to any tithe, toll, market, fair, or other franchise is in question, shall not be tried in a borough civil court which before the passing of the Municipal Corporations Act, 1835, had not authority to try actions wherein such titles were in question. If it appears to such a court that such a title is in question in an action the jurisdiction of the court in the matter of the action shall cease ; and the court may, if it thinks fit, award costs against the party commencing the action.

This is taken from sect. 118 of the Act of 1835.

184.—(1.) Nothing in this Act shall take away or abridge in respect of local extent, amount or otherwise, any power, jurisdiction, or authority of a borough civil court, or of a judge, or assessor, or registrar thereof, or of any deputy of a judge, or assessor, or registrar thereof, or affect the constitution or procedure thereof; and, subject to the express provisions of this Act, such power, jurisdiction, authority, constitution, and procedure, shall continue and be as if this Act had not been passed.

Saving for borough civil courts and for 35 & 36 Vict. c. 86.

(2.) Nothing in this Act shall affect the Borough and Local Courts of Record Act, 1872.

By the Borough and Local Courts of Record Act, 1872 (35 & 36 Vict. c. 86), the provisions of the Interpleader Act (1 & 2 Will. 4, c. 32), and also of the schedule to that Act, as to hearing motions

Act of 1882 s. 184. for new trials, &c., as to settlement of fees by the judge, as to statement of special case for the High Court, as to removal of actions into the High Court, and as to issuing a commission to examine witnesses abroad, may be extended to "all or any local court or Courts of Record in England or Wales by Order in Council." Sect. 6 of the same Act gives power to the court to send writs of execution for the recovery of sums not exceeding 20*l.* to the bailiffs of the County Courts.

Power to extend jurisdiction of borough civil court.   **185.** It shall be lawful for the Queen, by Order in Council, on the joint petition of the justices of a county in quarter sessions and of the council of a borough, to grant that the jurisdiction of the borough civil court shall extend over any district adjacent to the borough within the jurisdiction of those quarter sessions; and the same shall extend accordingly.

This is taken from sect. 184 of the Act of 1835.

Borough Juries.

Every burgess of quarter sessions borough liable to serve as juror.   **186.**—(1.) Every burgess of a borough having a separate court of quarter sessions or a borough civil court shall, unless by law exempt or disqualified, be qualified and liable to serve on grand juries in the borough, and on juries for the trial of issues joined in either of those courts.

Notice of sessions.   (2.) The clerk of the peace shall give public notice of the time and place of holding the court of quarter sessions ten days at least before the holding thereof, and shall, seven days at least before the holding thereof, summon a sufficient number of persons, qualified and liable, to serve as grand jurors at the sessions.

Summons of jurors.   (3.) The clerk of the peace and registrar of the borough civil court respectively shall also summon a sufficient number of persons, qualified and liable, to serve as jurors at every such sessions, and at the holding of every such civil court for the trial of causes, if there is any cause then to be tried.

(4.) The summons may be made by showing to the person to be summoned, or, if he is absent from his usual place of abode, by leaving with some person therein inhabiting a notice containing its substance, and signed by the clerk of the peace or registrar, as the case may be.

(5.) The clerk of the peace and registrar shall make out lists containing the surnames and other names, abodes, and descriptions of the persons summoned by them respectively.

(6.) No person shall be summoned under this section to

serve as a juror more than once in any year, unless every person qualified and liable so to serve has been already summoned once in that year.

(7.) If any person, having been duly summoned under this section, fails to attend according to the summons, or, being thrice called, does not answer to his name, or after his appearance wilfully withdraws himself from the court, he shall (unless some reasonable excuse is proved by him to the satisfaction of the court), be liable to pay a fine of such amount as the court thinks fit.

(8.) If the person on whom any such fine is imposed refuses to pay it to the person authorized by the court to receive it, the court may, then or at the next sitting, by order of the court signed by the clerk of the peace or registrar, cause to be levied, by distress and sale of the goods of the person on whom the fine is imposed the fine, and the reasonable charges of the distress and sale.

(9.) Nothing in this Act shall affect the Juries Act, 1870.

This is taken from sect. 121 of the Act of 1835, the amendment by 7 Will. 4 & 1 Vict. c. 78, being reproduced by paragraph six.

The exemptions and disqualifications from and for serving on juries will be found in the Juries Act, 1870 (33 & 34 Vict. c. 77). The principal exemptions are of—ministers of religion, lawyers actually practising, officers on full pay, medical practitioners, officers of the inland revenue, and officers of police. To the list of exemptions under the schedule of the Act of 1870 must be added income-tax commissioners, by 34 & 35 Vict. c. 103, s. 30; and dentists, by the Dentists Act, 1878 (41 & 42 Vict. c. 33), s. 30, "if they so desire."

By the schedule to the Act of 1870 there is also an exemption for:

"Members of the council of the municipal corporation of any borough, and every justice of the peace assigned to keep the peace therein, and the town clerk and treasurer for the time being of every such borough, *so far as relates to any jury summoned to serve in the county where such borough is situate;*" and for

"Burgesses of every borough in and for which a separate court of quarter sessions shall be holden, *so far as relates to any jury summoned for the trial of issues joined in any court of general or quarter sessions of the peace in the county wherein such borough is situate.*"

Where no express exemption can be found in any statute subsequent to 1870, a liability to serve on all juries is imposed by sect. 9 of the Juries Act, 1870.

Exceptional Provisions.

187. The grant to a borough of a separate commission of the peace, or of a separate court of quarter sessions, shall not be prejudicially affected by any subsequent grant to or

Act of 1882 s. 187.

for any county of a commission of the peace or other commission.

This section in substance re-enacts 2 & 3 P. & M. c. 18, repealed as to boroughs within this Act by sect. 5, ante, and Sched. I. Part 2, p. 141, post.

Trial of offences committed in counties of cities, &c.

188.—(1.) Until her Majesty is pleased to direct a commission of oyer and terminer and gaol delivery to be executed within any borough being a county of a city or county of a town, all bills of indictment for offences committed within that borough shall be preferred, and all proceedings thereon shall be had, in the manner authorized by the Act of the thirty-eighth year of the reign of King George the Third, chapter fifty-two, " to regulate the trial of causes, indictments, and other proceedings which arise within the counties of certain cities and towns corporate within the kingdom."

* Page 156.

(2.) For the purposes of that Act each borough named in the Sixth Schedule * shall be considered as next adjoining the county named in conjunction therewith.

This section is taken from sect. 109 of the Act of 1835. By 38 Geo. 3, c. 52 (Chit. Stat. vol. ii. tit. *"Criminal Law"*) indictments removed into the Queen's Bench by certiorari, if the venue be laid in the county or city of a town corporate, may be directed by the court at the instance of the prosecutor or defendant to be tried by a jury of the county next adjoining to the county of such city or town.

Jurisdiction in places separated from borough.

189. Where under any Act a place has ceased or ceases to be part of a borough or the liberties thereof, all matters by virtue of a local Act of Parliament or otherwise cognizable by a justice or by the quarter sessions having jurisdiction within that place shall be cognizable by the justices or the quarter sessions of the county, liberty, or jurisdiction within which the place is situate, in the same manner and subject to the same provisions as they were within the jurisdiction of the justices or the quarter sessions for that place.

This is taken from sect. 30 of the Act of 1835.

PART IX.—POLICE.

Watch Committee; Constables.

Council to appoint watch committee.

190.—(1.) The council shall from time to time appoint, for such time as they think fit, a sufficient number not exceeding one-third of their own body, who, with the mayor, shall be the watch committee.

(2.) The watch committee may act by a majority of those

present at a meeting thereof, but shall not act unless three are so present.

Act of 1882 s. 190.

This and the next section are taken from sects. 76 and 77 of the Act of 1835, the words "not exceeding one-third" in sub-s. 1 of this section being new.

The amendment was inserted for the purpose of giving an appeal from the watch committee to the town council against the dismissal of constables, &c. instead of the Home Secretary, as proposed in a certain " Police Bill," which was passing through Parliament contemporaneously with the present Act. The Police Bill was withdrawn, but this consequential amendment was not struck out.

Prior to this Act, it is understood to have been the practice in very many boroughs to place most, if not all, the councillors upon the watch committee. A committee exceeding in number the one-third, if appointed *before* 1st January, 1883, may (see sect. 260, sub-s. 3, p. 138) continue to act; but it is conceived that the acts of any such committee appointed *after* that date would be void.

191.—(1.) The watch committee shall from time to time appoint a sufficient number of fit men to be borough constables.

Appointment, duties, and powers of borough constables.

(2,) A borough constable shall be sworn in (¹) before a justice having jurisdiction in the borough, and when so sworn shall, in the borough, in the county in which the borough or any part thereof is situate, and in every county being within seven miles from any part of the borough, and in all liberties in any such county, have all such powers and privileges, and be liable to all such duties and responsibilities, as any constable has and is liable to for the time being in his constablewick, at common law or by statute, and shall obey all such lawful commands as he receives from any justice having jurisdiction in the borough or in any county in which the constable is called on to act.

(3.) The watch committee may from time to time frame such regulations as they deem expedient for preventing neglect or abuse, and for making the borough constables efficient in the discharge of their duties.

(4.) The watch committee, or any two justices having jurisdiction in the borough, may at any time suspend, and the watch committee may at any time dismiss, any borough constable whom they think negligent in the discharge of his duty, or otherwise unfit for the same.

(5.) When a borough constable is so dismissed, or ceases to belong to the constabulary force of the borough, all powers vested in him as a constable by virtue of this Act shall immediately cease.

Act of 1882
s. 191.

(6.) Nothing in this section shall interfere with the operation of an Act of the session of the third and fourth years of
her majesty's reign " to amend the Act for the establishment
of county and district constables ;" and throughout that Act
a reference to this Act shall be deemed to be substituted for a
reference to the Municipal Corporations Act, 1835, and any
Act amending it.

This is taken from sects. 76 and 77 of the Act of 1835.

By 3 & 4 Vict. c. 88, s. 14, the justices of any county and the
council of any borough situated in or adjoining to such county
may agree together for the consolidation of the county and borough
police establishments. By sect. 5 of 19 & 20 Vict. c. 69, the terms
of consolidation may be arranged, in case of a proposal by the
council to consolidate not being effected, by the Privy Council; and
by sect. 20 of the same Act an agreement for consolidation may not
be put an end to without the sanction of a Secretary of State.

(¹) *Sworn in.*]—There were corresponding words in the Act of
1835, s. 76, but the Promissory Oaths Act, 1868 (31 & 32 Vict. c. 72,
s. 12) so far (though not in express terms) amended that section as
to substitute a declaration for an oath. The operation of the Promissory Oaths Act is saved by sect. 239, sub-sect. 2, post, and it
is conceived that, looking to the consolidating character of this
statute, such saving will give that Act a prospective operation, and
substitute a declaration for the oath expressly prescribed by sub-
sect. 2 of the present section ; but the point is a doubtful one.

**Quarterly
returns as to
borough
constables.**

192. The watch committee shall, on the 1st of January,
the 1st of April, the 1st of July, and the 1st of October in
every year, send to the Secretary of State a copy of all rules
from time to time made by the watch committee or the council
for the regulation and guidance of the borough constables.

This is taken from sect. 86 of the Act of 1835.

**Power for
constables to
apprehend
disorderly
persons, &c.**

193. A borough constable may, while on duty, apprehend
any idle and disorderly person whom he finds disturbing the
public peace, or whom he has just cause to suspect of intention to commit a felony, and deliver him into the custody
of the borough constable in attendance at the nearest watch-
house, in order that he may either be secured until he can be
brought before a justice, or, where the constable in attendance
is empowered and thinks fit to take bail, give bail for his
appearance before a justice.

This is taken from sect. 78 of the Act of 1835.

**Penalties on
constables for
neglect of
duty.**

194. If a borough constable is guilty of neglect of duty, or
of disobedience to a lawful order, he shall for every such
offence be liable on summary conviction to imprisonment for

any time not exceeding ten days, or, in the discretion of the court, to a fine not exceeding forty shillings, or to be dismissed from his office.

Act of 1882
s. 194.

This and the next section are taken from sects. 80 and 81 of the Act of 1835.

195.—(1.) If any person assaults or resists a borough constable in the execution of his duty, or aids or incites any person so to assault or resist, he shall for every such offence be liable on summary conviction to a fine not exceeding five pounds.

Penalty for assaults on constables.

(2.) But nothing in this section shall prevent any prosecution by way of indictment against any such offender, except that he shall not be prosecuted both by indictment and in a summary manner for the same offence.

By sect. 38 of 24 & 25 Vict. c. 100, "whosoever shall assault any person with intent to commit felony, or shall assault, resist, or wilfully obstruct any peace officer in the due execution of his duty, or any person acting in aid of such officer, or shall assault any person with intent to resist or prevent the lawful apprehension or detainer of himself or of any other person for any offence, shall be guilty of a misdemeanour, and, being convicted thereof, shall be liable, at the discretion of the court, to be imprisoned for any term not exceeding two years, with or without hard labour."

Special Constables.

196.—(1.) Two or more of the justices having jurisdiction in a borough shall, in October, in every year, appoint, by precept signed by them, so many as they think fit of the inhabitants of the borough, not legally exempt from serving the office of constable, to act as special constables in the borough.

Appointment of special constables.

(2.) Every such special constable shall make a declaration to the effect of the oath set forth in the Act of the session of the first and second years of the reign of King William the Fourth, chapter forty-one, "for amending the laws relative to the appointment of special constables, and for the better preservation of the peace," and shall have the powers and immunities, and be liable to the duties and penalties, enacted by that Act.

Declaration.

(3.) He shall act when so required by the warrant of a justice having jurisdiction in the borough, but not otherwise.

(4.) The warrant shall recite that in the opinion of the justice the ordinary police force of the borough is insufficient

Warrant of justice of the peace.

Act of 1882 s. 196.

Special con- stables—*contd.*

at the date of the warrant to maintain the peace of the borough.

(5.) Nothing in this section shall make any person having a right to vote at a parliamentary election liable or compellable to serve as a special constable at or during the election.

(6.) Special constables shall be entitled to remuneration as appearing by the Fourth and Fifth Schedules.*

* Pages 152, 154.

This is taken from sect. 83 of the Act of 1835, the substitution of the declaration for the oath being new.

The exemptions under the first paragraphs are conceived to be the same as those fixed by 5 & 6 Vict. c. 109, s. 6, which exempts large classes of persons, *e.g.*, ministers of religion, solicitors, and medical practitioners from serving the office of parish constable *under that Act*, and by sect. 5, enacts that " every able-bodied man resident within" a parish "between the ages of twenty-five and fifty-five years, rated to the relief of the poor, or to the county rate on any tenements of the net yearly value of four pounds or upwards," except such persons as are exempt or disqualified by that Act, " shall be qualified and liable to serve as a constable of that parish." If this interpretation of the words " legally exempt, &c." be correct, the abolition of parish constables under the Parish Constables Act, 1872, will not affect it, nor will the fact that the Act 5 & 6 Vict. c. 109, does not apply to municipal corporations (sect. 21). The form of oath is set forth in 1 & 2 Will. 4, c. 41, s. 1.

The form of declaration will be :—

"I, A. B., do declare that I will well and truly serve our Sovereign Lady the Queen the office of special constable for the borough of   , without favour or affection, malice or ill will; and that I will to the best of my power cause the peace to be preserved, and prevent all offences against the persons and properties of her Majesty's subjects; and that while I continue to hold the said office, I will to the best of my skill and knowledge discharge all the duties thereof faithfully according to law."

By 1 & 2 Will. 4, c. 41, s. 6, special constables have "all such powers, authorities, advantages and immunities as any constable duly appointed *now* (*i.e.*, in 1831, when the Act was passed) has within his constablewick by virtue of the common law of the realm, or of any statute or statutes." By sect. 7 of the same Act there is a penalty not exceeding 5*l*. for refusing to take the oath [now declaration], and by sect. 8 a similar penalty for refusal to serve, or disobedience of orders. (See the Act, Chit. Stat. vol. iv. tit. "*Police.*")

Watch Rate.

Levy of watch rate.

197.—(1.) Where at the commencement of this Act any rate might be levied in a borough, or in any part of a borough, for the purpose of watching solely by day or by night, or for the purpose of watching by day or by night, conjointly with any other purpose, the council may from time to time make and levy a watch rate on the occupiers of all hereditaments within such parts of the borough as are watched by day and by night, and as are from time to time, by order of the council, declared liable to watch rate.

Act of 1882 s. 197.

(2.) The watch rate shall be made on an estimate of the net annual value of the several hereditaments rated thereto, that is to say, of the rent at which, one year with another, they might in their actual state be reasonably expected to let from year to year, the probable annual average cost of the repairs, insurances, and other expenses necessary to maintain them in their actual state, and all rates, taxes, and public charges, except tithes or tithe commutation rentcharge (if any), being paid by the tenant.

(3.) The watch rate may be made by one rate made yearly, or by two or more rates made half-yearly or otherwise, and may be of any amount, in the discretion of the council, not exceeding in any year eightpence in the pound on the net annual value of the hereditaments rated thereto.

Limit of watch rate to 8*d.* in the pound.

(4.) For the purposes of the watch rate the council and all persons concerned, including overseers, shall have all powers given to them in respect of the borough rate for ordering, making, assessing, levying, raising, collecting, or paying the same, or as near thereto as the nature of the case admits.

(5.) The provision of this Act* relating to orders of vestries for the rating, in some cases, of owners, instead of occupiers, shall extend to the watch rate.

*Sect. 147.

(6.) Nothing in the foregoing provisions of this section (except the general power to levy a watch rate) shall apply to any borough in which the borough fund is sufficient with the aid of the amount only of watch rate which could for the time being be raised therein under the Municipal Corporations Act, 1835, and without the aid of any borough rate, to defray the expenses of the constabulary force of the borough, with all other expenses legally payable out of the borough fund; but nothing in the present provision shall affect any benefit or right reserved by Part X., or make the borough fund liable to any expenses with which it would not be otherwise chargeable.

(7.) Nothing in this section shall affect the liability of the borough fund to make good any deficiency of the watch rate towards the expenses of the police.

(8.) Nothing in this section shall make liable to watch rate any hereditaments exempted by any local Act from payment of watch rate.

(9.) Nothing in this section shall alter the comparative liability to watch rate of any hereditaments which are under any local Act in respect of any watch rate entitled to any deduction from, or chargeable with any increase on, an equal pound rate; but the like comparative deductions and increased charges shall be made under this section.

This section (of which sub-s. 5 is new) is taken from sect. 92 of the Act of 1835 as amended by the Act of 1839 (2 & 3 Vict. c. 28), the Act of 1840 (3 & 4 Vict. c. 28), and the Act of 1859 (22 & 23 Vict. c. 32), s. 6, which latter enactment raised the limit from 6d. to 8d. in the pound, as now fixed by paragraph 3 of this section.

Watch rate in divided parish.

198.—(1.) Where part only of a parish is liable to watch rate, the overseers shall not pay out of the poor rate the amount of the watch rate charged by the council on that parish, but shall make a separate rate or assessment on the part or parts only of the parish liable to watch rate; which rate shall be made in like manner and under like regulations and with like means and remedies for recovery thereof as in the case of a rate levied in respect of the contribution towards a borough rate.

(2.) No such separate rate shall be demanded, collected, or payable until it has been allowed by two justices usually acting in and for the borough, and has been published as a poor rate is by law required to be allowed and published (¹).

(3.) Any person who thinks himself aggrieved by such a separate rate may appeal to the recorder at the next quarter sessions for the borough, or if there is none to the next court of quarter sessions for the county wherein the borough is situate, or whereto it is adjacent; and the recorder or court shall hear and determine the same, and shall award relief in the premises as in cases of appeal against a poor rate.

(4.) Every such separate rate may be of the rate in the pound necessary for raising the sum charged by the council, but not exceeding twopence in the pound beyond the rate in the pound at which the council have computed the watch rate charged by them.

(5.) The overseers shall account for money collected under such a separate rate as for money collected under a poor rate;

and if there is a surplus in their hands, they shall pay it to the treasurer, to go to the borough fund, to the credit of the place for which the rate was made, and in part payment of the next watch rate laid on that place by the council.

(6.) The council or a committee appointed for this purpose, on application on behalf of any person rated to such a separate rate to be discharged therefrom, and on proof of his inability through poverty to pay the amount charged on him, may order that he be excused from the payment thereof, and may strike out his name therefrom ; and the sum at which he was rated shall not thereafter be collected, nor shall any person be charged with it or be liable to account for it or for omitting to collect or receive it.

(7.) The overseers making any such separate rate may, by warrant from two justices usually acting in and for the borough, levy on every person refusing to pay the rate the amount charged on him, with the costs and charges of recovering and enforcing payment thereof, to be ascertained by the justices, by distress and sale of the offender's goods, rendering to him the overplus; and in default of such distress two justices may commit him to prison, there to remain without bail until payment of the amount and arrearages.

This section substantially reproduces sects. 2—7 of the Act of 1845 (8 & 9 Vict. c. 110).

(¹) *Allowance and Publication of Rate.*]—As to allowance of poor rate by justices of the peace, see 43 Eliz. c. 2; and as to publication, 17 Geo. 2, c. 3; which, as amended by 7 Will. 4 & 1 Vict. c. 45, s. 2, enacts that the overseers must affix on the church doors notice "of every rate for the relief of the poor allowed by the justices of the peace the next Sunday after the same shall have been so allowed;" and that no rate shall be valid, so as to collect the same, unless such notice shall have been given. This enactment is imperative (*Reg.* v. *Dyott*, 9 Q. B. D. 47); but by the Poor Rate Act, 1882 (45 & 46 Vict. c. 20), s. 4, publication in a conspicuous place in a parish not having a church or chapel is sufficient.

As to relief in cases of appeal, see 17 Geo. 2, c. 38.

199. Any warrant required for the levy or collection of a watch rate or separate rate may be issued by the mayor, signed by him, and sealed with the corporate seal.

This is taken from sect. 5 of the Act of 1836 (6 & 7 Will. 4, c. 104).

200. All money raised by a watch rate, or by a separate rate as last aforesaid, shall go to the borough fund.

This is taken from sect. 92 of the Act of 1835.

PART X.—FREEMEN.

Act of 1882 s. 201.

Definition of freeman.**201.** In this Part the term freeman includes any person of the class whose rights and interests were reserved by the Municipal Corporations Act, 1835, under the name either of freemen or of burgesses.

See sect. 2 of the Act of 1835, and *Hopkins* v. *Mayor of Swansea*, 8 M. & W. 901.

Freedom not by gift or purchase.

202. No person shall be admitted a freeman by gift or by purchase.

This is taken from sect. 3 of the Act of 1835.

The freemen's roll.

203. The town clerk of every borough for which at the commencement of this Act there is a Freemen's Roll shall continue to keep a list, called the Freemen's Roll.

This and the next section are taken from sect. 5 of the Act of 1835. As to right of freemen to vote at parliamentary elections if registered and resident, see note to sect. 209, post.

Admission to freedom.

204. Where a person is entitled to be admitted a freeman for the purposes of this Part in respect of birth, servitude, or marriage, and claims accordingly, the mayor shall examine into the claim, and on its being established the claimant shall be admitted and enrolled by the town clerk on the Freemen's Roll.

Reservation of rights of property to freemen and others.

205.—(1.) Every person who had before the passing of the Municipal Corporations Act, 1835, been admitted a freeman, or if that Act had not been passed might have been so admitted otherwise than by gift or purchase, and

(2.) Every person who for the time being is—

        (a.) An inhabitant of a borough, or

        (b.) Wife, widow, son, or daughter of a freeman, or

        (c.) Husband of a daughter or widow of a freeman, or

        (d.) Bound an apprentice,—

shall, subject to the provisions of this Part, have and enjoy and be entitled to acquire and enjoy the same share and benefit of the hereditaments, and of the rents and profits thereof, and of the common lands and public stock of any borough or body corporate, and of any property held in whole or in part for any charitable uses or trusts, as if the Municipal Corporations Act, 1835, or this Act, had not been passed.

This and the two next sections are taken from sects. 2 and 3 of the Act of 1835.

206.—(1.) The total amount to be divided among the persons whose rights are by the last foregoing section reserved shall not exceed the surplus remaining after payment of the interest of all lawful debts chargeable on the property out of which the sums so to be divided have arisen, together with the salaries of municipal officers and all other lawful expenses which, on the 5th of June, 1835, were defrayed out of or chargeable on the same.

(2.) Where, if the Municipal Corporations Act, 1835, or this Act, had not been passed, any such person would have been liable by statute, bye-law, charter, or custom, to pay any fine, fee, or sum of money to any body corporate, or to any member, officer, or servant thereof, in consideration of his freedom, or of his or her title to those reserved rights, or there was any condition precedent to any person being entitled to those rights, he or she shall not have any benefit in respect of those rights until he or she has paid that fine, fee, or sum to the treasurer on account of the borough fund, or has fulfilled that condition, as far as it is capable of being fulfilled according to the provisions of this Act.

207. Nothing in this Act shall strengthen or confirm any claim, right, or title of any freeman or of any person to the benefit of any right in this Part reserved, but the same may in every case be brought in question, impeached, and set aside, as if this Act had not been passed.

208.—(1.) Nothing before in this Part contained shall apply to any claim, right, or title of a freeman or of any person to any discharge or exemption from any tolls or dues levied wholly or in part by or for the use or benefit of any borough or body corporate.

(2.) No person shall have any such discharge or exemption except a person who, on the 5th of June, 1835, was an inhabitant, or was admitted or entitled to be admitted a freeman, or was the wife, widow, son, or daughter of a freeman, or was bound an apprentice ; and every such person shall be entitled to the same discharge or exemption as if the Municipal Corporations Act, 1835, or this Act, had not been passed.

(3.) But nothing in this Act shall affect the right of any person claiming such discharge or exemption otherwise than as inhabitant or freeman, or member of a municipal corporation, or widow or kin of such an inhabitant, freeman, or member.

This is taken from sect. 2 of the Act of 1835, and sect. 9 of the Act of 1836 (6 & 7 Will. 4, c. 104).

Reservation of parliamentary franchise, &c.

209.—(1.) Every person who, if the Municipal Corporations Act, 1835, had not been passed, would have enjoyed as a freeman, or might thereafter have acquired, in respect of birth or servitude, as a freeman, the right of voting in a parliamentary election, shall be entitled to enjoy or acquire that right as if that Act or this Act had not been passed.

(2.) No stamp duty shall be chargeable on the admission of any person as a freeman in respect of birth or servitude in a parliamentary borough.

(3.) The town clerk shall do all things appertaining by law to the registration of freemen for parliamentary elections.

The first and third paragraphs of this section are taken from sect. 4 of the Act of 1835; the second from 1 & 2 Vict. c. 35. By sect. 46, sub-sect. 9, no stamp duty is payable in respect of the enrolment as a burgess. The only stamp duty therefore payable is that upon admission as a freeman in a non-parliamentary borough, as to which, see Stamp Act, 1870 (33 & 34 Vict. c. 97), ss. 29, 30, and schedule, tit. "Admission."

The right of freemen to vote at parliamentary elections depends upon sect. 32 of the Reform Act, 1832, by which the franchise is reserved to registered freemen who have resided in the borough or within seven miles thereof for six months previous to the last day of (altered to 15th day by sect. 7 of the Parliamentary and Municipal Registration Act, 1878) July prior to registration, with the proviso, that freemen admitted since 1st March, 1831, otherwise than in respect of birth or servitude, shall not be entitled to vote or be registered.

PART XI.—GRANT OF CHARTERS.

Power to Crown in granting charter to borough to extend to it the provisions of the Municipal Corporations Acts.

210. If on the petition to the Queen of the inhabitant householders of any town or towns or district in England, or of any of those inhabitants, praying for the grant of a charter of incorporation, her Majesty, by the advice of her Privy Council, thinks fit by charter to create such town, towns or district, or any part thereof specified in the charter, with or without any adjoining place, a municipal borough, and to incorporate the inhabitants thereof, it shall be lawful for her Majesty by the charter to extend to that municipal borough and the inhabitants thereof so incorporated the provisions of the Municipal Corporations Acts.

This and the other sections of this "Part" (sect. 18 being new) of the Act reproduce "The Municipal Corporations (New Charters) Act, 1877" (40 & 41 Vict. c. 69), substituted for sect. 141 of the Act of 1835, and sect. 49 of 7 Will. 4 & 1 Vict. c. 78, repealed by that Act.

Since the Act of 1835 (which applied to 178 boroughs scheduled thereto), charters have been granted to about sixty boroughs.

Advisability of having Charter.]—The principal grounds of distinction between a local government district (as to the constitution of which, see Public Health Act, 1875, ss. 282, 312 and schedules 2 and 3) are that municipal corporation officers are elected by a purely popular franchise, whereas local board officers are elected by plural voting, and that municipal corporations are not so much under the control of the Local Government Board.

Peculiar, also, to a municipal corporation is a separate police; and by grant of the Crown, *upon further petition*, a separate court of quarter sessions, and a separate commission of the peace and coroner.

211.—(1.) Every petition for a charter under this Act shall be referred to a Committee of the Lords of Her Majesty's Privy Council (in this Part called the Committee of Council).

(2.) One month at least before the petition is taken into consideration by the Committee of Council, notice thereof and of the time when it will be so taken into consideration shall be published in the London Gazette, and otherwise in such manner as the Committee direct for the purpose of making it known to all persons interested.

Reference to Committee of Council, and notice of petition for charter.

212.—(1.) Where her Majesty by a charter extends the Municipal Corporation Acts to a municipal borough it shall be lawful for her Majesty, by the charter, to do all or any of the following things :

(a.) To fix the number of councillors, and to fix the number and boundaries of the wards (if any), and to assign the number of councillors to each ward ; and

(b.) To fix the years days and times for the retirement of the first aldermen and councillors ; and

(c.) To fix such days times and places, and nominate such persons to perform such duties, and make such other temporary modifications of the Municipal Corporations Acts, as may appear to her Majesty to be necessary or proper for making those Acts applicable in the case of the first constitution of a municipal borough.

Power by charter to settle wards, and by fixing dates and otherwise to adapt the Municipal Corporations Acts to first constitution of new borough.

(2.) The years days times and places fixed by the charter, and the persons nominated therein to perform any duties, shall, as regards the borough named in the charter, be respectively substituted in the Municipal Corporations Acts for the years, days, times, places, officers, and persons therein mentioned, and the persons so nominated shall have the like powers, and be subject to the like obligations and penalties, as the officers and persons mentioned in those Acts for whom they are respectively substituted.

(3.) Subject to the provisions of the charter authorized by this section, the Municipal Corporations Acts shall, on the charter coming into effect, apply to the municipal borough to which they are extended by the charter; and, where the first mayor aldermen and councillors or any of them are named in the charter, shall apply as if they were elected under the Municipal Corporations Acts, and where they are not so named, shall apply to their first election.

Scheme for
continuance
or abolition
of and ad-
justment of
rights of
existing local
authority and
officers.

213.—(1.) Where a petition for a charter is referred to the Committee of Council, and it is proposed by the charter to extend the Municipal Corporation Acts to the municipal borough to be created by the charter, the Committee of Council may settle a scheme for the adjustment of the powers, rights, privileges, franchises, duties, property, and liabilities of any then existing local authority whose district comprises the whole or part of the area of that borough, either with or without any adjoining or other place, and also of any officer of that authority.

(2.) The scheme, so far as it appears to the Committee of Council to be necessary or proper for carrying into effect the said adjustment as regards any local authority existing at the time of the making of the scheme, may contain provisions for the continuance of that authority, or for the abolition total or partial of that authority, or for the creation of another authority or authorities, and the alteration of the district of the existing local authority and the union or other relation of the existing local authority and the authority or authorities so created, and for the continuance, modification, transfer, vesting, and extension to the whole of the borough of all or any of the powers, rights, privileges, franchises, duties, property, and liabilities of the existing local authority, and may contain such provisions as appear to the Committee of Council to be necessary or proper for fully carrying into effect any such adjustment and provisions as aforesaid.

(3.) The scheme, when settled by the Committee of Council, shall be published in the London Gazette, and shall not be of any effect unless confirmed as hereinafter mentioned.

(4.) Where, within one month after the publication of the scheme in the London Gazette, a petition against it by any local authority affected thereby, or by not less than one-twentieth of the owners and ratepayers of the borough (such twentieth to be one-twentieth in number of the owners and ratepayers of the borough taken together, or the owners and ratepayers in respect of one-twentieth of the rateable property in the borough and the owners and ratepayers in all cases to include women not under coverture) has been received by the Committee of Council, and is not withdrawn, the scheme shall require the confirmation of Parliament, and the Committee of Council may, if they think fit, submit it to Parliament for confirmation ; but otherwise, at any time after the expiration of the said month, or after the withdrawal of any petition that has been presented, the Committee of Council may, if they think fit, submit the scheme for confirmation, either to Parliament or to her Majesty in Council, and in the latter case it shall be lawful for her Majesty to confirm the scheme by Order in Council.

(5.) A scheme, when confirmed by Parliament or by Order in Council, shall have full operation, with, in the former case, such modifications, if any, as are made therein by Parliament, as if the scheme were part of this Act.

(6.) A local authority for the purposes of this Part means a sanitary authority (not being the mayor, aldermen, and burgesses of a borough subject to the Municipal Corporations Acts), also the corporation of a borough not subject to the Municipal Corporations Acts, a burial board, trustees, commissioners or other persons who, as a public body and not for their own profit, act under any Act for paving, lighting, supplying with water or gas, cleansing, watching, regulating or improving any town or place, or for providing or maintaining a cemetery or market in or for any town or place, and any commissioners, trustees, or other persons (not being justices) maintaining any police force, and any other authority not in this section excepted, and not being a school board, and having powers of local government and of rating for public purposes.

(7.) The district of a local authority for the purposes of this section means the area within which such authority can exercise any powers or rights

Supplemental provisions as to scheme and charter.

214.—(1.) A scheme shall, before being settled by the Committee of Council, be referred for consideration to the Secretary of State and the Local Government Board, and, if and as far as it is intended to affect any authority which is a harbour authority within the meaning of the Harbours and Passing Tolls, &c. Act, 1861, to the Board of Trade.

(2.) A scheme shall in every case provide for placing the new borough within the jurisdiction of the council as the sanitary authority.

* Page 156.

(3.) The regulations contained in the Seventh Schedule * with respect to the scheme shall be observed.

(4.) If the Committee of Council are satisfied that a local authority or other petitioners have properly promoted or properly opposed a scheme before them, and that for special reasons it is right that the reasonable costs incurred by the authority or other petitioners in such promotion or opposition should be paid as expenses properly incurred by the local authority in the execution of their duties, the Committee of Council may order those costs to be so paid, and they shall be paid accordingly.

Provision as to police force in new borough.

215. Nothing in any scheme or in the Municipal Corporation Acts shall authorize the establishment in a borough to which a charter is granted under this Act of a new separate police force not consolidated with the county police force, unless the district incorporated by the charter contained twenty thousand inhabitants or upwards, according to the census taken next before the date of the incorporation.

Validity of charters.

216.—(1.) A charter creating a municipal borough which purports to be granted in pursuance of the royal prerogative and in pursuance of or in accordance with this Act, shall after acceptance be deemed to be valid and within the powers of this Act and her Majesty's prerogative, and shall not be questioned in any legal proceeding whatever.

(2.) Every such charter shall be laid before both Houses of Parliament within one month after it is granted, if Parliament is then sitting, or if not, within one month after the beginning of the then next sitting of Parliament.

Act of 1882 s. 216.

217. Where a charter was granted to a borough within seven years before the 14th of August, 1877, the Committee of Council, on the petition to the Queen of the council of the borough, or of any existing local authority whose district comprises the whole or any part of the area of the borough, either with or without any adjoining or other place, may settle a scheme under this Act in like manner as if the petition for the grant of a charter to the borough had been referred to the Committee of Council after the commencement of this Act, and the provisions of this Act with respect to a scheme shall apply accordingly, with the necessary modifications; and if within one month after the publication of the scheme in the London Gazette a petition against the scheme from the council of the borough has been received by the Committee of Council and s not withdrawn the scheme shall require the confirmation of Parliament.

Power to settle scheme in case of recent charters.

218.—(1.) Where a scheme for a borough has been confirmed under this Part, or any former enactment, and the municipal corporation of the borough or one-twentieth of the owners and ratepayers of the borough (estimated as in this Part mentioned), or a local authority affected by the scheme, petition the Queen for an amending scheme, the petition shall be referred to a Committee of the Lords of Her Majesty's Privy Council (included in the term the Committee of Council in this Part), and shall be proceeded on, and this Part shall apply thereto, as nearly as may be, as if the same were a petition for a charter extending the Municipal Corporations Acts to a municipal borough to be incorporated.

Power to amend scheme.

(2.) The Committee of Council, if they think fit to submit the amending scheme for confirmation, shall submit the same to Parliament, or they may submit the same to her Majesty in Council, if the original scheme was confirmed by Order in Council; and in the latter case it shall be lawful for her Majesty to confirm the amending scheme by Order in Council.

(3.) An amending scheme, when confirmed by Parliament,

or by Order in Council, as the case may require, shall have full operation, with, in the former case, such modifications, if any, as are made therein by Parliament, as if the amending scheme were part of this Act.

This section is new.

PART XII.—Legal Proceedings.

Information to be within six months.
219.—(1.) In summary proceedings for offences and fines under this Act the information shall be laid within six months after the commission of the offence.

Appeal.
(2.) Any person aggrieved by a conviction of a court of summary jurisdiction under this Act may appeal therefrom to a court of quarter sessions ([1]).

(3.) Any fine incurred under this Act and not recoverable summarily may be recovered by action in the High Court.

This is taken from sects. 127—132 of the Act of 1835, omitting such parts as have been rendered obsolete by the Summary Jurisdiction Acts of 1848 and 1879 (11 & 12 Vict. c. 43, and 42 & 43 Vict. c. 49).

([1]) *Appeal.*]—By virtue of the 31st section of the Summary Jurisdiction Act, 1879, the appeal must be (1) " to the next practicable court of quarter sessions having jurisdiction in the county, borough or place for which the court of summary jurisdiction acted, and holden not less than fifteen days after the day on which the decision was given upon which the conviction or order was founded;" and (2) the appellant must give a written notice of appeal, signed by him or his agent, within seven days after such day, which notice " may be transmitted as a registered letter by the post in the ordinary way, and shall be deemed to have been served at the time when it would be delivered in the ordinary course of the post;" and (3) the appellant must, within three days after the day on which he gave notice of appeal, enter into a recognizance conditioned to try the appeal, or give some security in lieu of a recognizance, upon entering into or giving which he may, if in custody, be released from custody; and see the same section as to adjournment and costs of appeal.

Exclusion of certiorari.
220. A conviction, order, warrant, or other matter made or done or purporting to be made or done by virtue of this Act shall not be quashed for want of form, and shall not, unless it is an order of the council for payment of money out of the borough fund, be removed by certiorari or otherwise into the High Court.

This is taken from sect. 132 of the Act of 1835. It would seem that the Crown, not being expressly named, is not bound thereby. Nor is the section applicable where there is a want or excess of jurisdiction (see Paley on Convictions, p. 430, citing *Ex parte Brad-laugh*, 3 Q. B. D. 509, and many other cases); or where the court was illegally constituted (see *ib.*, citing *Reg.* v. *Cheltenham Commissioners*, 1 Q. B. 467); or where the conviction, &c. was obtained by fraud (see *ib.*, citing *Reg.* v. *Gillyard*, 12 Q. B. 527).

Act of 1882 s. 220.

221.—(1.) Where by any Act passed or to be passed, any fine, penalty, or forfeiture is made recoverable in a summary manner before any justice or justices and payable to the Crown or to any body corporate, or to any person whomsoever, the same if recovered and adjudged before any justice of a borough having a separate court of quarter sessions shall, notwithstanding anything in the Act under which it is recovered, be recovered for and adjudged to be paid to the treasurer of the borough.

Application of penalties in quarter sessions boroughs.

(2.) But this section shall not apply to a fine, penalty, or forfeiture, or part thereof, where the Act under which it is recovered—

(a) Directs payment thereof to the informer or to any person aggrieved; or

(b) If passed since the Municipal Corporations Act, 1835, directs that the same shall go in any other manner and not to the borough fund; or

(c) Relates to the customs, excise, or post office, or to trade or navigation, or to any branch of the revenue of the Crown.

This substantially reproduces sect. 126 of the Act of 1835, held to be prospective in *Attorney-General* v. *Moore*, 3 Ex. D. 276; 47 L. J., M. C. 103; 38 L. T. 251; 26 W. R. 366—C. A., affirming judgment below, 47 L. J., M. C. 33.

222. Where the offices of town clerk and clerk of the peace for a borough are not held by the same person, the clerk of the peace shall perform all duties imposed on the town clerk by the Act of the third year of King George the Fourth, chapter forty-six, "for the more speedy return and levying of fines, penalties, and forfeitures, and recognizances estreated;" and the clerk of the peace shall make all returns, issue all processes, and do all other acts required by that Act to be made, issued, and done by the town clerk.

Duties of clerk of peace as to fines and forfeitures.

This substantially reproduces sect. 5 of the Act of 1857 (20 & 21 Vict. c. 50). For 3 Geo. 4, c. 46, see Chit. Stat. vol. v. tit. "*Sheriff.*"

Service of
summons or
warrant.

223. Any summons for appearance, warrant to enforce appearance, warrant for apprehension, or search warrant, may, if issued by a justice for a borough, be served or executed in any county wherein the borough or any part thereof is situate, or within any distance not exceeding seven miles from the borough, and, within those limits, shall have the same effect as if it had been issued or indorsed by a justice having jurisdiction in the place where it is served or executed, and may be served or executed by the constable or special constable to whom it is directed.

This is taken from sect. 101 of the Act of 1835, the words of which it so far follows as not to include a warrant to commit in default of payment of fine (*Reg.* v. *Cumpton*, 5 Q. B. D. 341; 49 L. J., M. C. 41; 42 L. T. 543; 28 W. R. 539).

As to measuring distance, see sect. 231, post.

Procedure in
penal actions
against corpo-
rate officers.

224.—(1.) An action to recover a fine from any person for acting in a corporate office without having made the requisite declaration, or without being qualified, or after ceasing to be qualified, or after becoming disqualified, may not be brought except by a burgess of the borough, and shall not lie unless the plaintiff has, within fourteen days after the cause of action arose, served a notice in writing personally on the person liable to the fine of his intention to bring the action, nor

Notice of ac-
tion of three
months'
limit.

unless the action is commenced within three months after the cause of action arose.

(2.) The court or a judge shall, on the application of the defendant within fourteen days after he has been served with writ of summons in the action, require the plaintiff to give security for costs.

(3.) Unless judgment is given for the plaintiff, the defendant shall be entitled to costs, to be taxed as between solicitor and client.

(4.) Where any such action is brought against a person on the ground of his not being qualified in respect of estate, it shall lie on him to prove that he was so qualified.

(5.) A moiety of the fine recovered shall, after payment of the costs of action, be paid to the plaintiff.

This is taken from sect. 53 of the Act of 1835. The third paragraph appears to override Ord. LV. of the Rules of the Supreme Court.

Quo warranto.

225.—(1.) An application for an information in the nature of a quo warranto against any person claiming to hold a corporate office shall not be made after the expiration of twelve months from the time when he became disqualified after election.

Act of 1882 s. 225.

(2.) In the case of such an application, or of an application for a mandamus to proceed to an election of a corporate officer, the applicant shall give notice in writing of the application to the person to be affected thereby (in this section called the respondent) at any time not less then ten days before the day in the notice specified for making the application.

Notice to respondent of application for quo warranto or mandamus.

(3.) The notice shall set forth the name and description of the applicant, and a statement of the grounds of the application.

(4.) The applicant shall deliver with the notice a copy of the affidavits whereby the application will be supported.

(5.) The respondent may show cause in the first instance against the application.

(6.) If sufficient cause is not shown, the court, on proof of due service of the notice, statement, and copy of affidavits used in support of the application, may, if it thinks fit, make the rule for the information or mandamus absolute.

(7.) The court may, if it thinks fit, direct that any issue of fact on an information be tried by jury in London or at Westminster.

Trial by jury of issue of fact.

(8.) The court may, if it thinks fit, direct that any writ of mandamus issued shall be peremptory in the first instance.

This is taken from sect. 23 of the Act of 1837 and sects. 1 and 5 of the Act of 1843.

226.—(1.) An action, prosecution, or proceeding against any person for any act done in pursuance or execution or intended execution of this Act, [or in respect of any alleged neglect or default in the execution of this Act,] shall not lie or be instituted unless it is commenced within six months next after the act or thing is done or omitted, or, in case of a continuance of injury or damage, within six months next after the ceasing thereof.

Provisions for protection of persons acting under Act.

(2.) Where the action is for damages, tender of amends before the action was commenced may, in lieu of or in addition to any other plea, be pleaded. If the action was commenced after the tender, or is proceeded with after payment into court

Act of 1882
s. 226.
of any money in satisfaction of the plaintiff's claim, and the plaintiff does not recover more than the sum tendered or paid, he shall not recover any costs incurred after the tender or payment, and the defendant shall be entitled to costs, to be taxed as between solicitor and client, as from the time of the tender or payment; but this provision shall not affect costs on any injunction in the action.

Council may pay costs of defendant officer.

(3.) Subject and without prejudice to any other powers, the council, where the defendant in any such action, prosecution, or other proceeding is their officer, agent, or servant, may, if they think fit, except so far as the court before which the action, prosecution or other proceeding is heard and determined otherwise directs, pay out of the borough fund or borough rate all or any part of any sums payable by the defendant in or in consequence of the action, prosecution, or proceeding, whether in respect of costs, charges, expenses, damages, fine, or otherwise.

This is taken from sect. 133 of the Act of 1835; the words in brackets, which are new, being added to meet the case of *Reg.* v. *Barrell*, 12 A. & E. 460. The third paragraph, which is also new, was perhaps suggested by *Reg.* v. *Mayor of Exeter* (6 Q. B. D. 135), in which it was held that the town council could not pay a chief constable's costs incurred in defending an action for malicious prosecution.

Power for borough constables to take bail if justice not sitting.

227.—(1.) Where a person charged with a petty misdemeanour is brought without the warrant of a justice into the custody of a borough constable during his attendance at a watch-house in the borough, at any time (by day or night) at which a justice is not actually sitting for the public administration of justice at the justices' room, or town hall, or other place used for that purpose in the borough, the constable may, if he thinks fit, take bail without fee from that person, by recognizance conditioned for his appearance for examination within two days before a justice in the borough at some time and place therein specified.

(2.) A recognizance so taken shall be of equal obligation on the parties entering into the same, and liable to the same proceedings for the estreating thereof, as if taken before a justice.

(3.) The constable shall enter in a book, kept for that purpose in every watch-house, the name, residence, and occupation of the person entering into the recognizance, and of his surety or sureties, if any, with the condition of the recognizance, and the sums acknowledged.

(4.) The constable shall lay the book before the justice present at the time when and place where the recognizor is required to appear.

(5.) If the recognizor does not appear at the time and place required, or within one hour after, the justice shall cause a record of the recognizance to be drawn up and signed by the constable, and shall return the same to the next court of quarter sessions for the borough, or, if the borough has no separate court of quarter sessions, for the county in which the borough is situate, with a certificate at the back thereof, signed by the justice, that the recognizor has not complied with the obligation therein contained.

(6.) The clerk of the peace shall make the like estreats and schedules of every such recognizance as of recognizances forfeited in quarter sessions.

(7.) If the recognizor applies by any person on his behalf to postpone the hearing of the charge against him, and the justice thinks fit to consent thereto, the justice may enlarge the recognizance to such further time as he appoints.

(8.) When the matter is heard and determined, either by the dismissal of the charge, or by binding over the recognizor to answer the matter of the complaint at quarter sessions, or otherwise, the recognizance for his appearance before a justice shall be discharged without fee.

This substantially reproduces sect. 79 of the Act of 1835, the power to take bail *by day* being new.

PART XIII.—General.

Boundaries.

228.—(1.) Every place at the commencement of this Act included within each borough then existing, and no other place, shall be part of the borough, and in each borough then existing which is a county of itself, shall be part of that county and of no other, as if this Act had not been passed.

Boundaries of boroughs and transfer of parts to counties.

(2.) Where under the Municipal Corporations Act, 1835, or any Act amending it, any such county or borough does not, at the commencement of this Act, include a place which, before

Act of 1882
s. 228.

the passing of the Municipal Corporations Act, 1835, was part
thereof, that place shall continue to be part of the county
wherein it is situate, or with which it has the longest common
boundary, as if this Act had not been passed.

(3.) But nothing in this Act shall prevent any gaol, house
of correction, lunatic asylum, court of justice, or judges'
lodging, which at the passing of the Municipal Corporations
Act, 1835, was, and at the commencement of this Act is,
taken to be, for any purpose, in any county, from being
still, for that purpose, taken to be in that county, as if this
Act had not been passed.

(4.) Any gaol, court, depôt for arms, and any land thereto
belonging, which at the commencement of this Act is parcel
of a county shall continue to be parcel of the county, and
under the exclusive jurisdiction of the authorities of the
county, as if this Act had not been passed.

(5.) Nothing in this Act shall be construed to affect the
assessments of the land tax or assessed taxes, as those assessments exist at the commencement of this Act, or to extend or
diminish the jurisdiction of any commissioners of those taxes,
as such commissioners then exist; but all lands, and all
parishes, parts of parishes, and places shall continue to be
charged as at the commencement of this Act towards the land
tax charged on the county or other district whereof at the
commencement of this Act they are part, and to be subject in
that behalf to the jurisdiction of the commissioners of the
same county or other district, as if this Act had not been
passed.

The first four paragraphs of this section are taken from sects. 7
and 8 of the Act of 1835, as amended by sects. 1, 2 and 5 of the
Act of 1836 (6 & 7 Will. 4, c. 103), and from sect. 41 of the Act of
1837 (7 Will. 4 & 1 Vict. c. 78).

Adjustment
between
boroughs and
counties on
change of
boundaries.

229. If any place, which under the Municipal Corporations
Act, 1835, or any Act amending it, ceased to be included in a
borough or county of a town or city, was before the passing of
the Municipal Corporations Act, 1835, liable to contribute to
any rate for satisfying any lawful debt to which the ratepayers of that borough or county were then liable, and if
after the commencement of this Act any difference arises concerning the proportion of that debt to be contributed in respect

of that place, the Secretary of State, on the application of the council, or of the chairman of a public meeting of the rate-payers of the place, may appoint by writing under his hand a barrister not having any interest in the question to arbitrate between the parties, and by his award under his hand and seal to assess the proportion aforesaid, if any; and the arbitrator shall assess the costs of the arbitration, and direct by whom and in what proportion and out of what fund they shall be paid; and the rate aforesaid shall continue to be levied by warrant of the council and to be paid by the place aforesaid to the treasurer of the borough, as if the Municipal Corporations Act, 1835, or any Act amending it, or this Act, had not been passed, until the proportion aforesaid is satisfied, and no longer.

Act of 1882 s. 229.

> This is taken from the first proviso to sect. 8 of the Act of 1835, under which, however, the arbitrator was appointed by the judge of assize.

Time.

230.—(1.) Where by this Act any limited time from or after any date or event is appointed or allowed for the doing of any act or the taking of any proceeding, then in the computation of that limited time the same shall be taken as exclusive of the day of that date or of the happening of that event, and as commencing at the beginning of the next following day; and the act or proceeding shall be done or taken at the latest on the last day of the limited time as so computed, unless the last day is a Sunday, Christmas Day, Good Friday, or Monday or Tuesday in Easter week, or a day appointed for public fast, humiliation, or thanksgiving, in which case any act or proceeding shall be considered as done or taken in due time if it is done or taken on the next day afterwards, not being one of the days in this section specified.

Computation of time.

(2.) Where by this Act any act or proceeding is directed or allowed to be done or taken on a certain day, then if that day happens to be one of the days in this section specified, the act or proceeding shall be considered as done or taken in due time if it is done or taken on the next day afterwards, not being one of the days in this section specified.

(3.) Where by this Act any act or proceeding is directed or allowed to be done or taken within any time not exceeding seven days, the days in this section specified shall not be reckoned in the computation of such time.

This section generalizes, with some slight alterations, the specific provisions of 3 & 4 Will. 4, c. 31, sect. 30 of the Act of 1835, sect. 25 of the Act of 1837, sect. 25 of the Act of 1832, and sect. 11 of the Act of 1875.

Observing of Greenwich Time.]—Where mention is made of an hour or hours, Greenwich time must be observed. Statutes (Definition of Time) Act, 1880 (43 & 44 Vict. c. 9). As to provision of public clocks, see Public Health Act, 1875 (38 & 39 Vict. c. 55, s. 165).

Distance.

Measurement of distances.

231. The distances mentioned in this Act shall be measured in a straight line on a horizontal plane, and may be determined by the map made under the survey commonly known as the ordnance survey.

This applies generally a similar specific provision of the Act of 1869.

Notices.

Notices on town hall.

232. Any notice or other document required by this Act to be fixed on the town hall shall be fixed in some conspicuous place on or near the outer door of the town hall, or, if there is no town hall, in some conspicuous place in the borough or ward to which the notice or document relates.

This section is new.

Inspection and Copies.

Inspection of documents.

233.—(1.) The minutes of proceedings of the council shall be open to the inspection of a burgess on payment of a fee of one shilling, and a burgess may make a copy thereof or take an extract therefrom.

(2.) A burgess may make a copy of or take an extract from an order of the council for the payment of money.

(3.) The treasurer's accounts shall be open to the inspection of the council, and a member of the council may make a copy thereof or take an extract therefrom.

(4.) The abstract of the treasurer's accounts shall be open to the inspection of all the ratepayers of the borough, and copies thereof shall be delivered to a ratepayer on payment of a reasonable price for each copy.

(5.) The freemen's roll shall be open to public inspection, and the town clerk shall deliver copies thereof to any person on payment of a reasonable price for each copy.

(6.) A document directed by this Act to be open to inspection shall be so open at any reasonable time during the ordinary hours of business, and without payment, unless it is otherwise expressed.

(7.) If a person having the custody of any document in this section mentioned,—

(a.) Obstructs any person authorized to inspect the same in making such inspection thereof as in this section mentioned; or

(b.) Refuses to give copies or extracts to any person entitled to obtain the same under this section;

he shall, on summary conviction, be liable to a fine not exceeding five pounds.

The first two paragraphs of this section are taken from sect. 69 of the Act of 1835, and sect. 22 of the Act of 1837; the third and fourth from sect. 93 of the Act of 1835; and the fifth from sect. 5 of the Act of 1835.

Fees.

234. The town clerk of every borough shall cause a true copy of the tables of fees for the time being authorized to be taken by the clerk of the peace (if any) for the borough, by the clerk to the justices (if any) for the borough, and by the registrar and officers of the borough civil court (if any), to be posted conspicuously in the following places : **Tables of fees to be posted.**

(a.) The room where the business of the town clerk's office is transacted;

(b.) The room, if any, where the justices of the borough sit for transacting their business;

(c.) The room, if any, where the court of quarter sessions of the borough is held; and

(d.) The room, if any, where the borough civil court is held.

This section is taken from sect. 125 of the Act of 1835.

Seals and Signatures.

235. If any person forges the seal or signature affixed or subscribed to a bye-law made under this Act, or the signature subscribed to any minute of proceedings of the council, or tenders in evidence any such document with a false or counterfeit seal or signature, knowing it to be false or counterfeit, he shall be liable to imprisonment with hard labour for any term not exceeding two years. **Forgery.**

This re-enacts sect. 4 of the Act of 1873, except that that section imposed a minimum term of imprisonment of one year.

s. 236.

Notice of
application
to and corre-
spondence
with
Treasury.

Applications to Treasury.

236.—(1.) Where the council intend to apply to the Treasury for their approval of any sale, loan, or other financial arrangement under this Act notice of the intention to make the application shall be fixed on the town hall one month at least before the application, and a copy of the intended application shall during that month be kept in the town clerk's office, and be open to public inspection.

(2.) If the Treasury either refuse their approval or grant it conditionally or under qualifications, notice of the correspondence between the Treasury and the council shall forthwith and during one month be fixed on the town hall, and a copy of the correspondence shall during that month be kept in the town clerk's office, and be open to public inspection.

This is taken from sect. 94 of the Act of 1835, and sects. 8 and 9 of the Act of 1860.

Deputy.

Acts of deputy
not to be
invalidated
by defect in
appointment.

237. No defect in the appointment of a deputy under this Act shall invalidate his acts.

This section is new.

Overseers.

Notices to
and acting of
overseers.

238.—(1.) Every matter by the Municipal Corporations Acts directed to be done by overseers may be lawfully done by the major part of them.

(2.) Any notice by the Municipal Corporations Acts required to be given to overseers may be delivered to any one of them, or left at his place of abode, or at his office for transacting parochial business.

This re-enacts sect. 14 of the Act of 1853.

Declarations and Oaths.

Power to
administer
oaths, &c.

239.—(1.) Where by or under this Act a declaration or oath is required to be made or taken by the holder of a corporate office or other person before the council or any members thereof, or any other persons, they shall have authority to receive and administer the same without any commission or authority other than this Act.

(2.) Nothing in this Act in any case shall require or authorize the taking or making of any oath or declaration that would not have been required or authorized under the Promissory Oaths Act, 1868, or otherwise by law, if this Act had not been passed, or interfere with the operation of the Promissory Oaths Act, 1868.

Act of 1882 s. 239.

Forms.

240. The forms in the Eighth Schedule * or forms to the like effect, varied as circumstances require, may be used, and shall be sufficient in law.

Forms in schedule.
* Page 157.

Misnomer or Inaccurate Description.

241. No misnomer or inaccurate description of any person, body corporate, or place named in any schedule to the Municipal Corporations Act, 1835, or in any roll, list, notice, or voting paper required by this Act, shall hinder the full operation of this Act with respect to that person, body corporate, or place, provided the description of that person, body corporate, or place be such as to be commonly understood.

Misnomer or inaccurate description not to hinder.

This is substantially identical with the concluding words of sect. 142 of the Act of 1835, which was held to cure only an inaccurate description of the real person, &c., and not a description of a person other than the real one. *Reg.* v. *Coward*, 16 Q. B. 819. Therefore, where voting papers described the place of abode of a candidate as " G. P.," in the said borough, whereas his place of abode was N. R. in the borough, this was not cured (*Reg.* v. *Coward*, 16 Q. B. 819); but an abbreviation by initials, such as W. for William, was held to be a misnomer curable by the section. *Reg.* v. *Plenty*, L. R., 4 Q. B. 346; 38 L. J., Q. B. 205; *Reg.* v. *Bradley*, 30 L. J., Q. B. 180; 3 E. & E. 634. See also *Reg.* v. *Gregory*, 1 E. & B. 600; *Reg.* v. *Thwaites*, ib. 704; *Reg.* v. *Spratley*, 6 E. & B. 363.

Substitution in former Acts.

242.—(1.) In the several enactments described in Part I. of the Ninth Schedule,† a reference to this Act shall be deemed to be substituted for a reference to the Municipal Corporations Act, 1835, and any Act amending it.

Provision for references in unrepealed enactments to 5 & 6 Will. 4, c. 76, &c.
† Page 165.
‡ Page 167.

(2.) In each of the enactments described in Part II. of the Ninth Schedule,‡ there shall be substituted for the respective provision of the Municipal Corporations Act, 1835, in that Part mentioned in connexion therewith, such provision of this Act as is also mentioned in connexion therewith.

(3.) Where any Act passed before this Act, and not specified in the First or in the Ninth Schedule, refers to the Municipal

Act of 1982
s. 242.
Corporations Act, 1835, or any Act amending it, or to boroughs or corporations subject to that Act or any Act amending it, the reference shall be deemed to be to this Act or to the corresponding provision of this Act, or to boroughs or corporations subject to this Act (as the case may require).

(4.) All enactments to which this section relates shall, except as in this section provided, continue to operate as if this Act had not been passed.

This enactment follows a common form in consolidating Acts. See, for instance, the Public Health Act, 1875, s. 313, and the Factory and Workshop Act, 1878, s. 102.

Short titles
of Acts partly
repealed.

* Page 130.

243. Such of the Acts specified in the First Schedule* as will remain in force to any extent after the commencement of this Act, may continue to be cited by the short titles in that schedule mentioned.

Returning Officers at Parliamentary Elections.

Mayor of
certain
boroughs to
be returning
officer in
parliamentary
elections.

244.—(1.) In boroughs, other than cities and towns being counties of themselves, the mayor shall be the returning officer at parliamentary elections; but this provision shall not extend to the borough of Berwick-upon-Tweed.

(2.) If there are more mayors than one within the boundaries of a parliamentary borough, the mayor of that borough to which the writ of election is directed shall be the returning officer.

(3.) If when a mayor is required to act as returning officer the mayor is absent, or incapable of acting, or there is no mayor, the council shall forthwith choose an alderman to be returning officer.

Disfranchised Parliamentary Boroughs.

Electors in
disfranchised
boroughs.

245. Where a borough has, in pursuance of the Representation of the People Act, 1867, or of any Act passed in the session of the thirty-first and thirty-second years of the reign of her Majesty, ceased to return a member to serve in Parliament, and the persons entitled to vote for the member or members formerly returned by the borough were by law electors for any other purpose, the burgesses of the borough shall be electors for that purpose, and shall in all respects, as regards that purpose, be substituted for the persons so entitled to vote.

This is a substantial re-enactment of the Borough Electors Act, 1868 (31 & 32 Vict. c. 41).

Licensing.

246. In the Act of the ninth year of the reign of King George the Fourth, chapter sixty-one, "to regulate the granting of licences to keepers of inns, alehouses, and victualling houses in England," the expressions "town corporate," "county or place," and "division or place," include every borough having a separate commission of the peace, and the expression "high constable" includes any constable of any such borough to whom the justices of the borough direct their precept under that Act.

Explanation of terms "town corporate," &c. in Licensing Act.

This is a substantial re-enactment of sect. 5 of the Act of 1861, which section was enacted to clear up the doubts raised by the conflicting cases of *Candlish* v. *Simpson* (30 L. J., M. C. 178) and *Brown* v. *Nicholson* (28 L. J., M. C. 49; 5 C. B., N. S. 468).

Freedom of Trading.

247. Notwithstanding any custom or bye-law, every person in any borough may keep any shop for the sale of all lawful wares and merchandizes by wholesale or retail, and use every lawful trade, occupation, mystery, and handicraft for hire, gain, sale, or otherwise within any borough.

Right of free trading in boroughs.

This is a re-enactment of sect. 14 of the Act of 1835.

Cinque Ports.

248.—(1.) The boroughs of Hastings, Sandwich, Dover, Hythe, being four of the Cinque Ports, and the borough of Rye, are in this section referred to as the five boroughs.

Special provisions as to certain of the Cinque Ports.

(2.) The jurisdiction, powers, and authorities of the court of quarter sessions, recorder, coroner, and clerk of the peace for each of the five boroughs shall extend to the non-corporate members and liberties thereof, and to such corporate members thereof as have not a separate court of quarter sessions.

(3.) The jurisdiction, powers, and authorities of the persons constituted justices within and throughout the liberties of the Cinque Ports by virtue of their commission, shall extend to all places being within the limits of the five boroughs or of their members or liberties, corporate or non-corporate, and not being within the limits of a borough having a separate commission of the peace.

(4.) The justices for the five boroughs respectively shall have all the jurisdiction, powers, and authorities of justices for a county relating to the granting of licences or authorities to persons to keep inns, ale-houses, or victualling houses, or to sell exciseable liquors by retail within any of the corporate or non-corporate members or liberties of the five boroughs respectively, not being within the limits of a borough having a separate commission of the peace.

(5.) The non-corporate members and liberties of the five boroughs and such corporate members thereof as have not a separate court of quarter sessions, shall be charged by the respective courts of quarter sessions of the five boroughs, with a due proportion of all those expenses of the five boroughs, to the payment whereof rates in the nature of county rates are applicable; and such rates may be assessed and levied in the manner in which rates of that description were assessed and levied before the passing of the Municipal Corporations Act, 1835, under any enactment then in force, but subject to the operation of any subsequent enactment affecting the same.

(6.) A due proportion of inhabitant householders to serve as grand jurors and jurors at the respective courts of quarter sessions of the five boroughs shall be summoned by the clerks of the peace thereof from the non-corporate members and liberties thereof, and such corporate members thereof as have not a separate court of quarter sessions; and the attendance of such jurors shall be enforced, and their defaults punished, in the manner by this Act directed with respect to jurors in boroughs.

(7.) Nothing in this section shall affect the Cinque Ports Act, 1869, or the Acts therein recited.

This is taken from sects. 134 and 135 of the Act of 1835, and sects. 10 and 11 of the Act of 1836.

Cambridge.

Vice-Chan-
cellor of
Cambridge.
249.—(1.) It shall be lawful for the Queen, from time to time, by her commission of the peace for the borough of Cambridge, to constitute the Vice-Chancellor for the time being of the University of Cambridge a justice for that borough.

(2.) He shall not, by reason of being so constituted, have any greater authority as to the grant of licences to alehouses than any other justice named in the commission.

(3.) But nothing in this section shall affect the rights and privileges which the Vice-Chancellor lawfully has or enjoys, or might have lawfully had or enjoyed if he were not so constituted a justice.

This is taken from sect. 12 of the Act of 1836.

Savings.

250.—(1.) Nothing in this Act shall prejudicially affect any charter granted before the commencement of this Act, or take away, abridge, or prejudicially affect any of the rights, powers, privileges, estates, property, duties, liabilities, or obligations vested in or imposed on any municipal corporation existing at the commencement of this Act, or in or on the mayor, or the council of a borough then existing, or any members or committee of the council, by the incorporation of the inhabitants of the borough, or by transfer from any other authority, or otherwise; but every such charter shall continue to operate, and every such corporation shall continue to have perpetual succession and a common seal, and to be capable in law by the council to do and suffer all acts which at the commencement of this Act they and their successors respectively may lawfully do or suffer, and the corporation and all members and officers thereof and their sureties, and every such mayor, and every such council and committee, and every such officer, shall continue to have, enjoy, and be subject to the like rights, powers, offices, privileges, estates, property, duties, liabilities, and obligations, as if this Act had not been passed, without prejudice, nevertheless, to the operation of the repeal of enactments by this Act, and to the other express provisions of this Act.

(2.) Nothing in this Act shall alter the boundaries ([1]) of any borough existing at the commencement of this Act, or the number, apportionment, or qualification of the aldermen or councillors thereof, or the division thereof into wards ([2]).

(3.) Nothing in this Act shall affect the right of the council of a borough to collect by their own officers the borough rate and watch rate, or either of them, where, at the commencement of this Act, they are authorized by law to so collect, and are so collecting, the same.

(4.) Nothing in this Act shall alter the respective jurisdiction of county and borough justices.

(5.) Nothing in this Act shall affect the right of any borough named in Schedule (A.) to the Municipal Corporations Act, 1835, to have a separate commission of the peace.

This general saving clause has no parallel in the Act of 1835, which, on the contrary, by sect. 1, in general terms abrogated all charters, &c. inconsistent with it.

(¹) *Boundaries.*]—See as to this, sect. 238, ante.

(²) *Number of Councillors.*]—See these numbers, &c., as settled by the Act of 1835, in the Schedules (A) and (B) to that Act; and see also Appendix, p. 343, post.

Saving for local Acts.

251. Nothing in this Act shall alter the effect of any local Act of Parliament.

Local Acts are in force in almost every borough of importance. A list of such Acts in force at the time of the passing of the Act of 1835 will be found in Schedule (E) to that Act.

For local Acts passed since that date, see Index to Local Acts, tit. *"Boroughs."*

Effect of Public Health Act.]—By sect. 303 of the Public Health Act, 1875 (38 & 39 Vict. c. 55), "the Local Government Board may, on the application of the local authority [*i.e.*, by sect. 6, in boroughs under this Act, the town council] of any district, by provisional order wholly or partially repeal, alter, or amend any local Act, other than an Act for the conservancy of rivers, which is in force in any area comprising the whole or part of any such district, and not conferring powers or privileges on any person or persons for his or their own pecuniary benefit, which relates to the same subject-matters as" the Public Health Act, 1875; and such a provisional order may provide for the extension or further limitation of the limits of such local Act.

And sect. 340 of the Public Health Act is as follows :—"Where within the district of a local authority any local Act is in force providing for purposes the same as or similar to the purposes of this Act, proceedings may be instituted at the discretion of the authority or person instituting the same, either under the local Act or this Act or under both, subject to these qualifications :—

(1.) That no person shall be punished for the same offence both under a local Act and this Act; and

(2.) That the local authority shall not by reason of any local Act in force within their district be exempted from the performance of any duty or obligation to which they may be subject under this Act."

Saving for Prison Acts.

* Sect. 242.

252. Nothing in this Act, except the provision * referring to the Ninth Schedule, shall affect the Prison Act, 1865, or the Prison Act, 1877, and nothing in this Act shall affect the

Act of the session of the fifth and sixth years of her Majesty, chapter ninety-eight, "to amend the laws concerning prisons," or revive or restore any enactment which, being contained in that Act, or in the Municipal Corporation (Justices) Act, 1850, or in any other Act, is virtually repealed or superseded by the Prison Act, 1865, or the Prison Act, 1877.

Act of 1882 s. 252.

The Prison Act, 1865 (28 & 29 Vict. c. 126), imposed an obligation on boroughs within this Act to erect and maintain prisons; but the Prison Act, 1877 (40 & 41 Vict. c. 21), by sect. 16 did away with that obligation. 5 & 6 Vict. c. 98, the greater part of which was repealed by the Prison Act, 1865, imposed a somewhat similar obligation to that contained in the Prison Act, 1877.

253. Nothing in this Act shall compel the acceptance of any office or duty whatever in any borough by any military, naval, or marine officer in her Majesty's service on full pay or half pay, or by any officer or other person employed and residing in any of her Majesty's dockyards, victualling establishments, arsenals, barracks, or other naval or military establishments.

Saving for military and naval officers, &c.

Army officers on full pay are also exempted from serving municipal offices by sect. 146 of the Army Act, 1881 (44 & 45 Vict. c. 58).

254. Nothing in this Act shall affect the watching, paving, or lighting, or the internal regulations for the government, of any of her Majesty's dockyards, victualling establishments, arsenals, barracks, or other naval or military establishments, or make the tenements therein or the inhabitants thereof liable to any rate for watching, paving, or lighting.

Saving for dockyards, barracks, &c.

This is taken from sects. 89 of the Act of 1835.

255. Nothing in this Act shall affect the authority of justices vested in the Commissioners for executing the office of Lord High Admiral of the United Kingdom, or any authority to appoint coroners to act within the jurisdiction of the Admiralty.

Saving as to Admiralty.

This is taken from sects. 64 and 89 of the Act of 1835.

256. Nothing in this Act shall affect the jurisdiction and office of the Lord Warden in his office of Admiral of the Cinque Ports.

Saving for Lord Warden.

This is taken from sect. 108 of the Act of 1835.

Saving for
universities.

257. Nothing in this Act shall—

(1.) Affect the rights, privileges, duties, or liabilities of the chancellor, masters, and scholars of the Universities of Oxford and Cambridge respectively, as by law possessed under the respective charters of those universities or otherwise; or

(2.) Entitle the mayors of Oxford and Cambridge respectively to any precedence over the vice-chancellors of those universities respectively; or

(3.) Entitle any person to be enrolled a citizen of the city of Oxford or burgess of the borough of Cambridge by reason of his occupation of any rooms, chambers, or premises in any college or hall of either of those universities; or

(4.) Compel any resident member of either of those universities to accept any office in or under the municipal corporation of Oxford or of Cambridge; or

(5.) Authorize the levy of any rate within the precincts of those universities, or of any of the colleges or halls thereof, which now by law cannot be levied therein, or make either of those universities, or the members thereof, liable to any rate to which they are not liable to contribute at the commencement of this Act; or

(6.) Authorize the transfer of any rights or liabilities by a local authority to the municipal corporation of the borough of Cambridge without the consent of the chancellor, master, and scholars of the University of Cambridge; or

(7.) Affect the rights or privileges granted by charter or Act of Parliament to the University of Durham.

This is taken from sects. 137 and 138 of the Act of 1835, as amended by sect. 2 of the Act of 1857 and sect. 2 of the Act of 1861.

Saving for
jurisdiction
over cathedral
precincts.

258. Nothing in this Act shall prevent any jurisdiction or authority exercised in or over the precinct or close of any cathedral from being continued concurrently with the jurisdiction and authority of the justices of the borough in which the precinct or close is situate.

This is taken from sect. 138 of the Act of 1835.

259. Nothing in this Act shall prejudicially affect her Majesty's royal prerogative; and the enabling provisions of this Act shall be deemed to be in addition to, and not in derogation of, the powers exerciseable by her Majesty by virtue of her royal prerogative.

Act of 1882 s. 259.

Saving for royal prerogative.

The first paragraph of this section is new, but seems to express what was implied before by virtue of the maxim, "Le roy n'est lie par aucun statut, s'il ne fût expressment nommé;" the second paragraph is taken from sect. 10 of the Municipal Corporations (New Charters) Act, 1877 (40 & 41 Vict. c. 69), replaced by Part XI. of this Act, ante, p. 112, which section, previously applicable to the grant of new charters only, it extends to the whole statute law of municipal corporations.

260.—(1.) The repeal effected by this Act* shall not affect—

Saving as to repealed enactments.

* Sect. 5.

(a.) Anything done or suffered before the commencement of this Act under any enactment repealed by this Act; or

(b.) Any proceeding or thing pending or in course of being done at the commencement of this Act under any enactment repealed by this Act; or

(c.) Any jurisdiction or practice established, confirmed, or transferred, or right or privilege acquired or confirmed, or duty or liability imposed or incurred, or compensation secured, by or under any enactment repealed by this Act; or

(d.) Any disability or disqualification existing at the commencement of this Act under any enactment repealed by this Act; or

(e.) Any fine, forfeiture, punishment, or other consequence incurred or to be incurred in respect of any offence committed before the commencement of this Act against any enactment repealed by this Act; or

(f.) The institution or the prosecution to its termination of any legal proceeding or other remedy for ascertaining, enforcing, or recovering any such jurisdiction, practice, right, privilege, duty, liability, compensation, disability, disqualification, fine, forfeiture, punishment, or consequence as aforesaid; or

(g.) The terms on which any money has been borrowed before the commencement of this Act under any enactment repealed by this Act.

Act of 1882 s. 160.

(2.) The repeal effected by this Act shall not extend to Scotland or Ireland, and shall not, as regards the enactments described in Part II. of the First Schedule, operate in respect of any place other than a borough to which this Act applies, and shall not revive or restore any statute, law, usage, custom, royal or other charter, grant, letters patent, bye-law, jurisdiction, office, right, title, claim, privilege, liability, disqualification, exemption, restriction, practice, procedure, or other matter or thing abolished by the Municipal Corporations Act, 1835, or not in force or existing at the commencement of this Act, or otherwise affect the past operation of any enactment repealed by this Act.

Validity of elections, appointments, &c.

(3.) All elections, declarations, appointments, bye-laws, rates, tables of fees, and regulations made, or pending, or in the course of being made, and all other things done, or pending, or in the course of being done, under the Municipal Corporations Act, 1835, or any other enactment repealed by this Act, before or at the commencement of this Act, shall for the purposes of this Act be of the like effect as if they had been made or done, or were pending, or in the course of being made or done under this Act, and shall, as far as may be requisite for the continuance, validity, and effect thereof, be deemed to have been made or done, or may be carried on and be made or done, as the case may require, under this Act.

[SCHEDULES.

SCHEDULES.

THE FIRST SCHEDULE.

ENACTMENTS REPEALED.

Act of 1882
Schedule 1.

PART I.—*Enactments repealed generally.*

[See sect. 5,
and sect. 7,
sub-s. 4.]

5 & 6 Will. 4 .. The Municipal Corporations Act, 1835.
c. 76.

6 & 7 Will. 4 .. An Act for carrying into effect the reports of the Com-
c. 77.   missioners appointed to consider the state of the
in part.   Established Church in England and Wales, with
            reference to ecclesiastical duties and revenues, so
            far as they relate to episcopal dioceses, revenues,
            and patronage;
            in part, namely,—
            section twenty-six.

6 & 7 Will. 4 .. The Municipal Corporation (Boundaries) Act, 1836;
c. 103.   except section six (Berwick).
in part.

6 & 7 Will. 4 .. The Municipal Corporation (Borough Fund) Act,
c. 104.   1836.

6 & 7 Will. 4 .. The Municipal Corporation (Justices, &c.) Act, 1836.
c. 105.

7 Will. 4 & .... The Municipal Corporation (General) Act, 1837.
1 Vict. c. 78.

7 Will. 4 & .... The Municipal Corporation (Watch Rate) Act, 1837.
1 Vict. c. 81.

1 & 2 Vict. .... The Municipal Corporation (Benefices) Act, 1838.
c. 31.

1 & 2 Vict. .... An Act to repeal the stamp duty now paid on ad-
c. 35.   mission to the freedom of corporations in England.

2 & 3 Vict. .... The Municipal Corporation (Borough Courts) Act,
c. 27.   1839.

2 & 3 Vict. .... The Municipal Corporation (Watch Rate) Act, 1839.
c. 28.

3 & 4 Vict. .... The Municipal Corporation (Watch Rate) Act, 1840.
c. 28.

4 & 5 Vict. .... An Act to render certain municipal corporations
c. 48.   rateable to the relief of the poor in certain cases.

6 & 7 Vict. .... The Municipal Corporation Act, 1843.
c. 89.

8 & 9 Vict. .... The Municipal Corporation (Rates) Act, 1845.
c. 110.

11 & 12 Vict... An Act to confirm the incorporation of certain
c. 93.   boroughs.

32 & 33 Vict... c. 55.	The Municipal Corporation (Election) Act, 1869.
32 & 33 Vict... c. 62. in part.	The Debtors Act, 1869 ; in part, namely,— section twenty-one.
34 & 35 Vict... c. 67.	The Municipal Corporations Act, 1859, Amendment Act.
35 & 36 Vict... c. 33. in part.	The Ballot Act, 1872 ; in part, namely,— sections twenty and twenty-one.
35 & 36 Vict... c. 60.	The Corrupt Practices (Municipal Elections) Act, 1872.
36 & 37 Vict... c. 33.	The Municipal Corporations Evidence Act, 1873.
37 & 38 Vict... c. 59.	The Working Men's Dwellings Act, 1874.
38 & 39 Vict... c. 40.	The Municipal Elections Act, 1875.
39 & 40 Vict... c. 61. in part.	The Divided Parishes and Poor Law Amendment Act, 1876 ; in part, namely,— section thirty.
40 & 41 Vict... c. 69.	The Municipal Corporations (New Charters) Act, 1877.
41 & 42 Vict... c. 26. in part.	The Parliamentary and Municipal Registration Act, 1878 ; in part, namely,— sections twenty, thirty-four, and forty-one.

PART II.—*Enactments repealed only as to Boroughs within this Act.*

[See sects. 5 and 7, sub-s. 4.]

3 Edw. 1 ..... c. 6. in part.	The Statutes of Westminster, the first. Amerciaments shall be reasonable ; in part, namely,— as far as it relates to a city, borough, or town.
3 Edw. 1 ..... c. 31. in part.	The Statutes of Westminster, the first. Excessive toll in market town. Murage ; in part, namely,— from "Touching citizens" to "the King," inclusive.
15 Rich. 2 .... c. 5. in part.	St. 7 Edw. I. de Religiosis. Converting land to a churchyard declared to be within that statute. Mortmain where any is seised of lands to the use of spiritual persons. Mortmain to purchase lands to gilds, fraternities, offices, commonalties ; or to their use ; in part, namely,— as far as it relates to mayors, bailiffs, and commons of cities, boroughs, and other towns which have a perpetual commonalty.

**Act of 1882
Schedule 1.
(*Part II.*)**

2 & 3 Phil. & Mary. c. 18.	An Act touching commissions of the peace and gaol delivery in towns corporate not being counties in themselves.
7 Jas. 1, c. 5 in part.	An Acte for ease in pleading against troublesome and contencious suites presented against justices of the peace, maiors, constables, and certaine other His Majesties officers for the lawful execution of their office; in part, namely,— as far as it relates to mayors of cities or towns corporate.
21 Jas. 1 c. 12. in part.	An Acte for ease in pleading against troublesome and contencious suites; in part, namely,— section three, as far as it relates to mayors of cities or towns corporate.
11 Geo. 1 c. 4.	An Act for preventing the inconvenience arising from want of elections of mayors or other chief magistrates of boroughs or corporations being made upon days appointed by charter or usage for that purpose, and directing in what manner such elections shall be afterwards made.
12 Geo. 3 c. 21.	An Act for giving relief in proceedings upon writs of mandamus for the admission of freemen into corporations and for other purposes therein mentioned.
32 Geo. 3. c. 58.	An Act for the amendment of the law in proceedings upon information in nature of quo warranto.
55 Geo. 3. c. 51.	An Act to amend an Act of His late Majesty King George the Second, for the more easy assessing, collecting, and levying of county rates.
57 Geo. 3. c. 91.	An Act to enable justices of the peace to settle the fees to be taken by clerks of the peace of the respective counties and other divisions of England and Wales.
2 & 3 Will. 4. c. 69.	An Act to prevent the application of corporate property to the purposes of election of members to serve in Parliament.
3 & 4 Will. 4, c. 31.	An Act to enable the election of officers of corporations and other public companies now required to be held on the Lord's Day to be held on the Saturday next preceding or on the Monday next ensuing.
4 & 5 Will. 4, c. 27.	An Act for the better administration of justice in certain boroughs and franchises.
7 Will. 4 & 1 Vict. c. 19.	An Act to empower the recorder or other person presiding at quarter sessions in corporate cities and towns, and justices of the peace for counties, ridings, or divisions, to divide their respective courts in certain cases.
5 & 6 Vict. c. 104.	The Municipal Corporation Act, 1842.

15 & 16 Vict. . . The Municipal Corporation Act, 1852.
   c. 5.

23 & 24 Vict. . . The Municipal Corporation (Mortgages, &c.) Act,
   c. 16.   1860.

23 & 24 Vict. . . The Local Taxation Returns Act, 1860;
   c. 51.   in part, namely,—
   in part.   so far as it relates to the receipts and expen-
                  diture of a municipal corporation.

23 & 24 Vict. . . The Lands Clauses Consolidation Acts Amendment
   c. 106.   Act, 1860;
   in part.   in part, namely,—
                  section six.

38 & 39 Vict. . . The Public Works Loans Act, 1875;
   c. 89.   in part, namely,—
   in part.   in section forty, the second paragraph (be-
                  ginning " The council" and ending " this
                  Act"), and the words " and the council
                  respectively" in the last paragraph.

39 & 40 Vict. . . The Statute Law Revision Act (Substituted Enact-
   c. 20.   ments) Act, 1876;
   in part.   in part, namely,—
                  section three.

40 & 41 Vict. . . An Act to amend the law relating to the division of
   c. 17.   courts of quarter sessions in boroughs.

40 & 41 Vict. . . The Local Taxation Returns Act, 1877;
   c. 66.   in part, namely,—
   in part.   so far as it relates to the receipts and expen-
                  diture of a municipal corporation.

42 & 43 Vict. . . The Sale of Food and Drugs Act, Amendment Act,
   c. 30.   1879;
   in part.   in part, namely,—
                  section eight.

43 Vict. c. 17 . . The Town Councils and Local Boards Act, 1880.

THE SECOND SCHEDULE.

Meetings and Proceedings of Council.

[See sect. 7, sub-s. 4, and sect. 22, sub-s. 1.]

Quarterly meetings.

1. The council shall hold four quarterly meetings in every year for the transaction of general business.

2. The quarterly meetings shall be held at noon on each 9th of November, and at such hour on such other three days before the 1st of November then next following as the council at the quarterly meeting in November decide or afterwards from time to time by standing order determine.

Special meetings.

3. The mayor may at any time call a meeting of the council.

4. If the mayor refuses to call a meeting after a requisition

for that purpose, signed by five members of the council, has been presented to him, any five members of the council may forthwith, on that refusal, call a meeting. If the mayor (without so refusing) does not within seven days after such presentation call a meeting, any five members of the council may, on the expiration of those seven days, call a meeting.

Notice of meeting.

5. Three clear days at least before any meeting of the council, notice of the time and place of the intended meeting, signed by the mayor, or if the meeting is called by members of the council, by those members, shall be fixed on the town hall. Where the meeting is called by members of the council, the notice shall specify the business proposed to be transacted thereat.

Summons to meeting.

6. Three clear days at least before any meeting of the council, a summons to attend the meeting, specifying the business proposed to be transacted thereat, and signed by the town clerk, shall be left [or delivered by post in a registered letter (¹)] at the usual place of abode of every member of the council, three clear days at least before the meeting.

7. Want of service of the summons on any member of the council shall not affect the validity of a meeting.

8. No business shall be transacted at a meeting other than that specified in the summons relating thereto, except in case of a quarterly meeting, business prescribed by this Act to be transacted thereat.

Chairman.

9. At every meeting of the council, the mayor, if present, shall be chairman. If the mayor is absent, then the deputy mayor, if chosen for that purpose by the members of the council then present, shall be chairman. If both the mayor and the deputy mayor are absent, or the deputy mayor, being present, is not chosen, then such alderman, or in the absence of all the aldermen, such councillor, as the members of the council then present choose, shall be chairman.

Quorum.

10. All acts of the council, and all questions coming or arising before the council, may be done and decided by the majority of such members of the council as are present [and vote (²)] at a meeting held in pursuance of this Act, the whole number present at the meeting, whether voting or not, not being less than one-third of the number of the whole council.

11. In case of equality of votes, the chairman of the meeting shall have a second or casting vote.

Act of 1882 Schedule 2.

Casting vote.

12. Minutes of the proceedings of every meeting shall be drawn up and fairly entered in a book kept for that purpose, and shall be signed in manner authorized by this Act.*

Minutes.

* Sect. 22, sub-s. 5.

13. Subject to the foregoing provisions of this Schedule, the council may from time to time make standing orders for the regulation of their proceedings and business, and vary or revoke the same.

Standing orders.

This Schedule, excepting rules 7 and 13, which are new, and the additions to rules 6 and 10, which are indicated in the notes thereto, substantially reproduces the greater part of section 69 of the Act of 1835.

([1]) *Or delivered, &c.*]—The words in brackets are new.

([2]) *And vote, &c.*]—The words in brackets are new, and place it beyond doubt that members present and not voting are absent in law, except for the purpose of estimating the quorum.

THE THIRD SCHEDULE.

Elections.

Part I. (*a*)— *Preparation and Revision of Parish Burgess Lists in Boroughs not Parliamentary.*

[See sect. 7, sub-s. 4, and sect. 44, sub-s. 2.]

1. On or before each 1st of September, the overseers of each parish shall make, sign, and deliver to the town clerk a list, called the parish burgess list, of all persons entitled to be enrolled in the burgess roll for the year in respect of property in that parish.

Parish burgess lists.

A majority of the overseers may act (sect. 238). For penalty for default, see sects. 75 and 226. For *form* of list, see sched. viii. pt. ii. Form (C.), post, p. 158.

2. The overseers shall keep a printed copy of the parish burgess list made by them open to public inspection on the first fifteen days of September.

No fee for inspection (sect. 233, sub-sect. 6).

3. The town clerk shall cause a printed copy of all the parish burgess lists to be fixed on the town hall, and to be kept so fixed during the last seven of those fifteen days.

(*a*) This Part is taken from sects. 14—19 of the Act of 1835, as amended by sect. 7 of the Act of 1857.

**Act of 1882
Schedule 3.
(*Part* 1.)**

Claim.

4. Every person whose name is not in a parish burgess list, and who claims to have it inserted therein (in this Act referred to as a claimant), shall, on or before the 15th of September, give notice in writing of his claim to the town clerk.

For *form* of claim, see sched. viii. pt. ii. Form (D.), post.

Objection.

5. Every person whose name is in a parish burgess list may object to any other person as not being entitled to have his name retained in that or any other parish burgess list.

Notice of objection.

6. Every person so objecting (in this Act referred to as an objector) shall, on or before the 15th of September, give to the town clerk, and also give to the person objected to, or leave at or on the property for which he appears in the parish burgess list to be rated, notice in writing of the objection.

For *form* of notice of objection, see sched. viii. pt. ii. Form (E.), post. It has been held that the parish in which the objector's qualifying property lies, need not be stated (*Reg.* v. *Mayor of Monmouth*, L. R., 5 Q. B. 251), but that there must be a statement of the property as well as of the abode (*Reg.* v. *Mayor of Harwich*, 8 Ad. & E. 919).

Lists of claimants and persons objected to.

7. The town clerk shall make two separate lists of the claimants and the persons objected to (in this Act referred to as respondents), and shall cause printed copies thereof to be fixed on the town hall, and to be kept so fixed during the last seven days of September.

For *form* of lists, see sched. viii. pt. ii. Forms (F.) and (G.), post.

8. He shall also keep a printed copy of each of these lists, open to public inspection on any day during the same seven days.

No fee (sect. 233, sub-sect. 6).

Revision.

9. The mayor and the two revising assessors shall in each year revise the parish burgess lists.

10. They shall for this purpose hold an open court in the borough on some or one of the first fifteen days of October.

11. They shall give three clear days' notice of the holding of the court, by notice fixed on the town hall.

12. The town clerk shall at the opening of the court pro-

duce the parish burgess lists, and a copy of the lists of claimants and respondents.

13. The court shall insert in the parish burgess lists the name of every person who has duly claimed to have his name inserted therein, and is proved to the satisfaction of the court to be so entitled.

14. The court shall expunge from the parish burgess lists the name of every person proved to the court to be dead.

15. Subject as aforesaid, the court shall retain in the parish burgess lists the name of every person to whom objection has not been duly made.

16. The court shall also retain therein the name of every respondent, unless the objector appears by himself, or by some person on his behalf, in support of the objection.

17. Where the objector so appears, the court shall require proof of the respondent's qualification, and, if it is not proved to the satisfaction of the court, shall expunge his name from the parish burgess list.

18. If the name of any person is entered in respect of property situate in more than one ward, the court may call upon him to choose, and if he does not choose, may determine in which of those wards he shall be entitled to vote.

19. The court shall correct any mistake and supply any omission proved to the court to have been made in any of the lists with respect to the name or abode of any person, or the description of any property.

20. The overseers, vestry clerks, and collectors of poor rates of every parish shall attend the court.

21. The court may require any overseer or person having the custody of any book containing any poor rate made in any year in any parish to produce the same at the court for inspection.

22. The court may examine on oath the town clerk, overseers, vestry clerks, and collectors, and any claimant, objector, respondent, or witness.

23. The court shall, on the hearing in open court, determine on the validity of all claims and objections.

24. The mayor shall, in open court, write his initials against each name inserted or expunged, and against any part of the lists in which a mistake has been corrected or omission supplied, and shall sign his name to every page of the lists so revised.

Act of 1882
Schedule 3.
(Part 1.)

Adjournment.

[See sect. 7,
sub-s. 4, and
sect. 55.]

Nomination
paper.

* Sect. 49.

Delivery of
nomination
paper.

25. The mayor may adjourn the court from time to time, so that no adjourned court be held after the 15th of October.

But a mandamus under sect. 47, sub-sect. 2, *ante*, may be granted to hold a court after the 15th October (*Reg.* v. *Mayor of Monmouth*, L. R., 5 Q. B. 251), and the mandamus may go to a succeeding mayor. (*Reg.* v. *Mayor of Rochester*, E., B. & E. 1024.)

PART. II.—*Rules as to Nomination in Elections of Councillors (a)*.

1. Every candidate for the office of councillor must be nominated in writing.

2. The writing must be subscribed by two burgesses of the borough, or, in the case of a ward election, of the ward, as proposer and seconder, and by eight other burgesses of the borough or ward, as assenting to the nomination.

A different proposer cannot be substituted without the further assent of the assenting burgesses. (*Harmon* v. *Park*, 7 Q. B. D. 369; 50 L. J., Q. B. 775.)

3. Each candidate must be nominated by a separate nomination paper, but the same burgesses, or any of them, may subscribe as many nomination papers as there are vacancies to be filled, but no more.

In *Northcote* v. *Pulsford*, L. R., 10 C. P. 476; 44 L. J., C. P. 217, a candidate was twice nominated, one nomination paper being good, the other bad, and his name appeared in the ballot papers in respect of both nominations. It was held, that the votes on the two sets of ballot papers might be added together.

4. Each person nominated must be enrolled in the burgess roll or entered in the separate non-resident list required by this Act * to be made.

5. The nomination paper must state the surname and other names of the candidate, with his abode and description.

6. The town clerk shall provide nomination papers, and shall supply any burgess with as many nomination papers as may be required, and shall, at the request of any burgess, fill up a nomination paper.

7. Every nomination paper subscribed as aforesaid must be delivered by the candidate, or his proposer or seconder, at the town clerk's office, seven days at least before the day of election, and before five oclock in the afternoon of the last day for delivery of nomination papers.

It was held in *Monks* v. *Jackson* (1 C. P. D. 683; 46 L. J., C. P.

(a) These rules seem substantially to re-enact sects. 1, 2 and 7 of the Municipal Elections Act, 1875 (38 & 39 Vict. c. 40).

162), that delivery by an agent was insufficient; but sect. 2, subsect. 3, of the Act of 1875, on which that decision was given, enacted, that the nomination paper "shall be delivered by the candidate himself, or" &c. The re-enactment of this, with the omission of the word "himself," appears to show that delivery by an agent would now be sufficient.

Act of 1882 Schedule 3. (*Part 2.*)

The nomination paper must be delivered seven clear days before the day of election, exclusive of nomination and election days (*Howes* v. *Turner*, 1 C. P. D. 670 ; 45 L. J., C. P. 550) and also of Sunday, &c., sect. 230, ante.

8. The town clerk shall forthwith send notice of every such nomination to each candidate.

Notice of nominations to candidates.

9. The mayor shall attend at the town hall on the day next after the last day for delivery of nomination papers for a sufficient time, between the hours of two and four in the afternoon, and shall decide on the validity of every objection made in writing to a nomination paper.

10. Where a person subscribes more nomination papers than one, his subscription shall be inoperative in all but the one which is first delivered.

Subscription of more nomination papers than one.

This rule is new : it will be observed that it includes the case of a subscription of more nomination papers than *two* or more in proportion to the number of vacancies, although, by rule 3, two or more nomination papers may be subscribed by the same burgesses.

There may, therefore, be a technical irregularity under rule 10, although rule 3 has been strictly complied with, and it is submitted (1) that the two rules must be read together, and that if rule 3 be complied with, rule 10 may pro tanto be disregarded ; or (2) that the difficulty may be got over by the application of sect. 72, p. 37, ante.

11. Each candidate may, by writing signed by him, or, if he is absent from the United Kingdom, then his proposer or seconder may, by writing signed by him, appoint a person (in this schedule referred to as the candidate's representative) to attend the proceedings before the mayor on behalf of the candidate, and this appointment must be delivered to the town clerk before five o'clock in the afternoon of the last day for delivery of nomination papers.

12. Each candidate and his representative, but no other person, except for the purpose of assisting the mayor, shall be entitled to attend the proceedings before the mayor.

13. Each candidate and his representative may, during the time appointed for the attendance of the mayor for the purposes of this schedule, object to the nomination paper of any other candidate for the borough or ward.

Act of 1882
Schedule 3.
(*Part 2.*)

14. The decision of the mayor shall be given in writing, and shall, if disallowing an objection, be final, but, if allowing an objection, shall be subject to reversal on petition questioning the election or return.

Public notice of nomination.

15. The town clerk shall at least four days before the day of election cause the surnames and other names of all persons validly nominated, with their respective abodes and descriptions, and the names of the persons subscribing their nomination papers as proposers and seconders, to be printed and fixed on the town hall, and in the case of a ward election, in some conspicuous place in the ward.

For *form* of public notice, see sched. viii. part ii., Form II., post.

Candidate abroad.

16. The nomination of a person absent from the United Kingdom shall be void, unless his written consent given within one month before the day of his nomination in the presence of two witnesses is produced at the time of his nomination.

Withdrawal.

17. Where the number of valid nominations exceeds that of the vacancies, any candidate may withdraw from his candidature by notice signed by him, and delivered at the town clerk's office not later than two o'clock in the afternoon of the day next after the last day for delivery of nomination papers: Provided that such notices shall take effect in the order in which they are delivered, and that no such notice shall have effect so as to reduce the number of candidates ultimately standing nominated below the number of vacancies.

Roll in force at day of election to be deemed "the roll."

18. In and for the purposes of the provisions of this Act relating to proceedings preliminary to election, the burgess roll or ward roll which will be in force on the day of election shall be deemed to be the burgess roll or ward roll, and a person whose name is inserted in one of the lists from which the burgess roll or ward roll will be made up, shall be deemed to be enrolled in that roll although that roll is not yet completed.

[See sect. 7,
sub-s. 4, and
sect. 58,
sub-s. 11.]

PART III.—*Modifications of the Ballot Act in its Application to Municipal Elections.*

1. The provisions of the Ballot Act, 1872, with respect to the voting of a returning officer, the use of a room for taking a poll, and the right to vote of persons whose names are on the register of voters, and rules 16 and 19 in the schedule to that Act, shall not apply in the case of a municipal election.

Act of 1882
Schedule 3.
(*Part* 3.)

2. The mayor shall at least four days before the day of election give public notice of the situation, division, and allotment of polling places for taking the poll at the election, and of the description of the persons entitled to vote thereat, and at the several polling stations.

3. The mayor shall provide everything which in the case of a parliamentary election is required to be provided by the returning officer for the purpose of a poll, and shall appoint officers for taking the poll and counting the votes.

4. The mayor shall furnish every polling station with such number of compartments in which the voters can mark their votes screened from observation, and furnish each presiding officer with such number of ballot papers, as in the judgment of the mayor may be necessary for effectually taking the poll at the election.

5. All expenses of the election shall be defrayed in manner by this Act provided.

6. No return shall be made to the clerk of the Crown in Chancery.

PART IV.—*Enactments which are to revive on the Expiration of the Ballot Act.*

[See sect. 7, sub-s. 4, and sect. 76, sub-s. 1.]

With respect to a contested election of councillors, elective auditors or revising assessors, the following rules shall be observed:

1. The returning officer shall cause the requisite polling booths to be erected, or the requisite rooms to be hired and used as polling booths.

2. The returning officer shall, at least two days before the day of election, give public notice of the situation, division, and allotment of the different booths.

3. Each booth shall be divided into compartments, and the returning officer shall appoint a clerk to take the poll at each compartment.

4. There shall be affixed on each booth a notice specifying the part of the borough for which it is allotted.

5. No person shall be admitted to vote at any booth except that allotted for the part in which his qualifying property is situate, unless no booth is allotted for that part, in which case he may vote at any booth.

Act of 1882
Schedule 3.
(*Part* 4.)

Enactments
to be revived
after ex-
piration of
Ballot Act.

6. If there is more than one booth, the returning officer may appoint a deputy to preside at each booth.

7. A burgess may vote by delivering to the returning officer or his deputy a voting paper containing the surnames and other names of the persons for whom he votes, with their abodes and descriptions. The voting paper must be signed by the burgess, and must state the qualifying property in respect of which he votes.

8. The returning officer or his deputy shall, if so required by two burgesses, put to any person offering to vote at the time of his delivering in his voting paper, but not afterwards, the following question :

"Are you the person whose name is signed as [*A. B.*] to the voting paper now delivered in by you?"

The vote of a person required to answer this question shall not be received until he has answered it. If any person wilfully makes a false answer thereto he shall be guilty of a misdemeanour.

9. The returning officer shall, at the close of the poll, examine the voting papers, and shall publish a list of the persons elected not later than two o'clock in the afternoon of the day next but one after the day of election.

10. The town clerk shall, for a period of six months from the day of election, keep at his office the voting papers used at the election, and shall permit any burgess to inspect the same on payment of one shilling for each search.

[See sect. 7,
sub-s. 4.]

THE FOURTH SCHEDULE.

FEES AND REMUNERATION.

The following fees and remuneration shall be payable :—

1. *Commissioner for Division into Wards or Alteration of Wards.*

[See sect. 30,
sub-s. 15.]

Five guineas for every day he is employed, over and above his travelling and other expenses.

2. *Assistant Recorder and Officers of Second Court of Quarter Sessions.*

[See sect. 168,
sub-sect. 8.]

For every day not exceeding two, or, by resolution of the council, with the sanction of the Secretary of State, not exceeding six—

To an assistant recorder - - - - Ten guineas.
To an assistant clerk of the peace - - Two guineas.
To an additional crier- - - - - Half a guinea.

The remuneration is payable on a certificate from the recorder showing the amount due.

3. *Coroner.*

Act of 1882
Schedule 4.

[See sect. 171,
sub-s. 4.]

To the borough coroner (subject to the provisions of any other Act relating to
coroners)—

For every inquisition which he duly takes in
the borough - - - - - - Twenty shillings.

and

For every mile exceeding two miles which he
is compelled to travel from his usual
place of abode to take such inquisition - Ninepence.

4. *Special Constables.*

To a special constable, for every day during) Three shillings
which he is called out to act as such- -) and sixpence.

[See sect. 196,
sub-s. 6.]

THE FIFTH SCHEDULE.

PAYMENTS OUT OF THE BOROUGH FUND (*a*).

[See sect. 7,
sub-s. 4, and
sect. 140.]

PART I.—*Payments which may be made without Order.*

1. The remuneration (if any) of the mayor, of the recorder
(if any) in his capacity either of recorder or of judge of a
borough civil court, of the stipendiary magistrate (if any), of
the town clerk, of the treasurer, of the clerk of the peace when
paid by salary, of every other officer appointed by the council,
and of the clerk to the justices.

2. The remuneration and allowances certified by the
Treasury to be payable to the Treasury in respect of an election
petition.

3. The remuneration certified by the recorder to be due to
any assistant recorder, assistant clerk of the peace, or additional crier.

PART II.—*Payments which may not be made without Order.*

1. The expenses incurred by overseers, and by the town Elections.
clerk and other municipal authorities, in relation to the
enrolment of burgesses and the holding of municipal elections,

-----

(*a*) The provisions of this Schedule, and of section 140, from
which it derives its force, are principally taken from sect. 92 of the
Act of 1835, the somewhat vague but important rule 12 of Part II.
being a substantial re-enactment of a similar clause of that section.

Act of 1882
Schedule 5.
_(Part 2.)

* Page 218.

or so much of those expenses as is not otherwise provided for under section thirty of the Parliamentary and Municipal Registration Act, 1878.*

2. The expenses incurred by the town clerk in providing accommodation for an election court held under this Act.

Corporate buildings. 3. The expenses of providing, furnishing, maintaining, or improving the corporate buildings, including the justices' room (if any), and the necessary expenses of that room.

Fees. 4. The fees payable to the clerk of the peace if not paid by salary, and under this Act to the borough coroner.

Police. 5. The payments to be made under this Act to or in respect of the borough police and to any special constable, including the following payments (namely);

    (a) Such salaries, wages, and allowances to the borough constables, and at such periods, as the watch committee, with the approbation of the council, direct; and

    (b) Such further sum as may be awarded by the watch committee, subject to the approbation of the council, or by the court of quarter or petty sessions, to a borough constable as a reward for extraordinary diligence or exertion, or as a compensation for wounds or severe injuries received in the performance of his duty, or as may be awarded by the watch committee, subject to the approbation of the council, to a borough constable, as an allowance to him when disabled by bodily injury, or worn out by length of service; and

    (c) Any extraordinary expenses which a borough constable appears to have necessarily incurred in apprehending offenders, and executing the orders of any justice having jurisdiction in the borough, such expenses having been first examined and approved by that justice; and

    (d) All other charges and expenses which the watch committee, subject to the approbation of the council, direct to be paid for the purposes of the borough constabulary force.

Prosecution, &c. of offenders. 6. The costs and expenses payable by the corporation in respect of the prosecution, maintenance, conveyance, transport, or punishment of offenders.

7. All sums payable under this Act by the corporation of the borough to the treasurer of a county.

County treasurer.

8. The expenses of and incidental to the division of a borough into wards or the alteration of wards, including the remuneration of the commissioner appointed for the purposes of the division or alteration.

Wards.

9. Such remuneration to the clerk to any commissioners for taxes in respect of making copies of assessments as the council think reasonable.

Clerk to tax commissioners.

10. The expenses of and relating to a charter of incorporation for a borough, and of and relating to all elections acts and proceedings under the charter.

Incorporation.

11. All expenses charged on the borough fund by any Act of Parliament or otherwise by law.

Statutory, &c.

12. All other expenses, not by this Act otherwise provided for, necessarily incurred in carrying this Act into effect.

Necessary expenses.

Application of Borough Fund.]—This 5th schedule must be read with sect. 140. Rule 12 substantially repeats a part of sect. 92 of the Act of 1835, upon which the borough fund had been held legally applicable to the following purposes:—

The costs of opposing any bill which attacks the existence, property or privileges of the corporation. (*Att.-Gen.* v. *Mayor of Brecon*, 10 Ch. D. 204; 48 L. J., Ch. 153; 40 L. T. 52; 27 W. R. 332, per Jessel, M. R.)

The costs of a mandamus unsuccessfully resisted on public grounds. (*Reg.* v. *Town Council of Lichfield*, 10 Q. B. 534; *Lewis* v. *Mayor of Rochester*, 30 L. J., C. P. 169.)

The expenses of a prosecution for riot and assault on a mayor while holding a revision court. (*Reg.* v. *Lichfield*, 4 Q. B. 893.)

Fees payable to the clerk to the justices. (*Reg.* v. *Mayor of Gloucester*, 5 Q. B. 862.) *This is now provided for by rule 1 of Part I. of this Schedule.*

Repairs of a corporation pew in a parish church. (*Reg.* v. *Mayor of Warwick*, 8 Q. B. 926; this item appears to fall within the discretionary powers of the court rather than the express words of the statute.)

But to the following purposes the borough fund has been held not legally applicable:—

The costs of opposing a waterworks bill. (*Reg.* v. *Mayor of Sheffield*, L. R., 6 Q. B. 652; 40 L. J., Q. B. 247; 24 L. T. 659; 19 W. R. 1159; this is the important case which led to the passing of the Borough Funds Act, 1872 (35 & 36 Vict. c. 91).)

The costs of opposing a quo warranto, and the costs of opposing a criminal information against a councillor. (*Reg.* v. *Mayor of Bridgwater*, *Reg.* v. *Paramore*, 10 Ad. & E. 281, 286.)

The costs of a prosecution for libel by an inspector of police. (*Reg.* v. *Mayor of Liverpool*, 41 L. J., Q. B. 175.)

The costs of a defence of a borough constable to an indictment,

Act of 1882
Schedule 5.
(Part 2.)
or of a chief constable to an action for malicious prosecution. (*Reg.* v. *Thompson*, 5 Q. B. 477; *Reg.* v. *Mayor of Exeter*, 6 Q. B. D. 135; *these are now made a legal charge, if the indictment be for a thing done in pursuance of the Act, by* sect. 226, sub-sect. 3, *ante*, p. 122.)

The costs of a charity petition. (*Reg.* v. *Mayor of Warwick*, 8 Q. B. 930.)

A gold chain for the mayor. (*Att.-Gen.* v. *Mayor of Batley*, 26 L. T. 392.)

THE SIXTH SCHEDULE.

[See sect. 7,
sub-s. 4, and
sect. 188,
sub-s. 2.]
COUNTIES TO WHICH CERTAIN BOROUGHS ARE TO BE CONSIDERED ADJOINING FOR PURPOSES OF CRIMINAL TRIALS.

Berwick-upon-Tweed ....Northumberland.
Bristol ....Gloucestershire.
Chester ....Cheshire.
Exeter ....Devonshire.
Kingston-upon-Hull ....Yorkshire.
Newcastle-upon-Tyne ....Northumberland.

THE SEVENTH SCHEDULE.

[See sect. 7,
sub-s. 4, and
sect. 214,
sub-s. 3.]
PROCEDURE FOR SCHEME ON GRANT OF NEW CHARTER.

1. The Committee of Council may, if they think fit, require the draft of a proposed scheme to be submitted to them, either together with the petition for a charter, or at any subsequent period.

2. The draft of a proposed scheme shall be published by advertisement, or placards, or handbills, or otherwise, as the Committee of Council think best calculated for giving notice thereof to all persons interested.

3. Before settling the scheme the Committee of Council shall consider any objections which may be made thereto by any local authority or persons affected thereby.

4. The scheme, when settled, shall, besides being published in the London Gazette, be published by advertisement, or

placards, or handbills, or otherwise, as the Committee of Council think best calculated for giving notice thereof to all person interested.

5. Where a scheme is submitted to Parliament for confirmation, the Committee of Council may introduce a bill for the confirmation of the scheme, which bill shall be a public bill.

6. Before such bill is introduced into Parliament the Committe of Council may alter the scheme in such manner as they think proper.

7. If while the bill confirming a scheme is pending in either House of Parliament a petition is presented against the scheme, the bill, so far as it relates to such scheme, may be referred to a select committee, and the petitioner shall be allowed to appear and oppose as in the case of a private bill.

8. A scheme shall come into operation at the date of its confirmation or any later date mentioned in the scheme.

9. The confirmation of a scheme shall be conclusive evidence that all the requirements of this Act with respect to proceedings required to be taken previously to the making of the scheme have been complied with, and that the scheme has been duly made, and is within the powers of this Act.

THE EIGHTH SCHEDULE.

FORMS.

PART I.—*Declarations on accepting Office.* [See sect. 7, sub-s. 4, and

FORM A. sects. 35, 240.]

FORM OF DECLARATION ON ACCEPTANCE OF CORPORATE OFFICE.

I, *A. B.*, having been elected mayor [*or* alderman, councillor, elective auditor, *or* revising assessor] for the borough of , hereby declare that I take the said office upon myself, and will duly and faithfully fulfil the duties thereof according to the best of my judgment and ability [*and in the case of the person being qualified by estate say*, And I hereby declare that I am seised or possessed of real or personal estate, or both [*as the case may be*], to the value or amount of one thousand pounds, or five hundred pounds [*as the case may require*], over and above what will satisfy my just debts].

FORM B.

DECLARATION BY RECORDER OR BOROUGH JUSTICE.

I, *A. B.*, hereby declare that I will faithfully and impartially execute the office of recorder [*or* justice of the peace] for the borough of   , according to the best of my judgment and ability.

PART II.—*Forms relating to Elections.*

FORM C.

The LIST of BURGESSES of the Borough of   in the Parish [*or* Township] of   .

Surname and other Names of each Person in full.	Nature of Property for which he is now rated.	Name and Situation of Property for which he is now rated.
Ashton, John. .	Shop .	No. 23, Church Street.
Bates, Thomas .	House .	Brook's Farm.

(Signed)   A. B. } Overseers.
                        C. D. }

FORM D.

NOTICE OF CLAIM.

To the Town Clerk of the Borough of   .

I hereby give you notice, that I claim to have my name inserted in the parish burgess lists of the borough of   that I occupy [*here describe the house, warehouse, counting-house, shop, or other building then occupied by the claimant*] in the borough, and that I have been rated in the parish of   [*here state the parish or several parishes, and the time during which the claimant has been rated in each of them within the borough, necessary for his qualification*].
Dated the   day of   in the year   .
(Signed)   John Allen of [*place of abode*].

FORM E.

NOTICE OF OBJECTION.

To the Town Clerk of the Borough of   [*or to the person objected to as the case may be*].

I hereby give you notice, that I object to the name of Thomas Bates of Brook's Farm, in the parish of   [*describe the person objected to as described in the parish burgess list*] being retained on the parish burgess lists of the borough of   .
Dated the   day of   in the year   .

(Signed)   John Ashton of [*here state the place of abode and the property for which he is said to be rated in the parish burgess lists*].

Form F.

List of Claimants.

Act of 1882
Schedule 8.
(*Part 2.*)

[See sect. 240,
and sched. iii.
pt. 1, rule 3.]

The following Persons claim to have their Names inserted in the Parish Burgess Lists of the Borough of   .

Surname and other Names of each Claimant.	Nature of Property for which he is now rated.	Situation of Property for which he is now rated.	Parish [*or* Parishes] in which he has been rated, as stated in the Claim.
Allen, John .	House . .	No. 17, High Street.	Rated in the last year in Saint Mary's parish in the borough, and in the two preceding years in Saint James's parish in the borough.

(Signed)   *A. B.*, Town Clerk.

Form G.

List of Persons Objected to.

The following Persons have been objected to as not being entitled to have their Names retained in the Parish Burgess Lists of the Borough of   .

Surname and other Names of each Person objected to.	Nature of Property for which he is now rated.	Situation of Property for which he is said to be now rated in the Overseers List.	Parish in which is the Property for which he is now said to be rated in the Overseers List.
Bates, Thomas.	House . .	Brook's Farm .	Saint James'.

(Signed)   *A. B.*, Town Clerk.

Form H.

Notice.

[See sect. 240,
and sched. iii.
part 2, rule
15.]

Borough of   . Election of councillors, [*or* elective auditors, *or* revising assessors, *as the case may be*] for the [Ward or several Wards of the] Borough.

Take Notice.

1. That an election of [*here insert the number of councillors, auditors, or assessors, as the case may be*] for the [ward or several wards of the] said borough will be held on the   day of   .

2. Candidates must be nominated by writing, subscribed by two

Act of 1882
Schedule 8.
(Part 2.)
burgesses as proposer or seconder, and by eight other burgesses as assenting to the nomination.

3. Candidates must be duly qualified for the office to which they are nominated, and the nomination paper must state the surname and other names of the person nominated, with his abode and description, and may be in the following form, or to the like effect:
(Set out Form I.)

4. Each candidate must be nominated by a separate nomination paper, but the same burgesses or any of them may subscribe as many nomination papers as there are vacancies to be filled for the borough [or ward], but no more.

5. Every person who forges a nomination paper, or delivers any nomination paper knowing the same to be forged, will be guilty of a misdemeanour, and be liable to imprisonment for any term not exceeding six months, with or without hard labour.

6. Nomination papers must be delivered by the candidate himself, or his proposer or seconder, at the town clerk's office before five o'clock in the afternoon of day the day of next.

7. The mayor will attend at the town hall on day the day of , for a sufficient time between the hours of two and four o'clock in the afternoon, to hear and decide objections to nomination papers.

8. Forms of nomination papers may be obtained at the town clerk's office; and the town clerk will, at the request of any burgess, fill up a nomination paper.

Dated this day of 18 . *A. B.*, Town Clerk.

[See sect. 240, and sched. iii. pt. 2, rules 1—3.]

Form I.—Nomination Paper.

Borough of . Election of councillors, [elective auditors, *or* revising assessors] for Ward in the said Borough [*or* the said Borough] to be held on the day of 18 .

We, the undersigned, being respectively burgesses, hereby nominate the following person as a candidate at the said election.

Surname.	Other Names.	Abode.	Description.

Signature.	Number (*a*) on Burgess Roll, with the Ward or Polling District, if any, having a distinct numbering.

A. B.
C. D.

We, the undersigned, being respectively burgesses, hereby assent

(*a*) To give a wrong number is fatal (*Gothard* v. *Clark*, 5 C. P. D. 253).

to the nomination of the above-named person as a candidate at the said election.

Dated this   day of   18 .

Signature.	Number on Burgess Roll, with the Ward or Polling District, if any, having a distinct numbering.
E. F. G. H. I. J. K. L. M. N. O. P. Q. R. S. T.	

FORM K.—BALLOT PAPER.
FORM of Front of Ballot Paper.

[See sect. 62.]

For Elective Auditors.

Counterfoil.

No.

Note. — The counterfoil is to have a number to correspond with that on the back of the ballot paper.

1	CADE. (John Cade, of 22, Wellclose Place, Accountant.)
2	JOHNSON. (Charles Johnson, of 7, Albion Street, Gentleman.)
3	THOMPSON. (William Thompson, of 14, Queen Street, Silversmith.)

For Revising Assessor.

1	BACON. (Charles Bacon, of 29, New Street, Solicitor.)
2	BYRON. (James Byron, of 45, George Street, Commission Agent.)
3	WILSON. (George Wilson, of 22, Hanover Square, Gentleman.)

FORM of Back of Ballot Paper.

No.   . Election of elective auditors [*or* revising assessors] for the borough of   to be held on the   day of   18 .

The number on the back of the ballot paper is to correspond with that on the counterfoil.

Act of 1882
Schedule 8.
(*Part 3.*)

[See sect. 7,
sub-s. 4, and
sects. 111,
240.]

PART III.—*Forms relating to Working Men's Dwellings.*

FORM L.

FORM OF GRANT BY CORPORATION.

The Municipal Corporations Act, 1882.

(Working Men's Dwellings.)

Borough of   .   Grant No.   .

The mayor, aldermen, and burgesses of the borough of   by virtue and in pursuance of the above-mentioned Act, and in consideration of   paid to them by *A. B.* of   hereby grant to the said *A. B.* (herein referred to as the grantee), and his heirs, the site following (that is to say) [*insert description*] with the appurtenances, subject to the following conditions (that is to say):

1. The grantee shall build on the site one working-man's or working-men's dwelling (and no more) according to the plan and specification deposited in the office of the town clerk, numbered   , and under the superintendence and to the satisfaction of the corporation.

2. The grantee, his heirs and assigns, shall always maintain and repair the building, and shall not sell or alienate the site or building in divisions or separate parts, and, in case of the taking down or destruction of the building shall not rebuild it except in manner approved by the corporation.

3. The grantee, his heirs or assigns, shall not add to or alter the character of the building without the consent of the corporation.

4. If at any time the grantee, his heirs or assigns, fail to fully observe and perform any stipulation of this grant, the corporation may, if they think fit, declare that the site is re-vested in the corporation; and thereupon the same, with the dwelling and other buildings thereon, shall become and be vested in the corporation, as if this grant had not been made.

In witness whereof, &c., this   day of   187   .

(*Corporate Seal.*)

FORM M.

FORM OF TRANSFER OF GRANT.

The Municipal Corporations Act, 1882.

(Working Men's Dwellings.)

Borough of   .   Transfer No.   .   (Grant No.   .)

A. B. of   , by virtue and in pursuance of the above-mentioned Act, and in consideration of   paid to him by *C. D.* of   , hereby grants and transfers to the said *C. D.* and his heirs the site comprised in the within-written* grant [*or* the grant No.   under the said Act, dated the   day of   187 †] with the appurtenances and with the dwelling and other buildings thereon, subject to the conditions on which that site is held immediately before the execution of this transfer.

[In case of transfer by indorsement.]

†[*In case of transfer by separate deed.*]

In witness whereof, &c., this   day of   18   .

A. B.   (L.S.)

FORM N.

FORM OF LEASE BY CORPORATION.

The Municipal Corporations Act, 1882.

(Working Men's Dwellings.)

Borough of . Lease No. .

The mayor, aldermen, and burgesses of the borough of   by virtue and in pursuance of the above-mentioned Act, and in consideration of the sum of   paid to them by *A.B.* of   and of the rent and stipulations in this lease reserved and contained, and to be by him, his executors, administrators, or assigns, paid and performed hereby lease to the said *A.B.* (herein referred to as the lessee), his executors and administrators, the site following (that is to say) [*insert description*] with the appurtenances, for the term of [*nine hundred and ninety-nine*] years from the   day of   , at the yearly rent (clear of all deductions) of   , payable by two equal half-yearly payments on the   day of   and the   day of   in every year, the first thereof to be made on the   day of   , and the last thereof to be made in advance on the   day of   next before the end of the term, and so that on the term being determined by re-entry a proportionate part of the rent for the fraction of the current half year up to re-entry be repayable.

And the lessee hereby covenants with the corporation that he, his executors, administrators, or assigns, will during the term pay the rent on the days and in manner aforesaid, and will pay all taxes, rates, and outgoings for the time being payable by the tenant in respect of the premises.

And this lease is made subject to the following conditions (that is to say):

1. The lessee shall build on the site one working-man's or working-men's dwelling (and no more) according to the plan and specification deposited in the office of the town clerk, and numbered   , under the superintendence and to the satisfaction of the corporation.

2. The lessee, his executors, administrators, and assigns, shall always during the term maintain and repair the building, and shall not sell or alienate the site or building in divisions or separate parts and, in case of the taking down or destruction of the building, shall not rebuild it, except in manner approved by the corporation.

3. The lessee, his executors, administrators, or assigns, shall not add to or alter the character of the building without the consent in writing of the corporation.

4. If at any time the lessee, his executors, administrators, or assigns, fail to duly pay the rent hereby reserved, or to fully observe and perform any stipulation herein contained, the corporation may, if they think fit, re-enter on any part of the site in the name of the whole, and thereupon the term of   years shall absolutely cease.

In witness whereof, &c., this   day of   187 .

(*Corporate Seal.*)
A.B. (L.S.)

M 2

FORM O.

FORM OF ASSIGNMENT OF LEASE.

The Municipal Corporations Act, 1882.

(Working Men's Dwellings.)

Borough of   . Transfer No.   . (Lease No.   .)

A. B. of   (herein referred to as the assignor) by virtue and in pursuance of the above-mentioned Act, and in consideration of paid to him by *C. D.* of   , hereby assigns to the said *C. D.* (herein referred to as the assignee,) his executors and administra-

* [In case of assignment by indorsement.]

† [In case of assignment by separate deed.]

tors, the site comprised in the within-written lease* [*or the lease No.   under the said Act, dated the   day of   187 †*], with the appurtenances, and with the dwelling and other buildings thereon, for the residue of the term of   years, at the rent and subject to the stipulations and conditions at and subject to which that site is held immediately before the execution of this assignment.

And the assignee for himself, his executors and administrators, covenants with the assignor, his executors and administrators, that the assignee, his executors or administrators, will pay the yearly rent and observe and perform the stipulations and conditions aforesaid, and will at all times keep the assignor, his executors and administrators, indemnified in respect thereof.

In witness whereof, &c., this   day of   187 .

A. B.   (L.S.)
C. D.   (L.S.)

PART IV.—*Forms relating to Borough Bridges.*

FORM P.

FORM OF MORTGAGE.

The Municipal Corporations Act, 1882.

(Borough Bridges.)

Borough of   . Mortgage No.   .

We, the mayor, aldermen, and burgesses of the borough of by virtue and in pursuance of the above-mentioned Act, and in consideration of the sum of   paid to them by *A. B.* of for the purposes of the said Act, do grant and assign unto the said *A. B.*, his executors, administrators, and assigns, such proportion of the borough fund and borough rate as the said sum of doth or shall bear to the whole sum which is or shall be borrowed on the credit of the said fund and rate, to hold to the said *A. B.*, his executors, administrators, and assigns, from the day of the date hereof, until the said sum of   with interest at the rate of per centum per annum for the same, shall be fully paid and satisfied. And it is hereby declared that the said principal sum shall be repaid on the   day of   at [*place of payment*].

In witness whereof, &c., this   day of   187 .

(*Corporate Seal.*)

Form Q.

Form of Transfer of Mortgage.

The Municipal Corporations Act, 1882.

(Borough Bridges.)

Borough of   Transfer No.   .   (Mortgage No.   .)

I *A. B.* of   , in consideration of the sum of   paid to me by *C. D.* of   , do hereby transfer to the said *C. D.*, his executors, administrators, and assigns, a certain mortgage, dated this   day of   , and made by the mayor, aldermen, and burgesses of the borough of   , under the above-mentioned Act, for securing the sum of   and interest thereon at   per centum per annum [*or, if the transfer is by indorsement on the mortgage, insert, instead of the words immediately following the word "assigns," the within security*], and all my right, estate, and interest in and to the money thereby secured, and in and to the fund and rate thereby assigned.

In witness whereof, &c., this   day of   , 187 .

$$A. B. \quad (\text{L.S.})$$

THE NINTH SCHEDULE.

Enactments in which a Reference to this Act is to be Substituted.

Part I.—*General References.*

2 & 3 Vict. c. 93.	An Act for the establishment of county and district constables by the authority of justices of the peace (section 24).
5 & 6 Vict. c. 109.	An Act for the appointment of parish constables (section 21).
9 & 10 Vict. c. 74.	An Act to encourage the establishment of public baths and wash-houses (section 1).
10 & 11 Vict. c. 62.	An Act for the establishment of naval prisons, and for the prevention of desertion from her Majesty's navy (section 13).
12 & 13 Vict. c. 35.	An Act for requiring annual returns of the expenditure on highways in England and Wales to be transmitted to the Secretary of State, and afterwards laid before Parliament (section 2).
12 & 13 Vict. c. 82.	An Act to relieve boroughs, in certain cases, from contribution to certain descriptions of county expenditure.
13 & 14 Vict. c. 20.	An Act to amend an Act of the fifth and sixth years of her present Majesty for the appointment and payment of parish constables (section 7.)
13 & 14 Vict. c. 105.	An Act for facilitating the union of liberties with the counties in which they are situate (section 10).

14 & 15 Vict... An Act for the well-ordering of common lodging-
c. 28.   houses (section 2).

14 & 15 Vict... An Act to encourage the establishment of lodging-
c. 34.   houses for the labouring classes (section 2).

16 & 17 Vict... An Act for the establishment of a body of naval
c. 73.   coast volunteers, and for the temporary transfer
         to the navy, in case of need, of seafaring men
         employed in other public services (section 24).

16 & 17 Vict... The Lunatic Asylums Act, 1853 (section 9).
c. 97

17 & 18 Vict... An Act to amend the law concerning the making of
c. 71.   borough rates in boroughs not within the Muni-
         cipal Corporation Acts.

17 & 18 Vict... An Act to make further provision for the burial of
c. 87.   the dead in England beyond the limits of the
         metropolis (section 3).

17 & 18 Vict... The Militia Law Amendment Act, 1854 (section 11).
c. 105.

18 & 19 Vict... An Act further to amend the laws relating to the
c. 57.   militia in England (section 7).

18 & 19 Vict... The Nuisances Removal Act for England, 1855.
c. 121.

19 & 20 Vict... An Act to render more effectual the police in coun-
c. 69.   ties and boroughs in England and Wales.

20 & 21 Vict... An Act to amend the Burial Acts.
c. 81.

22 & 23 Vict... An Act for the establishment of a reserve volunteer
c. 40.   force of seamen, and for the government of the
         same (section 25).

23 & 24 Vict... An Act for the better management and control of
c. 68.   the highways in South Wales.

25 & 26 Vict... An Act for the better management of highways in
c. 61.   England.

26 & 27 Vict... An Act for the protection of certain garden or
c. 13.   ornamental grounds in cities and boroughs.

26 & 27 Vict... The Stipendiary Magistrates Act, 1863 (section 2).
c. 97.

28 & 29 Vict... The Prison Act, 1865 (section 4).
c. 126.

30 & 31 Vict... The Representation of the People Act, 1867.
c. 102.

31 & 32 Vict... The Petty Sessions and Lock-up House Act, 1868
c. 22.   (section 3).

31 & 32 Vict... The Boundary Act, 1868 (First Schedule).
c. 46.

31 & 32 Vict... The Parliamentary Electors Registration Act, 1868.
c. 58.

31 & 32 Vict... The Parliamentary Elections Act, 1868 (sections 43
c. 125.   and 45).

31 & 32 Vict... The Artizans and Labourers Dwellings Act, 1868   **Act of 1882**
  c. 130.   (section 3).   **Schedule 9.**

33 & 34 Vict... The Elementary Education Act, 1870 (section 3).
  c. 75.

33 & 34 Vict... The Tramways Act, 1870 (Schedule A.).
  c. 78.

34 & 35 Vict... The Dogs Act, 1871 (Schedule).
  c. 56.

34 & 35 Vict... The Petroleum Act, 1871 (section 2).
  c. 105.

35 & 36 Vict... The Infant Life Protection Act, 1872 (First
  c. 38.   Schedule).

35 & 36 Vict... An Act to authorize the application of funds of
  c. 91.   municipal corporations and other governing
                   bodies in certain cases.

38 & 39 Vict... The Explosives Act, 1875 (section 108).
  c. 17.

38 & 39 Vict... The Public Health Act, 1875 (section 4).
  c. 55.

38 & 39 Vict... The Local Loans Act, 1875 (section 34).
  c. 83.

39 & 40 Vict... The Commons Act, 1876 (section 37).
  c. 56.

40 & 41 Vict... The Prison Act, 1877 (section 59).
  c. 21.

41 & 42 Vict... The Weights and Measures Act, 1878 (Fourth
  c. 49.   Schedule).

41 & 42 Vict... The Contagious Diseases (Animals) Act, 1878
  c. 74.   (sections 7 and 66).

41 & 42 Vict... The Highways and Locomotives (Amendment) Act,
  c. 77.   1878 (section 38).

PART II.—Particular References.   [See sect. 242,

14 & 15 Vict. c. 55.—An Act to amend the law relating to the sub-s. 2.]
expenses of prosecutions, and to make further provisions for the
apprehension and trial of offenders in certain cases:
In section 24, for Schedule C. to the Municipal Corporations Act,
1835, the Sixth Schedule to this Act.

33 & 34 Vict. c. 91.—The Clerical Disabilities Act, 1870:
In the First Schedule, for section 28 of the Municipal Corporations Act, 1835, so much of the provision of this Act relative to
disqualifications for being councillor as relates to being in holy
orders.

INCORPORATED ENACTMENTS.

I.

REGISTRATION.

II.

VOTING AT ELECTIONS.

III.

PERSONATION.

IV.

CORRUPT PRACTICES.

[*Asterisks denote the omission of sections or parts of sections applicable to parliamentary elections only.*]

INCORPORATED ENACTMENTS.

$\blacklozenge$

I.—REGISTRATION.

PARLIAMENTARY REGISTRATION ACT, 1843.

[Incorporated, as to parliamentary boroughs, by sect. 44 of the
Municipal Corporations Act, 1882, ante, p. 26 ; and sect. 18
of the Parliamentary and Municipal Registration Act, 1878,
p. 210, post.]

6 Vict. c. 18. *An Act to amend the Law for the Registra-*
tion of Persons entitled to vote, and to define certain
Rights of voting, and to regulate certain Proceedings
in the Election of Members to serve in Parliament for
England and Wales. [31st May, 1843

CONTENTS :

6 *Vict. c.* 18.

[The preceding sections relate to lists, &c. for county elections.]

10. And for the purpose of preparing like lists, and forming a register of all persons entitled to vote in the election of a member or members to serve in Parliament for any city or borough, be it enacted, that the town clerk of every such city or borough shall cause a sufficient number of forms of precepts, notices, and lists to be printed according to the forms numbered (1. 2. 3. 4. 8. 12.) in the Schedule (B.) and of the Table numbered (1.) in the Schedule (D.) to this Act annexed, and shall on or before the 10th day of June in every year make, and cause to be delivered to the overseers of the poor of every parish or township situate wholly or in part within such city or borough, or within any place sharing in the election for such city or borough, his precept according to the form numbered (1.) in the said Schedule (B.), and also a sufficient number of the said printed forms of notices and lists, and of the said table (*a*).

Forms of precepts.

11. And be it enacted, that the overseers of every such parish or township shall, on or before the 20th day of June in every year, publish a notice in writing according to form numbered (2.) in the said Schedule (B.), stating that no person will be entitled to have his name inserted in any list of voters for the city or borough then next to be made in respect of the occupation of premises of the clear yearly value of not less than ten pounds, situate wholly or in part within such parish or township, unless he shall pay, on or before the 20th day of July then next ensuing, all the poor's rates and assessed taxes which shall have become payable from him in respect of such premises during the twelve calendar months next before the *6th day of April* then last past (*b*).

Overseers to give public notice as to the payment of rates and taxes by occupiers of premises of the yearly value of 10l.

*   *   *   *   *   *   *

13. And be it enacted, that the overseers of every such parish or township shall, on or before the last day of July in every year, make out or cause to be made out, according to the form numbered (3.) in the Schedule (B.) to this Act annexed, an alphabetical list of all persons who may be entitled to vote in the election of a member or members to serve in Parliament for such city or borough in respect of the occupation of premises of the clear yearly value of not less than

Overseers to prepare and publish lists of persons (other than freemen) entitled to vote.

(*a*) These forms are superseded by the forms under the Act of 1878, post, p. 204.

(*b*) See sect. 10 of the Act of 1878, post p. 205, and Form B., post p. 226. Also sect. 9 of the Act of 1882, p. 5, ante, from which it appears that "5th January," is substituted for "6th April."

ten pounds, situate wholly or in part within such parish or township, and another alphabetical list, according to the form numbered (4.) in the said Schedule (B.) of all other persons (except freemen) who may be entitled to vote in the election of such city or borough by virtue of any other right whatsoever, and in each of the said lists the Christian name and surname of every such person shall be written at full length, together with the place of his abode and the nature of his qualification; and where any person shall be entitled to vote in respect of any property, then the name of the street, lane, and the number of the house (if any) or other description of the place where such property may be situate, shall be specified in the list; and the said overseers shall sign such lists, and shall forthwith cause a sufficient number of copies of each of the said lists to be written or printed, and shall publish copies of the said lists on or before the 1st day of August in

Copies of lists to be kept for inspection and sale. such year, and shall likewise keep a copy of each of the said lists, to be perused by any person without payment of any fee, at any time between the hours of ten of the clock in the forenoon and four of the clock in the afternoon of any day, except Sunday, during the first fourteen days after such lists shall have been so published, and shall deliver copies thereof to all persons applying for the same, on payment of a price for each copy after the rate contained in the table numbered (1.) in the Schedule (D.) to this Act annexed (*c*).

*   *   *   *   *   *   *

Persons omitted from the borough lists to give notice of their claims. **15.** And be it enacted, that every person whose name shall have been omitted in any such list of voters for any city or borough so to be made out as aforesaid, and who shall claim, as having been entitled on the *last* (*d*) day of July then next preceding, to have his name inserted therein, and every person desirous of being registered for a different qualification than that for which his name appears in the said list, shall, on or before the 25th day of August in that year, give or cause to be given a notice, according to the form numbered (6.) in the said Schedule (B.) or to the like effect, to

---

(*c*) See sect. 15, sub-s. 4, of the Act of 1878 (post, p. 208), the *forms* of which (post, p. 223) supersede the *forms* of this section, except (D.).
(*d*) 15th, Act of 1878, sect. 7, post, p. 203.

the overseers of that parish or township in the list whereof he shall claim to have his name inserted, or if he shall claim as a freeman of any city or borough, or place sharing in the election therewith, then he shall in like manner give or cause to be given to the town clerk of such city, borough, or place a notice according to the form numbered (7.) in the said Schedule (B.) or to the like effect; and the overseers and town clerks respectively shall include the names of all persons so claiming as aforesaid in lists, according to the forms numbered (8.) and (9.) respectively in the said Schedule (B.) (*e*).

Lists of claimants to be made.

16. And be it enacted, that it shall be lawful for any person whose name shall be on any list of voters for the time being for any city or borough, or for any person who shall have claimed to have his name inserted in any such list, upon request made by such person, at any time between the hours of ten of the clock in the forenoon and four of the clock in the afternoon of any day, except Sunday, between the 10th day of August and the last day of August, to any overseer or other officer having the custody of any poor-rate book, to inspect such poor-rate book, and make extracts therefrom for any purpose relating to any claim or objection made or intended to be made by or against such persons; and every such overseer or other officer as aforesaid is hereby required, upon such request as aforesaid, to permit such inspection, and the making of such extracts without payment of any fee.

Registered electors and claimants may inspect rate books.

17. And be it enacted, that every person whose name shall have been inserted in any list of voters for any city or borough may object to any other person as not having been entitled on the last day of July next preceding to have his name inserted in any list of voters for the same city or borough; and every person so objecting shall, on or before the 25th day of August in that year, give or cause to be given a notice according to the form numbered (10.) in the said Schedule (B.), or to the like effect, to the overseers who shall have made out the list in which the name of the person so objected to shall have been inserted, or if the person objected to shall

Objections.

Notice of objection.

(*e*) By virtue of sect. 8 of the Act of 1878, post, the *forms* scheduled to that Act are substituted for the *forms* scheduled to this.

6 *Vict. c.* 18.　have been inserted in the list of freemen of any city or borough, except the city of London, then to the town clerk of such city or borough; and every person so objecting shall also give or cause to be left at the place of abode of the person objected to, as stated in the said list, a notice according to the form numbered (11.) in the said Schedule (B.); and every notice of objection shall be signed by the person objecting (*f*).

List of persons objected to to be made.

18. And be it enacted, that the said overseers shall include the names of all persons so objected to in a list, according to the form numbered (12.) in the said Schedule (B); and every town clerk shall include the names of all persons so objected to as freemen in a list, according to the form numbered (13.) in the said Schedule (B.); and the said overseers and town clerks respectively shall sign each of the said lists, and cause copies thereof to be written or printed, and shall publish the said list of persons objected to, and the said list of claimants as aforesaid, on or before the 1st day of September in the said year; and shall keep copies of the said lists, and shall allow the same, and also the notices of objection which they shall have received, to be perused by any person, without payment of any fee, at any time between the hours of ten of the clock in the forenoon and four of the clock in the afternoon of any day, except Sunday, during the first fourteen days of September in the said year, and shall deliver copies of each of such lists to any person requiring the same, on payment of a price for each copy after the rate contained in the table numbered (1.) in the Schedule (D.) to this Act annexed.

Such lists and the lists of claimants to be published.

Copies of lists and notices of objection to be kept for inspection.

Overseers to deliver copies of lists to the town clerk.

19. And be it enacted, that the said overseers shall, on or before the 29th day of August in every year, deliver to the said town clerk a copy of the said list of voters, made out by them as aforesaid, and a copy of the said list of persons who shall have claimed as aforesaid, and a copy of the list of persons objected to as aforesaid.

*　　*　　*　　*　　*　　*　　*

(*f*) By virtue of sect. 8 of the Act of 1878, post, the forms scheduled to that Act are substituted for the forms scheduled to this; and by sect. 26 of the same Act, the notice to a person objected to must state the grounds of objection. A signature by stamped facsimile is good. *Bennett* v. *Brumfitt*, L. R., 3 C. P. 28.

22. And be it enacted, that every precinct or place, whether extra-parochial or otherwise, which shall have no overseers of the poor, shall, for the purpose of making any claim, and making out any list directed by this Act, be deemed to be within the parish or township adjoining thereto and sharing in the right of election to which such claim or list may relate; and if such parish or place shall adjoin two or more parishes or townships situated as aforesaid it shall be deemed to be within the least populous of such parishes or townships, according to the last census for the time being.

6 Vict. c. 18.

Provision as to places having no overseers.

23. And be it enacted, that every notice, list, register, or other document herein required to be published, shall be so published, except where some other mode or place of publication is herein expressly provided, by being fixed in some public and conspicuous situation on the outside of the outer door or outer wall near the door of the buildings hereinafter named for that purpose; (that is to say,) in the case of publication by overseers, every church and public chapel in their parish or township, including places of public worship which do not belong to the established church, and in the case of publication by a town clerk, the town hall, or in either case, if there be no such building as is hereinbefore named for that purpose, then in some public and conspicuous situation within the parish or township, city, borough, or place respectively (*g*).

What shall be publication of notice.

24. And be it enacted, that in all cases in which any notice, list, register, or other document shall, pursuant to the provisions aforesaid, be affixed on or near the door of any church, chapel, town hall, or other place, the same shall continue so fixed for a period including two consecutive Sundays at the least next after the day on or before which the same is hereinbefore required to be published; and in case the same shall be destroyed, mutilated, effaced, or removed before the expiration of such period, the party hereinbefore required to publish the same as aforesaid shall, as soon as conveniently may be, publish in like manner in its place another notice, list, register, or other document, to the like purport and effect with the notice, list, register, paper, or document so destroyed, mutilated, effaced, or removed.

Time for which publication shall be.

(*g*) See further, Act of 1878, sect. 9, post, p. 204.

6 *Vict. c.* 18.

Penalty for
hindering
publication.

25. And be it enacted, that every person who shall wilfully destroy, mutilate, efface, or remove any notice, list, register, or other document so affixed as aforesaid, during the period during which the same is hereinbefore required to remain so affixed, shall for every such offence forfeit any sum not exceeding forty shillings nor less than ten shillings to any person who will sue for the same, to be recovered in a summary manner before any two justices of the peace.

List not in-
validated by
imperfect
publication.

26. And be it enacted, that no list shall be invalidated by reason that it shall not have been affixed in every place and for the full time hereinbefore required for publication thereof, but that the barrister shall proceed to revise and adjudicate upon every such list which shall have been affixed in any place and for any part of the time hereinbefore mentioned in that behalf; but nothing herein contained shall be construed to exempt the overseer, town clerk, or other person charged with the duty of publishing such list as aforesaid from the penalties of his neglect or wilful default.

If no list
made out or
published,
former list to
be in force.

27. And be it enacted, that in case no list of voters shall have been made out for any parish, township, or place in any year, or in case such list shall not have been affixed in any place hereinbefore mentioned in that behalf, the register of voters for that parish, township, or place then in force shall be taken to be the list of voters for that parish, township, or place for the year then next ensuing, and the provisions herein contained respecting any such list of voters shall be taken to apply to such register as aforesaid.

[**28, 29.** Appointment of revising barristers.]

Barristers
may hold
separate
courts.

30. And be it enacted, that where two or more barristers shall be appointed for the same county, riding, parts, or division of a county, or for the same city or borough, they may hold separate courts at the same time and place for the despatch of business, or may hold separate courts at different times and places, as shall be deemed most expedient.

Barrister to
notify his
appointment
to town clerks,
who are to
transmit to
him abstracts
and lists.

31. And be it enacted, that every such revising barrister shall notify his appointment to the clerk of the peace of every county, and to the town clerk of every city and borough of which he shall be appointed to revise the lists; and each clerk of the peace shall, as soon as possible, transmit an abstract of the number of persons objected to by the overseers and by other persons in each parish and township in and for the same county, and the town clerk of every city or borough shall, as soon as possible, transmit an abstract of the said several lists of claimants, and the lists of persons objected to, in each parish or township in and for the same city or borough, to the said barrister, in order that proper times and places for holding courts for the revision of such lists respectively may be appointed.

6 *Vict. c.* 18.

*   *   *   *   *   *   *

33. And be it enacted, that the barrister or barristers appointed to revise the lists of voters for any city or borough shall hold an open court or courts for that purpose within such city or borough, and also within every place sharing in the election for such city or borough, between the 15th day of September inclusive and the *last* (*h*) day of October inclusive in the then current year, and such barrister or barristers shall, seven days at the least before holding any such court or courts, give notice to the town clerk of such city or borough of the time and place of holding the same; and if such barrister shall, in his discretion, deem it expedient to hold his courts at different times and places within the said city or borough, the said barrister shall in such case give notice to the said town clerk of such times and places so appointed, and of the parishes allotted to each court; and the town clerk shall forthwith publish a notice of the time and place of the holding of every such court as aforesaid on the town hall, and on every church and chapel within such city or borough, or, if there be no church or chapel or town hall therein, then in some public and conspicuous place therein.

Barristers to hold courts for revising the lists of voters for boroughs, and give notice thereof to the town clerk, who is to publish the same.

[**34** (*i*). And be it enacted, that the clerk of the peace of every county, at the opening of the first court to be so holden as aforesaid in and for the same county, shall deliver or cause to be delivered to the said barrister or barristers all the lists of voters for the then current year, with the marginal additions

Overseers to attend the courts for their respective parishes, and produce lists of voters, and answer questions.

(*h*) 12th, for municipal revision. Act of 1878, sect. 18, sub-s. 2, post, p. 210.

(*i*) This section appears to refer to county revisions only.

L.C.   N

6 *Vict. c.* 18. as aforesaid, and lists of persons objected to in the said year, relating to the said county, and also one or more printed copies of the register of voters then in force for the said county; and the overseers of every parish and township shall attend the court to be holden for revising the lists relating to their parish or township, and shall deliver to the barrister or barristers holding such court the original notices of claim and notices of objection given to them as aforesaid; and the said clerk of the peace and overseers shall (if required) answer upon oath all such questions as such barrister or barristers may put to them, and produce all documents, papers, and writings in their possession, custody, or power touching any matter herein mentioned (*j*).]

Town clerks, overseers, to attend courts, produce lists and answer questions, &c.

35. And be it enacted, that the town clerk of every city or borough, and the several overseers for the time being of every parish or township therein, and in the city of London the secondaries and the clerks of the several livery companies of such city, shall attend the first court to be holden before every such barrister for every such city or borough, unless they shall have been respectively required by notice to attend at some other court, in which case they shall attend the said court as required; and the said overseers, town clerks, and secondaries respectively shall, at the opening of the said court, deliver to the said barrister the several lists so made by them respectively as aforesaid, and also the original notices of claim and of objection received by them as aforesaid; and the said overseers shall also produce at the said court all rates made for the relief of the poor of their respective parishes or townships between the 6th day of April in the year then last passed and the last day of July in the then present year; and the said town clerks, overseers, secondaries, and clerks respectively shall answer upon oath all such questions as any such barrister may put to them or any of them, and produce all documents, papers, and writings in their possession, custody, or power touching any matter necessary for revising the list of voters;

Power of barrister to require attendance of overseer of past year.

and every such barrister shall have power to require any assessor, collector of taxes, or other officer having the custody of any tax assessment or duplicate, or any overseer or overseers of a past year, or other person having the custody of any

_____

(*j*) This section appears to refer to county revisions only.

poor rate of the then current or any past year, or any relieving officer, and in the city of London the chamberlain or his deputy, to attend before him at any court to be holden by him in pursuance of this Act, and they shall attend accordingly, and answer upon oath all such questions as such barrister may put to them.

6 Vict. c. 18.

*   *   *   *   *   *   *

38. And be it enacted, that the revising barrister shall insert in any list of voters for any city or borough the name of every person omitted who shall be proved to the satisfaction of such barrister to have given due notice of his claim to be inserted in such list, and to have been entitled on the last day of July then next preceding to have his name inserted therein in respect of the qualification described in such notice of claim.

Power of barrister to insert names in lists of borough voters.

39. And be it enacted, that it shall be lawful for any person whose name shall be on any list of voters for any county, city, or borough to oppose the claim of any person so omitted as aforesaid to have his name inserted in any list of voters for the same county, city, or borough; and such person intending to oppose any such claim shall, in the court to be holden as aforesaid for the revision of such list, and before the hearing of the said claim, give notice in writing to the revising barrister of his intention to oppose the said claim, and shall thereupon be admitted to oppose the same, by evidence or otherwise, without any previous or other notice, and shall have the same rights, powers, and liabilities as to costs, appeal, and other matters relating to the hearing and determination of the said claim, as any person who shall have duly objected to the name of any other person being retained on any list of voters, and who shall appear and prove the requisite notices as hereinafter mentioned.

Any person on list of voters may object to claimants.

[**40.** *Corrections by barrister in register*—Superseded by sect. 27 of the Act of 1878, post.]

41. And be it enacted, that every revising barrister holding any court under this Act shall have power to adjourn the same from time to time, and from any one place to any other place within the same county, or within the same city or borough, but so that no such adjourned court shall be holden after the

Power of revising barristers to adjourn their courts, administer oath, &c.

6 *Vict. c.* 18.

last (*i*) day of October in any year; and at every court to be holden as aforesaid by any revising barrister the said barrister shall have power to administer an oath to all persons examined before him, and all parties, whether claiming or objecting or objected to, and all persons whatsoever, may be examined upon oath touching the matters in question; and every person taking any oath or affirmation under this Act, who shall wilfully swear or affirm falsely, shall be deemed guilty of perjury, and at the holding of such respective courts no party or other person shall appear or be attended by counsel; and every such barrister shall upon the hearing in open court finally determine upon the validity of such claims and objections, and shall for that purpose have the same powers and proceed in the same manner (except where otherwise directed by this Act) as the returning officer of any county, city, or borough, according to the laws and usages observed at elections previous to the passing of the said recited Act; and such barrister shall in open court write his initials against the names respectively expunged or inserted, and against any part of the said lists in which any mistake shall have been corrected or any omission supplied or any insertion made by him, and shall sign his name to every page of the several lists so settled.

Persons swearing falsely guilty of perjury.

Barrister in open court to decide upon validity of claims and objections.

Appeal from revising barrister's decision on points of law.

42. And be it enacted, that it shall be lawful for any person who, under the provisions hereinbefore contained, shall have made any claim to have his name inserted in any list, or made any objection to any other person as not entitled to have his name inserted in any list, or whose name shall have been expunged from any list, and who in any such case shall be aggrieved by or dissatisfied with any decision of any revising barrister on any point of law material to the result of such case, either himself or by some person on his behalf, to give to the revising barrister in court, before the rising of the said court, on the same day on which such decision shall have been pronounced, a notice in writing that he is desirous to appeal, and in such notice shall shortly state the decision against which he desires to appeal; and the said

(*i*) 12th, for municipal revision. Act of 1878, sect. 18, sub-s. 2, post, p. 210.

barrister thereupon, if he thinks it reasonable and proper that such appeal should be entertained (*j*), shall state in writing the facts which according to his judgment shall have been established by the evidence in the case, and which shall be material to the matter in question, and shall also state in writing his decision upon the whole case, and also his decision upon the point of law in question appealed against; and such statement shall be made as nearly as conveniently may be in like manner as is now usual in stating any special case for the opinion of the Court of Queen's Bench upon any decision of any court of quarter sessions; and the said barrister shall read the said statement to the appellant in open court, and shall then and there sign the same; and the said appellant, or some one on his behalf, shall at the end of the said statement make a declaration in writing under his hand to the following effect, that is to say, "I appeal from this decision" (*k*); and the said barrister shall then indorse upon every such statement the name of the county and polling district, or city and borough, and of the parish or township to which the same shall relate, and also the Christian name and surname and place of abode of the appellant and of the respondent in the matter of the said appeal, and shall sign and date such indorsement; and the said barrister shall deliver such statement, with such indorsement thereon, to the said appellant, to be by him transmitted to her Majesty's Court of Common Pleas at Westminster in the manner hereinafter* mentioned; and the said barrister shall also deliver a copy of such statement, with the said indorsement thereon, to the respondent in such appeal who shall require the same.

6 Vict. c. 18.

Discretionary statement of case.

Appellant to make a declaration in writing.

Revising barrister to indorse on statement the names of parties, &c.;

and deliver a copy to either party requiring it.

* Sect. 62.

43. And be it enacted, that in the matter of every such appeal the party in whose favour the decision appealed against shall have been given shall be the respondent; but if there be no such party, or if such party, or some one on his behalf, shall in open court decline, and state in writing that he declines, to support the decision appealed against as respondent, then and in every such case it shall be lawful for the said

Who shall be respondent on appeal.

(*j*) As to *obligation* of revising barrister to state case, see Act of 1873, s. 37.

(*k*) The appellant may require the town clerk to be made respondent. Act of 1878, sect. 38, post.

6 *Vict. c.* 18.   revising barrister to name any person who may be interested
in the matter of the said appeal, and who may consent, or the
overseers of any parish or township, or the town clerk of any
city or borough to be, and such person so consenting, or such
overseers or town clerk respectively so named, shall be deemed
to be the respondent or respondents in such appeal (*l*).

Power to
consolidate
appeals.

44. And be it enacted, that if it shall appear to any
revising barrister that the validity of any number of such
claims or objections determined by him at any court as aforesaid depends and has been decided by him upon the same
point or points of law, and the parties or any of them
aggrieved, by or dissatisfied with his decision thereon, shall
have given notice of an intention to appeal therefrom, it shall
in such case be lawful for the said barrister to declare that the
appeals against such decision ought to be consolidated, and
the said barrister shall in such case state in writing the case,
and his decision thereon, in manner hereinbefore mentioned,
and that several appeals depend upon the same decision, and
ought to be consolidated, and shall read such statement, and
sign the same, as hereinbefore mentioned, and thereupon it
shall be lawful for the said barrister to name any person
interested, and consenting, for and on behalf of himself and
all other persons in like manner interested in such appeals,
to be the appellant or respondent respectively in such consolidated appeal, and to prosecute or answer the said appeal,
in like manner as any appellant or respondent might in his
own case under the provisions of this Act, and the person so
named appellant in such consolidated appeal, or some one on
his behalf, shall, at the end of the said statement, make and
sign a declaration in the form or to the effect following;
(that is to say,)

"I, for myself and on behalf of all the other persons who are
interested as appellants in this matter, and whose names are hereunder written, do appeal against this decision, and agree to prosecute
this appeal."

And the person so named respondent in such consolidated
appeal, or some one on his behalf, shall in like manner make

_____

(*l*) The town clerk may be named respondent either alone or in addition to any other person referred to in this section.   Act of 1878, sect. 38,
post.

and sign a declaration in writing in the form or to the effect following; (that is to say,)

" I, for myself and on behalf of all the other persons interested as respondents in this matter, and whose names are hereunder written, do agree to appear and answer this appeal."

And the name, and, where necessary, the particulars of the qualification of every party intended to be joined in such consolidated appeal, shall be written under the aforesaid declaration of the appellant or respondent respectively to which they may respectively refer: provided always, that it shall be lawful for the said barrister, if necessary, in any case to name the overseers of any parish or township, or the town clerk of any city or borough, to be, and they or he so named shall be, the respondents or respondent in such consolidated appeal, without any such declaration being made or signed by them or him as hereinbefore mentioned.

Overseers or town clerk may be named as respondents.

45. And be it enacted, that in and with regard to every such consolidated appeal the like proceeding shall be had and taken and the like rules and regulations shall apply as in the case of any other appeal under this Act; and that every order, judgment, or decision of the said Court of Common Pleas shall be equally valid and effectual for all the purposes of this Act, and binding and conclusive upon all the parties named in or referred to as parties to such consolidated appeal as aforesaid; and that if in any case all or any of the parties to such consolidated appeal shall make or enter into any agreement as to the mode of contributing among themselves to the costs and expenses of such appeal, the said agreement may, upon the application of any party or parties thereto, be made a rule of the said Court of Common Pleas, if the said court shall think fit: provided always, that if any such consolidated appeal shall not be duly prosecuted or answered, it shall be lawful for the said Court of Common Pleas, or for the Lord Chief Justice or any judge of the said court, to give to any party or parties interested in such appeal, upon his or their application, the conduct and direction of the said appeal, or of the answer thereto respectively, as the case may require, instead of or in addition to any person named as aforesaid as appellant or respondent, and in such manner and upon such terms

Consolidated appeals to be conducted as any single appeal.

Agreement for contribution to costs may be made rule of court.

If consolidated appeal not duly prosecuted or answered, court may give conduct of it or of answer to other persons.

6 *Vict. c.* 18.

as the said court or Lord Chief Justice or judge may think fit and order, or to make such other order in the case as may seem meet: provided also, that if after the said barrister shall as aforesaid have declared that the appeal in any case ought to be with others consolidated, any party interested in such appeal shall object and refuse to be a party to or to be bound by any such consolidated appeal, then and in such case the appeal in which such person is interested may proceed separately, but such person so refusing or objecting shall be liable to pay costs to the other party, but shall not be entitled to receive any costs of or in such appeal, unless the said court otherwise order.

Power to barrister to give costs in certain cases to parties claiming or objecting.

46. And be it enacted, that if in any case it shall appear to any revising barrister holding any court as aforesaid that any person shall under this Act have made or attempted to sustain any groundless or frivolous and vexatious claim or objection or title to have any name inserted or retained in any list of voters, it shall be lawful for the said barrister, in his discretion, to make such order as he shall think fit for the payment by such person of the costs or of any part of the costs of any person or persons in resisting such claim or objection or title; and in every such case the said barrister shall make an order in writing, specifying the sum which he shall order to be paid for such costs, and by and to whom and when and where the same sum shall be paid, and shall date and sign the said order, and deliver it to the person or persons to whom the said sum shall therein be ordered to be paid: provided always, that the said sum so ordered to be paid by way of costs shall not in any case exceed the sum of *twenty shillings* (*m*): provided also, that such order for the payment of costs as aforesaid may be made in any case, notwithstanding any party shall have given notice of his intention to appeal against any decision of the revising barrister in the same case; but in case of such appeal the said order for the payment of costs shall be suspended, and shall abide the event of such appeal, unless the Court of Appeal shall otherwise direct; but no appeal shall be allowed or entertained against or only in respect of any such order for the payment of costs:

(*m*) Forty shillings in some cases, by Act of 1878, sect. 27, sub-s. 3.

provided also, that whenever any revising barrister shall have 6 *Vict. c.* 18. made any such order for the payment of any sum of money for costs by any person who shall have made any objection as aforesaid, it shall not be lawful for the said barrister to hear or admit proof of any other objection or notice of objection made or signed by the same person until the sum of money so ordered to be paid by him for costs be paid to the person entitled to receive the same, or deposited in the hands of the said barrister in court, for the use of the person so entitled.

    *   *   *   *   *   *   *

48. And be it enacted, that the lists of voters for each city or borough, signed as aforesaid, shall be forthwith delivered by the revising barrister to the town clerk of the same city or borough; and the said town clerk shall forthwith cause the said lists to be copied and printed in a book; and in the said book the said lists shall be arranged and every name numbered according to the directions aforesaid with regard to the county lists, so far as the same are applicable; and the said town clerk shall sign and deliver the said book on or before the said last day of *November* (n) to the returning officer of the same city or borough, to be by him and his successors as returning officer safely kept for the purposes hereinafter mentioned.

Borough lists to be delivered to the town clerks, and copied into a book.

49. And be it enacted, that the said printed book or books so signed as aforesaid by the clerk of the peace or town clerk respectively, and given into the custody of the sheriff of any county, or the returning officer of any city or borough, as the case may be, shall be the register of persons entitled to vote at any election of a member or members to serve in Parliament which shall take place in and for the same county, city, or borough respectively, between the last day of November in the year wherein such register shall have been made and the 1st day of December in the succeeding year: provided always, that the register of electors now in force shall be the register in force until the 1st day of December, 1843; and the clerk of the peace of every county, and the town clerk of every city or borough respectively, shall keep printed copies of the said

Books to be the register of voters for one year.

Copies of registers to be printed for sale.

(n) December. Act of 1867, sect. 38, post.

register for such county, city, or borough, and shall deliver such copies of such register, or of any part thereof, to any person applying for the same, upon payment of a price after the rate contained in the table numbered (2.) in the Schedule (D.) to this Act annexed: provided always, that no person shall be entitled to a copy of any part of any register relating to any parish or township without taking or paying for the whole that relates to such parish or township.

Assessors and other officers neglecting to attend when summoned by revising barrister, liable to be fined.

50. And be it enacted, that any assessor or collector of taxes or other officer, or any overseer or overseers of the poor, or other persons having the custody of any poor-rate book for any past year, or any assistant overseer or relieving officer, who shall wilfully refuse or neglect, when duly required by summons under the hand of any revising barrister, to attend before such barrister at any court to be holden as aforesaid, according to the exigency of such summons, shall, upon proof before him of the service of such summons, be liable to pay by way of fine for every such offence a sum of money not exceeding five pounds nor less than twenty shillings, to be imposed by and at the discretion of the said barrister holding any such court as aforesaid.

Power to barristers to fine overseers for neglect of duty.

51. And be it enacted, that any overseer of any parish or township who shall wilfully refuse or neglect to make out any list, or who shall wilfully neglect to insert therein the name of any person who shall have given due notice of claim, or who in making out the list of voters for any city or borough shall wilfully and without any reasonable cause omit the name of any person duly qualified to be inserted in such list, or who shall wilfully and without reasonable cause insert in such list the name of any person not duly qualified, or who shall wilfully refuse or neglect to publish any notice or list, or copy of the part of the register of voters relating to his parish or township, at the time and in the manner required by this Act, or who shall wilfully refuse or neglect to deliver to the clerk of the peace the copy of the lists of claimants and of persons objected to, and the copies of the register, as required by this Act, or who shall wilfully refuse or neglect to deliver to the town clerk of the city or borough the copies of the several lists as required by this Act, or who shall wilfully refuse or neglect to attend the court for revising the lists of voters of his parish or township, or to attend any revising barrister when required by any summons as aforesaid, or who shall wilfully refuse or neglect to deliver to the barrister or barristers holding any such court the several lists to be made out by them as aforesaid, or who shall be wilfully guilty of any other breach of duty in the execution of this Act, shall for every such offence be liable to pay by way of fine a sum of money not exceeding five pounds nor less than twenty shillings, to be imposed by and at the discretion of any barrister holding any court for the revision of any list of the parish or township of such overseer: provided always, that nothing herein contained as to any fine as aforesaid shall affect or abridge any right of action against any overseer or other person liable to any fine as aforesaid, or any liability such overseer or other person may incur under or by virtue of this Act or the said recited Act (*o*).

6 *Vict. c.* 18.

52. And be it enacted, that every revising barrister, when and so often as he shall impose any such fine as aforesaid, shall at the same time in open court, by an order in writing under his hand, stating the sum payable for such fine, direct by and to whom and when the same shall be paid, and the person to whom the said sum shall be so ordered to be paid shall receive the same, and in every case where the offence for which the said fine shall have been so imposed shall relate to the formation of the register of voters for any county he shall pay over the sum so received by him to the clerk of the peace of the same county, and in every case where such offence shall relate to the formation of the register of voters for any city or borough he shall pay over the sum so received by him to the town clerk of the same city or borough, or to the said secondaries, as the case may require.

Fines, to whom payable, and to what purpose to be applied.

53. And be it enacted, that the clerk of the peace of every county and the town clerk of every city or borough respectively shall keep an account of all monies to be received by him or them for or on account of the sale of any copies of the register as aforesaid, or for or by way of fine imposed as

Clerk of the peace and town clerk to account for and pay over all monies received by them.

(*o*) This section is extended to cases under the Act of 1878 by sect. 29 of that Act, p. 218, *post*.

aforesaid; and the said clerk of the peace shall pay over or account for all such monies received by him to the treasurer of the same county, to be applied in aid of the county rate; and the said town clerk shall pay over or account for all such monies so received by them to and amongst the overseers of the several parishes and townships within every city or borough; and the share of each parish or township shall be calculated as nearly as may be according to the same relative proportion as the number of persons whose names shall appear in the list of the said parish or township shall bear to the number in all the other lists upon the same register, and the said monies, together with all monies received by any overseers from the sale by them of any lists, shall be paid and applied by the said overseers in aid of the monies collected for the relief of the poor.

*　　　*　　　*　　　*　　　*　　　*　　　*

Expenses of town clerks and returning officers, how to be defrayed.

55. And be it enacted, that all the expenses incurred by any town clerk or returning officer of any city or borough in carrying into effect the provisions of this Act, shall be defrayed out of the monies to be collected for the relief of the poor in the several parishes and townships within the same city or borough; and the sum to be contributed by every such parish or township shall be calculated, as nearly as may be, according to the same relative proportion as the number of persons whose names shall appear in the list of the said parish or township shall bear to the number in all the other lists upon the same register; and an account of all the said expenses so incurred, and also an account of the sum to be contributed for defraying the same by each parish or township as aforesaid, shall, as soon as may be after the said expenses shall have been so incurred, be laid before the common council or town council of the said city or borough, or if there be no such council in any city or borough, then before the justices of the peace at the quarter sessions to be holden in and for the county in which the same city or borough is situate; and the said council or the said justices respectively shall, when they allow the said accounts, make and give to the said town clerk a certificate of the total sum allowed by such council or justices in respect of the said expenses, and also a certificate of the sum to be paid by and as the contribution of each of the said parishes or townships towards defraying the same; and thereupon it shall be lawful for the overseers of every such parish or township, and they are hereby required, out of the first monies to be collected for the relief of the poor, to pay the sum in such certificate mentioned to be paid by and as the contribution of the said parish or township to the said town clerk (*p*).

*　　*　　*　　*　　*　　*　　*

57. And be it enacted, that an account of all expenses incurred by the overseers of every parish or township in carrying into effect the provisions of this Act, shall be laid before the revising barrister at the court at which the list of voters for such parish or township shall be revised; and the said barrister shall sign and give to the said overseers a certificate of the sum which he shall allow to be due to them in respect of the said expenses (*q*); and it shall be lawful for the said overseers to receive the sum so certified to be due to them from and out of the first monies thereafter to be collected for the relief of the poor in the same parish or township.

> Expenses of overseers, how to be defrayed.

*　　*　　*　　*　　*　　*　　*

59. And be it enacted, that every barrister appointed to revise any lists of voters under this Act shall be paid the sum of two hundred guineas, by way of remuneration to him, and in satisfaction of his travelling and other expenses; and every such barrister, after the termination of his last sitting, shall forward his appointment to the Commissioners of her Majesty's Treasury, who shall make an order for the payment of the above sums to every such barrister, and all such sums shall be paid out of the Consolidated Fund of the united kingdom of Great Britain and Ireland: provided always, that in the case of any barrister having been appointed under this Act to revise any lists of voters in addition to the barrister or barristers originally appointed, such barrister, instead of the sums above mentioned, shall be paid at the rate of five guineas for every day that he shall be so employed, together with three guineas each day for his travelling and other expenses; and every such last-mentioned barrister, after the termination of his last

> Remuneration of revising barristers.

(*p*) See sect. 31 of Act of 1867, post, p. 198.
(*q*) By sect. 32 of the Act of 1868, post, p. 200, this certificate is con clusive.

sitting, shall lay or cause to be laid before the Commissioners of her Majesty's Treasury his appointment, and a statement of the number of days during which he shall have been so employed; and the said commissioners shall make an order for the payment of such sum as shall thereupon appear to be due to every such last-mentioned barrister, and every such sum shall also be paid out of the said Consolidated Fund, but so that no such barrister shall be entitled to or in any case be paid more than the sum of two hundred guineas (*q*).

Appeals to be heard by Queen's Bench Division of High Court.

60. And be it enacted, that all appeals or matters of appeal from or in respect of any decision of any revising barrister entertained in manner hereinbefore mentioned shall be prosecuted, heard, and determined in and by her Majesty's Court of Common Pleas at Westminster (*r*), according to the ordinary rules and practice of that court with respect to special cases, so far as the same may be applicable, and not inconsistent with the provisions of this Act, or in such manner and form, and subject to such rules and regulations, as the said court from time to time, by any rule or order made for regulating the practice and proceedings in such appeals, shall order and direct.

*   *   *   *   *   *   *

Notice of appeal to be given by appellant.

62. And be it enacted, that every appellant who shall intend to prosecute his appeal shall, within the first four days in the Michaelmas term next after the decision to which such appeal shall relate, transmit to the masters of the said Court of Common Pleas the statement in writing so signed by the said revising barrister as aforesaid, and shall also therewith give or send a notice, signed by him, stating therein his intention to prosecute the said appeal, and the said appellant shall also give or send a notice, signed by him, to the respondent in the said appeal, stating his said intention duly to prosecute

Appeals to be entered in a book.

such appeal in the said court; and one of the masters of the said court, to be nominated for that purpose by the Lord Chief Justice of the said court, shall forthwith enter every appeal of which he shall have received due notice from the appellant as aforesaid in a book to be kept by him for that purpose.

(*q*) As to further remuneration in respect of municipal revision, see last paragraph of sect. 30 of the Act of 1878, post, p. 219.

(*r*) The appeal is now to the Queen's Bench Division of the High Court.

63. And be it enacted, that the judges of the said Court of Common Pleas shall, as soon as may be after the fourth day of Michaelmas term in every year, make arrangements for hearing the appeals entered as aforesaid, and shall appoint such certain day or days, either in term time or in time of vacation, as they may think fit and necessary, but as early as conveniently may be, for the purpose of hearing and deciding such appeals; and the said judges shall cause public notice to be given of the time and place so appointed by them for that purpose, and of the order in which such appeals will be heard.

6 *Vict. c.* 18.

Court to give notice of the time and place of hearing appeals.

64. And be it enacted, that no appeal or matter of appeal whatsoever shall, in any case, except where the conduct and direction of the appeal, or of the answer thereto, shall have been given by order of the Court of Common Pleas or of any judge thereof to any person, be entertained or heard by the said court unless notice shall have been given by the appellant to the masters of the said court at the time and in the manner hereinbefore mentioned; and no appeal shall be heard by the said court in any case where the said respondent shall not appear, unless the said appellant shall prove that due notice of his intention to prosecute such appeal was given or sent to the said respondent ten days at least before the day appointed for the hearing of such appeal: provided always, that if it shall appear to the said court that there has not been reasonable time to give or send such notice in any case, it shall be lawful for the said court to postpone the hearing of the appeal in such case, as to the said court shall seem meet.

No appeal to be entertained unless notice given.

65. And be it enacted, that no appeal or notice of appeal under this Act shall be received or allowed against any decision of any revising barrister upon any question of fact only, or upon the admissibility or effect of any evidence or admission adduced or made in any case to establish any matter of fact only: provided always, that if the said court shall be of opinion in any case that the statement of the matter of the appeal is not sufficient to enable them to give judgment in law, it shall be lawful for the said court to remit the said statement to the revising barrister by whom it shall have been signed, in order that the case may be more fully stated.

No appeal on fact or evidence.

Court may remit case to be more fully stated.

Decisions of High Court to be final.

66. And be it enacted, that every judgment or decision of the said court shall be final and conclusive in the case upon the point of law adjudicated upon (*r*), and shall be binding upon every committee of the House of Commons appointed for the trial of any petition complaining of an undue election or return of any member or members to serve in parliament.

Decisions of court to be notified to the sheriff or returning officer, and register to be altered conformably.

67. And be it enacted, that whenever by any judgment or order of the said court any decision or order of any revising barrister shall be reversed or altered, so as to require any alteration or correction of the register of voters for any county, or for any city or borough, notice of the said judgment or order of the said court shall be forthwith given by the said court to the sheriff or returning officer, as the case may be, having the custody of such register, and the said notice shall be in writing under the hand of one of the masters of the said court, and shall specify exactly every alteration or correction to be made, in pursuance of the said judgment or order, in the said register; and such sheriff or returning officer respectively shall, upon the receipt of the said notice, alter or correct the said register accordingly, and shall sign his name against every such alteration or correction, in the said register, and shall safely keep and hand over to his successor every such notice received by him from the said court as aforesaid, together with the said register.

Copies of decisions on appeals to be admissible in evidence.

68. And be it enacted, that a copy of any order or decision of the said court, such copy purporting to be signed by one of the masters of the said court, shall be sufficient evidence in all cases, without proof of the signature of the said master, and shall have the like force and effect as any entry made in any list or register of voters under this or the said recited Act.

＊　　＊　　＊　　＊　　＊　　＊　　＊

High Court may give costs of appeal.

70. And be it enacted, that it shall be lawful for the said court to make such order respecting the payment of the costs of any appeal, or of any part of such costs, as to the said court shall seem meet: provided always, that it shall not be

---

(*r*) By sect. 14 of the Judicature Act, 1881 (44 & 45 Vict. c. 68), there may, by leave of the High Court, be a further appeal to the Court of Appeal, whose decision would be final.

lawful for the said court in any case to make any order for costs against or in favour of any respondent or person named as respondent as aforesaid, unless he shall appear before the said court in support of the decision of the revising barrister in question.

6 *Vict. c.* 18.

71. And be it enacted, that in case any sum of money by the order of any revising barrister as aforesaid directed to be paid by any person by way of fine or for costs shall not be paid according to the terms of such order, it shall be lawful for any justice of the peace and he is hereby required, upon proof before him that a true copy of the said order hath been served upon or left at the usual place of abode of the person in the said order directed to pay such sum, and that the said sum hath been demanded of such person, and that he hath refused or neglected to pay the same, by warrant under his hand and seal to order the said sum of money, together with the costs of and attending the said warrant, to be levied by distress and sale of the goods and chattels of such person so making default which may be found within the jurisdiction of the said justice; and the overplus, if any, after the said sum of money and costs, and the charges of such distress and sale, are deducted, shall be returned, upon demand, to the owner of the said goods and chattels; provided always, that no certiorari or other writ or process for the removal of any such order or warrant, or of any order or warrant to be made or issued on account of a false charge of personation in the manner hereinafter provided, or any proceeding thereon respectively, into any of her Majesty's courts at Westminster, shall be allowed or granted.

Costs and fines to be recovered by distress and sale of the parties goods.

No certiorari allowed.

*   *   *   *   *   *   *

[**85—89.** *Personation.*—See these sections, post, p. 257.]

*   *   *   *   *   *   *

101. And be it enacted, that throughout this Act, in the construction thereof, except there be something in the subject or context inconsistent with or repugnant to such construction, the word "county" shall extend to and mean any county, riding, parts or division of a county, respectively returning a knight or knights of the shire to serve in Parliament; and the words "city or borough" shall extend to and

Interpretation clause.

Meaning of the word "county:"

"city or borough:"

L.C.   O

6 *Vict. c.* 18.　mean any city, borough, town corporate, cinque port, district, or place within England and Wales returning a member or members to serve in Parliament, other than counties at large, and ridings, parts and divisions of counties at large, and to every place sharing in the election of a member for any city or borough, and shall also include the town of Berwick-upon-Tweed; that the words "clerk of the peace" shall compre-

" clerk of the peace:"

" town clerk:"

hend and apply to any deputy or other person executing the duties of such clerk of the peace; and the words "town clerk" shall, except in regard to the cities of London and Westminster and the borough of Southwark, extend to and mean any person executing the duties of town clerk, or if in any city or borough there shall be no such officer as town clerk, then to any officer executing the same or like duties as usually devolve upon the town clerk, or if in any city or borough there be no such person, then to the returning officer of such city or borough, or to such person as the returning officer may appoint for that purpose, which he is hereby authorized to do; and the words "barrister" or "barristers"

" barrister:"

shall respectively be taken to include a serjeant or serjeants-at-law; and the words "returning officer" shall apply to every person or persons to whom by virtue of his or their office, under any law, custom, or statute, the execution of any writ or precept doth or shall belong for the election of a member or members to serve in Parliament, by whatever name or title such person or persons may be called; and the words "parish or township" shall extend to and mean every parish, township, village, hamlet, district, or place maintaining its own poor; and the words "overseers" or "overseers of the poor" shall extend to and mean all persons who by virtue of any office or appointment shall execute the duties of overseers of the poor, by whatever name or title such persons may be called, and in whatsoever manner they may be appointed, and that all matters by this Act directed to be done by the overseers of a parish or township may be lawfully done by the major part of such overseers; and that wherever any notice is by this Act (*s*) required to be given or sent to the overseers of any parish or township, it shall be sufficient

" returning officer:"

" parish or township:"

" overseers" or " overseers of the poor."

Provision as to service of notices.

(*s*) Or by the Act of 1878. See sect. 40 of that Act, post.

if such notice shall be delivered to any one of such overseers, or shall be left at his place of abode, or at his office or other place for transacting parochial business, or shall be sent by the post, free of postage, or the postage thereof being first paid, addressed to the overseers of the particular parish or township, naming the parish or township, and the county, city, or borough respectively, to which the notice to be so sent may relate, without adding any place of abode of such overseers ; and that wherever by this Act any notice is required to be given or sent to any person or persons whatsoever, or public officer, it shall be sufficient if such notice be sent by the post in the manner and subject to the regulations hereinbefore provided with respect to sending notices of objection by the post, free of postage, or the postage thereof being first paid, addressed with a sufficient direction to the person or persons to whom the same ought to be given or sent, at his or their usual place of abode; and that all provisions in this Act relative to any matters to be done by or with regard to justices of the peace for counties, or sessions of the peace for counties, or clerks of the peace for counties, or treasurers of counties, shall extend to the justices, sessions, clerks of the peace, and treasurers of the several ridings of Yorkshire and parts of Lincolnshire ; and that the town clerk for the time being for the borough of Newport in the Isle of Wight shall for the purposes of this Act be deemed and taken to be the clerk of the peace for the county of the Isle of Wight ; and that all the said respective justices, sessions, and clerks of the peace shall have power to do the several matters required by this Act, as well within places of exclusive jurisdiction as without ; and that no misnomer or inaccurate description of any person, place, or thing named or described in any schedule to this Act annexed, or in any list or register of voters, or in any notice required by this Act, shall anywise prevent or abridge the operation of this Act with respect to such person, place, or thing, provided that such person, place, or thing, shall be so denominated in such schedule, list, register, or notice, as to be commonly understood ; and that the word "oath" shall include affirmation, where by law such affirmation is required or allowed to be taken in place of an oath ; and where the subject or context requires it, every word importing the

[marginal notes:] Justices, sessions, clerks of the peace, and treasurers of counties.

Misnomer not to vitiate.

" Oath."

Singular.

6 *Vict. c.* 18.   singular number only shall extend and be applied to several
                    persons or things as well as one person or thing; and every
Plural.   word importing the plural number shall extend and be applied
                    to one person or thing as well as several persons or things.

*   *   *   *   *   *   *

SCHEDULE (D).

[See s. 18.]

No. 1.

TABLE of RATES of PAYMENT to be demanded and paid for any List
or Copy of a List (other than a Register), where a Payment is
required and authorized by this Act.

For any List or Copy of a List containing any Number of Persons
Names—

	s.	d.
Not exceeding 100 names	0	6
Exceeding 100 and not exceeding 200 . .	1	0
Exceeding 200 and not exceeding 300 . .	1	6
Exceeding 300 and not exceeding 400 . .	2	0
Exceeding 400	2	6

See s. 49.]

No. 2.

TABLE of RATES of PAYMENT to be demanded and paid for any
Copy of a Register or part of any Register, where a Payment
is required and authorized by this Act.

For every Copy of any Register or any part of any Register containing any Number of Persons Names—

	s.	d.
Not exceeding 1,000 names . . .	1	0
Exceeding 1,000 and not exceeding 3,000 .	2	6
Exceeding 3,000 and not exceeding 6,000 .	5	0
Exceeding 6,000 and not exceeding 9,000 .	7	6
Exceeding 9,000 . , . . .	10	0

COUNTY VOTERS REGISTRATION ACT, 1865.

28 Vict. c. 36.   *An Act to amend the Law relating to the
Registration of County Voters, and to the Powers and
Duties of Revising Barristers in certain cases.*

[2nd June, 1865.

[See sect. 26 of Act of 1878, post, p. 212.]

Person
objected to
need not give
evidence
except as to
ground of
objection.

7. No person objected to under the provisions of this Act
shall be required to give evidence before the revising barrister
in support of his right to be registered, otherwise than as such
right shall be called in question in such ground or grounds of
objection.

8. Every separate ground of objection shall be treated by the revising barrister as a separate objection; and for every ground of objection which, in the opinion of the revising barrister, shall have been groundlessly or frivolously and vexatiously stated in a notice of objection, he shall, on the application of the person objected to, or any one on his behalf, and upon production of the notice of objection, award costs against the objector to the amount at least of two shillings and sixpence, and this though the name of the person objected to be expunged upon some other ground of objection stated in the same notice of objection.

28 *Vict. c.* 36.

Every separate ground of objection to be treated separately.

Representation of the People Act, 1867.

30 & 31 Vict. c. 102. *An Act further to amend the Laws relating to the Representation of the People in England and Wales.* [15th August, 1867.

Whereas it is expedient to amend the laws relating to the representation of the people in England and Wales:

Be it enacted by the Queen's most excellent Majesty, by and with the advice and consent of the Lords spiritual and temporal, and Commons, in this present Parliament assembled, and by the authority of the same, as follows:

1. This Act shall be cited for all purposes as "The Representation of the People Act, 1867."

Short title.

*   *   *   *   *   *   *

28. Where any poor rate due on the 5th of January in any year from an occupier in respect of premises capable of conferring the franchise for a borough remains unpaid on the 1st of June following, the overseers whose duty it may be to collect such rates shall, on or before the 20th of the same month of June, unless such rate has previously been paid, or has been duly demanded by a demand note, to be served in like manner as the notice in this section referred to, give or cause to be given a notice *in the form set forth in the schedule* (*E*) *to this Act* (*t*) to every such occupier. The notice shall be deemed to be duly given if delivered to the occupier or left at

Notice of rate in arrear to be given by overseers to voters.

(*t*) Form C. under the Act of 1878 is substituted for this form by sect. 8 of that Act, post, p. 204.

Penalty for
wilfully with-
holding
notice.

his last or usual place of abode, or with some person on the premises in respect of which the rate is payable (*u*). Any overseer who shall wilfully withhold such notice, with intent to keep such occupier off the list or register of voters for the said borough, shall be deemed guilty of a breach of duty in the execution of the Registration Acts.

Overseers to
make out a
list of persons
in arrear of
rates, which
shall be open
to perusal
without fee.

29. The overseers of every parish wholly or partly within a borough shall, on or before the 22nd of July in every year, make out a list containing the name and place of abode of every person who shall not have paid, on or before the 20th of the same month, all poor rates which shall have become payable from him in respect of any premises within the said parish before the 5th of January then last past, and the overseers shall keep the said list, to be perused by any person, without payment of any fee, at any time between the hours of ten of the clock in the forenoon and four of the clock in the afternoon of any day except Sunday during the first fourteen days after the said 22nd of July. Any overseer wilfully

Penalty on
overseer for
neglect.

neglecting or refusing to make out such list, or to allow the same to be perused as aforesaid, shall be deemed guilty of a breach of duty in the execution of the Registration Acts.

*   *   *   *   *   *   *

Definition of
"expenses of
registration."

* Page 188.

31. The word "expenses" contained in the sections fifty-four and fifty-five of the said Registration Act of the session of the sixth year of the reign of her present Majesty, chapter eighteen,* shall be deemed to and shall include and apply to all proper and reasonable fees and charges of any clerk of the peace of any county, or of any town clerk of any city or borough, to be hereafter made or charged by him in any year for his trouble, care, and attention in the performance of the services and duties imposed upon him by the same Act or by this Act, in addition to any money actually paid or disbursed by him for or in respect of any such services or duties as aforesaid.

*   *   *   *   *   *   *

Alteration as
to time for
delivery of
lists and com-
mencement of
register of
voters.

38. The forty-seventh and forty-eighth sections of the Act of the sixth year of the reign of her present Majesty, chapter eighteen, relating to the transmission and delivery of the book

---

(*u*) See sect. 10 of the Act of 1878, post, p. 205.

or books containing the lists of voters to the sheriff and re- 30 & 31 *Vict.*
c. 102.
turning officer, shall be construed as if the word "December"
were substituted in those sections for the word "November,"
and the said book or books shall be the register of persons
entitled to vote for the county or borough to which such
register relates at any election which takes place during the
year commencing on the 1st day of January next after such
register is made.

*   *   *   *   *   *   *

59. This Act, so far as is consistent with the tenor thereof, This Act, as far as consistent, to be construed with enactments now in force.
shall be construed as one with the enactments for the time
being in force relating to the representation of the people and
with the Registration Acts.

Parliamentary Electors Registration Act, 1868.

31 & 32 Vict. c. 58. *An Act to amend the Law of Registration so far as relates to the Year One thousand eight hundred and sixty-eight, and for other purposes relating thereto.*   [16th July, 1868.

Whereas it is expedient to make provision for expediting
the completion of the registration of parliamentary electors
during the present year, and to make certain amendments in
the law relating to elections:

Be it enacted, as follows:

Preliminary.

1. "Principal Act" in this Act shall mean the Act passed Definition of principal Act.
in the session of the sixth and seventh years of the reign of
her present Majesty, chapter eighteen, intituled "An Act to
amend the Law for the Registration of Persons entitled to
Vote, and to define certain Rights of Voting, and to regulate
certain Proceedings in the Election of Members to serve in
Parliament for England and Wales," as amended by "The
County Voters Registration Act, 1865."

2. This Act shall be construed as one with the principal This and principal Act construed as one.
Act, and may be cited for all purposes as "The Parliamentary Electors Registration Act, 1868."

*   *   *   *   *   *   *

Recovery of
expenses by
town clerks
and returning
officers.

23. Whereas it is expedient to provide a summary remedy for the recovery by town clerks and returning officers of sums of money due to them in respect of expenses incurred in pursuance of the Registration Acts: be it enacted, that if the overseers of any parish or township refuse or neglect to pay to the town clerk or returning officer of any borough, out of the first monies to be collected for the relief of the poor, any contribution or sum required to be paid to him by the fifty-fifth section of the principal Act, or any Act amending the same, or any part of such contribution or sum, it shall be lawful for any justice of the peace for the county or place within which such parish or township is wholly or in part situate, upon information and complaint in writing, and after seven days' notice in writing to be served upon such overseers or one of them, by warrant under his hand to levy such contribution or sum by distress and sale of the goods of the offender or offenders, together with all costs occasioned by the making of such complaint, service of such summons, and the obtaining and executing such warrant.

*　　*　　*　　*　　*　　*　　*

Provision
when borough
situate partly
in one circuit
and partly in
another.

25. Where a borough is situated partly in one circuit and partly in another the judge of the circuit in which the greater part in extent of such borough is situate shall appoint the revising barrister for such borough.

*　　*　　*　　*　　*　　*　　*

Certificate of
revising
barrister to
be conclusive.
* Page 189.

32. The certificate given to the overseers by the revising barrister under section fifty-seven of the principal Act * for the expenses incurred by them in carrying into effect the provisions of the Registration Acts shall be final and conclusive; provided nevertheless, that such certificate shall be signed by the revising barrister in open court, and any ratepayer present shall have a right to inspect the account of expenses delivered in by the overseers, and to object to any item or items included therein, before such account is allowed by the revising barrister, who shall hear any such objection and make a decision respecting the same.

PARLIAMENTARY AND MUNICIPAL REGISTRATION ACT, 1878.

41 & 42 Vict. c. 26. *An Act to amend the Law relating to the Registration of Voters in Parliamentary Boroughs and the Enrolment of Burgesses in Municipal Boroughs, and relating to certain rights of voting and proceedings before and appeals from Revising Barristers.*
[22nd July, 1878.

CONTENTS:

41 & 42 *Vict*
c. 26.

Short titles.

BE IT ENACTED, as follows :

1. This Act may be cited as the Parliamentary and Municipal Registration Act, 1878.

The Acts referred to in this Act by short titles may be cited for all purposes by those titles respectively.

Extent of Act.

2. This Act shall not extend to Scotland or Ireland.

Commencement of Act.

3. This Act shall come into operation on the 1st of February, 1879, which date is in this Act referred to as the commencement of this Act.

Definitions.

4. In this Act—

The term "Reform Act, 1832," means the Act of the session of the second and third years of the reign of King William the Fourth, chapter forty-five, "to amend the representation of the people in England and Wales : "

The term "Municipal Corporation Acts" means the Municipal Corporation Act, 1835 (*x*), and the Acts amending the same (*y*) :

The term "Parliamentary Registration Act, 1843," means the Act of the session of the sixth and seventh years of the reign of her present Majesty, chapter eighteen, "to amend the law for the registration of persons entitled to vote, and to define certain rights of voting and to regulate certain proceedings in the election of members to serve in Parliament for England and Wales : "

The term "Parliamentary Registration Acts" means the Parliamentary Registration Act, 1843, and any enactment amending the same or otherwise relating to the registration of parliamentary electors :

The term "parliamentary borough" means any borough, city, county of a city, county of a town, place, or combination of places returning a member or members to serve in Parliament, and not being a county at large, or riding, part, or division of a county at large :

The term "municipal borough" means any place for the time being subject to the Municipal Corporation Acts :

(*x*) 5 & 6 Will. 4, c. 76, repealed but in great part re-enacted by the Act of 1882, ante.

(*y*) See the titles of these Acts, which are repealed, but in great part re-enacted by the Act of 1882, p. 139, ante.

The term "parliamentary voter" means a person entitled to be registered as a voter and when registered to vote at the election of a member or members to serve in Parliament for a parliamentary borough :

The term "burgess" has the same meaning as in the Municipal Corporation Acts :

The term "parish" means a place for which a separate poor rate is or can be made, or for which a separate overseer is or can be appointed :

Other terms used in this Act have the same meaning as in the Parliamentary Registration Acts.

5. (*z*) In and for the purposes of the Reform Act, 1832, and the Municipal Corporation Acts the terms "house, warehouse, counting-house, shop, or other building," shall include any part of a house where that part is separately occupied for the purpose of any trade, business, or profession ; and any such part may for the purpose of describing the qualification be described as "office," "chambers," "studio," or by any like term applicable to the case.

In and for the purposes of the Representation of the People Act, 1867, the term "dwelling-house" shall include any part of a house where that part is separately occupied as a dwelling, and the term "lodgings" shall include any apartments or place of residence, whether furnished or unfurnished, in a dwelling-house.

For the purposes of any of the Acts referred to in this section, where an occupier is entitled to the sole and exclusive use of any part of a house, that part shall not be deemed to be occupied otherwise than separately by reason only that the occupier is entitled to the joint use of some other part.

The interpretation contained in this section of "dwelling-house" shall be in substitution for the interpretation thereof contained in section sixty-one of the Representation of the People Act, 1867, but not so as to affect any of the other provisions of the said Act relating to rating.

*   *   *   *   *   *   *

7. In every parliamentary borough and in every municipal borough every period of qualification for parliamentary voters and burgesses respectively, which is now computed by refer-

Margin notes: 41 & 42 *Vict.* c. 26. — Explanation of terms. "House," &c. — "Dwelling-house." "Lodgings." — Separate occupation of part notwithstanding joint occupation of other part. — Period of qualification.

(*z*) Such parts of this section as relate to municipal elections are substantially repeated by sect. 31 of the Municipal Corporations Act, 1882, ante, p. 20. The paragraphs printed in small type have reference to parliamentary elections only.

ence to the last day of July (*a*), shall, instead of being so computed, be computed by reference to the 15th of July.

The term "period of qualification" in this section shall include any period of occupation, residence, possession, receipt of rents and profits, and non-receipt of parochial relief or other alms.

Forms relating to registration in parliamentary boroughs and burgess lists in certain municipal boroughs.

8. In every parliamentary borough and in every municipal borough the whole or part of the area whereof is co-extensive with or included in the area of a parliamentary borough, the forms in the schedule to this Act, or forms to the like effect, varied as circumstances require, shall be used for the purposes for which the same are applicable respectively, and shall, for the purposes of the Parliamentary Registration Acts and this Act be deemed to be substituted for any corresponding forms in the schedules to the Parliamentary Registration Acts.

The said schedule and the notes thereto shall be construed and have effect as if enacted in the body of this Act.

All precepts, instructions, proceedings, notices and lists relating to the registration of parliamentary voters or enrolment of burgesses shall be expressed in such manner and form as may be necessary to carry the provisions of this Act into effect.

Publication of notices and lists in post and telegraph offices, &c.

9. In every parliamentary borough and in every municipal borough the whole or part of the area whereof is co-extensive with or included in the area of a parliamentary borough, any notice or list which is by the Parliamentary Registration Acts or this Act directed to be published by overseers shall be published by them not only in the manner directed by those Acts, but also by being affixed and kept in some public and conspicuous position in or near every post office and telegraph office occupied by or on behalf of her Majesty's Postmaster General, and in or near every public or municipal or parochial office within the parish to which the list relates.

All the provisions of those Acts with respect to the publication of notices or lists shall apply to the publication to be made under this section.

(*a*) When this Act was passed the Municipal Corporations Act, 1869 (32 & 33 Vict. c. 55), was in force, and by sect. 1 of that Act (now replaced by sect. 9 of the Act of 1882), the period of qualification by occupation was computed with reference to the last day of July.

10. Where the whole or part of the area of a municipal borough is co-extensive with or included in the area of a parliamentary borough, section eleven of the Parliamentary Registration Act, 1843,* and section twenty-eight of the Representation of the People Act, 1867† (which relate to the notices to be published and given with respect to rates and taxes in arrear), shall, as amended by this Act, extend with the necessary modifications to the rates of which the payment is required as a condition of enrolment on the burgess roll, and all the provisions of those sections as so amended shall apply to the overseers of parishes situate wholly or partly in a municipal borough accordingly.

Any notice required to be given under this section shall be deemed to be duly given if delivered to the occupier or left at his last or usual place of abode, or with some person on the premises in respect of which the rate is payable.

In case no such person can be found, then the notice required to be given under this section or under section twenty-eight of the Representation of the People Act, 1867,* shall be deemed to be duly given if affixed upon some conspicuous part of the premises.

Any overseer who with intent to keep an occupier off the list or register of voters for a parliamentary borough, or off the burgess lists or burgess roll of a municipal borough, shall wilfully withhold any notice required by this section to be given to such occupier, shall be deemed guilty of a breach of duty in the execution of this Act.

Section twenty-nine of the Representation of the People Act, 1867, shall extend and be applicable to every parish situate wholly or partly within a municipal borough whose burgess lists are revised under this Act.

11. Every registrar of births and deaths whose sub-district includes the whole or part of any parliamentary borough or any municipal borough the whole or part of the area whereof is co-extensive with or included in the area of a parliamentary borough, shall transmit by post or otherwise to the overseers of every parish the whole or any part of which is included in the parliamentary borough or municipal borough and also in his sub-district, a return certified under his hand to be a true return of the names, ages, and residences of all male persons

margin notes:
41 & 42 *Vict.* c. 26.

Notice of rates in arrear.

* Ante, p. 171.
† Ante, p. 197.

* Page 197.

Registrars to furnish returns of deaths to overseers.

41 § 42 *Vict.*
c. 26.

Returns of
deaths—*contd.*

of full age dying within that parish or part, and also when
and as required by those overseers of the names, ages, and
residences of all women of full age dying within that parish
or part.

The returns shall state the names of all such persons in full
(where the names are known) and the dates of their deaths,
and the names and residences of the persons by whom information of the deaths was given to the registrar.

The returns shall be made four times a year; that is to say,

On or before the 7th of April for the three months
ending with the preceding 31st of March;

On or before the 22nd of July for the period beginning
with the preceding 1st of April and ending with the
15th of July;

On or before the 15th of September, or at such other
time before the completion of the revision of the lists of
the parliamentary borough or municipal borough to the
area of which the return relates as the barrister revising
the same shall appoint in that behalf for the period
beginning with the preceding 16th of July, and ending
with the time when such return is made, or as near
thereto as practicable;

And on or before the 7th of January for the period
beginning with the preceding 15th of September or from
the time for which the last preceding return was made,
and ending with the 31st of December:

The registrar making any such return shall be entitled to
fees at the rate specified in the twenty-eighth section of the
Births and Deaths Registration Act, 1874, in respect of the
returns therein mentioned, and such fees shall be paid by
the overseers as part of the expenses of carrying into effect
the provisions of this Act with respect to the lists of parliamentary voters and burgess lists.

Overseers to
omit name of
dead person.

The overseers shall omit from any list made by them the
name of any person who appears from such returns to be
dead, and shall allow any person who is registered as a parliamentary voter of the parliamentary borough or enrolled as a
burgess of the municipal borough to which the returns relate
to inspect any such returns in their custody at all reasonable
times free of charge.

12. The overseers of every parish situate wholly or partly either in a parliamentary borough or in a municipal borough the whole or part of the area whereof is co-extensive with or included in the area of a parliamentary borough, shall ascertain from the relieving officer acting for that parish the names of all persons who are disqualified for being inserted in the lists of parliamentary voters or burgess lists for that parish by reason of having received parochial relief, and the relieving officer, upon application from the overseers, shall produce to them at such place within the parish, and at such time as is required by them, the books in his possession containing the names of those persons.

41 & 42 Vict. c. 26.

List of persons disqualified by parochial relief.

13. In every parish situate wholly or partly either in a parliamentary borough or in a municipal borough the whole or part of the area whereof is co-extensive with or included in the area of a parliamentary borough, the books containing the poor rates made for the parish within the previous two years shall at all reasonable times be open, free of charge, to the inspection of any person who is registered as a parliamentary voter for the parliamentary borough, or enrolled as a burgess of the municipal borough, and any such voter or burgess may make any copy thereof or take any extract therefrom.

Inspection of rate books.

14. Whereas by section nineteen of the Poor Rate Assessment and Collection Act, 1869, the overseers in making out the poor rate are required in every case, whether the rate is collected from the owner or occupier, or the owner is liable to the payment of the rate instead of the occupier, to enter in the occupier's column of the rate book the name of the occupier of every rateable hereditament, and it is thereby declared that every such occupier shall be deemed to be duly rated for any qualification or franchise as therein mentioned; and whereas doubts (*b*) have been entertained as to the application of this enactment, and it is expedient to remove them: be it therefore enacted that the recited enactment shall not be deemed to apply exclusively to cases where an agreement has been made under section three of the same Act, or where an order

Explanation of 32 & 33 Vict. c. 41, s. 19, as to entering occupier's name in rate book.

(*b*) In the conflicting cases of *Cross* v. *Allsop*, L. R., 6 C. P. 315, and *Smith* v. *Seghill*, L. R., 10 Q. B. 422.

Revision
of lists of
parliamentary
voters and
burgess lists
together in
parliamentary
boroughs.

has been made under section four of the same Act, but shall be of general application.

15. Where the whole or part of the area of a municipal borough is co-extensive with or included in the area of a parliamentary borough, the lists of parliamentary voters and the burgess lists shall so far as practicable be made out and revised together.

In every such case the overseers of every parish situate wholly or partly either in the parliamentary borough or in the municipal borough shall, on or before the last day of July in every year make out a list of all persons entitled under any right conferred by the Reform Act, 1832, or by section three of the Representation of the People Act, 1867, to be registered as voters for the parliamentary borough in respect of the occupation of property situate wholly or partly within that parish, or entitled to be enrolled as burgesses of the municipal borough in respect of the occupation of any property so situate:

With respect to every list so made out the following provisions shall have effect:

(1.) The lists shall be in substitution for the lists of persons so entitled, which are required to be made out under the Parliamentary Registration Acts and the Municipal Corporation Acts:

(2.) Where the parish is situate wholly or partly both in the parliamentary borough and in the municipal borough, the list for the parish shall be made out in three divisions:

Division One shall comprise the names of the persons entitled both to be registered as parliamentary voters under a right conferred as aforesaid and to be enrolled as burgesses;

Division Two shall comprise the names of the persons entitled to be registered as parliamentary voters under a right conferred as aforesaid, but not to be enrolled as burgesses;

Division Three shall comprise the names of the persons entitled to be enrolled as burgesses, but not to be registered as parliamentary voters under a right conferred as aforesaid:

(3.) Each list shall state the surname and other name or names of every person whose name is inserted therein, his place of abode, the nature of his qualification, and the situation and description of the property in respect of which he is entitled:

(4.) Each list shall be signed and otherwise dealt with in manner directed by the Parliamentary Registration Acts with respect to the alphabetical lists mentioned in section thirteen of the Parliamentary Registration Act, 1843:

(5.) Where no part of the parish is situate within the municipal borough, the list for the parish shall be deemed to be a list of voters for the parliamentary borough:

(6.) Where no part of the parish is situate within the parliamentary borough, the list for the parish shall be deemed to be a burgess list for the municipal borough:

(7.) Where the list is made out in divisions, divisions one and two shall be deemed to be lists of voters for the parliamentary borough, and divisions one and three shall be deemed to be burgess lists for the municipal borough:

(8.) The lists, and if the lists are made out in divisions, each division thereof, shall, if and so far as the local authority from time to time direct, according to convenience for use, be framed in parts for polling districts or wards; and where the polling districts and wards are not conterminous, in such manner . that the parts may be conveniently compiled or put together to serve either as lists for polling districts or as ward lists.

16. In the case of any parliamentary borough in which any persons are entitled to be registered as freemen, or under any right other than a right conferred by the Reform Act, 1832, or the third section of the Representation of the People Act, 1867, the registration of such persons shall be carried out in the manner directed by the Parliamentary Registration Acts, as modified by this Act.

Sidenote: 41 & 42 Vict. c. 26.

Sidenote: Freemen's and other rights.

41 & 42 Vict. c. 26.

Provision where several municipal boroughs included in one parliamentary borough.

17. In the case of a parliamentary borough which includes in whole or in part more municipal boroughs than one, each such municipal borough shall, for the purposes of this Act, be dealt with separately and as if each were the only municipal borough included in whole or in part in such parliamentary borough, and if any parish is partly in one and partly in another or others of such municipal boroughs, so much thereof as is in any one of such municipal boroughs shall, for the purposes of this Act, be dealt with as a separate parish.

The town clerk of each such municipal borough shall, so far as regards the area of such municipal borough, issue the precepts and perform the other duties to be performed by the town clerk under and shall be the town clerk for the purposes of the Parliamentary Registration Acts and this Act.

Application of Parliamentary Registration Acts to burgess lists made out under this Act.

18. The Municipal Corporation Acts shall not, as to anything prior to the completion of the revision of the burgess lists, apply to any burgess list made out under this Act, and instead thereof the Parliamentary Registration Acts, as modified by this Act, shall, up to the completion of the revision of the burgess lists, apply to every such burgess list, as if it were a list of parliamentary voters made out under those Acts, and as if the municipal borough to which such burgess lists relate were a parliamentary borough : provided as follows :

(1.) Nothing in this Act shall authorize a person entered on a burgess list, not being also entered on a list of parliamentary voters, to make any objection in respect of a list of parliamentary voters, or authorize any person entered on a list of parliamentary voters, not being also entered on a burgess list, to make any objection in respect of a burgess list;

(2.) The last day for revising a burgess list made out under this Act shall be the 12th of October ; and

(3.) The burgess lists when revised shall be copied for the burgess roll in manner directed by the Municipal Corporation Acts.

19. Where the whole or part of the area of a municipal borough is co-extensive with or included in the area of a

parliamentary borough, the separate lists of the persons entitled to be elected councillors or aldermen of the municipal
borough, though not entitled to be on the burgess roll, shall
be made out at the same time and in the same manner as the
burgess lists, and all the provisions of this Act with respect
to the burgess lists shall apply to those separate lists.

41 & 42 Vict. c. 26.

Lists of per-
sons qualified
to be aldermen
or councillors,
but not to be
burgesses.

[**20.** *Abolition of assessors in parliamentary boroughs.*—Repealed by Municipal Corporations Act, 1882. See sect. 29 of
that Act.]

21. If and so far as the local authority so direct, the lists
of parliamentary voters and registers of parliamentary voters
in parliamentary boroughs, and the burgess lists and burgess
rolls in municipal boroughs, and the lists of claimants and
persons objected to in parliamentary boroughs and municipal
boroughs respectively, or any of those documents, shall, so far
as they relate to persons qualified in respect of the owner-
ship or occupation of property (including persons qualified in
respect of lodgings), be arranged in the same order in which
the qualifying premises appear in the rate book for the parish
in which those premises are situate, or as nearly thereto as
will cause those lists, registers, and rolls to record the qualifying premises in successive order in the street or other place
in which they are situate, subject in the case of a municipal
borough divided into wards to the division of the burgess roll
into ward lists. The local authority in this Act means as regards a parliamentary borough the authority having power
to divide the parliamentary borough into polling districts,
and as regards a municipal borough the council of the
municipal borough.

Lists and
registers may
be arranged
according to
streets.

*　　*　　*　　*　　*　　*　　*

24. Any person who is entered on any list of voters for a
parliamentary borough or any burgess list, subject to revision
under this Act, for a municipal borough, and whose name or
place of abode or the nature of whose qualification or the
name or situation of whose qualifying property is not correctly
stated in such list, or in respect of whom there is any other
error or omission in the said list, may, whether he has
received a notice of objection or not, if he thinks fit, make and
subscribe a declaration in the form in that behalf in the

Declaration
as to mis-
description.

41 & 42 *Vict.*
c. 26.

Declaration
as to misde-
scription—
continued.

schedule to this Act, or as near thereto as the circumstances will admit, before any justice of the peace or any commissioner or other person authorized to administer oaths in the Supreme Court of Judicature.

The declaration shall be duly dated and shall on or before the 12th of September be sent to the town clerk, who forthwith shall indorse on the declaration a memorandum signed or initialed by him, stating the date when he received it, and naming the declarant, and the list to which the declaration refers, and shall deliver all such declarations to the revising barrister at his first court.

If the declaration is sent as aforesaid in due time (of which the said indorsement shall be primâ facie proof), the revising barrister shall receive the declaration as evidence of the facts declared to, and that without proof of the signature of the declarant, or of the justice, commissioner, or person before whom the declaration purports to have been subscribed, unless he has good reason to doubt the genuineness of any signature thereto.

The declarations shall be open free of charge to public inspection at the office of the said town clerk, at any time between the hours of ten of the clock in the forenoon and four of the clock in the afternoon of any day except Sunday, before the 15th of September, and he shall deliver copies thereof on application and payment of the price of fourpence per folio of seventy-two words.

Penalty for
false declara-
tion.

25. If any person falsely or fraudulently signs any such declaration as last aforesaid, or any declaration either as claimant or witness in respect of a claim to vote as a lodger in the name of any other person, whether that person is living or dead, or in a fictitious name, or sends as genuine any false or falsified declaration knowing the same to be false or falsified, or knowingly and wilfully makes any false statement of fact in any declaration of the nature aforesaid, he shall be guilty of a misdemeanor and punishable by fine or by imprisonment for a term not exceeding one year, and the revising barrister shall have power to impound the declaration.

Notice of ob-
jection must
state grounds.

26. The notice required by the seventeenth and twentieth sections of the Parliamentary Registration Act, 1843, to be given to persons objected to in boroughs for the purposes of the revision of the lists of voters for the parliamentary borough and the burgess lists for a municipal borough whose burgess lists are revised under this Act, shall state specifically the ground or grounds of objection, and sections seven and eight of the County Voters Registration Act, 1865, shall extend to such objections.

41 & 42 Vict.
c. 26.

27. For the purposes of the revision of the lists of voters for a parliamentary borough, and the burgess lists for a municipal borough whose burgess lists are revised under this Act—

Revision of lists of voters.

(1.) An objection may be withdrawn by a notice to that effect in writing, signed by the objector, and given to the person objected to and to the town clerk not less then seven days before the day which shall be appointed for the holding of the first court of revision of the list to which the objection relates :

Objections may be withdrawn.

(2.) Any objection by a qualified objector may, after his death, be revived by any other person qualified to have made the objection originally by a notice to that effect in writing signed by him, and given to the person objected to and to the town clerk at or before the time of the revision of the entry to which the objection relates :

Reviver of objections on death of objector.

A person reviving an objection shall be deemed to have made the objection originally, and he shall be responsible in respect thereof, and the proceedings thereon shall be continued accordingly :

(3.) Where objection is made otherwise then by an overseer to any person whose name appears on a list of voters or burgesses and the name is retained on the list, the revising barrister shall, unless he is of opinion that the objection was reasonably made either because of a defect or error in the entry to which the objection relates, or because of a difficulty in verifying or identifying the particulars comprised in such entry, or unless the objection is duly withdrawn, or unless for some other special reason he otherwise determines, order costs not exceeding forty shillings to be paid by the objector to the person objected to.

Costs of objections.

Duties and
powers of
revising
barrister.
Correction of
mistakes.

28. A revising barrister shall, with respect to the lists of voters for a parliamentary borough and the burgess lists for a municipal borough which he is appointed to revise, perform the duties and have the powers following:

(1.) He shall (c) correct any mistake which is proved to him to have been made in any list:

(2.) He may correct any mistake which is proved to him to have been made in any claim or notice of objection (d):

Expunging
of names,
whether
objected to
or not.

(3.) He shall expunge the name of every person, whether objected to or not, whose qualification as stated in any list is insufficient in law to entitle such person to be included therein:

(4.) He shall expunge the name of every person who, whether objected to or not, is proved to the revising barrister to be dead:

(5.) Where an entry in any list and an entry in a return made to the overseers of deaths appear to relate to the same person, the revising barrister shall inquire whether such entries relate to the same person, and on proof being made to him that the entries relate to the same person shall expunge the entry in the list therefrom:

(6.) The revising barrister shall expunge the name of every person, whether objected to or not, whose name or place of abode, or the nature of whose qualification, or the name or situation of whose qualifying property if the qualification is in respect of property, or any other particulars respecting whom by law required to be stated in the list, is or are either wholly omitted or in the judgment of the revising barrister insufficiently described for the purpose of being identified, unless the matter or matters so omitted or insufficiently described be supplied to the satisfaction of the revising barrister before he

---

(c) The distinction between the "shall" of par. (1) and the "may" of par. (2) is pretty obvious. "Shall" is absolutely imperative; "may" gives an absolute discretion to the revising barrister. See *Pickard* v. *Baylis*, 5 C. P. D. 235.

(d) See *James* v. *Howarth*, 5 C. P. D. 225; *Adams*, app., *Bostock*, resp., 8 Q. B. D. 259.

41 & 42 *Vict.* c. 26.

shall have completed the revision of the list in which the omission or insufficient description occurs, and in case such matter or matters shall be so supplied, he shall then and there insert the same in such list:

(7.) He shall expunge the name of every person, whether objected to or not, where it is proved to the revising barrister that such person was, on the last day of July then next preceding, incapacitated (*e*) by any law or statute from voting at an election for the parliamentary borough or an election for the municipal borough, as the case may be, to which the list relates:

(8.) Before expunging from a list the name of any person not objected to, the revising barrister shall cause such notice, if any, as shall appear to him necessary or proper under the circumstances of the proposal to expunge the name, to be given to or left at the usual or last known place of abode of such person:

(9.) Subject as herein and otherwise by law provided, the revising barrister shall retain the name of every person not objected to, and also of every person objected to, unless the objector appears by himself or by some person on his behalf in support of his objection: *Retention of names not objected to, and of names objected to, unless objector appears.*

(10.) If the objector so appears the revising barrister shall require him, unless he is an overseer, to prove that he gave the notice or notices of objection required by law to be given by him, and to give primâ facie proof of the ground of objection, and for that purpose may himself examine and allow the objector to examine the overseers or any other person on oath touching the alleged ground of objection, and unless such proof is given to his satisfaction shall, subject as herein and otherwise by law provided, retain the name of the person objected to: *Burden of proof upon objector, unless he is an overseer.*

An objection made under this Act by overseers

(*e*) This means permanently incapacitated, and not temporarily as by receipt of parochial relief (*Hayward* v. *Scott*, 5 C. P. D. 231). See Act of 1882, s. 9, and notes, ante, p. 5.

**Duties and
powers of
revising
barrister—
*continued.***

shall be deemed to cast upon the person objected to
the burden of proving his right to be on the list:

The primâ facie proof shall be deemed to be given
by the objector if it is shown to the satisfaction of
the revising barrister by evidence, repute, or otherwise that there is reasonable ground for believing
that the objection is well founded, and that by reason
of the person objected to not being present for examination, or for some other reason, the objector
is prevented from discovering or proving the truth
respecting the entry objected to:

**Expunging of
name upon
objection
being proved,
&c.**

(11.) If such proof is given by the objector as herein
prescribed, or if the objection is by overseers, then
unless the person objected to appears by himself
or by some person on his behalf, and proves that
he was entitled on the last day of July then next
preceding to have his name inserted in the list in
respect of the qualification described in such list,
the revising barrister shall expunge the name of
the person objected to:

**Correction of
entry.**

(12.) Where the matter stated in a list or claim, or proved
to the revising barrister in relation to any alleged
right to be on any list, is in the judgment of the
revising barrister insufficient in law to constitute a
qualification of the nature or description stated or
claimed, but sufficient in law to constitute a qualification of some other nature or description, the
revising barrister, if the name is entered in a list
for which such true qualification in law is appropriate, shall correct such entry by inserting such
qualification accordingly, and in any other case shall
insert the name with such qualification in the appropriate list, and shall expunge it from the other list,
if any, in which it is entered:

(13.) Except as herein provided, and whether any person
is objected to or not, no evidence shall be given of
any other qualification than that which is described
in the list or claim, as the case may be, nor shall the
revising barrister be at liberty to change the description of the qualification as it appears in the list

except for the purpose of more clearly and accurately defining the same: 41 & 42 *Vict.* *c.* 26.

(14.) Where the name of any person appears to be entered Double entry. more than once as a parliamentary voter on the lists of voters for the same parliamentary borough, or more than once as a burgess on the burgess lists for the same municipal borough, the revising barrister shall inquire whether such entries relate to the same person, and on proof being made to him that such entries relate to the same person shall retain one of the entries for voting, and place against the other or others a note to the effect that the person is not entitled to vote in respect of the qualification therein contained for the parliamentary borough or for the municipal borough, as the case may be, he being on the list for voting in respect of another qualification:

Any such person may, by notice in writing delivered to the revising barrister at the opening of his first revision court, select the entry to be retained for voting, and in making such selection may select one entry to be retained for voting for the parliamentary borough, and another entry to be retained for voting as a burgess for the municipal borough, but if he does not make any selection the entry to be so retained shall be selected by the revising barrister, except in the case of freemen, in which case the entry to be retained by the revising barrister for voting shall be that on the freemen's list:

If any question on appeal, or otherwise, arise as to the validity of the qualification for which the parliamentary voter or burgess is on the list for voting, recourse may be had for supporting the right of the voter or burgess to be on the parliamentary register or burgess roll for voting to any other qualification of such person appearing on the register or burgess roll:

Provided always, that in the case of a municipal borough divided into wards a vote given in or the right to vote in one ward shall not be supported by a qualification appearing on the burgess roll for some other ward:

41 & 42 Vict. c. 26, s. 28.

Placing of name in right division.

(15.) Where a list is made out in divisions the revising barrister shall place the name of any person in the division in which it should appear according to the result of the revision, regard being had to the title of the person to be on the list both as a parliamentary voter and as a burgess, or only in one of those capacities, and shall expunge the name from the other division (if any) in which it appears.

Substitution of sect. 28 for sect. 40 of Act of 1843.

This section shall, as regards every parliamentary borough and every municipal borough whose burgess lists are revised under this Act, take effect instead of section forty of the Parliamentary Registration Act, 1843.

Power to fine overseers for neglect.

* Page 186.

29. The provisions of the fifty-first section of the Parliamentary Registration Act, 1843,* relating to the power of the revising barrister to fine overseers for neglect of duty, shall extend to every wilful refusal, neglect, or breach of duty on the part of overseers in the execution of this Act.

xp enses and receipts.

* Page 198.

30. Where the whole or part of the area of a municipal borough is co-extensive with or included in the area of a parliamentary borough, the expenses properly incurred by the town clerk (including in his expenses the matters mentioned in section thirty-one of the Representation of the People Act, 1867*), and the expenses properly incurred by the overseers in carrying into effect the provisions of this Act with respect to the lists of parliamentary voters and burgess lists, and all moneys received in respect of any of those lists, or in respect of any fine imposed by the revising barrister on the revision of the lists, shall be respectively paid and applied as follows:

(1.) If the area of the parliamentary borough and the area of the municipal borough are co-extensive, one-half of the expenses shall be defrayed in the manner provided by the Parliamentary Registration Acts as expenses incurred thereunder, and the other half shall be defrayed out of the borough fund, and one-half of the moneys received as aforesaid shall be applied in the manner directed in those Acts, and the other half shall be paid to the borough fund:

(2.) In all other cases the expenses and receipts in respect of the area common to the parliamentary borough and to a municipal borough shall, as to one-half thereof, be defrayed and applied as expenses and receipts under the Parliamentary Registration Acts, and shall, as to the other half thereof, be defrayed out of and paid to the borough fund of such municipal borough :

And the expenses and receipts in respect of an area exclusively parliamentary shall be defrayed and applied as expenses and receipts under the Parliamentary Registration Acts :

And the expenses and receipts of an area exclusively municipal shall be defrayed out of and paid to the borough fund of the municipal borough comprising such area :

Any expenses and receipts incurred or arising in respect of more than one such area shall be apportioned between the several areas in respect of which they are incurred or arise, in the proportion as nearly as may be in which the same are incurred and arise in respect of the several areas, regard being had to the number of parliamentary voters or burgesses in each area, or any other circumstances occasioning the expenses or giving rise to the receipts :

The revising barrister shall, as part of the business of the revision, determine, if necessary, in respect of what area or areas any expenses or receipts are incurred or arise, and how much thereof is attributable to each area.

The remuneration of the revising barrister shall be paid as heretofore under the Parliamentary Registration Acts (*f*) : provided always, that in the case of a municipal borough whose burgess lists are revised under this Act, there shall be paid out of the borough fund to the revising barrister, by way of additional remuneration in respect of his additional work on account of the municipal revision for such municipal borough, a remuneration at the rate mentioned in the third section of the Municipal Corporation Act, 1859 (*g*).

41 & 42 Vict. c. 26.

Remuneration of revising barrister.

(*f*) See sect. 59 of Act of 1843, ante.
(*g*) The Municipal Corporation Act, 1859 (22 Vict. c. 35), is repealed by the Municipal Corporation Act, 1882 (p. 140, ante), but for the pur-

Delivery and
custody of
revised lists.

31. The lists, if made out in divisions under this Act, shall, when revised, be delivered to the town clerk to whom in respect of the area to which the lists relate revised parliamentary lists ought to be delivered.

The revising barrister shall, as part of the business of the revision, at the request of the town clerk of any municipal borough the whole or part of the area of which is co-extensive with or included in the area of a parliamentary borough, sign and deliver to him a duplicate of the whole or part of any revised list made out in divisions and relating to that municipal borough.

Every such duplicate shall be prepared by the town clerk at whose request it is so signed, and shall be kept by him for use for municipal purposes.

*   *   *   *   *   *   *

Commence-
ment and
duration of
burgess roll.

33. The burgess roll made up from revised lists under this Act of burgesses for any municipal borough shall come into operation on the 1st of November next after the revision, and shall continue in operation for the year commencing with such 1st of November.

[**34.** *Expressions in Municipal Elections Act*, 1875, *referring to burgess roll, &c., to refer to new burgess roll or ward list.*— Repealed by Municipal Corporations Act, 1882.]

Appeal and
correction of
burgess roll
where burgess
lists are re-
vised under
this Act.

35. Where burgess lists are revised under this Act, the provisions of the Parliamentary Registration Acts, as to appeal from the decision of the revising barrister, shall apply to a decision on the revision of the burgess lists, and the provisions of the said acts as to the alteration or correction of the register, in pursuance of any judgment or order of the court of appeal, shall apply to the alteration or correction of the burgess roll made up from the burgess lists as if it were a register of parliamentary voters, except that the notice of the judgment or order shall be given to the town clerk having the custody of the burgess roll, and the alteration or correction shall be made and signed by him.

poses of this section, such part of the 3rd section of that Act as is applicable thereto is still in force (see *Reg.* v. *Smith*, L. R., 8 Q. B. 146; 42 L. J., M. C. 46; 28 L. T. 129; 21 W. R. 382). The 3rd section in question provides that the barrister "shall be remunerated at the rate of five guineas for every day he shall be employed, over and above his travelling expenses, out of the borough fund."

36. A revising barrister may by summons under his hand require any person to attend at the court and give evidence or produce documents for the purpose of the revision, and any person who, after the tender to him of a reasonable amount for his expenses, fails so to attend, or who fails to answer any question put to him by the revising barrister in pursuance of this section, or to produce any document which he is required, in pursuance of this section, to produce, shall be liable to pay such fine not exceeding five pounds as may be imposed by the revising barrister, and such fine may be recovered, and when recovered shall be applied in like manner as any other fine imposed by the revising barrister under the Parliamentary Registration Acts.

41 & 42 Vict.
c. 26.

Power for revising barrister to summon witnesses.

37. If any person feels aggrieved by a revising barrister neglecting or refusing to state any case (*h*), he may, within one month after such neglect or refusal, apply to the High Court of Justice upon affidavit of the facts for a rule calling on the revising barrister, and also on the person, if any, in whose favour the decision from which the applicant desires to appeal was given, to show cause why a rule should not be made directing the appeal to be entertained and the case to be stated, and thereupon the High Court, or any judge thereof in chambers, may make such rule to show cause, and make the same absolute, or discharge it with or without payment of costs as seems just, and the revising barrister, on being served with any such rule absolute, shall state the case accordingly, and the case shall be stated and the appeal entertained and heard, notwithstanding any limitations of time or place contained in the Parliamentary Registration Act, 1843.

Appeal where revising barrister neglects or refuses to state case.

38. The costs of an appellant against a decision of a revising barrister may, if the appeal is successful, be ordered by the court hearing the appeal to be paid by the clerk of the peace or town clerk named as respondent in the said appeal, whether he shall or shall not appear before the said court in support of the decision.

Costs of appeal.

For enabling an appellant to obtain such an order, he may, at or before the time of making his declaration of appeal

(*h*) As to discretionary statement of case under Act of 1843, see sect. 42 of that Act, ante, p. 180.

41 & 42 Vict.
c. 26.

* Page 180.

under section forty-two of the Parliamentary Registration Act, 1843,* require the revising barrister to name the clerk of the peace for the county or the town clerk for the parliamentary borough or municipal borough, as the case may be, to which the appeal relates, to be respondent in the appeal.

The revising barrister, if so required, shall, and in any case may, name such clerk of the peace or town clerk, as the case may be, to be respondent in an appeal, either alone or in addition to any other person referred to in section forty-three

* Page 181.

of the Parliamentary Registration Act, 1843.*

The expenses properly incurred by a clerk of the peace or town clerk as respondent, including any costs which he may be ordered to pay to the appellant in any such appeal, shall be allowed to him as part of the expenses incurred by him in respect of the revision of the list to which the appeal relates. The term "expenses" in this section shall include all matters mentioned in section thirty-one of the Representation of the

* Page 188.

People Act, 1867.*

The costs of an appeal against a decision of a revising barrister shall be in the discretion of the court hearing the appeal, subject, except as aforesaid, to the proviso contained in section seventy of the Parliamentary Registration Act, 1843.

Power to make rules for proceedings at revision courts.

39. The authority having power to make rules for regulating the practice and procedure in her Majesty's High Court of Justice may from time to time make, and when made alter and annul, rules for regulating the practice and procedure in the courts of revising barristers for the purposes of the Parliamentary Registration Acts and of this Act.

Rules to be laid before Parliament.

All rules made under this section shall be laid before each House of Parliament within forty days next after the same are made, if Parliament is then sitting, and if not, within forty days after the beginning of the then next sitting of Parliament; and if an address is presented to her Majesty by either of the said Houses within the next subsequent forty days on which the said House shall have sat, praying that any such rule be annulled, her Majesty may, by Order in Council, annul the same, and any rule so annulled shall thenceforth be of no effect, but without prejudice to the validity of any proceedings in the meantime taken thereunder.

All such rules shall, while in force, have effect as if enacted in this Act.

41 & 42 *Vict.* c. 26.

40. The provisions of section one hundred and one of the Parliamentary Electors Registration Act, 1843, as to the service of notices, shall apply to the service of notices under this Act.

Service of notices.

The term "notice" in the Parliamentary Registration Acts and this Act shall include any document required to be sent or delivered.

* * * * * * *

42. Nothing in this Act shall affect any register of parliamentary voters or burgess roll in force at the commencement of this Act.

Saving for existing registers and burgess rolls.

43. Nothing in this Act shall affect the provisions contained in section seventy-eight of the Reform Act, 1832.

Saving for 2 & 3 Will. 4, c. 45, s. 78.

SCHEDULE.

Form (A.)

Form of Precept of the Town Clerk or other Officer issuing the Precept to the Overseers of any Parish situate wholly or partly in a Parliamentary Borough, or in a Municipal Borough the whole or part of the area of which is co-extensive with or included in the area of a Parliamentary Borough.

† Parliamentary borough of † * Municipal borough of * to wit.

To the overseers of the poor of the parish of [*or* township of]

Omit part between crosses if no part of parish is in a parliamentary borough. Omit part between asterisks if no part of parish is in a municipal borough.

In pursuance of the provisions of the Parliamentary and Municipal Registration Act, 1878, and the Acts therein referred to, I require your attention to the following:

Instructions.

On or before the 20th of June you are to publish a notice [*or* notices], signed by you according to the form marked B. among the printed forms herewith sent.

Note.—Form B. in this schedule must be sent.

The manner in which you are required to publish that notice is as follows: (that is to say,) you are to fix one of the printed copies (each copy being first signed by you), on or near the outside of the outer door or of the outer wall near the door of every church and public chapel in your parish [*or* township], including chapels which do not belong to the Established Church, and also in some public and conspicuous position on or near every post office or telegraph office occu-

41 & 42 *Vict. c.* 26.

pied by or on behalf of her Majesty's Postmaster General, and every public or municipal or parochial office in your parish [*or* township], or if there is no such church, chapel, or office, then in some public situation in your parish [*or* township], and it must remain there during a period including two Sundays at the least.

Note.—Form C. in this schedule must be sent.

Omit part between crosses if no part of parish is in a parliamentary borough.

Omit part between asterisks if no part of parish is in a municipal borough.

Where any poor rate was on the 1st of June due from an occupier in respect of any premises capable of conferring the franchise for the said †Parliamentary *or† municipal* borough, you are on or before the 20th of June to give to that occupier a notice in the form marked C. sent herewith, by delivering it to the occupier, or leaving it at his last or usual place of abode, or with some person on the premises in respect of which the rate is payable, and in case no such person can be found, then by affixing the notice upon some conspicuous part of such premises. You need not give this notice if the rate has been previously duly demanded by a demand note served in the like manner as the last-mentioned notice.

When a borough rate is levied as a separate rate and not as part of the poor rate, the precept should be altered accordingly so as to contain a reference to the borough rate.

On or before the 22nd of July next you are to make out a list containing the name and place of abode of every person who has not paid on or before the 20th of the same month all poor rates which have become due from him in respect of any premises within your parish [*or* township] before the 5th of January last, and you are to keep that list to be perused by any person gratis at any time between 10 a.m. and 4 p.m. on any day, except Sunday, during the first fourteen days after the said 22nd of July.

Omit part between crosses if no part of parish is in a parliamentary borough.

Omit part between asterisks if no part of parish is in a municipal borough.

Omit part between asterisks if no part of parish is in a municipal borough, or if no part of parish is in a parliamentary borough.

On or before the last day of July you are to make out a list of all persons †entitled under any right conferred by the Reform Act, 1832 (2 & 3 Will. 4, c. 45), or by section three of the Representation of the People Act, 1867, to be registered as parliamentary voters to vote at the election of a member [*or* members] to serve in parliament for the parliamentary borough of   in respect of the occupation of property situate wholly or partly within your parish [*or* township], *or† entitled to be enrolled as burgesses of the municipal borough of   in respect of the occupation of property situate wholly or partly within your parish [*or* township].*

*This list is to be made out in three divisions :

Division One is to comprise the names of the persons entitled both to be registered as parliamentary voters under a right conferred as aforesaid, and to be enrolled as burgesses.

Division Two is to comprise the names of the persons entitled to be registered as parliamentary voters under a right conferred as aforesaid, but not to be enrolled as burgesses.

Division Three is to comprise the names of the persons entitled to be enrolled as burgesses, but not to be registered as parliamentary voters under a right conferred as aforesaid. *

†On or before the last day of July you are also to make

out a list of all persons who are entitled within your parish [*or* township] to be registered as parliamentary voters to vote at the election of a member [*or* members] to serve in parliament for the said parliamentary borough in respect of any other right than a right conferred by the Reform Act, 1832, or by section three of the Representation of the People Act, 1867 (except as freemen or as lodgers).

41 & 42 *Vict.* c. 26.
Omit part between crosses if no part of parish is in a parliamentary borough.

On or before the last day of July you are also to make out a list of all persons who being on the register of voters now in force for the said parliamentary borough in respect of residence in lodgings within your parish [*or* township] have duly claimed, on or before the 25th day of July, to have their names inserted in the lists of parliamentary voters for the said borough in respect of residence in the same lodgings.†

These lists are [*or* this list is] to be in the Form D. (*or, as the case may be*, E. *or* F.) sent herewith.

Note.—The appropriate form must be sent.

*On or before the last day of July you are also to make out a list (in the Form G. sent herewith) of all persons who are entitled, in respect of the occupation of property within your parish [*or* township], to be elected councillors or aldermen of the said municipal borough, but who are not entitled to be on the burgess roll thereof.*

Omit part between asterisks if no part of parish is in a municipal borough, but unless it is omitted, send Form G.

In making out each of these lists you will follow the directions of which a copy is enclosed.

On or before the 1st day of August you are to sign and publish written or printed copies of these lists, in the same manner as before mentioned with respect to the notice.

Note.—A printed copy of the directions in the schedule for the guidance of overseers in making out the lists must be enclosed.

You are to keep a copy of these lists signed by you, †and also a copy of the list of defaulters in payment of assessed taxes sent to you by the collector of taxes,† to be open to public inspection at any time between the hours of ten o'clock in the forenoon and four o'clock in the afternoon of any day, except Sunday, during the first fourteen days after the publication of the said lists, and to deliver copies of any such lists to any person on payment of a price for each copy after the rate contained in the table marked "Parliamentary Registration Act, 1843, Schedule (D.), No. 1," sent herewith.

Omit part between crosses if no part of parish is in a parliamentary borough.
Note.—A printed copy of the Table, No. 1, in Schedule (D.) to the Parliamentary Registration Act, 1843 (6 & 7 Vict. c. 18), must be enclosed.

You are to make out lists according to the forms marked K. sent herewith, containing the names of every person who has given or caused to be given to you, or any one of you, on or before the 25th day of August, notice of his claim to have his name inserted in any list of voters making separate lists of—

Note.—Forms marked K. and L. must be sent.

> (1.) Persons claiming to be entered in the lists of parliamentary voters otherwise than as freemen or lodgers; and
>
> (2.) Persons claiming to be entered in the lists of parliamentary voters as lodgers who are not comprised in the above-mentioned list of lodger voters; *and
>
> (3.) Persons claiming to be entered in the burgess lists.*

Omit part between asterisks if no part of parish is in a municipal borough.

You are also to make out lists according to the forms marked L. sent herewith, containing the names of every person against whom a notice of objection has been given to you, or any of you, on or before the 25th day of August, as

41 & 42 Vict. c. 26.

not being entitled to have his name retained in any list for your parish [or township], giving in separate lists the objections made to—

(1.) Any person on the list of parliamentary voters other than the above-mentioned list of lodger voters :

(2.) Any person on the above-mentioned list of lodger voters :

(3.) Any person on the burgess list.

Omit part between asterisks if no part of parish is in a municipal borough.

On or before the 29th day of August you are to deliver to me copies of the lists so respectively made out and signed by you as aforesaid.

On or before the 1st day of September you are to sign and publish each of the lists of claimants and persons objected to in the same manner as before mentioned with respect to the notice.

You are to keep a copy of each of the lists of claimants and persons objected to, signed by you, and these copies, and also the original notices of claims and of objections, are to be open to public inspection at any time between the hours of ten of the clock in the forenoon and four of the clock in the afternoon of any day, except Sunday, during the first fourteen days of September, and you are to deliver copies of each of these lists to any person on payment of a price for each copy after the rate contained in the table marked "Parliamentary Registration Act, 1843, Schedule (D.), No. 1," sent herewith.

If you find any such notice, list, or other document published by you as aforesaid to be destroyed, mutilated, effaced, or removed, you are forthwith to place another in its room to the same effect.

You are to attend at the court to be holden for the revision of the said lists, of the time of holding which notice will be given ; and at the opening of the court you are there to deliver to the barrister before whom the same is holden the several lists made out and signed by you, and the original notices of claims and of objections given to you.

If the officer issuing precept is not the town clerk of a municipal borough, he should append to his signature his proper official description.

Herein if you fail you will be liable to the penalties in that case provided.

Dated the   day of   , 18

(Signed)   *A. B.,*
        Town Clerk of the Municipal
        Borough of   .

FORM (B.)

NOTICE to be published by the OVERSEERS in a MUNICIPAL BOROUGH.

Note.—This form is to be used only where the whole or part of the area of the municipal borough is co-extensive with or included in the area of a parliamentary borough.

Municipal borough of   , to wit. } We hereby give notice that no person will be entitled to have his name inserted in any list of burgesses of the municipal borough   , now about to be made in respect of the occupation of any property situate wholly or partly within this parish [or township], unless he pays on or before the 20th day of July all poor rates and borough rates (if any) which have become due from him in respect of those premises up to the 5th day of January last past; and all persons who omit to make such payment will be incapable of being upon the next burgess roll for this borough in respect of those premises.

41 & 42 *Vict. c.* 26.

Dated the   day of June, 18

(Signed) *A. B.* } Overseers of the parish [*or*
     C. D. } township] of .

Note.—Where a parish is situate within both a parliamentary borough and a municipal borough, both the above notices must be issued.

Form (C.)

To *A. B.*

† Parliamentary borough of †

* Municipal borough of *

Take notice that you will not be entitled to have your name inserted †in the list of parliamentary voters for the parliamentary borough of * or † in the burgess lists for the municipal borough of * now about to be made in respect of the premises in your occupation in [*street or place*], unless you pay on or before the 20th day of July next all the poor rates * (including borough rates, if any) * due from you in respect of those premises up to the 5th day of January last, amounting to £ , and if you omit to make such payment you will be incapable of being on the next † register of parliamentary voters for the said parliamentary borough * or † burgess roll for the said municipal borough. *

Dated the day of June, 18

(Signed) *C. D.* } Overseers,
     E. F. }

or

G. H., Assistant Overseer,

or

I. K., Collector

of the parish [*or* township] of .

Note.—This form is to be used in every parliamentary borough, but only in a municipal borough the whole or part of the area of which is co-extensive with or included in the area of a parliamentary borough.

If no part of the parish is in a parliamentary borough the parts between crosses are to be omitted.

If no part of the parish is in a municipal borough the parts between asterisks are to be omitted.

Where a borough rate is levied as a separate rate and not as part of the poor rate, the form should be altered accordingly, so as to distinguish the borough rate from the poor rate, and to state that omission to pay the borough rate will disqualify for enrolment as a burgess.

Form (D.)

Form of Lists of Parliamentary Voters and Burgesses for a Parish wholly or partly situate both in a Parliamentary Borough and in a Municipal Borough.

No. 1.—List of

† The persons entitled under any right conferred by the Reform Act, 1832, or by section three of the Representation of the People Act, 1867, to be registered as parliamentary voters to vote at the election of a member [*or* members] to serve in Parliament for the parliamentary borough of in respect of the occupation of property situate wholly or partly within this parish [*or* township],* and † the persons

N.B.—This list (No. 1) does not contain the names of any parliamentary voters except those entitled under some right conferred by the Reform Act, 1832, or by section 3 of the Representation of the People Act, 1867.

41 & 42 *Vict. c.* 26.　entitled to be enrolled as burgesses for the municipal borough of ⸻ in respect of the occupation of property situate wholly or partly within this parish [*or* township]*.

Division One.　Persons entitled both to be Registered as Parliamentary Voters under a right conferred as aforesaid, and to be Enrolled as Burgesses.

1. Names of Voters in full, Surname being first.	2. Place of Abode.	3. Nature of Qualification.	4. Name and Situation of Qualifying Property.
Abrahams, Samuel	4, Brick Street	House (joint)	4, Brick Street.
Brown, Thomas ..	4, Brick Street	Shop	4, Brick Street.
Masters, Abel	1, Brick Street	House	1. Brick Street.
Smith, William ..	Wood Villa, Gainsborough	Building ..	2, Brick Street.

Division Two.　Persons entitled to be Registered as Parliamentary Voters under a right conferred as aforesaid, but not to be Enrolled as Burgesses.

Names of Voters in full, Surname being first.	Place of Abode.	Nature of Qualification.	Name and Situation of Qualifying Property.
Adams, John	24, Duke Street	House	7, Brick Street.
Stubbs, Thomas ..	10, High Street	Shop	4, Brick Street.

Division Three.　Persons entitled to be Enrolled as Burgesses, but not to be Registered as Parliamentary Voters under a right conferred as aforesaid.

Names of Voters in full, Surname being first.	Place of Abode.	Nature of Qualification.	Name and Situation of Qualifying Property.
Gardener, Mary ..	10, Brick Street	House	10, Brick Street.
Thompson, Henry	14, John Street	Warehouse .	3, Brick Street.

(Signed)　　A.B. } Overseers of the Parish [*or*
　　　　　　　C.D. }　Township] of

FORM (F.)

41 & 42 *Vict. c.* 26.

FORM of LIST of Burgesses for a PARISH wholly or partly situate in a MUNICIPAL BOROUGH, but not in a PARLIAMENTARY BOROUGH.

Note.—This form is to be used only where the whole or part of the area of the municipal borough is co-extensive with or included in the area of a parliamentary borough.

This form is to be the same as Form D., No. 1, omitting the parts between crosses, and omitting the words "*Division One. Persons entitled, &c.*," forming the heading of Division One, and omitting Divisions Two and Three.

FORM (G.)

FORM of LIST of Occupiers in any PARISH entitled to be elected Councillors or Aldermen of a MUNICIPAL BOROUGH, though not entitled to be on the Burgess Roll of that BOROUGH.

Note.—This form is to be used only where the whole or part of the area of the municipal borough is co-extensive with or included in the area of a parliamentary borough.

List of the persons who are entitled to be elected councillors or aldermen of the municipal borough of , in respect of the occupation within the parish [*or* township] of , of any property, but who are not entitled to be on the Burgess Roll of that borough.

1. Name of Persons in full, Surname being first.	2. Place of Abode.	3. Nature of Qualification.	4. Name and Situation of Qualifying Property.

(Signed) A. B. } Overseers of the Parish [*or*
C. D. } township] of .

FORM (H.)

FORM OF NOTICE OF CLAIM.

No. 3.—MUNICIPAL.

To the overseers of the parish [*or* township] of
I claim to have my name inserted in the list made by you of burgesses of the municipal borough of in respect of the qualification named below.

Note.—This form is to be used only where the whole or part of the area of the municipal borough is co-extensive with or included in the area of a parliamentary borough.

Dated the day of 18 .

Name of Claimant in full, Surname being first.	Place of Abode.	Nature of Qualification.	Name and Situation of Qualifying Property.

(Signed) A. B.

FORM (I.)

FORM OF NOTICE OF OBJECTION.

No 3.—(MUNICIPAL).

Note.—This form is to be used only where the whole or part of the area of the municipal borough is co-extensive with or included in the area of a parliamentary borough.

NOTICE of OBJECTION to be given to OVERSEERS.

To the overseers of the parish [*or* township] of

I hereby give you notice that I object to the name of being retained on the list of burgesses of the municipal borough of   .

Dated the   day of   18 .

(Signed)   *A. B.* of [*place of abode*], on the List of Burgesses for the parish of

No. 4 (MUNICIPAL).

Note.—This form is to be used only where the whole or part of the area of the municipal borough is co-extensive with or included in the area of a parliamentary borough.

NOTICE of OBJECTION to be given to PERSON objected to.

To Mr.

I hereby give you notice that I object to your name being retained on the lists of burgesses of the municipal borough of , on the following grounds, viz. :—

1. *e. g.*, that you have not occupied for twelve months to July 15th.

2. That

3.

Dated the   day of   18 .

(Signed)   *A. B.*, of [*place of abode*], on the List of Burgesses for the parish of   .

Note.—If there is more than one burgess list, the notice of objection in each of the above two cases, Nos. 3 and 4, should specify the list to which the objection refers (*i*), and if the list is made out in divisions, the notice of objection should specify the division to which the objection refers; and if the list contains two or more persons of the same name, the notice should distinguish the person intended to be objected to.

(*i*) It was held in a parliamentary revision case that the particular parochial list to which the objection refers need not be stated (*Mortlock* v. *Farrer, Hall* v. *Cropper*, 5 C. P. D. 73 ; 49 L. J., C. P. 160 ; 42 L. T. 55 ; 28 W. R. 395) ; but in that case the court, appearing to think that there is but one burgess list, appeared also to doubt whether this note could have any meaning. It is suggested, however, that the explanation is to be found by reference to Form F.

Form (K.)

41 & 42 *Vict. c.* 26.

Form of List of Claimants to be Published by the Overseers.

No. 3.—List of Claimants (Municipal).

The following persons claim to have their names inserted in the Burgess Roll for the municipal borough of :—

Note.—This form is to be used only where the whole or part of the area of the municipal borough is co-extensive with or included in a parliamentary borough.

Name of Claimant in full, Surname being first.	Place of Abode.	Nature of Qualification.	Name and Situation of Qualifying Property.

(Signed) *A. B.* ⎫ Overseers of the Parish [*or*
  C. D. ⎭ Township] of .

Form (L.)

Form of List of Persons Objected to, to be Published by the Overseers.

No. 3.—List of Persons objected to (Municipal).

The following persons have been objected to as not being entitled to have their names retained on the burgess lists for the municipal borough of .

Note.—This form is to be used only where the whole or part of the area of the municipal borough is co-extensive with or included in a parliamentary borough.

Name of Person objected to in full, Surname being first.	Place of Abode.	Nature of the supposed Qualification.	Name and Situation of Qualifying Property.

(Signed) *A. B.* ⎫ Overseers of the parish [*or*
  C. D. ⎭ township] of .

Form (M.)

Declaration for correcting misdescription in List.

I, of No. in the parish of in the parliamentary borough of , and in the municipal borough of [*as the case may be*], do solemnly and sincerely declare as follows:—

1. I am the person referred to in division of the list of parliamentary voters and burgesses made out in divisions

41 & 42 *Vict. c.* 26.　[or in the list of 　　　] (*specifying the particular list*) made
　　　　　　　　　　　out for the parish of 　　　, by an entry as follows :—

Name as described in List.	Place of Abode as described in List.	Nature of Qualification as described in List.	Name and Situation of Qualifying Property.
Brown, John....	High Street	Shop	2, Shire Lane.

　　2. My correct name and place of abode, and the correct
particulars respecting my qualification, are, and ought to be
stated for the purposes of the register about to be made up of
voters for the parliamentary borough of 　, and the burgess
roll about to be made up of burgesses for the municipal
borough of 　　(*as the case may be*), as follows :—

Correct Name.	Correct Place of Abode.	Correct nature of Qualification (k).	Correct Name and Situation of Qualifying Property.
Brown, Joseph ..	15, High Street	House	24, Shire Lane.

　　　　Dated this 　　　day of 　　　18 .
　　　Made and subscribed before ⎫
　　　　me this 　　day of 　　⎬　　(Signed)
　　　18 , 　　　　　　　　　⎭
　　　　A. B.,
　　Justice of the peace for 　　　　.

The person before whom the declaration is made should affix his official description.

FORM (N.)

NOTICE of WITHDRAWAL of OBJECTION.

The list should be referred to in the manner prescribed for the notice of objection.
Omit the words between crosses if the objection is wholly withdrawn.
The notice should be signed in the manner prescribed for the notice of objection.

　　No. 1.—NOTICE to the PERSON objected to.

　　To Mr. 　　　
　　I hereby give you notice that I withdraw my objection to
your name being retained on the list of 　　† so far as
regards the ground of objection numbered 　　in my notice
to you of such objection.†
　　Dated the 　　day of 　　18 . 　　(Signed)

The list should be referred to in the manner prescribed for the notice of objection.
Omit the words between crosses if the objection is wholly withdrawn.
The notice should be signed in the manner prescribed for the notice of objection.

　　No. 2.—NOTICE to the TOWN CLERK.

　　To the Town Clerk of 　　　.
　　I hereby give you notice that I withdraw my objection to
the name of 　　being retained on the list of 　　† so far
as regards the ground of objection numbered 　　in my
notice to him of such objection.†
　　Dated the 　　day of 　　18 . 　　(Signed)

　　(*k*) A substitution of "houses in succession," for houses have
been held to be a change not authorized by sect. 28 (*Porrett v.
Lord*, 5 C. P. D. 65; 49 L. J., C. P. 176; 42 L. T. 28; 28 W. R.
393).

Form (O.)

Notice of Reviving an Objection.

No. 1.—Notice to the Person objected to.

To Mr.   .

I hereby give you notice that I revive the objection which was made by   , since deceased, to your name being retained on the list of   † so far as regards the ground of objection numbered   in the notice to you of such objection.†

.   Dated the   day of   18   .

              (Signed)

The list should be referred to in the manner prescribed for the notice of objection.

Omit the words between crosses if the objection is wholly revived.

The notice should be signed in the manner prescribed for the notice of objection.

No. 2.—Notice to the Town Clerk.

To the Town Clerk of   .

I hereby give you notice that I revive the objection which was made by   , since deceased, to the name of being retained on the list of   † so far as regards the ground of objection numbered   in the notice to the person objected to of such objection.†

    Dated the   day of   18   .

              (Signed)

The list should be referred to in the manner prescribed for the notice of objection.

Omit the words between crosses if the objection is wholly revived.

The notice should be signed in the manner prescribed for the notice of objection.

Note (P.)

Directions for the Guidance of Overseers in making out the Lists.

The following directions should be observed by overseers in making out the lists of parliamentary voters and burgesses, and also the lists of claimants and persons objected to as parliamentary voters and burgesses.

(1.) The surname and other name or names of each person are to be written at full length, the surname being placed first.

(2.) Each list, and where the list is made out in divisions, each division of each list should be made out in alphabetical order.

(3.) The place of abode should be entered with the name of the street, lane, or other locality, and the number in such street, lane, or other locality of such place of abode, where there is any such name or number, and should be entered in all cases in such a manner as will afford a full and sufficient address for a person entered if a letter is addressed to him by post.

(4.) The nature of the qualification should be entered as nearly as possible in the words of the statute conferring the franchise, for instance:

    (a) The nature of the qualification of a person under the Reform Act, 1832 (2 & 3 Will. 4, c. 45), or under the Municipal Corporation Acts, should be stated thus: "house," or in the case of a joint occupa-

Note.—If the local authority has given any special directions as to the mode of making out the list the town clerk, or other officer issuing the precepts must modify direction (2) accordingly.

tion, "house (joint)," or "warehouse," "counting-house," "shop," or "building," or in the manner provided by the Parliamentary and Municipal Registration Act, 1878, as the case may be:

(b) The nature of the qualification of a person under section 3 of the Representation of the People Act, 1867, should be stated thus, "dwelling-house."

(5.) The name and situation of the qualifying property, if the qualification is in respect of property, should be entered with the name of the street, lane, or other locality, and the number in such street, lane, or other locality of such property, where there is any such name or number, and should be entered in all cases in such a manner as will afford full and sufficient means of identifying such property.

(6.) Where several qualifications are possessed by the same person, the particulars respecting each qualification should be stated in the list; and in the case of a list made out in divisions, where a person is entered in Division 1 in respect of one qualification for parliamentary purposes, and in respect of another qualification for municipal purposes, each such qualification should be distinguished in the list by a note to the effect that the qualification is for parliamentary purposes only, or for municipal purposes only, as the case may be.

(7.) In making out the list of lodger claimants who claim on or before the 25th day of July, and are then on the register in respect of the same lodgings, if you have reason to believe that any person whose name is entered on that list is dead, or is not entitled to vote, you should make a note to that effect in the last column of the list, being the column headed "Objections by overseers."

(8.) You should omit from any list of parliamentary voters or burgesses the name of any person who appears from the returns furnished by the registrar of births and deaths to be dead, and the name of any person who is ascertained to be disqualified for being inserted in the list by reason of having received parochial relief or other alms.

Note (Q.)

Directions for Guidance in the formation of the Parliamentary Register and Burgess Roll.

In copying and printing Divisions 1 and 2 for the parliamentary register, and Divisions 1 and 3 for the burgess roll, of any revised list made out in divisions under this Act, the two divisions in each set may, and, if and so far as the local authority under the Act shall so direct, shall be combined or kept separate, and be arranged according to convenience for use in parts for polling districts or wards, and where the polling districts and wards are not conterminous in such manner that the parts may be conveniently compiled or put together to serve either as lists for polling districts or as ward lists; and the names may, and, if and so far as the said local authority shall so direct, shall be distinguished by

41 & 42 *Vict. c.* 26.

a number either alone, or in combination with a letter or other distinguishing mark according to the parts, and any arrangement may, and, if and so far as the said local authority shall so direct, shall be adopted according to convenience, so that one print or edition of Division 1 may be available for both sets.

Each entry for voting on the parliamentary register of every parliamentary borough, and on the burgess roll of every municipal borough whose burgess lists are revised under this Act, is to be distinguished by a number, either alone or in combination with a letter or distinguishing mark.

Any entry of a person not entitled to vote in respect of the qualification therein contained, he being on the list for voting in respect of another qualification, is to be denoted by an asterisk in the manner provided by section forty-seven of the Parliamentary Registration Act, 1843, with respect to similar entries in the registers for counties.

The officer having the custody of any revised lists under this Act shall permit access thereto for the purpose of the same being copied for the parliamentary register of the parliamentary borough, and for the burgess roll of any municipal borough to which such revised lists relate.

II.

BALLOT ACT, 1872.

[Incorporated by sect. 58 of the Municipal Corporations Act, 1882, p. 31, *ante, with modifications* as specified by sched. iii. part 3, p. 150, ante.]

35 & 36 Vict. c. 33.—*An Act to amend the Law relating to Procedure at Parliamentary and Municipal Elections.*

[18th July, 1872

WHEREAS it is expedient to amend the law relating to procedure at parliamentary and municipal elections:

Be it enacted, as follows:

PART I.—PARLIAMENTARY ELECTIONS.

Procedure at Elections.

*   *   *   *   *   *   *

Poll at elections.

2. In the case of a poll at an election the votes shall be given by ballot. The ballot of each voter shall consist of a paper (in this Act called a ballot paper) showing the names 35 & 36 *Vict.* c. 33. and description of the candidates. Each ballot paper shall have a number printed on the back, and shall have attached a counterfoil with the same number printed on the face. At the time of voting, the ballot paper shall be marked on both sides with an official mark, and delivered to the voter within the polling station (*l*), and the number of such voter on the register of voters shall be marked on the counterfoil, and the voter having secretly marked his vote on the paper, and folded it up so as to conceal his vote, shall place it in a closed box in the presence of the officer presiding at the polling station (in this Act called "the presiding officer") after having shown to him the official mark at the back.

Any ballot paper which has not on its back the official mark, **What ballot papers void.** or on which votes are given to more candidates than the voter is entitled to vote for, or on which anything, except the said number on the back, is written or marked by which the voter can be identified, shall be void and not counted (*m*).

After the close of the poll the ballot boxes shall be sealed **Sealing and opening ballot boxes.** up, so as to prevent the introduction of additional ballot papers, and shall be taken charge of by the returning officer, and that officer shall, in the presence of such agents, if any, of the candidates as may be in attendance, open the ballot boxes, and ascertain the result of the poll by counting the votes given to each candidate, and shall forthwith declare to be elected the candidates or candidate to whom the majority of votes have been given [*and return their names to the Clerk of the Crown in Chancery*] (*n*). The decision of the returning officer as to any question arising in respect of any ballot paper shall be final, subject to reversal on petition questioning the election or return.

* * * * * * *

(*l*) This is *primâ facie* the duty of the presiding officer (*Pickering* v. *James*, L. R., 8 C. P. 489; 42 L. J., C. P. 217; 29 L. T. 210; 21 W. R. 786), for the breach of which he may be sued by a candidate by such breach prevented from being elected (*ib.*).

(*m*) See *Woodward* v. *Sarsons*, L. R., 10 C. P. 733, and p. 255, post.

(*n*) Omit words in brackets: Act of 1882, sched. iii. part 3, rule 6, p. 151, ante.

Offences at Elections.

Offences in
respect of
nomination
papers, ballot
papers, and
ballot boxes.

3. Every person who,—

(1.) Forges or fraudulently defaces or fraudulently destroys
any nomination paper, or delivers to the returning
officer any nomination paper, knowing the same to
be forged ; or

(2.) Forges or counterfeits or fraudulently defaces or
fraudulently destroys any ballot paper or the official
mark on any ballot paper ; or

(3.) Without due authority supplies any ballot paper to
any person ; or

(4.) Fraudulently puts into any ballot box any paper other
than the ballot paper which he is authorised by law
to put in ; or

(5.) Fraudulently takes out of the polling station any
ballot paper ; or

(6.) Without due authority destroys, takes, opens, or otherwise interferes with any ballot box or packet of
ballot papers then in use for the purposes of the
election ;

shall be guilty of a misdemeanor, and be liable, if he is a
returning officer or an officer or clerk in attendance at a
polling station, to imprisonment for any term not exceeding
two years, with or without hard labour, and if he is any other
person, to imprisonment for any term not exceeding six
months, with or without hard labour.

Any attempt to commit any offence specified in this section
shall be punishable in the manner in which the offence itself
is punishable.

In any indictment or other prosecution for an offence in
relation to the nomination papers, ballot boxes, ballot papers,
and marking instruments at an election, the property in such
papers, boxes, and instruments may be stated to be in the
returning officer at such election, as well as the property in
the counterfoils.

Infringement
of secrecy.

4. Every officer, clerk, and agent in attendance at a polling
station shall maintain and aid in maintaining the secrecy of
the voting in such station, and shall not communicate, except
for some purpose authorised by law, before the poll is closed,

35 & 36 *Vict.* c. 33.

to any person any information as to the name or number on the register of voters of any elector who has or has not applied for a ballot paper or voted at that station, or as to the official mark, and no such officer, clerk, or agent, and no person whosoever, shall interfere with or attempt to interfere with a voter when marking his vote, or otherwise attempt to obtain in the polling station information as to the candidate for whom any voter in such station is about to vote or has voted, or communicate at any time to any person any information obtained in a polling station as to the candidate for whom any voter in such station is about to vote or has voted, or as to the number on the back of the ballot paper given to any voter at such station. Every officer, clerk, and agent in attendance at the counting of the votes shall maintain and aid in maintaining the secrecy of the voting, and shall not attempt to ascertain at such counting the number on the back of any ballot paper, or communicate any information obtained at such counting as to the candidate for whom any vote is given in any particular ballot paper. No person shall directly or indirectly induce any voter to display his ballot paper after he shall have marked the same, so as to make known to any person the name of the candidate for or against whom he has so marked his vote.

Every person who acts in contravention of the provisions of this section shall be liable, on summary conviction before two justices of the peace, to imprisonment for any term not exceeding six months, with or without hard labour (*o*).

* * * * * * *

Duties of Returning and Election Officers.

8. Subject to the provisions of this Act, every returning officer shall provide such nomination papers, polling stations, General powers and duties of returning officer.

(*o*) The offence of communicating information is not committed unless the alleged offender actually makes known the information to another person, it is not enough that he gives the means of acquiring information (*Stannanought* v. *Hazeldine*, 4 C. P. D. 191; 48 L. J., M. C. 89; 40 L. T. 589; 27 W. R. 620.) In this case the alleged offender, a personating agent at a Liverpool municipal election, attended at the polling booth with a copy of the burgess roll, and, having marked it with the names of numerous voters, took it to the committee-room of the candidate employing him.

35 & 36 Vict. c. 33.

ballot boxes, ballot papers, stamping instruments, copies of register of voters, and other things, appoint and pay such officers, and do such other acts and things as may be necessary for effectually conducting an election in manner provided by this Act.

*   *   *   *   *   *   *

Keeping of order in station.

9. If any person misconducts himself in the polling station, or fails to obey the lawful orders of the presiding officer, he may immediately, by order of the presiding officer, be removed from the polling station by any constable in or near that station, or any other person authorised in writing by the returning officer to remove him; and the person so removed shall not, unless with the permission of the presiding officer, again be allowed to enter the polling station during the day.

Any person so removed as aforesaid, if charged with the commission in such station of any offence, may be kept in custody until he can be brought before a justice of the peace.

Provided that the powers conferred by this section shall not be exercised so as to prevent any elector who is otherwise entitled to vote at any polling station from having an opportunity of voting at such station.

Powers of presiding officer and administration of oaths, &c.

10. For the purpose of the adjournment of the poll, and of every other enactment relating to the poll, a presiding officer shall have the power by law belonging to a deputy returning officer; and any presiding officer and any clerk appointed by the returning officer to attend at a polling station shall have the power of asking the questions and administering the oath authorised by law to be asked of and administered to voters, and any justice of the peace and any returning officer may take and receive any declaration authorised by this Act to be taken before him.

Liability of officers for misconduct.

11. Every returning officer, presiding officer, and clerk who is guilty of any wilful misfeasance or any wilful act or omission in contravention of this Act shall, in addition to any other penalty or liability to which he may be subject, forfeit to any person aggrieved by such misfeasance, act, or omission a penal sum not exceeding one hundred pounds.

Section fifty of the Representation of the People Act, 1867, (which relates to the acting of any returning officer, or his partner or clerk, as agent for a candidate,) shall apply to any returning officer or officer appointed by him in pursuance of this Act, and to his partner or clerk.

Miscellaneous.

12. No person who has voted at an election shall, in any legal proceeding to question the election or return, be required to state for whom he has voted.

Prohibition of compulsory disclosure of vote.

13. No election shall be declared invalid by reason of a non-compliance with the rules contained in the First Schedule to this Act, or any mistake in the use of the forms in the Second Schedule to this Act, if it appears to the tribunal having cognizance of the question that the election was conducted in accordance with the principles laid down in the body of this Act, and that such non-compliance or mistake did not affect the result of the election (*p*).

Non-compliance with rules not to invalidate election.

14. Where a parliamentary borough and municipal borough occupy the whole or any part of the same area, any ballot boxes or fittings for polling stations and compartments provided for such parliamentary borough or such municipal borough may be used in any municipal or parliamentary election in such borough free of charge, and any damage other than reasonable wear and tear caused to the same shall be paid as part of the expenses of the election at which they are so used.

Use of municipal ballot boxes, &c. for parliamentary election, and vice versâ.

15. This part of this Act shall, so far as is consistent with the tenor thereof, be construed as one with the enactments for the time being in force relating to the representation of the people, and to the registration of persons entitled to vote at the election of members to serve in Parliament, and with any enactments otherwise relating to the subject matter of this part of this Act, and terms used in this part of this Act shall have the same meaning as in the said enactments; and in con-

Construction of Act.

(*p*) This section, which was held (in *Woodward* v. *Sarsons*, L.R., 10 C. P. 733; 44 L. J., C. P. 293) to mean that an election could be declared invalid only for a non-observance so great as to nullify election by ballot, and affect the result of the election, should be compared with sect. 72 of the Act of 1882, ante, p. 37, which repeats it, *omitting*, however, the words " and that such non-compliance or mistake did not affect the result of the election."

struing the said enactments relating to an election or to the
poll or taking the votes by poll, the mode of election and of
taking the poll established by this Act shall for the purposes
of the said enactments be deemed to be substituted for the
mode of election or poll, or taking the votes by poll, referred
to in the said enactments; and any person applying for a
ballot paper under this Act shall be deemed "to tender his
vote," or "to assume to vote," within the meaning of the
said enactments; and any application for a ballot paper under
this Act, or expressions relative thereto, shall be equivalent
to "voting" in the said enactments and any expressions relative thereto; and the term "polling booth" as used in the
said enactments shall be deemed to include a polling station;
and the term "proclamation" as used in the said enactments
shall be deemed to include a public notice given in pursuance
of this Act.

✻   ✻   ✻   ✻   ✻   ✻   ✻

[**24.** PERSONATION.—See this section, p. 260, post.]

✻   ✻   ✻   ✻   ✻   ✻   ✻

PART IV.—MISCELLANEOUS.

Effect of
schedules.
28. The schedules to this Act, and the notes thereto, and
directions therein, shall be construed and have effect as part
of this Act (q).

Definitions.
"Municipal
borough:"

"Municipal
Corporation
Acts:"
29. In this Act—

The expression "municipal borough" means any place
for the time being subject to the Municipal Corporation Acts, or any of them:

The expression "Municipal Corporation Acts" means—

(a.) As regards England, the Act of the session of the
fifth and sixth years of the reign of King William
the Fourth, chapter seventy-six, intituled "An Act
to provide for the regulation of municipal corporations in England and Wales," and the Acts amending the same.

✻   ✻   ✻   ✻   ✻   ✻   ✻

(q) The Act has been said to be "imperative," and the schedules
"directory." See *Woodward* v. *Sarsons*, L. R., 10 C. P. 733.

The expression "municipal election" means—

(a.) As regards England, an election of any person to serve the office of councillor, auditor, or assessor of any municipal borough, or of councillor for a ward of a municipal borough.

35 & 36 Vict.
c. 33.
<hr>"Municipal election."

*　　*　　*　　*　　*　　*　　*

Repeal.

[**32.** Repeal of Acts in schedules].

33. This Act may be cited as the Ballot Act, 1872, and shall continue in force till the 31st day of December, 1880, and no longer, unless Parliament shall otherwise determine; and on the said day the Acts in the fourth, fifth, and sixth schedules shall be thereupon revived; provided that such revival shall not affect any act done, any rights acquired, any liability or penalty incurred, or any proceeding pending under this Act, but such proceeding shall be carried on as if this Act had continued in force (r). *(right margin: Short title.)*

SCHEDULES.

FIRST SCHEDULE.

PART I.—RULES FOR PARLIAMENTARY ELECTIONS.

*　　*　　*　　*　　*　　*　　*

The Poll.

14. *The poll shall take place on such day as the returning officer may appoint, not being in the case of an election for a county or a district borough less than two nor more than six clear days, and not being in the case of an election for a borough other than a district borough more than three clear days after the day fixed for the election (s).* *(right margin: Day of poll.)*

15. At every polling place the returning officer shall provide a sufficient number of polling stations for the accommodation of the electors entitled to vote at such polling place, *(right margin: Polling stations.)*

(r) The Act has been continued by successive "Expiring Laws Continuance" Acts, of which the latest, the Expiring Laws Continuance Act, 1882 (45 & 46 Vict. c. 64), continues it till the 31st December, 1883.

(s) This rule is printed for the sake of uniformity; but its operation seems wholly excluded by Rule 64 (c), post.

35 & 36 *Vict.*
c. 33.
and shall distribute the polling stations amongst those electors in such manner as he thinks most convenient, provided
that in a district borough there shall be at least one polling
station at each contributory place of such borough.

*   *   *   *   *   *   *

17. A separate room or separate booth may contain a
separate polling station, or several polling stations may be
constructed in the same room or booth.

18. No person shall be admitted to vote at any polling
station except the one allotted to him.

*   *   *   *   *   *   *

20. The returning officer shall provide each polling station
with materials for voters to mark the ballot papers, with instruments for stamping thereon the official mark, and with
copies of the register of voters, or such part thereof as contains the names of the voters allotted to vote at such station.
He shall keep the official mark secret, and an interval of not
less than seven years shall intervene between the use of the
same official mark at elections for the same county or borough.

Presiding officers.   21. The returning officer shall appoint a presiding officer to
preside at each station, and the officer so appointed shall keep
order at his station, shall regulate the number of electors to
be admitted at a time, and shall exclude all other persons except the clerks, the agents of the candidates (*t*), and the constables on duty.

Form of ballot paper.   22. Every ballot paper shall contain a list of the candidates
described as in their respective nomination papers, and ar-
ranged alphabetically in the order of their surnames, and (if
there are two or more candidates with the same surname) of
their other names : it shall be in the form set forth in the

* Page 255.   second schedule to this Act,* or as near thereto as circumstances
admit, and shall be capable of being folded up.

Ballot box.   23. Every ballot box shall be so constructed that the ballot
papers can be introduced therein, but cannot be withdrawn
therefrom, without the box being unlocked. The presiding
officer at any polling station, just before the commencement
of the poll, shall show the ballot box empty to such persons,

---

(*t*) The candidate himself may be present (*Clementson* v. *Mason*,
L. R., 10 C. P. 209, and p. 252, note (*e*), post).

35 & 36 *Vict.* c. 33.

if any, as may be present in such station, so that they may see that it is empty, and shall then lock it up, and place his seal upon it in such manner as to prevent its being opened without breaking such seal, and shall place it in his view for the receipt of ballot papers, and keep it so locked and sealed.

24. Immediately before a ballot paper is delivered to an elector, it shall be marked on both sides with the official mark, either stamped or perforated, and the number, name, and description of the elector as stated in the copy of the register shall be called out, and the number of such elector shall be marked on the counterfoil, and a mark shall be placed in the register against the number of the elector, to denote that he has received a ballot paper, but without showing the particular ballot paper which he has received. *Delivery of ballot paper to elector.*

25. The elector, on receiving the ballot paper, shall forthwith proceed into one of the compartments in the polling station, and there mark his paper, and fold it up so as to conceal his vote, and shall then put his ballot paper, so folded up, into the ballot box; he shall vote without undue delay, and shall quit the polling station as soon as he has put his ballot paper into the ballot box. *Marking of ballot paper by elector.*

26. The presiding officer, on the application of any voter who is incapacitated by blindness or other physical cause from voting in manner prescribed by this Act, or (if the poll be taken on Saturday) of any voter who declares that he is of the Jewish persuasion, and objects on religious grounds to vote in manner prescribed by this Act, or of any voter who makes such a declaration as hereinafter mentioned that he is unable to read, shall, in the presence of the agents of the candidates, cause the vote of such voter to be marked on a ballot paper in manner directed by such voter, and the ballot paper to be placed in the ballot box, and the name and number on the register of voters of every voter whose vote is marked in pursuance of this rule, and the reason why it is so marked, shall be entered on a list, in this Act called "the list of votes marked by the presiding officer." *Blind, illiterate, &c. voters.*

The said declaration, in this Act referred to as "the declaration of inability to read," shall be made by the voter at the time of polling, before the presiding officer, who shall attest it in the form hereinafter mentioned, and no fee, stamp, or other payment shall be charged in respect of such declaration, and the said declaration shall be given to the presiding officer at the time of voting.

Tendered ballot paper.

27. If a person, representing himself to be a particular elector named on the register, applies for a ballot paper after another person has voted as such elector, the applicant shall, upon duly answering the questions and taking the oath permitted by law to be asked of and to be administered to voters at the time of polling, be entitled to mark a ballot paper in the same manner as any other voter, but the ballot paper (in this Act called a tendered ballot paper) shall be of a colour differing from the other ballot papers, and, instead of being put into the ballot box, shall be given to the presiding officer and endorsed by him with the name of the voter and his number in the register of voters, and set aside in a separate packet, and shall not be counted by the returning officer. And the name of the voter and his number on the register shall be entered on a list, in this Act called the tendered votes list.

Spoilt ballot paper.

28. A voter who has inadvertently dealt with his ballot paper in such manner that it cannot be conveniently used as a ballot paper, may, on delivering to the presiding officer the ballot paper so inadvertently dealt with, and proving the fact of the inadvertence to the satisfaction of the presiding officer, obtain another ballot paper in the place of the ballot paper so delivered up (in this Act called a spoilt ballot paper), and the spoilt ballot paper shall be immediately cancelled.

Sealing up ballot boxes, &c.

29. The presiding officer of each station, as soon as practicable after the close of the poll, shall, in the presence of the agents of the candidates, make up into separate packets sealed with his own seal and the seals of such agents of the candidates as desire to affix their seals,—

 (1.) Each ballot box in use at his station, unopened but with the key attached; and

 (2.) The unused and spoilt ballot papers, placed together; and

 (3.) The tendered ballot papers; and

 (4.) The marked copies of the register of voters, and the counterfoils of the ballot papers; and

 (5.) The tendered votes list, and the list of votes marked by the presiding officer, and a statement of the number of the voters whose votes are so marked by

the presiding officer under the heads "physical in-   35 & 36 *Vict.*
capacity," "Jews," and "unable to read," and the   *c.* 33.
declarations of inability to read;

and shall deliver such packets to the returning officer.

30. The packets shall be accompanied by a statement made
by such presiding officer, showing the number of ballot
papers entrusted to him, and accounting for them under the
heads of ballot papers in the ballot box, unused, spoilt, and
tendered ballot papers, which statement is in this Act referred
to as the ballot paper account.

Counting Votes.

31. The candidates may respectively appoint agents to   Counting
attend the counting of the votes.   votes.

32. The returning officer shall make arrangements for
counting the votes in the presence of the agents of the candidates as soon as practicable after the close of the poll, and
shall give to the agents of the candidates appointed to attend
at the counting of the votes notice in writing of the time and
place at which he will begin to count the same.

33. The returning officer, his assistants and clerks, and the
agents of the candidates, and no other person, except with the
sanction of the returning officer, may be present at the counting of the votes.

34. Before the returning officer proceeds to count the votes,
he shall, in the presence of the agents of the candidates, open
each ballot box, and, taking out the papers therein, shall
count and record the number thereof, and then mix together
the whole of the ballot papers contained in the ballot boxes.
The returning officer, while counting and recording the
number of ballot papers and counting the votes, shall keep
the ballot papers with their faces upwards, and take all proper
precautions for preventing any person from seeing the numbers
printed on the backs of such papers.

35. The returning officer shall, so far as practicable, proceed continuously with counting the votes, allowing only time
for refreshment, and excluding (except so far as he and the
agents otherwise agree) the hours between seven o'clock at
night and nine o'clock on the succeeding morning. During
the excluded time the returning officer shall place the ballot

papers and other documents relating to the election under his own seal and the seals of such of the agents of the candidates as desire to affix their seals, and shall otherwise take proper precautions for the security of such papers and documents.

Rejection of ballot papers by returning officer.

36. The returning officer shall endorse "rejected" on any ballot paper which he may reject as invalid, and shall add to the endorsement "rejection objected to," if an objection be in fact made by any agent to his decision. The returning officer shall report *to the Clerk of the Crown in Chancery* (*u*) the number of ballot papers rejected and not counted by him under the several heads of—

1. Want of official mark;
2. Voting for more candidates than entitled to;
3. Writing or mark by which voter could be identified;
4. Unmarked or void for uncertainty;

and shall on request allow any agents of the candidates, before such report is sent, to copy it.

Verification of ballot paper account.

37. Upon the completion of the counting, the returning officer shall seal up in separate packets the counted and rejected ballot papers. He shall not open the sealed packet of tendered ballot papers or marked copy of the register of voters and counterfoils, but shall proceed, in the presence of the agents of the candidates, to verify the ballot paper account given by each presiding officer by comparing it with the number of ballot papers recorded by him as aforesaid, and the unused and spoilt ballot papers in his possession and the tendered votes list, and shall reseal each sealed packet after examination. The returning officer shall report *to the Clerk of the Crown in Chancery* (*u*) the result of such verification, and shall, on request, allow any agents of the candidates, before such report is sent, to copy it.

Delivery of ballot papers to town clerk.

38. Lastly, the returning officer shall forward to *the Clerk of the Crown in Chancery* (*u*) (in manner in which the poll books are by any existing enactment required to be forwarded to such clerk, or as near thereto as circumstances admit) all the packets of ballot papers in his possession, together with the

---

(*u*) Read "Town Clerk," rule 64, post.

35 & 36 *Vict.*
c. 33.

said reports, the ballot paper accounts, tendered votes lists, lists of votes marked by the presiding officer, statements relating thereto, declarations of inability to read, and packets of counterfoils, and marked copies of registers, sent by each presiding officer, indorsing on each packet a description of its contents and the date of the election to which they relate, and the name of the county or borough for which such election was held; and the term poll book in any such enactment shall be construed to include any document forwarded in pursuance of this rule.

39. *The Clerk of the Crown* (*x*) shall retain for a year all documents relating to an election forwarded to him in pursuance of this Act by a returning officer, and then, unless otherwise directed by an order of the House of Commons, or of one of Her Majesty's Superior Courts, shall cause them to be destroyed.

40. No person shall be allowed to inspect any rejected ballot papers in the custody of the *Clerk of the Crown in Chancery* (*x*), except under the order of the *House of Commons or under the order of one of Her Majesty's Superior Courts* (*y*), to be granted by such court on being satisfied by evidence on oath that the inspection or production of such ballot papers is required for the purpose of instituting or maintaining a prosecution for an offence in relation to ballot papers, or for the purpose of a petition questioning an election or return; and any such order for the inspection or production of ballot papers may be made subject to such conditions as to persons, time, place, and mode of inspection or production as the *House or* (*z*) court making the same may think expedient, and shall be obeyed by the *Clerk of the Crown in Chancery* (*x*). Any power given to a court by this rule may be exercised by any judge of such court at chambers.

41. No person shall, except by order of the *House of Commons* (*y*) or any tribunal having cognizance of petitions com-

(*x*) Read "Town Clerk," Rule 64, post.
(*y*) Read "County Court," Rule 64, post.
(*z*) Omit, Rule 64, post.

35 & 36 Vict. c. 33. plaining of undue returns or undue elections, open the sealed packet of counterfoils after the same has been once sealed up, or be allowed to inspect any counted ballot papers in the custody of the *Clerk of the Crown in Chancery* (*d*), such order may be made subject to such conditions as to persons, time, place, and mode of opening or inspection as the *House or* tribunal(*d*) making the order may think expedient; provided that on making and carrying into effect any such order, care shall be taken that the mode in which any particular elector has voted shall not be discovered until he has been proved to have voted, and his vote has been declared by a competent court to be invalid.

Public inspection of documents. 42. All documents forwarded by a returning officer in pursuance of this Act to the *Clerk of the Crown in Chancery*, other than ballot papers and counterfoils, shall be open to public inspection at such time and under such regulations as may be prescribed *by the Clerk of the Crown in Chancery*, with the consent of *the Speaker of the House of Commons*, and the *Clerk of the Crown* shall supply copies of or extracts from the said documents to any person demanding the same, on payment of such fees and subject to such regulations as may be sanctioned by the Treasury (*d*).

Compliance with order for production of documents. 43. Where an order is made for the production by the *Clerk of the Crown in Chancery* (*d*) of any document in his possession relating to any specified election, the production by such clerk or his agent of the document ordered, in such manner as may be directed by such order, or by a rule of the court having power to make such order, shall be conclusive evidence that such document relates to the specified election; and any endorsement appearing on any packet of ballot papers produced by such *Clerk of the Crown* (*d*) or his agent shall be evidence of such papers being what they are stated to be by the endorsement. The production from proper custody of a ballot paper purporting to have been used at any election, and of a counterfoil marked with the same printed number and having

---

(*d*) For Clerk of the Crown substitute "Town Clerk," and for House of Commons, "County Court," Rule 64, post.

a number marked thereon in writing, shall be primâ facie evidence that the person who voted by such ballot paper was the person who at the time of such election had affixed to his name in the register of voters at such election the same number as the number written on such counterfoil.

35 & 36 *Vict.* c. 33.

General Provisions.

* * * * * * *

45. The returning officer shall, as soon as possible, give public notice of the names of the candidates elected, and, in the case of a contested election, of the total number of votes given for each candidate, whether elected or not.

Notice of result of election.

46. Where the returning officer is required or authorised by this Act to give any public notice, he shall carry such requirement into effect by advertisements, placards, handbills, or such other means as he thinks best calculated to afford information to the electors.

47. The returning officer may, if he think fit, preside at any polling station, and the provisions of this Act relating to a presiding officer shall apply to such returning officer with the necessary modifications as to things to be done by the returning officer to the presiding officer, or the presiding officer to the returning officer.

48. In the case of a contested election for any county or borough, the returning officer may, in addition to any clerks, appoint competent persons to assist him in counting the votes.

49. No person shall be appointed by a returning officer for the purposes of an election who has been employed by any other person in or about the election.

50. The presiding officer may do, by the clerks appointed to assist him, any act which he is required or authorised to do by this Act at a polling station except ordering the arrest, exclusion, or ejection from the polling station of any person.

51. A candidate may himself undertake the duties which any agent of his if appointed might have undertaken, or may assist his agent in the performance of such duties, and may be

present at any place at which his agent may, in pursuance of this Act, attend (e).

52. The name and address of every agent of a candidate appointed to attend the counting of the votes shall be transmitted to the returning officer one clear day at the least before the opening of the poll; and the returning officer may refuse to admit to the place where the votes are counted any agent whose name and address has not been so transmitted, notwithstanding that his appointment may be otherwise valid, and any notice required to be given to an agent by the returning officer may be delivered at or sent by post to such address.

Death of agent.

53. If any person appointed an agent by a candidate for the purposes of attending at the polling station or at the counting of the votes dies, or becomes incapable of acting during the time of the election, the candidate may appoint another agent in his place, and shall forthwith give to the returning officer notice in writing of the name and address of the agent so appointed.

Declaration of secrecy.

54. Every returning officer, and every officer, clerk, or agent authorised to attend at a polling station, or at the counting of the votes, shall, before the opening of the poll, make a statutory declaration of secrecy, in the presence, if he is the returning officer, of a justice of the peace, and if he is any other officer or an agent, of a justice of the peace or of the returning officer; but no such returning officer, officer, clerk, or agent as aforesaid shall, save as aforesaid, be required, as such, to make any declaration or take any oath on the occasion of any election.

55. Where in this Act any expressions are used requiring or authorising or inferring that any act or thing is to be done in the presence of the agents of the candidates, such expressions shall be deemed to refer to the presence of such agents of the candidates as may be authorised to attend, and as have in fact attended, at the time and place where such act or thing is being done, and the non-attendance of any agents or

(e) E. g. at a polling station (*Clementson* v. *Mason*, L. R., 10 C. P. 209; 44 L. J., C. P. 171; 32 L. T. 325; 23 W. R. 620).

agent at such time and place shall not, if such act or thing be otherwise duly done, in anywise invalidate the act or thing done.

35 & 36 *Vict.* c. 33.

56. In reckoning time for the purposes of this Act, Sunday, Christmas Day, Good Friday, and any day set apart for a public fast or public thanksgiving, shall be excluded; and where anything is required by this Act to be done on any day which falls on the above-mentioned days such thing may be done on the next day, unless it is one of the days excluded as above mentioned.

Computation of time.

57. In this Act—

The expression "district borough" means the borough of Monmouth and any of the boroughs specified in Schedule E. to the Act of the session of the second and third years of the reign of King William the Fourth, chapter forty-five, intituled "An Act to amend the Representation of the People in England and Wales;" and

The expression "polling place" means, in the case of a borough, such borough or any part thereof in which a separate booth is required or authorised by law to be provided; and

The expression "agents of the candidates," used in relation to a polling station, means agents appointed in pursuance of section eighty-five of the Act of the session of the sixth and seventh years of the reign of her present Majesty, chapter eighteen.

*   *   *   *   *   *   *

PART II.—RULES FOR MUNICIPAL ELECTIONS.

64. In the application of the provisions of this schedule to municipal elections the following modifications (*f*) shall be made :—

(a.) The expression "register of voters" means the burgess roll of the burgesses of the borough, or, in the case of an election for the ward of a borough, the ward list; and the mayor shall provide true copies of such register for each polling station :

(b.) All ballot papers and other documents which, in the

(*f*) See also Act of 1882, sched. iii. part 3, p. 150, ante.

case of a parliamentary election, are forwarded to the Clerk of the Crown in Chancery shall be delivered to the town clerk of the municipal borough in which the election is held, and shall be kept by him among the records of the borough; and the provisions of part one of this schedule with respect to the inspection, production, and destruction of such ballot papers and documents, and to the copies of such documents, shall apply respectively to the ballot papers and documents so in the custody of the town clerk, with these modifications; namely,

(a.) An order of the county court having jurisdiction in the borough, or any part thereof, or of any tribunal in which a municipal election is questioned, shall be substituted for an order of the House of Commons, or of one of Her Majesty's Superior Courts; but an appeal from such county court may be had in like manner as in other cases in such county court;

(b.) The regulations for the inspection of documents and the fees for the supply of copies of documents of which copies are directed to be supplied, shall be prescribed by the council of the borough with the consent of one of Her Majesty's Principal Secretaries of State; and, subject as aforesaid, the town clerk, in respect of the custody and destruction of the ballot papers and other documents coming into his possession in pursuance of this Act, shall be subject to the directions of the council of the borough:

(c.) Nothing in this schedule with respect to the day of the poll shall apply to a municipal election.

*   *   *   *   *   *   *

SECOND SCHEDULE.

Note.—The forms contained in this schedule, or forms as nearly resembling the same as circumstances will admit, shall be used in all cases to which they refer and are applicable, and when so used shall be sufficient in law.

*   *   *   *   *   *   *

Form of Ballot Paper (*f*).

Form of front of Ballot Paper.

Counterfoil No.	1	**BROWN** (John Brown, of 52, George St., Bristol, merchant.)	
NOTE: *The counterfoil is to have a number to correspond with that on the back of the Ballot Paper.*	2	**JONES** (William David Jones, of High Elms, Wilts, esquire.)	
	3	**MERTON** (Hon. George Travis, commonly called Viscount Merton, of Swanworth, Berks.)	
	4	**SMITH** (Henry Sydney Smith, of 72, High Street, Bath, attorney.)	

Form of back of Ballot Paper.

No.

Election for   county [*or* borough, *or* ward].

18   .

Note.—The number on the ballot paper is to correspond with that in the counterfoil.

Directions as to printing Ballot Paper.

Nothing is to be printed on the ballot paper except in accordance with this schedule.

The surname of each candidate, and if there are two or more candidates of the same surname, also the other names of such candidates, shall be printed in large characters, as shown in the form, and the names, addresses, and descriptions, and the number on the back of the paper, shall be printed in small characters.

(*f*) A paper marked with the name of the voter, or with the name of the candidate voted for, written opposite to the name of the latter and not marked with a cross, is bad; but a paper marked with two crosses, or with three crosses, or a single stroke, or a straight line, or a star, or a blurred cross, or a line drawn through the name of the candidate not voted for (in addition to a cross), or a cross on the left hand side, is, *in the absence of evidence of connivance or prearrangement*, good (*Woodward* v. *Sarsons*, L. R., 10 C. P. 733; 44 L. J., C. P. 293; 32 L. T. 867). In this case a Birmingham municipal ward election was held not to be avoided by the presiding officer having delivered nearly 300 ballot papers marked with the *number* of the voter on the burgess roll.

Form of Directions for the Guidance of the Voter in voting, which shall be printed in conspicuous Characters, and placarded outside every Polling Station and in every Compartment of every Polling Station.

The voter may vote for   candidate .

The voter will go into one of the compartments, and, with the pencil provided in the compartment, place a cross on the right-hand side, opposite the name of each candidate for whom he votes, thus **X**

The voter will then fold up the ballot paper so as to show the official mark on the back, and leaving the compartment will, without showing the front of the paper to any person, show the official mark on the back to the presiding officer, and then, in the presence of the presiding officer, put the paper into the ballot box, and forthwith quit the polling station.

If the voter inadvertently spoils a ballot paper, he can return it to the officer, who will, if satisfied of such inadvertence, give him another paper.

If the voter votes for more than   candidate , or places any mark on the paper by which he may be afterwards identified, his ballot paper will be void, and will not be counted.

If the voter takes a ballot paper out of the polling station, or deposits in the ballot box any other paper than the one given him by the officer, he will be guilty of a misdemeanor, and be subject to imprisonment for any term not exceeding six months, with or without hard labour.

Note.—These directions shall be illustrated by examples of the ballot paper.

Form of Statutory Declaration of Secrecy.

I solemnly promise and declare, That I will not at this election for   do anything forbidden by section four of The Ballot Act, 1872, which has been read to me.

Note.—The section must be read to the declarant by the person taking the declaration.

Form of Declaration of inability to read.

I, *A. B.*, of   , being numbered   on the Register of Voters for the county [*or* borough] of   , do hereby declare that I am unable to read.

                                     A. B.,   his mark.

      day of   .

I, the undersigned, being the presiding officer for the polling station for the county [*or* borough] of   , do hereby certify, that the above declaration, having been first read to the above-named *A. B.*, was signed by him in my presence with his mark.

                     Signed, *C. D.*,
             Presiding officer for   polling station for
                the county [*or* borough] of   .

      day of

III.
PERSONATION.

[Incorporated by Municipal Corporations Act, 1882, s. 86, ante.]

PARLIAMENTARY REGISTRATION ACT, 1843 (6 VICT. c. 18).

85. And for the more effectual detection of the personation of voters at elections, be it enacted, that it shall be lawful for any candidate, at any election of a member or members to serve in Parliament for any county, city, or borough, previous to the time fixed for taking the poll at such election, to nominate and appoint an agent or agents on his behalf to attend at each or any of the booths appointed for taking the poll at such election, for the purpose of detecting personation; and such candidate shall give notice in writing to the returning officer, or his respective deputy, of the name and address of the person or persons so appointed by him to act as agents for such purpose; and thereupon it shall be lawful for every such agent to attend during the time of polling at the booth or booths for which he shall have been so appointed.

Agents may be appointed by candidates to detect personation at the time of polling.

86. And be it enacted, that if at the time any person tenders his vote at such election, or after he has voted, and before he leaves the polling booth, any such agent so appointed as aforesaid shall declare to the returning officer, or his respective deputy, presiding therein, that he verily believes and undertakes to prove, that the said person so voting is not in fact the person in whose name he assumes to vote, or to the like effect, then and in every such case it shall be lawful for the said returning officer, or his said deputy, and he is hereby required, immediately after such person shall have voted, by word of mouth to order any constable or other peace officer to take the said person so voting into his custody, which said order shall be a sufficient warrant and authority to the said constable or peace officer for so doing: provided always, that nothing herein contained shall be construed or taken to authorise any returning officer, or his deputy, to reject the vote of any person who shall answer in the affirmative the questions authorised by this Act to be put to him at the time of polling, and shall take the oaths or make the affirmations authorised and required of him; but the said returning officer, or his deputy, shall cause the words, "protested against for per-

Returning officer may order persons charged with personation to be taken into custody.

Vote not to be rejected if questions answered in the affirmative.

L..C.   s

sonation," to be placed against the vote of the person so charged with personation when entered in the poll book.

Persons charged with personation to be taken before two justices.

Bail to be taken in certain cases.

87. And be it enacted, that every such constable or peace officer shall take the person so in his custody, at the earliest convenient time, before some two justices of the peace acting in and for the county, city, or borough within which the said person shall have so voted as aforesaid; provided always, that in case the attendance of two such justices as aforesaid cannot be procured within the space of three hours after the close of the poll on the same day on which such person shall have been so taken into custody, it shall be lawful for the said constable or peace officer, and he is hereby required, at the request of such person so in his custody, to take him before any one justice of the peace acting as aforesaid, and such justice is hereby authorised and required to liberate such person on his entering into a recognizance, with one sufficient surety, conditioned to appear before any two such justices as aforesaid, at a time and place to be specified in such recognizance, to answer the said charge; and if no such justice shall be found within four hours after the closing of the said poll then such person shall forthwith be discharged from custody: provided also, that if in consequence of the absence of such justices as aforesaid, or for any other cause, the said charge cannot be inquired into within the time aforesaid, it shall be lawful nevertheless for any two such justices as aforesaid to inquire into the same on the next or on some other subsequent day, and, if necessary, to issue their warrant for the apprehension of the person so charged.

If justices are satisfied that the person charged has been guilty of personation, they are to commit him for trial.

88. And be it enacted, that if on the hearing of the said charge the said two justices shall be satisfied, upon the evidence on oath of not less than two credible witnesses, that the said person so brought before them has knowingly personated and falsely assumed to vote in the name of some other person within the meaning of this Act, and is not in fact the person in whose name he voted, then it shall be lawful for the said two justices to commit the said offender to the gaol of the county, city, or borough within which the offence was committed, to take his trial according to law, and to bind over the witnesses in their respective recognizances to appear and give evidence on such trial as in the case of other misdemeanors.

89. And be it enacted, that if the said justices shall on the hearing of the said charge be satisfied that the said person so charged with personation is really and in truth the person in whose name he voted, and that the charge of personation has been made against him without reasonable or just cause, or if the agent so declaring as aforesaid, or some one on his behalf, shall not appear to support such charge before the said justices, then it shall be lawful for the said justices and they are hereby required to make an order in writing under their hands, on the said agent so declaring as aforesaid, to pay to the said person so falsely charged, if he shall consent to accept the same, any sum not exceeding the sum of ten pounds nor less than five pounds, by way of damages and costs; and if the said sum shall not be paid within twenty-four hours after such order shall have been made, then the same shall be levied, by warrant under the hand and seal of any justice of the peace acting as aforesaid, by distress and sale of the goods and chattels of the said agent; and in case no sufficient goods or chattels of the said agent can be found on which such levy can be made, then the same shall be levied in like manner on the goods and chattels of the candidate by whom such agent was so appointed to act; and in case the said sum shall not be paid or levied in the manner aforesaid, then it shall be lawful for the said person to whom the said sum of money was so ordered to be paid to recover the same from the said agent or candidate, with full costs of suit, in an action of debt to be brought in any one of her Majesty's Superior Courts of Record at Westminster: provided always, that if the person so falsely charged shall have declared to the said justices his consent to accept such sum as aforesaid by way of damages and costs, and if the whole amount of the sum so ordered to be paid shall have been paid or tendered to such person, in every such case, but not otherwise, the said agent, candidate, and every other person shall be released from all actions or other proceedings, civil or criminal, for or in respect of the said charge and apprehension.

6 Vict. c. 18.

If justices are satisfied that the charge is unfounded, they are to order compensation.

If party falsely charged accepts compensation, no action to be brought.

* * * * * *

[**101.** Interpretation clause. See ante, p. 193.]

———◆———

s 2

Ballot Act, 1872 (35 & 36 Vict. c. 33).

Definition and punishment of personation.

24. The following enactments shall be made with respect to personation at parliamentary and municipal elections:

A person shall for all purposes of the laws relating to parliamentary and municipal elections be deemed to be guilty of the offence of personation who at an election for a county or borough, or at a municipal election, applies for a ballot paper in the name of some other person, whether that name be that of a person living or dead, or of a fictitious person, or who having voted once at any such election applies at the same election for a ballot paper in his own name.

The offence of personation, or of aiding, abetting, counselling, or procuring the commission of the offence of personation by any person, shall be a felony, and any person convicted thereof, shall be punished by imprisonment for a term not exceeding two years, together with hard labour. It shall be the duty of the returning officer to institute a prosecution against any person whom he may believe to have been guilty of personation, or of aiding, abetting, counselling, or procuring the commission of the offence of personation by any person, at the election for which he is returning officer, and the costs and expenses of the prosecutor and the witnesses in such case, together with compensation for their trouble and loss of time, shall be allowed by the court in the same manner in which courts are empowered to allow the same in cases of felony.

The provisions of the Registration Acts, specified (*g*) in the Third Schedule to this Act, shall in England and Ireland respectively apply to personation under this Act in the same manner as they apply to a person who knowingly personates and falsely assumes to vote in the name of another person as mentioned in the said Acts.

(*g*) The provisions so specified are 6 Vict. c. 18, ss. 85—89, ante, p. 257—9.

◆

IV.

CORRUPT PRACTICES.

[Incorporated by Municipal Corporations Act, 1882, sect. 77, p. 39, ante.]

Corrupt Practices Prevention Act, 1854.

17 & 18 Vict. c. 102. *An Act to consolidate and amend the Laws relating to Bribery, Treating, and undue Influence at Elections of Members of Parliament.*

[10th August, 1854.

CONTENTS.

Whereas the laws now in force for preventing corrupt practices in the election of members to serve in Parliament have been found insufficient: And whereas it is expedient to consolidate and amend such laws, and to make further provision for securing the freedom of such elections: BE IT ENACTED, as follows:

[1. Repeal of Acts in the schedule.]

2. The following persons shall be deemed guilty of bribery, and shall be punishable accordingly: Bribery defined.

    1. Every person who shall, directly or indirectly, by himself, or by any other person on his behalf, give, lend, or agree to give or lend, or shall offer, promise, or promise to procure or to endeavour to procure, any money or valuable consideration (*h*) to or for any voter, or to or for any person on behalf of any voter, or to or for any other person, in order to induce any voter to vote, or refrain from voting, or shall corruptly do any such act as aforesaid, on account of such voter having voted or refrained from voting at any election:

___

(*h*) This includes an offer to remunerate for loss of time (*Simpson v. Yeend*, L. R., 4 Q. B. 626; 38 L. J., Q. B. 313; 21 L. T. 56; 17 W. R. 1100; 10 B. & S. 752).

2. Every person who shall, directly or indirectly, by himself
or by any other person on his behalf, give or procure,
or agree to give or procure, or offer, promise, or promise to procure or to endeavour to procure, any office,
place, or employment to or for any voter, or to or for
any person on behalf of any voter, or to or for any
other person, in order to induce such voter to vote, or
refrain from voting, or shall corruptly do any such act
as aforesaid, on account of any voter having voted or
refrained from voting at any election :

3. Every person who shall, directly or indirectly, by himself
or by any other person on his behalf, make any such
gift, loan, offer, promise, procurement, or agreement
as aforesaid, to or for any person, in order to induce
such person to procure, or endeavour to procure, the
return of any person to serve in Parliament, or the
vote of any voter at any election (*i*) :

4. Every person who shall, upon or in consequence of any
such gift, loan, offer, promise, procurement, or agreement, procure or engage, promise, or endeavour to
procure the return of any person to serve in Parliament,
or the vote of any voter at any election :

5. Every person who shall advance or pay, or cause to be
paid, any money to or to the use of any other person,
with the intent that such money, or any part thereof,
shall be expended in bribery at any election, or who
shall knowingly pay, or cause to be paid, any money to
any person in discharge or re-payment of any money
wholly or in part expended in bribery at any election :

and any person so offending shall be guilty of a misdemeanor,
and in Scotland of an offence punishable by fine and imprisonment, and shall also be liable to forfeit the sum of one hundred
pounds (*k*) to any person who shall sue for the same, together
with full costs of suit : provided always, that the aforesaid

(*i*) This includes a corrupt inducement to vote at a " test ballot"
(*Brett* v. *Robinson*, L. R., 5 C. P. 503 ; 39 L. J., C. P. 265 ; 23 L. T.
188 ; 18 W. R. 866.)
(*k*) In respect of each act of bribery, if more than one act committed (*Milnes* v. *Lea*, L. R., 10 C. P. 591 ; 44 L. J., C. P. 336 ;
33 L. T. 174 ; 23 W. R. 660.)

enactment shall not extend, or be construed to extend, to any
money paid, or agreed to be paid, for or on account of any
legal expenses bonâ fide incurred at or concerning any election.

3. The following persons shall also be deemed guilty of
bribery, and shall be punishable accordingly :

1. Every voter who shall, before or during any election,
   directly or indirectly, by himself or by any other person on his behalf, receive, agree or contract for any
   money, gift, loan, or valuable consideration, office,
   place, or employment, for himself or for any other
   person, for voting or agreeing to vote, or for re-
   fraining or agreeing to refrain from voting, at any
   election :
2. Every person who shall, after any election, directly or
   indirectly, by himself or by any other person on his
   behalf, receive any money or valuable consideration on
   account of any person having voted or refrained from
   voting, or having induced any other person to vote or
   to refrain from voting, at any election :

And any person so offending shall be guilty of a misdemeanor, and in Scotland of an offence punishable by fine
and imprisonment, and shall also be liable to forfeit the sum
of ten pounds to any person who shall sue for the same,
together with full costs of suit.

4. Every candidate at an election, who shall corruptly by
himself, or by or with any person, or by any other ways or
means on his behalf, at any time, either before, during, or
after any election, directly or indirectly give or provide, or
cause to be given or provided, or shall be accessory to the
giving or providing, or shall pay, wholly or in part, any
expenses incurred for any meat, drink, entertainment or provision to or for any person, in order to be elected, or for being
elected, or for the purpose of corruptly influencing such person
or any other person to give or refrain from giving his vote at
such election, or on account of such person having voted or
refrained from voting, or being about to vote or refrain from
voting, at such election, shall be deemed guilty of the offence
of treating, and shall forfeit the sum of fifty pounds to any
person who shall sue for the same, with full costs of suit :

17 & 18 Vict. c. 102.

Bribery further defined.

Penalty.

Treating defined.

Penalty.

and every voter who shall corruptly accept or take any such meat, drink, entertainment or provision, shall be incapable of voting at such election, and his vote, if given, shall be utterly void and of none effect.

Undue influence defined. **5.** Every person who shall, directly or indirectly, by himself, or by any other person on his behalf, make use of, or threaten to make use of, any force, violence or restraint, or inflict or threaten the infliction, by himself or by or through any other person, of any injury, damage, harm, or loss, or in any other manner practise intimidation upon or against any person in order to induce or compel such person to vote or refrain from voting, or on account of such person having voted or refrained from voting, at any election, or who shall, by abduction, duress or any fraudulent device or contrivance, impede, prevent or otherwise interfere with the free exercise of the franchise of any voter, or shall thereby compel, induce, or prevail upon any voter, either to give or to refrain from giving his vote at any election, shall be deemed to have committed the offence of undue influence, and shall be guilty of a misdemeanor, and in Scotland of an offence punishable by **Penalty.** fine or imprisonment, and shall also be liable to forfeit the sum of fifty pounds to any person who shall sue for the same, together with full costs of suit.

Names of offenders to be struck out of register, and inserted in separate list. **6.** Whenever it shall be proved before the revising barrister that any person who is or claims to be placed on the list or register of voters for any county, city or borough has been convicted of bribery or undue influence at an election, or that judgment has been obtained against any such person for any penal sum hereby made recoverable in respect of the offences of bribery, treating, or undue influence, or either of them, then and in that case such revising barrister shall, in case the name of such person is in the list of voters, expunge the same therefrom, or shall, in case such person is claiming to have his name inserted therein, disallow such claim ; and the names of all persons whose names shall be so expunged from the list of voters, and whose claims shall be so disallowed, shall be thereupon inserted in a separate list, to be entitled "The list of persons disqualified for bribery, treating or undue influence," which last-mentioned list shall be appended to the list or

register of voters, and shall be printed and published therewith, wherever the same shall be or is required to be printed
or published.

7. No candidate before, during, or after any election shall No cockades,
&c. to be
given at
elections.
in regard to such election, by himself or agent, directly or in-
directly, give or provide to or for any person having a vote at
such election, or to or for any inhabitant of the county, city,
borough, or place for which such election is had, any cockade,
ribbon, or other mark of distinction; and every person so Penalty.
giving or providing shall for every such offence forfeit the
sum of two pounds to such person as shall sue for the same,
together with full costs of suit; and all payments made for or
on account of any chairing, or any such cockade, ribbon, or
mark of distinction as aforesaid, or of any bands of music or
flags or banners, shall be deemed illegal payments within this
Act.

*   *   *   *   *   *   *

9. The pecuniary penalties hereby imposed for the offences Penalties,
how to be
recovered.
of bribery, treating, or undue influence respectively shall be
recoverable by action or suit by any person who shall sue for
the same in any of her Majesty's superior courts at Westminster, if the offence be committed in England or Wales,
and in any of her Majesty's superior courts in Dublin if the
offence be committed in Ireland, and in or before the Court
of Session if the offence be committed in Scotland, and not
otherwise.

*   *   *   *   *   *   *

14. No person shall be liable to any penalty or forfeiture Limitation of
actions.
hereby enacted or imposed, unless some prosecution, action,
or suit for the offence committed shall be commenced against
such person within the space of one year next after such
offence against this Act shall be committed, and unless such
person shall be summoned or otherwise served with writ or
process within the same space of time, so as such summons or
service of writ or process shall not be prevented by such person
absconding or withdrawing out of the jurisdiction of the
court out of which such writ or other process shall have
issued; and in case of any such prosecution, suit, or process

17 & 18 *Vict.* *c.* 102.

as aforesaid, the same shall be proceeded with and carried on without any wilful delay (*k*).

*   *   *   *   *   *   *

Refreshments to voters on the days of nomination or polling declared illegal.

23. And whereas doubts have also arisen as to whether the giving of refreshment to voters on the day of nomination or day of polling be or be not according to law, and it is expedient that such doubts should be removed : be it declared and enacted, that the giving or causing to be given to any voter on the day of nomination or day of polling, on account of such voter having polled or being about to poll, any meat, drink, or entertainment by way of refreshment, or any money or ticket to enable such voter to obtain refreshment, shall be deemed an illegal act, and the person so offending shall forfeit the sum of forty shillings for each offence, to any person who shall sue for the same, together with full costs of suit (*l*).

*   *   *   *   *   *   *

In actions for penalties, parties, &c. to be competent witnesses.

35. On the trial of any action for recovery of any pecuniary penalty under this Act, the parties to such action, and the husbands and wives of such parties respectively, shall be competent and compellable to give evidence in the same manner as parties, and their husbands and wives, are competent and compellable to give evidence in actions and suits under the Act of the fourteenth and fifteenth Victoria, chapter ninety-nine, and "The Evidence Amendment Act, 1853," but subject to and with the exceptions contained in such several Acts : provided always, that any such evidence shall not thereafter be used in any indictment or criminal proceeding under this Act against the party giving it.

Candidate declared guilty of bribery incapable of being elected during Parliament then in existence.

36. If any candidate at an election for any county, city, or borough shall be declared by any election committee guilty, by himself or his agents, of bribery, treating, or undue influence at such election, such candidate shall be incapable

(*k*) It was held to be "wilful delay" in a case where the plaintiff did not declare until eleven months after issue of writ, and the proceedings were stayed (*Taylor* v. *Vergette*, 30 L. J., Ex. 400 ; 7 H. & N. 143). See this section extended to misdemeanors, &c., by sect. 5 of the Act of 1863, post.

(*l*) This section was held to apply to municipal elections in *Hargreaves* v. *Simpson*, 4 Q. B. D. 403; 48 L. J., Q. B. 607; 41 L. T. 216; 27 W. R. 885.

of being elected or sitting in Parliament for such county, city, or borough during the Parliament then in existence.

37. In citing this Act in any instrument, document, or proceeding, or for any purpose whatsoever, it shall be sufficient to use the expression " The Corrupt Practices Prevention Act, 1854."

Short title.

38. Throughout this Act, in the construction thereof, except there be something in the subject or context repugnant to such construction, the word " county " shall extend to and mean any county, riding, parts, or division of a county, stewartry, or combined counties respectively returning a member or members to serve in Parliament; and the words " city or borough " shall mean any university, city, borough, town coporate, county of a city, county of a town, cinque port, district of burghs, or other place or combination of places (not being a county as hereinbefore defined) returning a member or members to serve in Parliament; and the word " election " shall mean the election of any member or members to serve in Parliament; and the words " returning officer " shall apply to any person or persons to whom, by virtue of his or their office, under any law, custom, or statute, the execution of any writ or precept doth or shall belong for the election of a member or members to serve in Parliament, by whatever name or title such person or persons may be called; and the words " revising barrister " shall extend to and include an assistant barrister and chairman presiding in any court held for the revision of the lists of voters, or his deputy in Ireland, and a sheriff or sheriff's Court of Appeal in Scotland, and every other person whose duty it may be to hold a court for the revision and correction of the lists or registers of voters in any part of the United Kingdom; and the word " voter " shall mean any person who has or claims to have a right to vote in the election of a member or members to serve in Parliament; and the words " candidate at an election " shall include all persons elected as members to serve in Parliament at such election, and all persons nominated as candidates, or who shall have declared themselves candidates at or before such election; and the words " per-

Interpretation of terms.

17 & 18 *Vict.*
c. 102.

sonal expenses," as used herein with respect to the expenditure of any candidate in relation to any election, shall include the reasonable travelling expenses of such candidate, and the reasonable expenses of his living at hotels or elsewhere for the purposes of and in relation to such election.

39. [Duration of Act (*m*).]

---

26 & 27 Vict. c. 29. *An Act to amend the Law relating to Corrupt Practices at Elections of Members of Parliament.* [8th June, 1863.

Legal Proceedings.

Sect. 14 of 17 & 18 Vict. c. 102, extended to misdemeanors, &c.

5. The provisions of the fourteenth section of the Corrupt Practices Prevention Act, 1854, shall extend to a misdemeanor or to any other offence under the Corrupt Practices Prevention Acts not punishable by a penalty or forfeiture, as well as to proceedings for any offence punishable by a penalty or forfeiture.

General allegations sufficient in indictments.

6. In any indictment or information for bribery or undue influence, and in any action or proceeding for any penalty for bribery, treating, or undue influence, it shall be sufficient to allege that the defendant was at the election at or in connection with which the offence is intended to be alleged to have been committed guilty of bribery, treating, or undue influence (as the case may require); and in any criminal or civil proceedings in relation to any such offence the certificate of the returning officer in this behalf shall be sufficient evidence of the due holding of the election, and of any person therein named having been a candidate thereat.

(*m*) The Act, originally limited to expire at the end of five years, and of the then next session of Parliament, has been continued by successive statutes, and lastly by the Expiring Laws Continuance Act, 1882 (45 & 46 Vict. c. 64), until the 31st December, 1883.

30 & 31 Vict. c. 102. *An Act further to amend the Laws relating to the Representation of the People in England and Wales.* [15th August, 1867.

49. Any person either directly or indirectly, corruptly paying any rate on behalf of any ratepayer for the purpose of enabling him to be registered as a voter, thereby to influence his vote at any future election, and any candidate or other person, either directly or indirectly, paying any rate on behalf of any voter for the purpose of inducing him to vote or refrain from voting, shall be guilty of bribery, and be punishable accordingly ; and any person on whose behalf and with whose privity any such payment as in this section is mentioned is made shall also be guilty of bribery, and punishable accordingly.

Corrupt payment of rates punishable as bribery.

SUPPLEMENTARY ENACTMENTS.

Towns Improvement Clauses Act, 1847.

[Incorporated with Public Health Act by sect. 160 of that Act, p. 305, post.]

10 & 11 Vict. c. 34. *An Act for consolidating in one Act certain Provisions, usually contained in Acts, for Paving, Draining, Cleansing, Lighting, and Improving Towns.* [21st June, 1847.

CONTENTS.

And with respect to naming the streets and numbering the houses, be it enacted as follows :

64. The commissioners (*a*) shall from time to time cause the houses and buildings in all or any of the streets to be marked with numbers as they think fit, and shall cause to be put up or painted on a conspicuous part of some house, building, or place at or near each end, corner, or entrance of every such street the name by which such street is to be known ; and every person who destroys, pulls down, or defaces any such number or name, or puts up any number or name different from the number or name put up by the commissioners, shall be liable to a penalty not exceeding forty shillings for every such offence.

Houses to be numbered and streets named.

65. The occupiers of houses and other buildings in the streets shall mark their houses with such numbers as the commissioners approve of, and shall renew such numbers as often as they become obliterated or defaced ; and every such occupier who fails, within one week after notice for that purpose from the commissioners, to mark his house with a number approved of by the commissioners, or to renew such number when obliterated, shall be liable to a penalty not exceeding forty shillings ; and the commissioners shall cause such numbers to be marked or to be renewed, as the case

Numbers of houses to be renewed by occupiers.

(*a*) Read, "The Town Council."

may require, and the expense thereof shall be repaid to them by such occupier, and shall be recoverable as damages.

And with respect to improving the line of the streets, and removing obstructions, be it enacted as follows:

Houses may be set forward for improving line of street.

66. The commissioners may allow, upon such terms as they think fit, any building within the limits of the special Act to be set forward, for improving the line of the street in which such building, or any building adjacent thereto, is situated.

Commissioners may purchase houses or ground for effecting additional improvements.

67. The commissioners may agree with the owners of any lands within the limits of the special Act for the absolute purchase thereof, for the purpose of widening, enlarging, or otherwise improving any of the streets, and they shall re-sell any parts of the land so purchased which shall not be wanted for the enlargement of the street.

Houses projecting beyond line of street, when taken down, to be set back.

68. When any house or building, any part of which projects beyond the regular line of the street, or beyond the front of the house or building on either side thereof, has been taken down in order to be rebuilt or altered, the commissioners may require the same to be set backwards to or toward the line of the street, or the line of the adjoining houses or buildings, in such manner as the commissioners direct, for the improvement of such street: provided always, that the commissioners shall make full compensation to the owner of any such house or building for any damage he thereby sustains.

Future projections of houses, &c. to be removed, on notice.

69. The commissioners may give notice to the occupier of any house or building to remove or alter any porch, shed, projecting window, step, cellar, cellar door or window, sign, signpost, signiron, showboard, window shutter, wall, gate, or fence, or any other obstruction or projection erected or placed, after the passing of the special Act, against or in front of any house or building within the limits of the special Act, and which is an obstruction to the safe and convenient passage along any street; and such occupier shall, within fourteen days after the service of such notice upon him, remove such obstruction, or alter the same in such manner as shall have been directed by the commissioners, and in default thereof shall be liable to a penalty not exceeding forty shillings; and the commissioners in such case may remove such obstruction or projection, and the expense of such removal shall be paid by the occupier so making default, and shall be recoverable as damages: provided always, that, except in the case in which such obstructions or projections were made or put up by the occupier, such occupier shall be entitled to deduct the expense of removing the same from the rent payable by him to the owner of the house or building.

10 & 11 *Vict.* c. 34.

70. If any such obstructions or projections were erected or placed against or in front of any house or building in any such street before the passing of the special Act, the commissioners may cause the same to be removed or altered as they think fit; provided that they give notice of such intended removal or alteration to the occupier of the house or building against or in front of which such obstruction or projection shall be thirty days before such alteration or removal is begun, and, if such obstructions or projections shall have been lawfully made, they shall make reasonable compensation to every person who suffers damage by such removal or alteration.

Commissioners may cause existing projections to be removed, and compensation to be made.

71. All doors, gates, and bars put up after the passing of the special Act, within the limits thereof, and which open upon any street, shall be hung or placed so as not to open outwards, except when, in the case of public buildings, the commissioners allow such doors, gates, or bars to be otherwise hung or placed; and if, except as aforesaid, any such door, gate, or bar be hung or placed so as to open outwards on any street, the occupier of such house, building, yard, or land shall, within eight days after notice from the commissioners to that effect, cause the same to be altered so as not to open outwards; and in case he neglect so to do, the commissioners may make such alteration, and the expenses of such alteration shall be paid to the commissioners by such occupier, and shall be recoverable from him as damages, and he shall, in addition, be liable to a penalty not exceeding forty shillings.

Doors in future to be made to open inwards.

72. If any such door, gate, or bar was before the passing of the special Act hung so as to open outwards upon any street, the commissioners may alter the same, so that no part thereof when open shall project over any public way.

Doors opening outwards may be altered.

73. When any opening is made in any pavement or footpath within the limits of the special Act, as an entrance into

Coverings for cellar doors to be made by occupier.

10 & 11 *Vict.*
c. 34.

any vault or cellar, a door or covering shall be made by the occupier of such vault or cellar, of iron or such other materials, and in such manner as the commissioners direct, and such door or covering shall from time to time be kept in good repair by the occupier of such vault or cellar; and if such occupier do not within a reasonable time make such door or covering, or if he make any such door or covering contrary to the directions of the commissioners, or if he do not keep the same when properly made in good repair, he shall for every such offence be liable to a penalty not exceeding five pounds.

Penalty for neglect.

Waterspouts to be affixed to houses or buildings.

74. The occupier of every house or building in, adjoining, or near to any street shall, within seven days next after service of an order of the commissioners for that purpose, put up and keep in good condition a shoot or trough of the whole length of such house or building, and shall connect the same either with a similar shoot on the adjoining house or with a pipe or trunk to be fixed to the front or side of such building from the roof to the ground, to carry the water from the roof thereof, in such manner that the water from such house, or any portico or projection therefrom, shall not fall upon the persons passing along the street, or flow over the footpath; and in default of compliance with any such order within the period aforesaid such occupier shall be liable to a penalty not exceeding forty shillings for every day that he shall so make default.

And with respect to ruinous or dangerous buildings, be it enacted as follows:

Ruinous or dangerous buildings to be taken down or secured by owners, &c.

75. If any building or wall, or any thing affixed thereon, within the limits of the special Act, be deemed by the surveyor of the commissioners to be in a ruinous state, and dangerous to passengers or to the occupiers of the neighbouring buildings, such surveyor shall immediately cause a proper hoard or fence to be put up for the protection of passengers, and shall cause notice in writing to be given to the owner of such building or wall, if he be known and resident within the said limits, and shall also cause such notice to be put on the door or other conspicuous part of the said premises, or otherwise to be given to the occupier thereof, if any, requiring such owner or occupier forthwith to take down, secure, or repair such building, wall, or other thing, as the case shall require; and if such owner or occupier do not begin to repair, take down, or secure such building, wall, or other thing within the space of three days after any such notice has been so given or put up as aforesaid, and complete such repairs, or taking down or securing, as speedily as the nature of the case will admit, the said surveyor may make complaint thereof before two justices, and it shall be lawful for such justices to order the owner, or in his default the occupier (if any), of such building, wall, or other thing, to take down, rebuild, repair, or otherwise secure, to the satisfaction of such surveyor, the same, or such part thereof as appears to them to be in a dangerous state, within a time to be fixed by such justices; and in case the same be not taken down, repaired, rebuilt, or otherwise secured within the time so limited, or if no owner or occupier can be found on whom to serve such order, the commissioners shall with all convenient speed cause all or so much of such building, wall, or other thing as shall be in a ruinous condition, and dangerous as aforesaid, to be taken down, repaired, rebuilt, or otherwise secured in such manner as shall be requisite; and all the expenses of putting up every such fence, and of taking down, repairing, rebuilding, or securing such building, wall, or other thing, shall be paid by the owner thereof.

10 & 11 Vict. c. 34.

If owner, &c. neglect to repair, commissioners may cause the same to be done, charging owner, &c. with the expenses.

76. If such owner can be found within the limits of the special Act, and if, on demand of the expenses aforesaid, he neglect or refuse to pay the same, then such expenses may be levied by distress, and any justice may issue his warrant accordingly.

The expenses to be levied by distress on the owner.

77. If such owner cannot be found within the said limits, or sufficient distress of his goods and chattels within the said limits cannot be made, the commissioners, after giving twenty-eight days' notice of their intention to do so, by posting a printed or written notice in a conspicuous place on such building, or on the land whereon such building stood, may take such building or land, provided that such expenses be not paid or tendered to them within the said twenty-eight days, making compensation to the owner of such building or land in the manner provided by the Lands Clauses Consolidation Act, 1845, in the case of lands taken otherwise than

If owner cannot be found, commissioners may take the house or ground, making compensation provided by 8 Vict. c. 18.

T 2

10 & 11 *Vict.*
c. 34.

with the consent of the owners and occupiers thereof, and the commissioners shall be entitled to deduct out of such compensation the amount of the expenses aforesaid, and may thereupon sell or otherwise dispose of the said building or land for the purposes of this Act.

Commissioners may sell the materials, restoring to the owner overplus arising from the sale.

78. If any such house or building as aforesaid, or any part of the same, be pulled down by virtue of the powers aforesaid, the commissioners may sell the materials thereof, or so much of the same as shall be pulled down, and apply the proceeds of such sale in payment of the expenses incurred in respect of such house or building; and the commissioners shall restore any overplus arising from such sale to the owner of such house or building, on demand; nevertheless, the commissioners, although they sell such materials for the purposes aforesaid, shall have the same remedies for compelling the payment of so much of the said expenses as may remain due after the application of the proceeds of such sale as are hereinbefore given to them for compelling the payment of the whole of the said expenses.

And with respect to precautions during the construction and repair of the sewers, streets, and houses, be it enacted as follows:

Bars to be erected across streets while repairs or alterations are making, and lights placed at night.

79. The commissioners shall, during the construction or repair of any of the streets vested in them, and during the construction or repair of any sewers or drains, take proper precaution for guarding against accident, by shoreing-up and protecting the adjoining houses, and shall cause such bars or chains to be fixed across or in any of the streets, to prevent the passage of carriages and horses while such works are carried on, as to them shall seem proper; and the commissioners shall cause any sewer or drain or other works, during the construction or repair thereof by them, to be lighted and guarded during the night, so as to prevent accidents; and every person who takes down, alters, or removes any of the said bars or chains, or extinguishes any light, without the authority or consent of the commissioners, shall for every such offence be liable to a penalty not exceeding five pounds.

Hoards to be set up during repairs.

80. Every person intending to build or take down any building within the limits of the special Act, or to cause the same to be so done, or to alter or repair the outward part of any such building, or to cause the same to be so done, where any street or footway will be obstructed or rendered inconvenient by means of such work, shall before beginning the same cause sufficient hoards or fences to be put up, in order to separate the building where such works are being carried on from the street, with a convenient platform and handrail, if there be room enough, to serve as a footway for passengers, outside of such hoard or fence, and shall continue such hoard or fence, with such platform and handrail as aforesaid, standing and in good condition, to the satisfaction of the commissioners, during such time as the public safety or convenience requires, and shall in all cases in which it is necessary, in order to prevent accidents, cause the same to be sufficiently lighted during the night; and every such person who fails to put up such fence or hoard, or platform with such handrail as aforesaid, or to continue the same respectively standing and in good condition as aforesaid during the time aforesaid, or who does not, while the said hoard or fence is standing, keep the same sufficiently lighted in the night, or who does not remove the same, when directed by the commissioners, within a reasonable time afterwards, shall for every such offence be liable to a penalty not exceeding five pounds, and a further penalty not exceeding forty shillings for every day while such default is continued.

81. When any building materials, rubbish, or other things are laid, or any hole made, in any of the streets, whether the same be done by order of the commissioners or not, the person causing such materials or other things to be so laid, or such hole to be made, shall at his own expense cause a sufficient light to be fixed in a proper place upon or near the same, and continue such light every night from sun-setting to sun-rising while such materials or hole remain; and such person shall, at his own expense, cause such materials or other things and such hole to be sufficiently fenced and inclosed until such materials or other things are removed or the hole filled up or otherwise made secure; and every such person who fails so to light, fence, or inclose such materials or other things, or such hole, shall for every such offence be liable to a penalty not exceeding five pounds, and a further penalty not exceeding forty shillings for every day while such default is continued.

Penalty for continuing deposits of building materials or excavations an unreasonable time.

82. In no case shall any such building materials or other things or such hole be allowed to remain for an unnecessary time, under a penalty not exceeding five pounds to be paid for every such offence by the person who causes such materials or other things to be laid or such hole to be made, and a further penalty not exceeding forty shillings for every day during which such offence is continued after the conviction for such offence; and in any such case the proof that the time has not exceeded the necessary time shall be upon the person so causing such materials or other things to be laid, or causing such hole to be made.

Dangerous places to be repaired or inclosed.

83. If any building or hole or any other place near any street be, for want of sufficient repair, protection, or inclosure, dangerous to the passengers along such street, the commissioners shall cause the same to be repaired, protected, or inclosed, so as to prevent danger therefrom; and the expenses of such repair, protection, or inclosure shall be repaid to the commissioners by the owner of the premises so repaired, protected, or inclosed, and shall be recoverable from him as damages.

TOWNS POLICE CLAUSES ACT, 1847.

[Incorporated with Public Health Act by sect. 171 of that Act, p. 307, post.]

10 & 11 Vict. c. 89. *An Act for consolidating in one Act certain provisions usually contained in Acts for regulating the Police of Towns.* [22nd July, 1847.

CONTENTS.

And with respect to obstructions and nuisances in the streets, be it enacted as follows:

21. The commissioners may from time to time make orders for the route to be observed by all carts, carriages, horses, and persons, and for preventing obstruction of the streets within the limits of the special Act, in all times of public processions, rejoicings, or illuminations, and in any case when the streets are thronged or liable to be obstructed, and may also give directions to the constables for keeping order and preventing any obstruction of the streets in the neighbourhood of theatres and other places of public resort, and every wilful breach of any such order shall be deemed a separate offence against this Act, and every person committing any such offence shall be liable to a penalty not exceeding forty shillings (*b*).

10 & 11 Vict. c. 89.

Power to prevent obstructions in the streets during public processions, &c.

22. On application to the commissioners by the minister or churchwardens or chapelwardens of any church, chapel, or other place of public worship within the limits of the special Act, the commissioners may make orders for regulating the route by which persons shall drive any cart or carriage, or cattle, or the manner in which they shall drive them, in the neighbourhood of such places of worship, during the hours of divine service on Sunday, Christmas-day, Good Friday, or any day appointed for a public fast or thanksgiving, and any orders so made shall be printed and put up on or near the church, chapel, or place of public worship to which the same refer, and in some conspicuous places near and leading thereto, and elsewhere as the commissioners direct, and every wilful breach of any such order shall be deemed a separate offence against this Act, and every person committing any such offence shall be liable to a penalty not exceeding forty shillings.

Power to regulate the route of persons driving stage carriages, &c. during divine service.

23. No proprietor of any stage carriage duly licensed to carry passengers for hire shall be liable to any penalty for any deviation from the route or line of route specified in his licence which the driver of such stage carriage makes in consequence of any regulation or direction made or given by the commissioners.

Proprietors of stage carriages deviating from route by order free from penalty.

24. If any cattle be at any time found at large in any street within the limits of the special Act, without any person having the charge thereof, any constable or officer of police, or

Power to impound stray cattle.

(*b*) This section would seem to have the effect of recognizing the legality of processions for any purpose.

10 & 11 Vict.
c. 89.
any person residing within the limits of the special Act, may seize and impound such cattle in any common pound within the said limits, or in such other place as the commissioners appoint for that purpose, and may detain the same therein until the owner thereof pay to the commissioners a penalty not exceeding forty shillings, besides the reasonable expenses of impounding and keeping such cattle.

Power to sell stray cattle for penalty and expenses.

25. If the said penalty and expenses be not paid within three days after such impounding, the pound-keeper, or other person appointed by the commissioners for that purpose, may proceed to sell or cause to be sold any such cattle; but previous to such sale seven days notice thereof shall be given to or left at the dwelling-house or place of abode of the owner of such cattle, if he be known, or if not, then notice of such intended sale shall be given by advertisement, to be inserted seven days before such sale in some newspaper published or circulated within the limits of the special Act; and the money arising from such sale, after deducting the said sums, and the expenses aforesaid, and all other expenses attending the impounding, advertising, keeping, and sale of any such cattle so impounded, shall be paid to the commissioners, and shall be by them paid, on demand, to the owner of the cattle so sold.

Persons guilty of pound-breach to be committed for three months.

26. Every person who releases or attempts to release any cattle from any pound or place where the same are impounded under the authority of this or the special Act, or who pulls down, damages, or destroys the same pound or place, or any part thereof, with intent to procure the unlawful release of such cattle, shall, upon conviction of such offence before any two justices, be committed by them to some common gaol or house of correction for any time not exceeding three months.

Power to provide a pound.

27. The commissioners may purchase a piece of land within the limits of the special Act for the purpose of a pound for stray animals, and may erect a pound thereon, and such pound when made shall be kept in repair by the commissioners.

Penalty on persons committing in a street any of the offences herein named.

28. Every person who in any street, to the obstruction, annoyance, or danger of the residents or passengers, commits any of the following offences, shall be liable to a penalty not exceeding forty shillings for each offence, or, in the discretion of the justice before whom he is convicted, may be committed to prison, there to remain for a period not exceeding fourteen days, and any constable or other officer appointed by virtue of this or the special Act shall take into custody, without warrant, and forthwith convey before a justice, any person who within his view commits any such offence; (that is to say,)

Every person who exposes for show, hire, or sale (except in a market or market-place or fair lawfully appointed for that purpose) any horse or other animal, or exhibits in a caravan or otherwise any show or public entertainment, or shoes, bleeds, or farries any horse or animal (except in cases of accident), or cleans, dresses, exercises, trains or breaks, or turns loose any horse or animal, or makes or repairs any part of any cart or carriage (except in cases of accident where repair on the spot is necessary):

Showing animals, &c.

Every person who suffers to be at large any unmuzzled ferocious dog, or sets on or urges any dog or other animal to attack, worry, or put in fear any person or animal:

Dogs.

Every owner of any dog who suffers such dog to go at large, knowing or having reasonable ground for believing it to be in a rabid state, or to have been bitten by any dog or other animal in a rabid state:

Every person, who after public notice given by any justice, directing dogs to be confined on account of suspicion of canine madness, suffers any dog to be at large during the time specified in such notice (*a*):

Every person who slaughters or dresses any cattle, or any part thereof, except in the case of any cattle over-driven which may have met with any accident, and which for the public safety or other reasonable cause ought to be killed on the spot:

Slaughtering cattle.

Every person having the care of any waggon, cart, or carriage who rides on the shafts thereof, or who without having reins, and holding the same, rides upon such waggon, cart, or carriage, or on any animal drawing the same, or who is at such a distance from such waggon, cart, or carriage as not to have due control over every animal drawing the same, or who does not, in meeting any other carriage, keep his waggon, cart, or carriage to the left or

Driving, &c.

(*a*) See also " The Dogs Act, 1871" (34 & 35 Vict. c. 56), p. 346, post.

10 & 11 *Vict.*
c. 89.

near side, or who in passing any other carriage, does not keep his waggon, cart, or carriage on the right or off side of the road (except in cases of actual necessity, or some sufficient reason for deviation), or who, by obstructing the street, wilfully prevents any person or carriage from passing him, or any waggon, cart, or carriage under his care:

Every person who at one time drives more than two carts or waggons, and every person driving two carts or waggons who has not the halter of the horse in the last cart or waggon securely fastened to the back of the first cart or waggon, or has such halter of a greater length from such fastening to the horse's head than four feet:

Every person who rides or drives furiously any horse or carriage, or drives furiously any cattle:

Every person who causes any public carriage, sledge, truck, or barrow, with or without horses, or any beast of burden, to stand longer than is necessary for loading or unloading goods, or for taking up or setting down passengers (except hackney carriages, and horses and other beasts of draught or burthen, standing for hire in any place appointed for that purpose by the commissioners or other lawful authority), and every person who, by means of any cart, carriage, sledge, truck, or barrow, or any animal, or other means, wilfully interrupts any public crossing, or wilfully causes any obstruction in any public footpath or other public thoroughfare:

Every person who causes any tree or timber or iron beam to be drawn in or upon any carriage without having sufficient means of safely guiding the same:

Every person who leads or rides any horse or other animal, or draws or drives any cart or carriage, sledge, truck, or barrow upon any footway of any street, or fastens any horse or other animal so that it stands across or upon any footway:

Obstructing footway. Every person who places or leaves any furniture, goods, wares, or merchandize, or any cask, tub, basket, pail, or bucket, or places or uses any standing-place, stool, bench, stall, or showboard on any footway, or who places any blind, shade, covering, awning, or other projection over or along any such footway, unless such blind, shade, covering, awning, or other projection is eight feet in height at least in every part thereof from the ground:

10 & 11 *Vict.* *c.* 89.

Every person who places, hangs up, or otherwise exposes to sale any goods, wares, merchandize, matter, or thing whatsoever, so that the same project into or over any footway, or beyond the line of any house, shop, or building at which the same are so exposed, so as to obstruct or incommode the passage of any person over or along such footway:

Every person who rolls or carries any cask, tub, hoop, or wheel, or any ladder, plank, pole, timber, or log of wood, upon any footway, except for the purpose of loading or unloading any cart or carriage, or of crossing the footway:

Every person who places any line, cord, or pole across any street, or hangs or places any clothes thereon: Clothes-line.

Every common prostitute or nightwalker loitering and importuning passengers for the purpose of prostitution: Indecent behaviour.

Every person who wilfully and indecently exposes his person:

Every person who publicly offers for sale or distribution, or exhibits to public view any profane, indecent, or obscene book, paper, print, drawing, painting, or representation, or sings any profane or obscene song or ballad, or uses any profane or obscene language:

Every person who wantonly discharges any firearm, or throws or discharges any stone or other missile, or makes any bonfire, or throws or sets fire to any firework: Firearms, &c.

Every person who wilfully and wantonly disturbs any inhabitant, by pulling or ringing any door bell, or knocking at any door, or who wilfully and unlawfully extinguishes the light of any lamp: Ringing bells —extinguishing lamps.

Every person who flies any kite, or who makes or uses any slide upon ice or snow: Sliding.

Every person who cleanses, hoops, fires, washes, or scalds any cask or tub, or hews, saws, bores, or cuts any timber or stone, or slacks, sifts, or screens any lime: Cleansing casks.

Every person who throws or lays down any stones, coals, slate, shells, lime, bricks, timber, iron, or other materials (except building materials so inclosed as to prevent mischief to passengers): Laying down stones.

10 & 11 Vict.
c. 89.

Carpets.

Every person who beats or shakes any carpet, rug, or mat (except door mats, beaten or shaken before the hour of eight in the morning):

Flower-pots.

Every person who fixes or places any flower-pot or box, or other heavy article, in any upper window, without sufficiently guarding the same against being blown down:

Throwing brick from roof.

Every person who throws from the roof or any part of any house or other building any slate, brick, wood, rubbish, or other thing, except snow thrown so as not to fall on any passenger:

Permitting servant to stand on window-sill.

Every occupier of any house or other building or other person who orders or permits any person in his service to stand on the sill of any window, in order to clean, paint, or perform any other operation upon the outside of such window, or upon any house or other building within the said limits, unless such window be in the sunk or basement story:

Leaving open cellar.

Every person who leaves open any vault or cellar, or the entrance from any street to any cellar or room underground, without a sufficient fence or handrail, or leaves defective the door, window, or other covering of any vault or cellar, or who does not sufficiently fence any area, pit, or sewer left open, or who leaves such open area, pit, or sewer without a sufficient light after sunset to warn and prevent persons from falling thereinto:

Throwing dirt.

Every person who throws or lays any dirt, litter, or ashes, or nightsoil, or any carrion, fish, offal, or rubbish, on any street, or causes any offensive matter to run from any manufactory, brewery, slaughter-house, butcher's shop, or dunghill into any street: provided always, that it shall not be deemed an offence to lay sand or other materials in any street in time of frost, to prevent accidents, or litter or other suitable materials to prevent the freezing of water in pipes, or in case of sickness to prevent noise, if the party laying any such things causes them to be removed as soon as the occasion for them ceases:

Pigstye.

Every person who keeps any pigstye to the front of any street, not being shut out from such street by a sufficient wall or fence, or who keeps any swine in or near any street, so as to be a common nuisance.

29. Every person drunk in any street, and guilty of any riotous or indecent behaviour therein, and also every person guilty of any violent or indecent behaviour in any police office or any police station house within the limits of the special Act, shall be liable to a penalty not exceeding forty shillings for every such offence, or, in the discretion of the justice before whom he is convicted, to imprisonment for a period not exceeding seven days (*c*).

10 & 11 *Vict.* c. 89.

Penalty on drunken persons, &c. guilty of riotous or indecent behaviour.

And with respect to fires, be it enacted as follows:

30. Every person who wilfully sets or causes to be set on fire any chimney within the limits of the special Act shall be liable to a penalty not exceeding five pounds: provided always, that nothing herein contained shall exempt the person so setting or causing to be set on fire any chimney from liability to be indicted for felony.

Penalty for setting chimneys wilfully on fire.

31. If any chimney accidentally catch or be on fire within the said limits the person occupying or using the premises in which such chimney is situated shall be liable to a penalty not exceeding ten shillings: provided always, that such forfeiture shall not be incurred if such person prove to the satisfaction of the justice before whom the case is heard that such fire was in nowise owing to omission, neglect, or carelessness of himself or servant.

Penalty for accidentally allowing chimneys to catch fire.

32. The commissioners may purchase or provide such engines for extinguishing fire, and such water buckets, pipes, and other appurtenances for such engines, and such fire escapes and other implements for safety or use in case of fire, and may purchase, keep, or hire such horses for drawing such engines as they think fit, and may build, provide, or hire places for keeping such engines with their appurtenances, and may employ a proper number of persons to act as firemen, and may make such rules for their regulation as they think proper, and give such firemen and other persons such salaries

Fire-engines and firemen may be provided by the commissioners.

(*c*) Drunkenness unaccompanied by disorder is punishable under sect. 12 of the Licensing Act, 1872 (35 & 36 Vict. c. 94), which section also authorizes the punishment of hard labour for drunkenness accompanied by disorder.

It has been held that a person summoned for drunkenness accompanied by disorder cannot be convicted of simple drunkenness. (*Martin* v. *Pridgeon*, 28 L. J., M. C. 179.)

10 & 11 Vict.
c. 89.

and such rewards for their exertions in cases of fire, as they think fit.

Fire police permitted to go beyond the limits of the Act in certain cases.

33. The commissioners may send such engines, with their appurtenances, and the said firemen, beyond the limits of the special act, for extinguishing fire in the neighbourhood of the said limits; and the owner of the lands or buildings where such fire shall have happened shall in such case defray the actual expense which may be thereby incurred, and shall also pay to the commissioners a reasonable charge for the use of such engines with their appurtenances, and for the attendance of such firemen; and in case of any difference between the commissioners and the owner of the said lands or buildings, the amount of the said expenses and charge, as well as the propriety of sending the said engines and firemen as aforesaid for extinguishing such fire, (if the propriety thereof be disputed,) shall be determined by two justices, whose decision shall be final; and the amount of the said expenses and charge shall be recovered by the commissioners as damages.

And with respect to places of public resort (*d*), be it enacted as follows:

Penalty on victuallers harbouring constables while on duty.

34. Every victualler or keeper of any public house, or person licensed to sell wine, spirits, beer, cider, or other fermented or distilled liquors by retail, to be drunk or consumed on the premises, within the limits of the special Act, who knowingly harbours or entertains or suffers to remain in his public-house or place wherein he carries on his business any constable during any part of the time appointed for his being on duty, unless for the purpose of quelling any disturbance or restoring order, shall, for every such offence, be liable to a penalty not exceeding twenty shillings.

Penalty on coffee-shop keepers harbouring disorderly persons.

35. Every person keeping any house, shop, room, or other place of public resort within the limits of the special act for the sale or consumption of refreshments of any kind who knowingly suffers common prostitutes or reputed thieves to

---

(*d*) The penalties under the Licensing Act, 1872 (35 & 36 Vict. c. 94), ss. 14, 16, are cumulative upon, not substitutionary of, the penalties under this section. See sect. 340 of the Public Health Act, 1875, post, p. 312.

assemble at and continue in his premises shall, for every such
offence, be liable to a penalty not exceeding five pounds.

10 & 11 Vict.
c. 89.

36. Every person who within the limits of the special Act
keeps or uses or acts in the management of any house, room,
pit, or other place for the purpose of fighting, baiting, or
worrying any animals shall be liable to a penalty of not more
than five pounds, or, in the discretion of the justices before
whom he is convicted, to imprisonment, with or without hard
labour, for a time not exceeding one month; and the commissioners may, by order in writing, authorise the superintendent
constable, with such constables as he thinks necessary, to
enter any premises kept or used for any of the purposes aforesaid, and take into custody all persons found therein without
lawful excuse, and every person so found shall be liable to a
penalty not exceeding five shillings, and a conviction for this
offence shall not exempt the owner, keeper, or manager of any
such house, room, pit, or place from any penal consequence to
which he is liable for the nuisance thereby occasioned (*e*).

Penalty on persons keeping places for bear-baiting, cock-fighting, &c.

And with respect to hackney carriages, be it enacted as
follows:

37. The commissioners may from time to time license to
ply for hire within the prescribed distance, or if no distance
is prescribed, within five miles from the General Post Office
of the city, town, or place to which the special Act refers,
(which in that case shall be deemed the prescribed distance,)
such number of hackney coaches or carriages of any kind or
description adapted to the carriage of persons as they think
fit.

Hackney carriages to be licensed.

38. Every wheeled carriage, whatever may be its form or
construction, used in standing or plying for hire in any street
within the prescribed distance, and every carriage standing
upon any street within the prescribed distance, having thereon
any numbered plate required by this or the special Act to be
fixed upon a hackney carriage, or having thereon any plate
resembling or intended to resemble any such plate as aforesaid, shall be deemed to be a hackney carriage within the
meaning of this Act; and in all proceedings at law or other-

What to be hackney car-riages.

(*e*) See also 12 & 13 Vict. c. 92, s. 3.

10 & 11 *Vict.*
c. 89.wise the term "hackney carriage" shall be sufficient to describe any such carriage: provided always, that no stage coach used for the purpose of standing or plying for passengers to be carried for hire at separate fares, and duly licensed for that purpose, and having thereon the proper numbered plates required by law to be placed on such stage coaches, shall be deemed to be a hackney carriage within the meaning of this Act.

Fee to be paid for licence.

39. For every such licence there shall be paid to the clerk of the commissioners, or other person appointed by them to receive the same, such sum as the commissioners direct, not exceeding five shillings.

Persons applying for licence to sign a requisition for same.

40. Before any such licence is granted a requisition for the same, in such form as the commissioners from time to time provide for that purpose, shall be made and signed by the proprietor or one of the proprietors of the hackney carriage in respect of which such licence is applied for, and in every such requisition shall be truly stated the name and surname and place of abode of the person applying for such licence, and of every proprietor or part proprietor of such carriage, or person concerned, either solely or in partnership with any other person, in the keeping, employing, or letting to hire of such carriage ; and any person who, on applying for such licence, states in such requisition the name of any person who is not a proprietor or part proprietor of such carriage, or who is not concerned as aforesaid in the keeping, employing, or letting to hire of such carriage, and also any person who wilfully omits to specify truly in such requisition as aforesaid the name of any person who is a proprietor or part proprietor of such carriage, or who is concerned as aforesaid in the keeping, employing, or letting to hire of such carriage, shall be liable to a penalty not exceeding ten pounds.

What shall be specified in the licences.

41. In every such licence shall be specified the name and surname and place of abode of every person who is a proprietor or part proprietor of the hackney carriage in respect of which such licence is granted, or who is concerned, either solely or in partnership with any other person, in the keeping, employing, or letting to hire of any such carriage, and also the number of such licence which shall correspond with the number to be painted or marked on the plates to be fixed on such carriage, together with such other particulars as the commissioners think fit. 10 & 11 *Vict.* c. 89.

42. Every licence shall be made out by the clerk of the commissioners, and duly entered in a book to be provided by him for that purpose, and in such book shall be contained columns or places for entries to be made of every offence committed by any proprietor or driver or person attending such carriage, and any person may at any reasonable time inspect such book without fee or reward. Licences to be registered.

43. Every licence so to be granted shall be under the common seal of the commissioners, if incorporated, or if not incorporated, shall be signed by two or more of the commissioners, and shall not include more than one carriage so licensed, and shall be in force for one year only from the day of the date of such licence, or until the next general licensing meeting, in case any general licensing day be appointed by the commissioners. Licence to be in force for one year only.

44. So often as any person named in any such licence as the proprietor or one of the proprietors, or as being concerned either solely or in partnership with any person in the keeping, employing, or letting to hire of any such carriage, changes his place of abode, he shall, within seven days next after such change, give notice thereof in writing, signed by him, to the commissioners, specifying in such notice his new place of abode; and he shall at the same time produce such licence at the office of the commissioners, who shall, by their clerk, or some other officer, endorse thereon and sign a memorandum specifying the particulars of such change; and any person named in any such licence as aforesaid as the proprietor, or one of the proprietors, of any hackney carriage, or as being concerned as aforesaid, who changes his place of abode, and neglects or wilfully omits to give notice of such change, or to produce such licence in order that such memorandum as aforesaid may be endorsed thereon within the time and in the manner limited and directed by this or the special Act, shall be liable to a penalty not exceeding forty shillings. Notice to be given by proprietors of hackney carriages of any change of abode.

45. If the proprietor or part proprietor of any carriage, or any person so concerned as aforesaid, permits the same to Penalty for plying for hire without a licence.

be used as a hackney carriage plying for hire within the pre-scribed distance without having obtained a licence as afore-said for such carriage, or during the time that such licence is suspended as hereinafter provided, or if any person be found driving, standing, or plying for hire with any carriage within the prescribed distance, for which such licence as aforesaid has not been previously obtained, or without having the number of such carriage corresponding with the number of the licence openly displayed on such carriage, every such person so offend-ing shall for every such offence be liable to a penalty not exceeding forty shillings.

Drivers not to act without first obtaining a licence.

46. No person shall act as driver of any hackney carriage licensed in pursuance of this or the special Act to ply for hire within the prescribed distance without first obtaining a licence from the commissioners, which licence shall be registered by the clerk to the commissioners, and a fee of one shilling shall be paid for the same ; and every such licence shall be in force until the same is revoked, except during the time that the same may be suspended as after mentioned.

Penalty on drivers acting without licence.

47. If any person acts as such driver as aforesaid without having obtained such licence or during the time that his licence is suspended, or if he lend or part with his licence, except to the proprietor of the hackney carriage, or if the proprietor of any such hackney carriage employ any person as the driver thereof who has not obtained such licence, or during the time that his licence is suspended, as hereinafter provided, every such driver and every such proprietor shall, for every such offence, respectively be liable to a penalty not exceeding twenty shillings.

Proprietor to retain licence of drivers when in his employ, and to produce the same when sum-moned.

Justices may endorse con-victions upon licences.

48. In every case in which the proprietor of any such hackney carriage permits or employs any licensed person to act as the driver thereof, such proprietor shall cause to be delivered to him, and shall retain in his possession, the licence of such driver while such driver remains in his employ ; and in all cases of complaint, where the proprietor of a hackney carriage is summoned to attend before a justice, or to produce the driver, the proprietor so summoned shall also produce the licence of such driver, if he be then in his employ; and if any driver complained of be adjudged guilty of the offence alleged against him, such justice shall make an endorsement upon the licence of such driver, stating the nature of the offence and the amount of the penalty inflicted; and if any such proprietor neglect to have delivered to him and to retain in his possession the licence of any driver while such driver remains in his employ, or if he refuse or neglect to produce such licence as aforesaid, such proprietor shall for every such offence be liable to a penalty not exceeding forty shillings.

Penalty on proprietors for neglect.

49. When any driver leaves the service of the proprietor by whom he is employed without having been guilty of any misconduct, such proprietor shall forthwith return to such driver the licence belonging to him; but if such driver have been guilty of any misconduct, the proprietor shall not return his licence, but shall give him notice of the complaint which he intends to prefer against him, and shall forthwith summon such driver to appear before any justice to answer the said complaint; and such justice, having the necessary parties before him, shall inquire into and determine the matter of complaint, and if upon inquiry it appear that the licence of such driver has been improperly withheld, such justice shall direct the immediate re-delivery of such licence, and award such sum of money as he thinks proper to be paid by such proprietor to such driver by way of compensation.

Proprietor to return licence to drivers when quitting his service if they behave well, if otherwise, proprietors to summon them.

Compensation in case of licence being improperly withheld.

50. The commissioners may, upon the conviction for the second time of the proprietor or driver of any such hackney carriage for any offence under the provisions of this or the special Act with respect to hackney carriages, or any bye-law made in pursuance thereof, suspend or revoke, as they deem right, the licence of any such proprietor or driver.

Licences to be suspended or revoked for misconduct.

51. No hackney carriage shall be used or employed or let to hire, or shall stand or ply for hire within the prescribed distance, unless the number of persons to be carried by such hackney carriage, in words at length, and in form following, (that is to say,) "To carry   persons," be painted on a plate placed on some conspicuous place on the outside of such carriage, and in legible letters, so as to be clearly distinguishable from the colour of the ground whereon the same are painted, one inch in length, and of a proportionate breadth; and the driver of any such hackney carriage shall not be

Number of persons to be carried in a hackney carriage to be painted thereon.

10 & 11 *Vict.*
c. 89.

required to carry in or by such hackney carriage a greater number of persons than the number painted thereon.

Penalty for neglect or for refusal to carry the prescribed number.

52. If the proprietor of any hackney carriage permit the same to be used, employed, or let to hire, or if any person stand or ply for hire with such carriage, without having the number of persons to be carried thereby painted and exhibited in manner aforesaid, or if the driver of any such hackney carriage refuse, when required by the hirer thereof, to carry in or by such hackney carriage the number of persons painted thereon, or any less number, every proprietor or driver so offending shall be liable to a penalty not exceeding forty shillings.

Penalty on driver for refusing to drive.

53. Any driver of a hackney carriage standing at any of the stands for hackney carriages appointed by the commissioners, or in any street, who refuses or neglects, without reasonable excuse, to drive such carriage to any place within the prescribed distance, or the distance to be appointed by any bye-law of the commissioners not exceeding the prescribed distance, to which he is directed to drive by the person hiring or wishing to hire such carriage, shall for every such offence be liable to a penalty not exceeding forty shillings.

Penalty for demanding more than the sum agreed for, though less than the legal fare.

54. If the proprietor or driver of any such hackney carriage, or if any other person on his behalf, agree beforehand with any person hiring such hackney carriage to take for any job a sum less than the fare allowed by this or the special Act, or any bye-law made thereunder, such proprietor or driver shall be liable to a penalty not exceeding forty shillings if he exact or demand for such job more than the fare so agreed upon.

Agreement to pay more than the legal fare not to be binding, and sum paid beyond the proper fare may be recovered back.

55. No agreement whatever made with the driver, or with any person having or pretending to have the care of any such hackney carriage, for the payment of more than the fare allowed by any bye-law made under this or the special Act, shall be binding on the person making the same, and any such person may, notwithstanding such agreement, refuse, on discharging such hackney carriage, to pay any sum beyond the fare allowed as aforesaid, and if any person actually pay to the driver of any such hackney carriage, whether in pursuance of any such agreement or otherwise, any sum exceeding the fare to which such driver was entitled, the person paying the same shall be entitled, on complaint made against such driver before any justice of the peace, to recover back the sum paid beyond the proper fare, and moreover such driver shall be liable to a penalty for such exaction not exceeding the sum of forty shillings, and in default of the repayment by such driver of such excess of fare, or of payment of the said penalty, such justice shall forthwith commit such driver to prison, there to remain for any time not exceeding one month, unless the said excess of fare and the said penalty be sooner paid.

56. If the proprietor or driver of any such hackney carriage, or if any other person on his behalf, agree with any person to carry in or by such hackney carriage persons not exceeding in number the number so painted on such carriage as aforesaid, for a distance to be in the discretion of such proprietor or driver, and for a sum agreed upon, such proprietor or driver shall be liable to a penalty not exceeding forty shillings if the distance which he carries such persons be under that to which they were entitled to be carried for the sum so agreed upon according to the fare allowed by this or the special Act, or any bye-law made in pursuance thereof.

Driver to carry, under an agreement for a discretionary distance, the distance to which hirer is entitled for the fare.

57. When any hackney carriage is hired and taken to any place, and the driver thereof is required by the hirer there to wait with such hackney carriage, such driver may demand and receive from such hirer his fare for driving to such place, and also a sum equal to the fare of such carriage for the period, as a deposit over and above such fare, during which he is required to wait as aforesaid, or if no fare for time be fixed by the bye-laws, then the sum of one shilling and sixpence for every half hour during which he is so required to wait, which deposit shall be accounted for by such driver when such hackney carriage is finally discharged by such hirer; and if any such driver who has received any such deposit as aforesaid refuses to wait as aforesaid, or goes away or permits such hackney carriage to be driven or taken away without the consent of such hirer, before the expiration of the time for which such deposit was made; or if such driver, on the final discharge of such hackney carriage, refuse duly to account for

Deposit to be made for carriages waiting.

Penalty on the driver refusing to wait, or to account for the deposit.

10 & 11 Vict.
c. 89.

such deposit, every such driver so offending shall be liable to a penalty not exceeding forty shillings.

Overcharge by hackney coachmen, &c. to be included in conviction, and returned to aggrieved party.

58. Every proprietor or driver of any such hackney carriage who is convicted of taking as a fare a greater sum than is authorized by any bye-law made under this or the special Act shall be liable to a penalty not exceeding forty shillings, and such penalty may be recovered before one justice ; and in the conviction of such proprietor or driver an order may be included for payment of the sum so overcharged, over and above the penalty and costs ; and such overcharge shall be returned to the party aggrieved, whose evidence shall be admissible in proof of the said offence.

Penalty for permitting persons to ride without consent of the hirer.

59. Any proprietor or driver of any such hackney carriage which is hired who permits or suffers any person to be carried in or upon or about such hackney carriage during such hire, without the express consent of the person hiring the same, shall be liable to a penalty not exceeding twenty shillings.

No person to act as driver of any carriage without the consent of the proprietor.

60. No person authorized by the proprietor of any hackney carriage to act as driver of such carriage shall suffer any other person to act as driver of such carriage without the consent of the proprietor thereof, and no person, whether licensed or not, shall act as driver of any such carriage without the consent of the proprietor, and any person so suffering another person to act as driver, and any person so acting as driver without such consent as aforesaid, shall be liable to a penalty not exceeding forty shillings for every such offence.

Penalty on drivers misbehaving.

61. If the driver or any other person having or pretending to have the care of any such hackney carriage be intoxicated while driving, or if any such driver or other person by wanton and furious driving, or by any other wilful misconduct, injure or endanger any person in his life, limbs or property, he shall be liable to a penalty not exceeding five pounds, and in default of payment thereof the justice before whom he is convicted of such offence may commit him to prison, there to remain for any time not exceeding two months.

Penalty for leaving carriages unattended at places of public resort.

62. If the driver of any such hackney carriage leave it in any street, or at any place of public resort or entertainment, whether it be hired or not, without some one proper to take

care of it, any constable may drive away such hackney carriage and deposit it, and the horse or horses harnessed
thereto, at some neighbouring livery stable or other place of
safe custody ; and such driver shall be liable to a penalty not
exceeding twenty shillings for such offence, and in default of
payment of the said penalty upon conviction, and of the expenses of taking and keeping the said hackney carriage and
horse or horses, the same, together with the harness belonging thereto, or any of them, shall be sold by order of the
justice before whom such conviction is made, and after deducting from the produce of such sale the amount of the said
penalty, and of all costs and expenses, as well of the proceedings before such justice as of the taking, keeping and
sale of the said hackney carriage, and of the said horse or
horses and harness, the surplus (if any) of the said produce
shall be paid to the proprietor of such hackney carriage.

10 & 11 Vict. c. 89.

63. In every case in which any hurt or damage has been
caused to any person or property as aforesaid by the driver of
any carriage let to hire, the justice before whom such driver
has been convicted may direct that the proprietor of such carriage shall pay such a sum not exceeding five pounds as
appears to the justice a reasonable compensation for such
hurt or damage ; and every proprietor who pays any such
compensation as aforesaid may recover the same from the
driver, and such compensation shall be recoverable from such
proprietor, and by him from such driver, as damages.

Damage done by driver may be recovered from the proprietor.

64. Any driver of any hackney carriage who suffers the
same to stand for hire across any street or alongside of any
other hackney carriage, or who refuses to give way, if he
conveniently can, to any other carriage, or who obstructs or
hinders the driver of any other carriage in taking up or setting down any person into or from such other carriage, or
who wrongfully in a forcible manner prevents or endeavours
to prevent the driver of any other hackney carriage from
being hired, shall be liable to a penalty not exceeding twenty
shillings.

Improperly standing with carriage ; re-fusing to give way to, or obstructing any other driver ; or de-priving him of his fare.

65. If the driver of any such hackney carriage be summoned or brought before any justice to answer any complaint
or information touching or concerning any offence alleged to

10 & 11 *Vict.*
c. 89.

Justices empowered to award compensation to drivers for loss of time in attending to answer complaints not substantiated.

have been committed by such driver against the provisions of this or the special Act, or any bye-law made thereunder, and such complaint or information be afterwards withdrawn or quashed or dismissed, or if such driver be acquitted of the offence charged against him, the said justice, if he think fit, may order the complainant or informant to pay to the said driver such compensation for his loss of time in attending the said justice touching or concerning such complaint or information as to the said justice seems reasonable, and in default of payment of such compensation, the said justice may commit such complainant or informant to prison for any time not exceeding one month, unless the same shall be sooner paid.

Penalty for refusing to pay the fare.

66. If any person refuse to pay on demand to any proprietor or driver of any hackney carriage the fare allowed by this or the special Act, or any bye-law made thereunder, such fare may, together with costs, be recovered before one justice as a penalty.

Penalty for damaging carriage.

67. Any person using any hackney carriage plying under a licence granted by virtue of this or the special Act, who wilfully injures the same, shall for every such offence be liable to a penalty not exceeding five pounds, and shall also pay to the proprietor of such hackney carriage reasonable satisfaction for the damage sustained by the same; and such satisfaction shall be ascertained by the justices before whom the conviction takes place, and shall be recovered by the same means as the penalty.

Commissioners may make bye-laws for regulating hackney carriages.

68. The commissioners may from time to time (subject to the restrictions of this and the special Act) make bye-laws for all or any of the purposes following; (that is to say,)

For regulating the conduct of the proprietors and drivers of hackney carriages plying within the prescribed distance in their several employments, and determining whether such drivers shall wear any and what badges, and for regulating the hours within which they may exercise their calling:

For regulating the manner in which the number of each carriage, corresponding with the number of its licence, shall be displayed:

For regulating the number of persons to be carried by such hackney carriages, and in what manner such number is to be shown on such carriage, and what number of horses or other animals is to draw the same, and the placing of check strings to the carriages, and the holding of the same by the driver, and how such hackney carriages are to be furnished or provided :

For fixing the stands of such hackney carriages and the distance to which they may be compelled to take passengers, not exceeding the prescribed distance :

For fixing the rates or fares, as well for time as distance, to be paid for such hackney carriages within the prescribed distance, and for securing the due publication of such fares :

For securing the safe custody and re-delivery of any property accidentally left in hackney carriages, and fixing the charges to be made in respect thereof.

And with respect to public bathing, be it enacted as follows :—

69. Where any part of the sea-shore or strand of any river used as a public bathing-place is within the limits of the special Act the commissioners may make bye-laws for the following purposes ; (that is to say,)

Bathing machines.

For fixing the stands of bathing machines on the sea-shore or strand, and the limits within which persons of each sex shall be set down for bathing, and within which persons shall bathe :

For preventing any indecent exposure of the persons of the bathers :

For regulating the manner in which the bathing machines shall be used, and the charges to be made for the same :

For regulating the distance at which boats and vessels let to hire for the purpose of sailing or rowing for pleasure shall be kept from persons bathing within the prescribed limits.

35 & 36 Vict. c. 91. *An Act to authorize the application of Funds of Municipal Corporations and other governing Bodies in certain cases* (*f*).   [10th August, 1872

Whereas by the Act passed in the session holden in the twentieth and twenty-first years of the reign of her Majesty, intituled An Act to amend the Acts concerning the Municipal Corporations (*g*), the trustees acting under any Act of Parliament for supplying any borough, or any district within or in certain cases beyond the limits of a borough, with water or gas, or having powers for providing or maintaining any cemetery or market in or for any borough, or otherwise improving the same, are authorized and empowered to transfer to the body corporate of such borough all their rights, estates, properties, and liabilities:

And whereas by the ninety-second section of the Act passed in the session holden in the fifth and sixth years of the reign of King William the Fourth, chapter seventy-six, to provide for the regulation of municipal corporations in England and Wales (*h*), in each borough the annual proceeds of all property and hereditaments belonging to the body corporate, and fines and rates levied in the borough, are directed to form the borough fund, and such fund is directed to be applied in the payment of certain salaries and certain expenses and the expenses necessarily incurred in carrying into effect the provisions of the said Act, and the surplus (if any)

(*f*) This Act, commonly called "Leeman's Act," and sometimes also conveniently (though incorrectly, inasmuch as it applies to other places besides boroughs) the "Borough Funds Act," was passed in consequence of the decision in *Reg.* v. *Mayor of Sheffield* (L. R., 6 Q. B. 652; 40 L. J., Q. B. 247; ante, p. 155), that the expenses of opposing a certain waterworks extension bill could not be legally charged upon the borough fund.

The Act does not affect the right of a municipal corporation, under the general law applicable to trustees, to defray out of their general funds or rates the expenses of opposing a bill attacking their existence as a corporation, or their property, rights, or privileges. (*Attorney-General* v. *Mayor of Brecon*, 10 Ch. D. 204; 48 L. J., Ch. 153; 40 L. T. 52; 27 W. R. 332—per Jessel, M. R.)

(*g*) 20 & 21 Vict. c. 50, s. 2, re-enacted by sect. 136 of the Act of 1882, ante, p. 74.

(*h*) Re-enacted by sect. 140 and 143 of the Act of 1882, ante, p. 76.

of such fund is directed to be applied, under the direction of the council, for the public benefit of the inhabitants and the improvement of the borough :

And whereas the Public Health Act, 1848 (*i*), the Local Government Act, 1858(*i*), and various local Acts of Parliament, have conferred powers of improving, cleansing, paving, lighting, and otherwise governing places or districts upon boards of health, commissioners, trustees, or other persons :

And whereas it is expedient to extend the powers of governing bodies so as to enable them to apply the borough or other funds under the control of such governing body towards such costs, charges, and expenses as may be incurred for the purposes and in the manner herein provided :

Be it therefore enacted by the Queen's most excellent Majesty, by and with the advice and consent of the lords spiritual and temporal and commons, in this present Parliament assembled, and by the authority of the same, as follows :

1. The term "governing body" in this Act shall mean the council of any municipal borough, the board of health, local board, commissioners, trustees, or other body acting under any general or local Act of Parliament for the management, improvement, cleansing, paving, lighting, and otherwise governing places or districts, and the term "district" shall mean the borough, place, township, or district within which the governing body may for the time being have jurisdiction : provided, however, that in the borough of Cambridge, in any matters affecting the constitution, power, or functions of the Board of Cambridge Improvement Commissioners, as defined in the several Acts of Parliament relating thereto, the term "governing body" shall mean such board of improvement commissioners, and not the council of the borough of Cambridge. *Interpretation of terms.*

2. When in the judgment of a governing body in any district it is expedient for such governing body to promote or oppose any local and personal Bill or Bills in Parliament, or to prosecute or defend any legal proceedings necessary for the promotion or protection of the interests of the inhabitants of *Costs of promoting or opposing parliamentary and other proceedings for benefit of inhabitants to be charge on borough funds, except in certain cases.*

(*i*) Repealed, but in great part re-enacted by the Public Health Act, 1875.

the district, it shall be lawful for such governing body to apply the borough fund, borough rate, or other the public funds or rates under the control of such governing body, to the payment of the costs and expenses attending the same; and when there are several funds or rates under the control of the governing body, such governing body shall determine out of which fund or funds, rate or rates, such expense shall be payable, and in what proportions: provided that nothing in this Act contained shall authorise any governing body to promote any Bill in Parliament for the establishment of any gas or waterworks to compete with any existing gas or water company established under any Act of Parliament: provided that no powers contained in this clause shall apply in any case where the promotion of or opposition to a Bill by a governing body has been decided by a committee of either House of Parliament to be unreasonable or vexatious (*k*).

No payment to member of governing body to be so charged.

3. No payment to any member of a governing body for acting as counsel or agent in promoting or opposing any such Bill shall be charged as aforesaid.

Costs of promoting or opposing Bills to require sanction of special meetings.

4. No expense in relation to promoting or opposing any Bill or Bills in Parliament shall be charged as aforesaid unless incurred in pursuance of a resolution of an absolute majority of the whole number of the governing body at a meeting of the governing body, after ten clear days notice by public advertisement of such meeting and of the purpose thereof in some local newspaper published or circulating in the district, such notice to be in addition to the ordinary notices required for summoning such meeting, nor unless such resolution shall have been published twice in some newspaper or newspapers circulating in the district, and shall have received, in respect of matters within the jurisdiction of the Local Government Board, the approval of such board, and in respect of other matters, the approval of one of her Majesty's Secretaries of State, and in case of the promotion of a Bill in Parliament no further expense shall be incurred or charged as aforesaid after the deposit of the Bill, unless the propriety of

---

(*k*) As to recovery of costs in such a case from promoters or opponents, see 28 Vict. c. 27.

such promotion shall be confirmed by such absolute majority at a further special meeting to be held in pursuance of a similar notice not less than fourteen days after the deposit of the Bill in Parliament : provided further, that no expense in promoting or opposing any Bill in Parliament shall be charged as aforesaid unless such promotion or opposition shall have had the consent of the owners and ratepayers of that district, to be expressed by resolution in the manner provided in the Local Government Act (1858) (*l*) for the adoption of that Act (*m*).

5. The approval of the Local Government Board or one of her Majesty's principal Secretaries of State, as the case may be, shall not be given to any such resolution as aforesaid until the expiration of seven days after the second publication thereof, as provided by this Act, and in the meantime any ratepayer within the district of the governing body may give notice in writing to the Local Government Board or Secretary of State objecting to such approval.

Proviso as to approval of Local Government Board, &c. to any such resolution.

6. All costs, charges, and expenses incurred under the provisions of this Act shall, before the same become chargeable, be examined and allowed by some person to be authorized by one of her Majesty's principal Secretaries of State or by the Local Government Board, as the case may be.

Costs to be examined.

7. The Local Government Board, or one of her Majesty's principal Secretaries of State, shall have power to direct a local inquiry to be held upon any application under this Act, by any person or persons whom they may respectively nominate for the purpose, and to charge the costs and expenses of such local inquiry upon the governing body or the person by whom such application shall be made.

Power to direct local inquiry.

(*l*) 21 & 22 Vict. c. 98, ss. 12, 13. But the Act is repealed by the Public Health Act, 1875, which by sect. 313 substitutes Schedule 3 to that Act for sects. 12 and 13 of the Local Government Act, 1858. See that section and Schedule 3, pp. 312, 313, post.

The court in its discretion refused to grant a mandamus for a poll applied for by a promoter of a bill in *Reg.* v. *Mayor of Peterborough*, 44 L. J., Q. B. 85.

(*m*) All these conditions precedent must be fully performed in order to give the promoters of a bill, if a town council, a locus standi, and the Act when passed will be found to contain a recital to that effect.

35 & 36 Vict. c. 91.

Saving clause.

8. Nothing in this Act shall extend or be construed to alter or affect any special provision which is or shall be contained in any other Act for the payment of the costs, charges, and expenses intended to be provided for by this Act, or to take away or diminish any rights or powers now possessed or enjoyed by any governing body, or which are or shall be vested in or exerciseable by the inhabitants of any district under any general or special Act.

Towns Improvement Clauses Act, 1847, s. 142, repealed.

9. The one hundred and forty-second section of "The Towns Improvement Clauses Act, 1847," is hereby repealed so far as the same is inconsistent with the provisions of this Act.

Act not to extend to bills if object attainable by provisional order.

10. The provisions of this Act shall not extend to applications for any Bill in Parliament for any object which would, for the time being, be obtainable by provisional order.

Act not to apply to the Metropolis.

11. This Act shall not extend or apply to Ireland or the city of London or the metropolitan area as defined by the Metropolitan Local Management Act, 1855.

PUBLIC HEALTH ACT, 1875.

38 & 39 Vict. c. 55. *An Act for consolidating and amending the Acts relating to Public Health in England.* [11th August, 1875

CONTENTS.

BE IT ENACTED as follows:

Definitions.

4. In this Act, if not inconsistent with the context, the

following words and expressions have the meanings hereinafter respectively assigned to them; that is to say,

"Borough" means any place for the time being subject to
  the Act of the session of the fifth and sixth years of the
  reign of King William the Fourth, chapter seventy-six,
  intituled "An Act to provide for the Regulation of Municipal Corporations in England and Wales," and any Act
  amending the same :

*   *   *   *   *   *

"Bakehouse Regulation Act" means 26 & 27 Vict. c. 40
  (Bakehouse Regulation Act, 1863) (*n*).

"Artizans and Labourers Dwellings Act" means 31 & 32
  Vict. c. 130 (Artizans and Labourers Dwellings Act,
  1868):

"Baths and Washhouses Acts" means 9 & 10 Vict. c. 74
  (An Act to encourage the establishment of Public Baths
  and Washhouses); 10 & 11 Vict. c. 61 (An Act to amend
  the Act for the establishment of Public Baths and Washhouses):

"Labouring Classes Lodging Houses Act" means 14 & 15
  Vict. c. 34 (Labouring Classes Lodging Houses Act,
  1851); 29 & 30 Vict. c. 28 (Labouring Classes Dwelling
  Houses Act, 1866); 30 & 31 Vict. c. 28 (Labouring
  Classes Dwelling Houses Act, 1867) (*o*):

*   *   *   *   *   *

PART II.—Authorities for Execution of Act.

Constitution of Districts and Authorities.

5. For the purposes of this Act England, except the metro- Urban and
polis, shall consist of districts to be called respectively— rural sanitary
districts.

(1.) Urban sanitary districts, and

(2.) Rural sanitary districts,

(in this Act referred to as urban and rural districts); and such
urban and rural districts shall respectively be subject to the

---

(*n*) This Act is repealed by the Factory and Workshop Act, 1878
(41 Vict. c. 16), but replaced by that Act. See especially sects. 34
and 35.

(*o*) For other Acts investing town councils with special power as
to their subject-matter, see post, p. 346.

38 & 39 *Vict.*
c. 55.

jurisdiction of local authorities, called urban sanitary authorities and rural sanitary authorities (in this Act referred to as urban and rural authorities), invested with the powers in this Act mentioned.

Borough, urban district, and town council, urban authority.

6. Urban districts shall consist of the places in that behalf mentioned in the first column of the table in this section contained, and urban authorities shall be the several bodies of persons specified in the second column of the said table in relation to the said places respectively.

Urban District.	Urban Authority.
Borough constituted such either before or after the passing of this Act.	The mayor, aldermen and burgesses acting by the council.

*   *   *   *   *   *

Powers and duties of urban authorities.

10. In addition to the powers, rights, duties, capacities, liabilities, and obligations exerciseable by or attaching to an urban authority under this Act, every urban authority shall within their district (to the exclusion of any other authority which may have previously exercised or been subject to the same) have, exercise, and be subject to all the powers, rights, duties, capacities, liabilities, and obligations within such district exerciseable or attaching by and to the local authority under the Bakehouse Regulation Act, and the Artizans and Labourers Dwellings Act, or any Acts amending the same.

Where the Baths and Washhouses Acts and the Labouring Classes Lodging Houses Acts, or any of them, are in force within the district of any urban authority, such authority shall have all powers, rights, duties, capacities, liabilities, and obligations in relation to such Acts exerciseable by or attaching to the council, incorporated commissioners, local board improvement commissioners, and other commissioners, or persons acting in the execution of the said Acts or any of them.

Where the Baths and Washhouses Acts are not in force within the district of any urban authority, such authority may adopt such Acts; and where the Labouring Classes

Lodging Houses Acts are not in force within the district of any urban authority, such authority may adopt such Acts.

38 & 39 Vict. c. 55.

Where any local Act other than an Act for the conservancy of any river is in force within the district of an urban authority, conferring on any commissioners, trustees, or other persons, powers, for purposes the same as, or similar to, those of this Act (but not for their own pecuniary benefit), all the powers, rights, duties, capacities, liabilities, and obligations of such commissioners, trustees, or other persons in relation to such purposes shall be transferred and attach to the said urban authority.

*   *   *   *   *   *   *

12. From and after the passing of this Act, all such property, real and personal, including all interests, rights, and easements in, to, and out of, property, real and personal (including things in action), as belongs to or is vested in, or would but for this Act have belonged to or been vested in, the council of any borough, or any improvement commissioners or local board as the urban sanitary authority of any district under the Sanitary Acts, or any board of guardians as the rural sanitary authority of any district under those Acts, shall continue vested or vest in such council, improvement commissioners, or local board, or board of guardians as the local authority of their district under this Act, subject to all debts, liabilities, and obligations affecting the same property.

Vesting of property in local authorities.

All debts, liabilities, and obligations incurred by any authority, whose powers, rights, duties, liabilities, capacities and obligations are under this Act exerciseable by, or attached to, a local authority, may be enforced against the local authority to the same extent and in the same manner as they might have been enforced against the authority which incurred the same.

*   *   *   *   *   *   *

160. The provisions of the Towns Improvement Clauses Act, 1847, with respect to the following matters; that is to say,

Incorporation of certain provisions of 10 & 11 Vict. c. 34.

    (1.) With respect to naming the streets and numbering the houses; and

L.C.   x

(2.) With respect to improving the line of the streets and removing obstructions; and

(3.) With respect to ruinous or dangerous buildings; and

(4.) With respect to precautions during the construction and repair of the sewers, streets and houses,

shall, for the purpose of regulating such matters in urban districts, be incorporated with this Act.

Notices for alterations under the sixty-ninth, seventieth, and seventy-first sections, directions under the seventy-third section, and orders under the seventy-fourth section of the said Towns Improvement Clauses Act, may, at the option of the urban authority, be served on owners instead of occupiers, or on owners as well as occupiers, and the cost of works done under any of these sections may, when notices have been so served on owners, be recovered from owners instead of occupiers; and when such cost is recovered from occupiers so much thereof may be deducted from the rent of the premises where the work is done as is allowed in the case of private improvement rates under this Act.

Lighting Streets, &c.

161. Any urban authority may contract with any person for the supply of gas, or other means of lighting the streets, markets, and public buildings in their district, and may provide such lamps, lamp posts and other materials and apparatus as they may think necessary for lighting the same.

Where there is not any company or person (other than the urban authority) authorized by or in pursuance of any Act of Parliament, or any order confirmed by Parliament, to supply gas for public and private purposes, supplying gas within any part of the district of such authority, such authority may themselves undertake to supply gas for such purposes or any of them throughout the whole or any part of their district; and if there is any such company or person so supplying gas, but the limits of supply of such company or person include part only of the district, then the urban authority may themselves undertake to supply gas throughout any part of the district not included within such limits of supply.

Where an urban authority may under this Act themselves undertake to supply gas for the whole or any part of their

Powers of urban authority for lighting their district.

district, a provisional order authorizing a gas undertaking 38 & 39 *Vict.*
may be obtained by such authority under and subject to the *c.* 55.
provisions of the Gas and Water Works Facilities Act, 1870,
and any Act amending the same; and in the construction of
the said Act the term "the undertakers" shall be deemed to
include any such urban authority: provided that for the
purposes of this Act the Local Government Board shall
throughout the said Act be deemed to be substituted for the
Board of Trade.

162. [Power for sale of undertaking of gas company to
urban authority.]

* * * * * * *

Police Regulations.

171. The provisions of the Towns Police Clauses Act, 1847, Incorporation
with respect to the following matters, (namely,)   of certain
provisions of
 (1.) With respect to obstructions and nuisances in the 10 & 11 Vict.
  streets; and   c. 89.

 (2.) With respect to fires; and

 (3.) With respect to places of public resort; and

 (4.) With respect to hackney carriages; and

 (5.) With respect to public bathing;

shall, for the purpose of regulating such matters in urban districts, be incorporated with this Act.

The expression in the provisions so incorporated "the superintendent constable," and the expression "any constable or
other officer appointed by virtue of this or the special Act,"
shall, for the purposes of this Act, respectively include any
superintendent of police, and any constable or officer of police
acting for or in the district of any urban authority; and the
expression "within the prescribed distance" shall, for the
purposes of this Act, mean within any urban district.

Notwithstanding anything in the provisions so incorporated,
a license granted to the driver of any hackney carriage in
pursuance thereof shall be in force for one year only from the
date of the license, or until the next general licensing meeting, where a day for such meeting is appointed.

172. Any urban authority may license the proprietors,
drivers and conductors of horses, ponies, mules or asses
standing for hire within the district in like manner and with

38 & 39 *Vict.*
c. 55.

Urban authority may make bye-laws for licensing horses, boats, &c. for hire.

the like incidents and consequences as in the case of proprietors and drivers of hackney carriages, and may make bye-laws for regulating stands and fixing rates of hire, and as to the qualification of such drivers and conductors, and for securing their good and orderly conduct while in charge.

Any urban authority may also license the proprietors of pleasure boats and vessels, and the boatmen or other persons in charge thereof, and may make bye-laws for regulating the numbering and naming of such boats and vessels, and the number of persons to be carried therein, and the mooring places for the same, and for fixing rates of hire, and the qualification of such boatmen or other persons in charge, and for securing their good and orderly conduct while in charge.

*   *   *   *   *   *   *

Bye-laws (a).

Authentication and alteration of bye-laws.

182. All bye-laws made by a local authority under and for the purposes of this Act shall be under their common seal; and any such bye-law may be altered or repealed by a subsequent bye-law made pursuant to the provisions of this Act: provided that no bye-law made under this Act by a local authority shall be of any effect if repugnant to the laws of England or to the provisions of this Act.

Power to impose penalties on breach of bye-laws.

183. Any local authority may, by any bye-laws made by them under this Act, impose on offenders against the same such reasonable penalties as they think fit, not exceeding the sum of five pounds for each offence, and in the case of a continuing offence a further penalty not exceeding forty shillings for each day after written notice of the offence from the local authority; but all such bye-laws imposing any penalty shall be so framed as to allow of the recovery of any sum less than the full amount of the penalty.

Nothing in the provisions of any Act incorporated herewith shall authorize the imposition or recovery under any bye-laws made in pursuance of such provisions of any greater penalty than the penalties in this section specified.

Confirmation of bye-laws.

184. Bye-laws made by a local authority under this Act shall not take effect unless and until they have been sub-

---

(*a*) See sect. 23, sub-sect. 6 of the Act of 1882, p. 15, ante.

mitted to and confirmed by the Local Government Board, which board is hereby empowered to allow or disallow the same as it may think proper; nor shall any such bye-laws be confirmed—

Unless notice of intention to apply for confirmation of the same has been given in one or more of the local newspapers circulated within the district to which such bye-laws relate, one month at least before the making of such application; and

Unless for one month at least before any such application a copy of the proposed bye-laws has been kept at the office of the local authority, and has been open during office hours thereat to the inspection of the ratepayers of the district to which such bye-laws relate, without fee or reward.

The clerk of the local authority shall, on the application of any such ratepayer, furnish him with a copy of such proposed bye-laws or any part thereof, on payment of sixpence for every hundred words contained in such copy.

A bye-law required to be confirmed by the Local Government Board shall not require confirmation, allowance, or approval by any other authority.

185. All bye-laws made by a local authority under this Act, or for purposes the same as or similar to those of this Act under any local Act, shall be printed and hung up in the office of such authority; and a copy thereof shall be delivered to any ratepayer of the district to which such bye-laws relate, on his application for the same; a copy of any bye-laws made by a rural authority shall also be transmitted to the overseers of every parish to which such bye-laws relate, to be deposited with the public documents of the parish, and to be open to the inspection of any ratepayer of the parish at all reasonable hours.

Bye-laws to be printed, &c.

186. A copy of any bye-laws made under this Act by a local authority (not being the council of a borough), signed and certified by the clerk of such authority to be a true copy and to have been duly confirmed, shall be evidence until the contrary is proved in all legal proceedings of the due making,

Evidence of bye-laws.

confirmation and existence of such bye-laws without further or other proof.

Bye-laws made under sect. 90 of 5 & 6 Will. 4, c. 76, to be submitted to Local Government Board.

187. Bye-laws made by the council of any borough under the provisions of section ninety of the Act of the sixth year of King William the Fourth, chapter seventy-six, for the prevention and suppression of certain nuisances, shall not be required to be sent to a Secretary of State, nor shall they be subject to the disallowance in that section mentioned; but all the provisions of this Act relating to bye-laws shall apply to the bye-laws so made as if they were made under this Act.

As to regulations of local authority.

188. The provisions of this Act relating to bye-laws shall not apply to any regulations which a local authority is by this Act authorized to make; nevertheless, any local authority may cause any regulations made by them under this Act to be published in such manner as they see fit.

*   *   *   *   *   *   *

Power to borrow on credit of rates.

233. Any local authority may, with the sanction of the Local Government Board, for the purpose of defraying any costs, charges, and expenses incurred, or to be incurred, by them in the execution of the Sanitary Acts or of this Act, or for the purpose of discharging any loans contracted under the Sanitary Acts or this Act, borrow or re-borrow, and take up at interest, any sums of money necessary for defraying any such costs, charges, and expenses, or for discharging any such loans as aforesaid.

An urban authority may borrow or re-borrow any such sums on the credit of any fund or all or any rates or rate out of which they are authorized to defray expenses incurred by them in the execution of this Act, and for the purpose of securing the repayment of any sums so borrowed, with interest thereon, they may mortgage to the persons by or on behalf of whom such sums are advanced any such fund or rates or rate.

*   *   *   *   *   *   *

Regulations as to exercise of borrowing powers.

234. The exercise of the powers of borrowing conferred by this Act shall be subject to the following regulations; (namely,)

    (1.) Money shall not be borrowed except for permanent works, (including under this expression any works

of which the cost ought in the opinion of the Local
Government Board to be spread over a term of
years):

(2.) The sum borrowed shall not at any time exceed, with
the balances of all the outstanding loans contracted
by the local authority under the Sanitary Acts and
this Act, in the whole the assessable value for two
years of the premises assessable within the district
in respect of which such money may be borrowed:

(3.) Where the sum proposed to be borrowed with such
balances (if any) would exceed the assessable value
for one year of such premises, the Local Government Board shall not give their sanction to such
loan until one of their inspectors has held a local
inquiry and reported to the said board:

(4.) The money may be borrowed for such time, not
exceeding sixty years, as the local authority, with
the sanction of the Local Government Board, determine in each case; and, subject as aforesaid, the
local authority shall either pay off the moneys so
borrowed by equal annual instalments of principal
or of principal and interest, or they shall in every
year set apart as a sinking fund, and accumulate
in the way of compound interest by investing the
same in the purchase of exchequer bills or other
Government securities, such sum as will with accu-
mulations in the way of compound interest be
sufficient, after payment of all expenses, to pay
off the moneys so borrowed within the period
sanctioned:

(5.) A local authority may at any time apply the whole or
any part of a sinking fund set apart under this Act
in or towards the discharge of the moneys for the
repayment of which the fund has been established:
provided that they pay into the fund in each year
and accumulate until the whole of the moneys
borrowed are discharged, a sum equivalent to the
interest which would have been produced by the
sinking fund or the part of the sinking fund so
applied:

(6.) Where money is borrowed for the purpose of discharging a previous loan, the time for repayment of the money so borrowed shall not extend beyond the unexpired portion of the period for which the original loan was sanctioned, unless with the sanction of the Local Government Board, and shall in no case be extended beyond the period of sixty years from the date of the original loan.

Where any urban authority borrow any money for the purpose of defraying private improvement expenses, or expenses in respect of which they have determined a part only of the district to be liable, it shall be the duty of such authority, as between the ratepayers of the district, to make good, so far as they can, the money so borrowed, as occasion requires, either out of private improvement rates, or out of a rate levied in such part of the district as aforesaid.

*   *   *   *   *   *   *

Substitution in other Acts of provisions of this Act for provisions of repealed Acts.

313. Where in any Act, or order made by one of her Majesty's principal Secretaries of State or by the Local Government Board and in force at the time of the passing of this Act, or in any document, any provisions of any of the Sanitary Acts which are repealed by this Act are mentioned or referred to, such Act, order or document shall be read as if the provisions of this Act applicable to purposes the same as or similar to those of the repealed provisions were therein mentioned or referred to instead of such repealed provisions and were substituted for the same; nevertheless those substituted provisions shall have effect subject to any modification or restriction in such Act order or document expressed in relation to the repealed provisions therein mentioned or referred to.

*   *   *   *   *   *   *

Saving for proceedings under local Acts.

340. Where within the district of a local authority any local Act is in force, providing for purposes the same as or similar to the purposes of this Act, proceedings may be instituted at the discretion of the authority or person instituting the same, either under the local Act or this Act, or under both, subject to these qualifications:

(1.) That no person shall be punished for the same offence both under a local Act and this Act; and

38 & 39 *Vict.*
c. 55.

(2.) That the local authority shall not, by reason of any local Act in force within their district, be exempted from the performance of any duty or obligation to which they may be subject under this Act.

341. All powers given by this Act shall be deemed to be in addition to and not in derogation of any other powers conferred by Act of Parliament, law or custom, and such other powers may be exercised in the same manner as if this Act had not passed; and nothing in this Act shall exempt any person from any penalty to which he would have been subject if this Act had not passed. *Powers of Act to be cumulative.*

Provided that no person who has been adjudged to pay any penalty in pursuance of this Act shall for the same offence be liable to a penalty under any other Act.

*　　*　　*　　*　　*　　*　　*

SCHEDULE III.

[Incorporated by 35 & 36 Vict. c. 91, s. 4, ante, p. 301.]

Rules as to Resolutions of Owners and Ratepayers.

(1.) For the purpose of passing a resolution of owners and ratepayers under this Act, a meeting shall be summoned on the requisition of any twenty ratepayers or owners, or of any twenty ratepayers and owners, resident in the district or place with respect to which the resolution is to be passed.

(2.) The summoning officer of such meeting shall be—

In boroughs, the mayor;

*　　*　　*　　*　　*　　*

(3.) Ratepayers or owners making a requisition for the summoning of such meeting shall, if required, give security in a bond, with two sufficient sureties, for repayment to the summoning officer, in the event of the resolution not being passed, of the costs incurred in relation to such meeting or any poll taken in pursuance of any demand made thereat; the amount of the security to be given by such sureties, and their sufficiency, and the amount of such costs, to be settled by agreement between the summoning officer and such ratepayers or owners, or, in case of dispute, by a court of summary jurisdiction.

(4.) The summoning officer shall, on such requisition as aforesaid, fix a time and place for holding such meeting, and shall forthwith give notice thereof—

By advertisement in some one or more of the local newspapers circulated in the district or place;

By causing such notice to be affixed to the principal doors of every church and chapel in the place to which notices are usually affixed.

(5.) The summoning officer shall be the chairman of the meeting unless he is unable or unwilling to preside, in which case the meeting on assembling shall choose one of its number as chairman, who may, with the consent of a majority of the persons present, adjourn the same from time to time.

(6.) The chairman shall propose to the meeting the resolution, and the meeting shall decide for or against its adoption: provided, that if any owner or ratepayer demands that such question be decided by a poll of owners and ratepayers, such poll shall be taken by voting papers in the Form O. in Schedule IV. to this Act, in the same way and with the same incidents and conditions as to the qualification of electors and scale of voting, as to notice to be given by the returning officer, delivery, filling up and collection of voting papers, as to the counting of votes, as to penalties for neglect or refusal to comply with the provisions of the Act, and in all respects whatsoever as is provided by the rules for the election of local boards in Schedule II. to this Act; except that in districts or places where there is no register of owners and proxies under this Act, any owner or proxy shall be entitled to have a voting paper delivered to him if at least fourteen days before the last day appointed for delivery of the voting papers he sends a claim in writing to the summoning officer containing the particulars required by Schedule II. to this Act to be contained in claims to be entered on the register of owners and proxies, and except that the provisions with respect to certain specified days of the month shall not apply.

Poll.

For the purposes of such poll the summoning officer shall be the returning officer, and shall have the powers and perform the duties of a returning officer under Schedule II. to this Act, so far as the same are applicable to a poll under this schedule.

If no poll is demanded, or the demand for a poll is withdrawn by the persons making the same, a declaration by the chairman shall, in the absence of proof to the contrary, be sufficient evidence of the decision of such meeting.

* * * * * * *

Form O.

Form of Voting Paper for Poll taken under Schedule III.

Voting Paper No. (   ).

At a meeting held on the   day of   , at   , in the county of   , it was agreed that the following resolution should be proposed to the owners and ratepayers of   .

(*Set out the resolution.*)

———	In favour of.	Against.	Number of Votes.	
			As Owner.	As Ratepayer.
Do you vote in favour of or against the adoption of this resolution.				

(Signed) _____

or the mark of_____

Witness to the mark_____

or proxy for_____

Directions to the Voter.

The voter must write his initials under the heading "in favour" or "against," according as he votes for or against the resolution, and must subscribe his name and address at full length.

If the voter cannot write he must make his mark instead of initials, but such mark must be attested by a witness, and such witness must write the initials of the voter against his mark.

If a proxy votes he must in like manner write his initials, subscribe his own name and address, and add after his signature the words "as proxy for," with the name of the body of persons for whom he is proxy.

This paper will be collected on the   of   , between the hours of   and   .

ELECTRIC LIGHTING ACT, 1882.

45 & 46 Vict. c. 56. *An Act to facilitate and regulate the supply of Electricity for Lighting and other purposes in Great Britain and Ireland* (*p*). [18th August, 1882.

CONTENTS.

BE IT ENACTED as follows :

Short title.   **1.** This Act may be cited for all purposes as the Electric Lighting Act, 1882.

(*p*) See Fitzgerald's Electric Lighting Act.

2. The provisions of this Act shall apply to every local authority, company, or person who may by this Act or any license or provisional order granted under this Act, or by any special Act to be hereafter passed, be authorized to supply electricity within any area (in this Act referred to as "the undertakers"), and to every undertaking so authorized, except so far as may be expressly provided by any such special Act; and every such license, provisional order, and special Act, is in this Act included in the expression "license, order, or special Act" (*q*).

45 & 46 Vict. c. 56.

Application of act.

3. The Board of Trade may from time to time license any local authority as defined by this Act,* or any company or person, to supply electricity under this Act for any public or private purposes within any area, subject to the following provisions :

Board of Trade licenses authorizing supply of electricity.

* Sect. 31.

(1.) The consent of every local authority having jurisdiction within the area or any part of the area within which a supply is licensed to be furnished shall be required to the application for a license, which consent such local authority is hereby authorized to give, with such conditions (if any) as, subject to the approval of the Board of Trade, the local authority may prescribe :

Consent of local authority.

(2.) A license shall be for any period not exceeding seven years, but may, at or after the expiration of such license, be renewed from time to time for a like period with such consent as above mentioned upon such terms and conditions as the Board of Trade may determine :

Term of license.

(3.) "Public purposes" shall mean lighting any street or any place belonging to or subject to the control of the local authority, or any church or registered place of public worship, or any hall or building belonging to or subject to the control of any public authority, or any public theatre, but shall not in-

---

(*q*) There is no provision to the effect that electricity may not be supplied otherwise than in accordance with this Act; so that sect. 161 of the Public Health Act, 1875, ante, p. 306, is legally applicable, so as to enable a local authority to proceed under that section independently of the Board of Trade.

clude any other purpose to which electricity may be applied :

(4.) " Private purposes " shall include any purposes whatever to which electricity may for the time being be applicable, not being public purposes, except the transmission of any telegram :

Public notice of application.

(5.) Every local authority, company, or person applying for a license shall publish notice of their application by public advertisement in such manner and including such particulars as the Board of Trade may from time to time direct or approve (r); and such license shall not be granted by the Board of Trade until after the expiration of a period of three months from the date of the first publication of such advertisement, nor until opportunity has been given to all parties interested to make representations or objections to the Board of Trade with reference to the application :

Preliminary resolution of local authority.

(6.) No application for a license shall be made by any local authority except in pursuance of a resolution to be passed at a special meeting of the local authority, and such special meeting shall only be held after one month's previous notice of the same and of the purpose thereof has been given in the manner in which notices of meetings of such local authority are usually given :

(7.) A license may, subject to the provisions of this Act, be granted to a local authority, authorizing them to supply electricity within any area, although the same or some part thereof may not be included within their own district :

Terms of license.

(8.) The license may make such regulations as to the limits within which and the conditions under which a supply of electricity is to be compulsory or permis-

---

(r) Compare sect. 5, post, which partly repeats this provision, and requires the Board of Trade Regulations to be laid before Parliament ; but there is no provision for publication of such regulations in the Gazette or elsewhere, although the parties concerned appear, by the effect of sect. 5, to have constructive notice of them.

sive, and for enforcing the performance by the licensees of their duties in relation to such supply, and for the revocation of the license where the licensees fail to perform such duties, and generally may contain such regulations and conditions as the Board of Trade may think expedient :

45 & 46 *Vict.*
c. 56.

Revocation
license.

(9.) Where in any area or part of an area in which any undertakers are authorized to supply electricity under any license the undertakers are not themselves the local authority, the license may contain any provisions and restrictions for enabling the local authority within whose jurisdiction such area or part of an area may be to exercise any of the powers of the undertakers under this Act with respect to the breaking up of any street repairable by such local authority within such area or part of an area, and the alteration of the position of any pipes or wires being under such street, and not being the pipes or wires of the undertakers, on behalf and at the expense of the undertakers, and for limiting the powers and liabilities of the undertakers in relation thereto, which the Board of Trade may think expedient.

Concurrent
powers of local
authority, if
not licensees.

4. The Board of Trade may, from time to time, by provisional order authorize any local authority, company, or person to supply electricity for any public or private purposes within any area, without requiring such consents as are required to the granting a license under this Act, and for such period, whether limited or unlimited, as the Board of Trade may think proper, but in all other respects subject to the like provisions as in the last section contained with respect to licenses, and subject also to the following provisions : —

Board of
Trade provisional orders
authorizing
the supply of
electricity.

(1.) No provisional order shall authorize the supply of electricity by any undertakers within the district of any local authority (not being themselves the undertakers), unless notice that such provisional order has been or is intended to be applied for has been given to such local authority by the applicants in

Notice to local
authority.

such manner as the Board of Trade may direct or approve (s), on or before the 1st day of July in the year in which such application is made; provided that in the case of any application made during the present year such notice shall be deemed to have been given in due time if the same is given within one month after the passing of this Act (t):

Confirmation of provisional order by Parliament.

(2.) The Board of Trade may submit to Parliament for confirmation any provisional order granted by it in pursuance of this Act, but any such order shall be of no force unless and until it is confirmed by Act of Parliament (u):

(3.) If, while the bill confirming any such order is pending in either House of Parliament, a petition is presented against any order comprised therein, the bill, so far as it relates to such order, may be referred to a select committee, and the petitioner shall be allowed to appear and oppose as in the case of private bills (v):

(4.) Any Act confirming any provisional order granted in pursuance of this Act may, on the application of the undertakers thereby authorised to supply electricity, be repealed, altered, or amended by any subsequent provisional order granted by the Board of Trade and confirmed by Parliament.

Board of Trade rules as to application, &c., under Act.

5. The Board of Trade may from time to time make, and when made may rescind, alter, or repeal rules* in relation to the applications for licenses or provisional orders, and to the

* See p. 336, post.

(s) See sect. 5 as to effect of Board of Trade Rules. The object of the notice is to enable the local authority to oppose the provisional order. See ib. and see sect. 7 as to expenses.

(t) The Act passed on the 18th of August.

(u) This sub-section follows the words of the Public Health Act, 1875 (38 & 39 Vict. c. 55), s. 297, sub-s. 3. It will be observed that no time is limited for submitting the order to Parliament, nor is there even any *obligation* upon the Board of Trade to bring in a bill at all; whereas a draft certificate under the Railways Construction Facilities Act, 1864, must, by sect. 12 of that Act (Chit. Stat. vol. v. tit. "*Railway*"), be submitted to Parliament in seven days.

(v) As to costs, see 34 Vict. c. 3, and other Acts, Chit. Stat. vol. i. tit "*Bill in Parliament.*"

payments to be made in respect thereof, and to the publication of notices and advertisements, and the manner in which and the time within which representations or objections with reference to any application are to be made, and to the holding of local inquiries in such cases as they may think it advisable, and to any other matters arising under this Act.

Any rules made in pursuance of this section shall be deemed to be within the powers conferred by this Act, and shall be of the same force as if enacted in this Act, and shall be judicially noticed.

Any rules made in pursuance of this section shall be laid before Parliament within three weeks after they are made if Parliament be then sitting, and if Parliament be not then sitting, within three weeks after the beginning of the next session of Parliament (x).

6. The undertakers shall be subject to such regulations and conditions as may be inserted in any license, order, or special act (y), affecting their undertaking with regard to the following matters:

(a.) The limits within which and the conditions under which a supply of electricity is to be compulsory or permissive;

(b.) The securing a regular and efficient supply of electricity;

(c.) The securing the safety of the public from personal injury, or from fire or otherwise;

(d.) The limitation of the prices to be charged in respect of the supply of electricity (z);

(e.) The authorizing inspection and inquiry from time to time by the Board of Trade and the local authority;

(f.) The enforcement of the due performance of the duties of the undertakers in relation to the supply of electricity by the imposition of penalties or otherwise,

Side notes: 45 & 46 Vict. c. 56. — Regulations in licenses, &c. — Regular supply. — Safety. — Limit of charges. — Inspection. — Enforcement of supply.

(x) As to costs, see 34 Vict. c. 3, and other Acts, Chit. Stat. vol. i. tit. "*Bill in Parliament.*"

(y) There can be no effective order without a special Act confirming it, but there may, if the promoters can succeed in Parliament without such a preliminary, be a special Act without a provisional order preceding it.

(z) See further, sect. 20, post.

and the revocation of the license, order, or special Act where the undertakers have, in the opinion of the Board of Trade, practically failed to carry the powers granted to them into effect within a reasonable time, or discontinued the exercise of such powers; and

General.

(g.) Generally with regard to any other matters in connexion with the undertakings.

Provided always, that the Board of Trade may, from time to time, make such regulations as they may think expedient for securing the safety of the public from personal injury or from fire or otherwise, and may from time to time amend or repeal any regulations which may be contained in any such license, order, or special act in relation thereto; and any regulations so made or amended by the Board of Trade shall, from and after the date thereof, have the like effect in every respect as though they had been originally inserted in the license, order, or special Act authorizing the undertaking, and every regulation so repealed shall, from and after the date thereof, be repealed accordingly, but such repeal shall not affect any liability or penalty incurred in respect thereof prior to the date of such repeal or any proceeding or remedy which might have been had in relation thereto.

Any local authority within any part of whose district electricity is authorized to be supplied under any license, order, or special act may, in addition to any regulations which may be made under the preceding provisions of this section for securing the safety of the public, from time to time make, rescind, alter, or repeal bye-laws for further securing such safety; and there may be annexed to any breach of such bye-laws such penalties to be recovered in a summary manner as they may think necessary: provided always, that no such bye-laws shall have any force or effect unless and until they have been confirmed by the Board of Trade and published in such manner as the Board of Trade may direct.

Expenses of local authority.

7. Any expenses incurred by a local authority under this Act, and not otherwise provided for, including any expenses incurred in connection with the obtaining by them, or any opposition to the obtaining by any other local authority, company, or person, of any license, order, or special Act under this Act, may be defrayed out of the local rate as defined in the schedule to this Act, and the local authority may from time to time cause such rates to be levied as may be necessary for the purpose of defraying such expenses : provided that where such local authority is a rural sanitary authority such expenses shall be deemed to be special expenses within the meaning of the Public Health Act, 1875 (*a*).

8. A local authority authorized to supply electricity by any license, order, or special Act, may from time to time borrow money on such security, with such consent and subject to such provisions and restrictions with respect to borrowing and the repayment of loans, as are in the schedule to this Act in that behalf mentioned, and the money so borrowed shall be deemed to be borrowed under the enactments subject to the provisions and restrictions of which it is borrowed, and the accounts of all receipts and expenditure by the local authority in pursuance of this Act, or any license, order, or special Act, shall be subject to such audit as is in the said schedule in that behalf mentioned : provided always, that any moneys borrowed under this section by the local authority of any district to which the Local Loans Act, 1875 (*b*), extends, may, if it is thought fit, be borrowed in manner provided by that Act; and in the construction of the said Act for the purposes of this Act the expression "prescribed" means prescribed by any conditions imposed by the authority whose consent is required to borrowing under this section.

(margin: Power of local authority to borrow money.)

Where any local authority is authorized by any Act to raise any money which they may be empowered to borrow for certain purposes by the issue of corporation or other stock, any money which a local authority may be authorized to borrow under this section may, if it is thought fit, be raised by them by the issue of such stock as aforesaid.

This section shall not apply to the mayor, commonalty, and citizens of the city of London or to the Metropolitan Board of Works, except in so far as the Metropolitan Board of Works

---

(*a*) 38 & 39 Vict. c. 55, s. 229.
(*b*) 38 & 39 Vict. c. 83.

45 & 46 *Vict.* c. 56.

may be concerned in the borrowing of any money by any vestry or district board.

Accounts.

9. The undertakers shall, on or before the 25th day of March in every year, fill up an annual statement of accounts of the undertaking made up to the 31st day of December then next preceding; and such statement shall be in such form and shall contain such particulars and shall be published in such manner as may from time to time be prescribed in that behalf by the Board of Trade.

The undertakers shall keep copies of such annual statement at their office, and sell the same to any applicant at a price not exceeding one shilling a copy.

In case the undertakers make default in complying with the provisions of this section, they shall be liable to a penalty not exceeding forty shillings for each day during which such default continues.

General powers of undertakers under license or provisional order.

10. The undertakers may, subject to and in accordance with the provisions and restrictions of this Act, and of any rules made by the Board of Trade in pursuance of this Act, and of any license, order, or special Act authorizing or affecting their undertaking, and for the purpose of supplying electricity, acquire such lands by agreement, construct such works, acquire such licenses for the use of any patented or protected processes, inventions, machinery, apparatus, methods, materials, or other things, enter into such contracts, and generally do all such acts and things as may be necessary and incidental to such supply.

Power for local authority to contract for execution of works, &c.

Restrictions on assignments of powers, &c.

11. Any local authority who have obtained a license, order, or special Act for the supply of electricity, may contract with any company or person for the execution and maintenance of any works needed for the purposes of such supply, or for the supply of electricity within any area mentioned in such license, order, or special Act, or in any part of such area; but no local authority, company, or person shall, by any contract or assignment transfer to any other company or person or divest themselves of any legal powers given to them, or any legal liabilities imposed on them by this Act, or by any license, order, or special Act, without the consent of the Board of Trade.

12. The provisions of the following Acts shall be incorporated with this Act; that is to say—

45 & 46 *Vict.* c. 56.

Incorporation of part of Lands Clauses Acts.

(1.) The Lands Clauses Acts (*c*), except the enactments with respect to the purchase and taking of lands otherwise than by agreement, and except the enactments with respect to the entry upon lands by the promoters of the undertaking ; and

(2.) The provisions of the Gasworks Clauses Act, 1847 (*d*), with respect to breaking up streets for the purpose of laying pipes, and with respect to waste or misuse of the gas or injury to the pipes and other works, except so much thereof as relates to the use of any burner other than such as has been provided or approved of by the undertakers ; and

Incorporation of part of Gasworks Clauses Acts.

(3.) Sections thirty-eight to forty-two inclusive, and sections forty-five and forty-six, of the Gasworks Clauses Act, 1871 (*e*).

For the purposes of this Act, in the construction of all the enactments incorporated by this section " the special Act " means this Act inclusive of any license, order, or special Act ; and the " promoters " or " undertakers," and " the undertaking," as the case may be, mean the undertakers and the undertaking respectively under this Act.

In the construction of the said Lands Clauses Acts, " land " includes easements in or relating to lands.

In the construction of the said Gasworks Clauses Act, 1847, and the Gasworks Clauses Act, 1871, the said Acts shall be construed as if " gas " meant " electricity," and as if " pipe " meant electric line, and " works " meant " works " as defined by this Act, and as if " the limits of the special Act " meant the area within which the undertakers are authorized to supply electricity under any license, order, or special Act.

(*c*) See sect. 32, and note. As to the absence of the *compulsory powers*, compare sect. 10 of the Gas and Water Facilities Act, 1870.
(*d*) 10 & 11 Vict. c. 15.
(*e*) 34 & 35 Vict. c. 41.

45 & 46 Vict. c. 56.

All offences, forfeitures, penalties and damages under the said incorporated provisions of the said Acts or any of them may be prosecuted and may be recovered in manner by the said Acts respectively enacted in relation thereto, provided that sums recoverable under the provisions of section forty of the Gasworks Clauses Act, 1871, shall not be recovered as penalties, but may be recovered summarily as civil debts.

Restriction on breaking up of private streets, railways and tramways.

13. Nothing in this Act, or in any Act incorporated therewith, shall authorize or empower the undertakers to break up any street which is not repairable by such local authority, or any railway or tramway, without the consent of the authority, company or person by whom such street, railway or tramway is repairable, unless in pursuance of special powers in that behalf inserted in the license, order or special Act, or with the written consent of the Board of Trade, and the Board of Trade shall not in any case insert any such special powers in any license or provisional order, or give any such consent until notice has been given to such authority, company or person, by advertisement or otherwise, as the Board of Trade may direct, and an opportunity has been given to such authority, company or person to state any objections they may have thereto.

Restrictions as to above-ground works.

14. Notwithstanding anything in this Act, or in any Act incorporated therewith, the undertakers shall not be authorized to place any electric line above ground, along, over, or across any street, without the express consent of the local authority; and the local authority may require the undertakers to forthwith remove any electric line placed by them contrary to the provisions of this section, or may themselves remove the same, and recover the expenses of such removal from the undertakers in a summary manner; and where any electric line has been placed above ground by the undertakers in any position, a court of summary jurisdiction, upon complaint made, if they are of opinion that such electric line is or is likely to become dangerous to the public safety, may, notwithstanding any such consent as aforesaid, make an order directing and authorizing the removal of such electric line by such person and upon such terms as they may think fit.

15. Subject to the provisions of this Act and of the license, order, or special Act authorizing them to supply electricity, and to any bye-laws made under this Act, the undertakers may alter the position of any pipes or wires being under any street or place authorized to be broken up by them which may interfere with the exercise of their powers under this Act on previously making or securing such compensation to the owners of such pipes or wires, and on complying with such conditions as to the mode of making such alterations as may before the commencement of such alterations be agreed upon between the undertakers and owners, or, in case of difference, as may be determined in manner prescribed by the license or provisional order authorizing the undertakers to supply electricity, or, where no such manner is prescribed, as may be determined by arbitration; and any local or other public authority, company or person may in like manner alter the position of any electric lines or works of the undertakers, being under any such street or place as aforesaid, which may interfere with the lawful exercise of any powers vested in such local or other public authority, company or person in relation to such street or place, subject to the like provisions, conditions and restrictions as are in this section contained with reference to the alteration of the position of any pipes or wires by the undertakers.

45 & 46 Vict. c. 56.

Power to undertakers to alter position of pipes and wires.

16. If at any time after the undertakers have placed any works under, in, upon, over, along or across any canal, any person having power to construct docks, basins or other works upon any land adjoining to or near such canal, constructs any dock, basin or work on such land, but is prevented by the works of the undertakers from forming a communication for the convenient passage of vessels with or without masts between such dock, basin or other work, and such canal; or if the business of such dock, basin or other work is interfered with by reason or in consequence of any such works of the undertakers, then the undertakers, at the request of such person, and on having reasonable facilities afforded them by him for placing works round such dock, basin or other work, under, in, upon, over, along or across land belonging to or under his control, shall remove and place their work accord-

Clause for protection of canals.

ingly. If any dispute arises between the undertakers and such person as to the facilities to be afforded to the undertakers, or as to the direction in which the works are to be placed, it shall be determined by arbitration.

Compensation for damage.

17. In the exercise of the powers in relation to the execution of works given them under this Act, or any license, order, or special Act, the undertakers shall cause as little detriment and inconvenience and do as little damage as may be, and shall make full compensation to all bodies and persons interested for all damage sustained by them by reason or in consequence of the exercise of such powers, the amount and application of such compensation in case of difference to be determined by arbitration.

Undertakers not to prescribe special form of lamp or burner.

18. The undertakers shall not be entitled to prescribe any special form of lamp or burner to be used by any company or person, or in any way to control or interfere with the manner in which electricity supplied by them under this Act, and any license, order or special Act is used : provided always that no local authority, company or person shall be at liberty to use any form of lamp or burner, or to use the electricity supplied to them for any purposes, or to deal with it in any manner so as to unduly or improperly interfere with the supply of electricity supplied to any other local authority, company or person by the undertakers, and if any dispute or difference arises between the undertakers and any local authority, company or person entitled to be supplied with electricity under this Act, or any license, order or special Act, as to the matters aforesaid, such dispute or difference shall be determined by arbitration.

Obligation on undertakers to supply electricity.

19. Where a supply of electricity is provided in any part of an area for private purposes, then, except in so far as is otherwise provided by the terms of the license, order or special Act authorizing such supply, every company or person within that part of the area shall, on application, be entitled to a supply on the same terms on which any other company or person in such part of the area is entitled under similar circumstances to a corresponding supply.

Charges for electricity.

20. The undertakers shall not, in making any agreements for a supply of electricity, show any undue preference to any local authority, company or person, but, save us aforesaid, they may make such charges for the supply of electricity, as may be agreed upon, not exceeding the limits of price imposed by or in pursuance of the license, order or special Act authorizing them to supply electricity.

21. If any local authority, company or person neglect to pay any charge for electricity, or any other sum due from them to the undertakers in respect of the supply of electricity to such local authority, company or person, the undertakers may cut off such supply, and for that purpose may cut or disconnect any electric line or other work through which electricity may be supplied, and may, until such charge or other sum, together with any expenses incurred by the undertakers in cutting off such supply of electricity as aforesaid, are fully paid, but no longer, discontinue the supply of electricity to such local authority, company or person.

Recovery of charges, &c.

22. Any person who unlawfully and maliciously cuts or injures any electric line or work with intent to cut off any supply of electricity shall be guilty of felony, and be liable to be kept in penal servitude for any term not exceeding five years, or to be imprisoned with or without hard labour for any term not exceeding two years; but nothing in this section shall exempt a person from any proceeding for any offence which is punishable under any other provision of this Act, or under any other Act, or at common law, so that no person be punished twice for the same offence.

Injuring works with intent to cut off supply of electricity.

23. Any person who maliciously or fraudulently abstracts, causes to be wasted or diverted, consumes, or uses any electricity shall be guilty of simple larceny and punishable accordingly.

Stealing electricity.

24. Any officer appointed by the undertakers may at all reasonable times enter any premises to which electricity is or has been supplied by the undertakers, in order to inspect the electric lines, meters, accumulators, fittings, works, and apparatus for the supply of electricity belonging to the undertakers, and for the purpose of ascertaining the quantity of electricity consumed or supplied, or where a supply of electricity is no longer required, or where the undertakers are authorized to take away and cut off the supply of electricity

Power to enter lands or premises for ascertaining quantities of electricity consumed or to remove fittings, &c.

45 & 46 Vict.
c. 56.

from any premises, for the purpose of removing any electric
lines, accumulators, fittings, works, or apparatus belonging to
the undertakers, repairing all damage caused by such entry,
inspection, or removal.

Electric lines,
&c. not to be
subject to
distress in
certain cases.

25. Where any electric lines, meters, accumulators, fittings,
works, or apparatus belonging to the undertakers are placed
in or upon any premises not being in the possession of the
undertakers for the purpose of supplying electricity under this
Act, or any license, order, or special Act, such electric lines,
meters, accumulators, fittings, works, or apparatus shall not be
subject to distress or to the landlord's remedy for rent of the
premises where the same may be, nor to be taken in execution
under any process of a court of law or equity, or any proceedings in bankruptcy against the person in whose possession the
same may be.

Provision for
protection
of the Post-
master-
General.

26. No alteration in any telegraph line of the Postmaster-
General shall be made by the undertakers except subject to
the provisions of the Telegraph Act, 1878 (*f*).

The undertakers shall not in the exercise of the powers
conferred by this Act, or by any license, order, or special Act,
lay down any electric line or do any other work for the supply
of electricity whereby any telegraphic line of the Postmaster-
General is or may be injuriously affected, and before any such
electric line is laid down or work is done within ten yards of
any part of a telegraphic line of the Postmaster-General
(other than repairs or the laying of connexions with mains
where the direction of the electric lines so laid down crosses
the line of the Postmaster-General at right angles at the point
of shortest distance and continues the same for a distance of
six feet on each side of such point) the undertakers or their
agents not more than twenty-eight nor less than seven clear
days before commencing such work shall give written notice
to the Postmaster-General specifying the course and nature of
the work, including the gauge of any electric lines, and the
undertakers and their agents shall conform with such reasonable requirements either general or special as may from time
to time be made by the Postmaster-General for the purpose of

(*f*) 41 & 42 Vict. c. 76.

45 & 46 Vict.
c. 56.

preventing any telegraphs of the Postmaster-General from being injuriously affected by the said work.

Any difference which arises between the Postmaster-General and the undertakers or their agents with respect to any requirements so made, shall be determined by arbitration.

In the event of any contravention of or wilful non-compliance with this section by the undertakers or their agents the undertakers shall be liable to a fine not exceeding ten pounds for every day during which such contravention or non-compliance continues, or, if the telegraphic communication is wilfully interrupted, not exceeding fifty pounds for every day on which such interruption continues.

Provided that nothing in this section shall subject the undertakers or their agents to a fine under this section, if they satisfy the court having cognizance of the case that the immediate execution of the work was required to avoid an accident, or otherwise was a work of emergency, and that they forthwith served on the postmaster or sub-postmaster of the postal telegraph office nearest to the place where the work was done a notice of the execution thereof, stating the reason for executing the same without previous notice.

For the purposes of this section a telegraphic line of the Postmaster-General shall be deemed to be injuriously affected by a work if telegraphic communication by means of such line is, whether through induction or otherwise, in any manner affected by such work, or by any use made of such work.

For the purposes of this section, and subject as therein provided, sections two, seven, eight, nine, ten, eleven and twelve of the Telegraph Act, 1878, shall be deemed to be incorporated with this Act, as if the undertakers were undertakers within the meaning of those sections, without prejudice nevertheless to any operation which the other sections of the said Act would have had if this section had not been enacted.

27. Where any undertakers are authorized by a provisional order or special Act to supply electricity within any area, any local authority within whose jurisdiction such area or any part thereof is situated may, within six months after the expiration of a period of twenty-one years (*g*), or such shorter period as

Purchase of undertaking by local authority.

(*g*) Compare the Tramways Act, 1870 (33 & 34 Vict. c. 78), s. 43.

is specified in that behalf in the application for the provisional order or in the special Act, from the date of the passing of the Act confirming such provisional order, or of such special Act, and within six months after the expiration of every subsequent period of seven years, or such shorter period as is specified in that behalf in the application for the provisional order or in the special Act, by notice in writing require such undertakers to sell, and thereupon such undertakers shall sell to them their undertaking, or so much of the same as is within such jurisdiction, upon terms of paying the then value of all lands, buildings, works, materials, and plant of such undertakers suitable to and used by them for the purposes of their under-taking within such jurisdiction, such value to be in case of difference determined by arbitration: provided that the value of such lands, buildings, works, materials, and plant shall be deemed to be their fair market value at the time of the purchase, due regard being had to the nature and then con-dition of such buildings, works, materials, and plant, and to the state of repair thereof, and the suitability of the same to the purposes of the undertaking, and, where a part only of the undertaking is purchased, to any loss occasioned by severance; but without any addition in respect of compulsory purchase or of goodwill or of any profits which may or might have been or be made from the undertaking, or of any similar considerations (h). The Board of Trade may determine any other questions which may arise in relation to such purchase, and may fix the date from which such purchase is to take effect. and from and after the date so fixed, or such other date as may be agreed upon between the parties, all lands, buildings, works, materials, and plant so purchased as afore-said shall vest in the local authority which has made the purchase, freed from any debts, mortgages, or similar obliga-tions of such undertakers or attaching to the undertaking, and the powers of such undertakers in relation to the supply of electricity under this Act or such provisional order or special Act as aforesaid within such area or part thereof as aforesaid shall absolutely cease and determine, and shall vest in the local authority aforesaid.

Arbitration.   **28.** Where any matter is by this Act, or any license, order

(h) Compare the Tramways Act, 1870 (33 & 34 Vict. c. 78), s. 43.

or special Act, directed to be determined by arbitration, such 45 & 46 *Vict.* matter shall, except as otherwise expressly provided, be *c.* 56. determined by an engineer or other fit person to be nominated as arbitrator by the Board of Trade on the application of either party, and the expenses of the arbitration shall be borne and paid as the arbitrator directs.

Any license or provisional order granted under this Act shall be deemed to be a special Act within the meaning of the Board of Trade Arbitrations, &c. Act, 1874 (*i*).

29. Where a supply of electricity is authorized in any area by any license, order, or special Act, and a supply of gas by any gas undertakers is also authorized within such area or any part thereof by any provisional order or special Act under the provisions of which such gas undertakers are under any general or limited obligation to supply gas upon demand, the Board of Trade may, upon the application of such gas undertakers, inquire into the circumstances of the case, and if they are satisfied that any specified part of such area is sufficiently supplied with electric light, and that the supply of gas in such specified part has ceased to be remunerative to the gas undertakers, and that it is just that such gas undertakers should be relieved from the obligation to supply gas upon demand as aforesaid, the Board of Trade may in their discretion make an order relieving the gas undertakers from such obligation, within such specified part of such area, either wholly or in part, and upon such terms and conditions as they may think proper; and from and after the date of such order such gas undertakers shall be so relieved accordingly. All expenses of the Board of Trade in connexion with any such inquiry or order shall be borne and paid by the gas undertakers upon whose application the inquiry or order was made.

Power for Board of Trade to relieve gas undertakers from obligation to supply gas in certain cases.

30. Not later than the 1st day of July in each year the Board of Trade shall lay before both Houses of Parliament a report respecting the applications to and proceedings of the Board of Trade under this Act during the year then last past.

Annual report by Board of Trade.

31. In this Act, unless the context otherwise requires, the expressions " local authority " and " local rate " mean, as

Definition of local authority, &c.

(*i*) 37 & 38 Vict. c. 40, s. 4; Chit. Stat. vol. v. tit. "*Railways.*"

respects each district set forth in the first column of the schedule to this Act annexed, the authority and rate mentioned opposite to that district in the second and third columns of that schedule; and such schedule, and the notes appended thereto, shall be of the same validity as if enacted in the body of the Act.

Interpretation.

32. In this Act, unless the context otherwise requires:

The expression "electricity" means electricity, electric current, or any like agency.

The expression "electric line" means a wire or wires, conductor, or other means used for the purpose of conveying, transmitting, or distributing electricity with any casing, coating, covering, tube, pipe, or insulator enclosing, surrounding, or supporting the same, or any part thereof, or any apparatus connected therewith for the purpose of conveying, transmitting, or distributing electricity or electric currents:

The expression "works" means and includes electric lines, also any buildings, machinery, engines, works, matters, or things of whatever description required to supply electricity and to carry into effect the object of the undertakers under this Act:

The expression "company" means any body of persons corporate or unincorporate:

The expression "Lands Clauses Acts" means the Lands Clauses Consolidation Acts, 1845, 1860, and 1869 (i):

The expression "street" includes any square, court, or alley, highway, lane, road, thoroughfare or public passage, or place, within the area in which the undertakers are authorized to supply electricity by this Act or any license, order, or special Act:

The expression "telegram" has the same meaning as in the Telegraph Act, 1869 (k).

(i) 8 Vict. c. 18; 23 & 24 Vict. c. 106, and 32 & 33 Vict. c. 18; Chit. Stat. vol. iii. tit. "*Lands Clauses.*"

(k) 32 & 33 Vict. c. 73, by sect. 3 of which "the term 'telegram' shall mean any message or other communication transmitted or intended to be transmitted by telegraph."

33. Nothing in this Act shall limit or interfere with the rights of any owner, lessee, or occupier of any mines or minerals lying under or adjacent to any road along or across which any electric lines shall be laid to work such mines and minerals.

45 & 46 *Vict.*
c. 56.

Protection of mines.

34. Nothing in this Act shall exempt the undertakers or their undertaking from the provisions of any general act relating to the supply of electricity which may be passed in this or any future session of Parliament (*l*).

Provision as to general Acts.

35. Nothing in this Act or in any license, order, or special Act, shall affect the exclusive privileges conferred upon the Postmaster-General by the Telegraph Act, 1869, or authorize or enable any local authority, company, or person to transmit any telegram or to perform any of the incidental services of receiving, collecting, or delivering telegrams, or give to any local authority, company, or person, any power, authority, or facility of any kind whatever, in connexion with the transmission of telegrams, or the performance of any of the incidental services of receiving, collecting, or delivering telegrams.

Saving for privileges of Postmaster-General.

[**36, 37.** Application of Act to Scotland and Ireland.]

(*l*) This section follows, *mutatis mutandis*, a common form clause to be found in all special Acts, passed in or after 1845, authorizing the construction of railways; and also in the Gasworks Clauses Act, 1847, sect. 49.

[SCHEDULE.

SCHEDULE.

[See Sect. 31.]

ENGLAND AND WALES.

Districts of Local Authorities.	Description of Local Authority of District set opposite its Name.	The Local Rate.	Security upon which Loans are to be contracted.	Authority whose Consent is required to borrowing by Local Authority.	Provisions and Restrictions as to Borrowing and the Repayment of Loans.	Mode of Audit of Accounts of Local Authority.
Urban sanitary district (1).	The urban sanitary authority(1).	The fund or rate applicable to the general purposes of the Public Health Act, 1875, in the district, or any other fund or rate applicable to lighting under any local Act.	The local rate as herein defined and any property of the local authority.	The authority whose consent is required to loans under section two hundred and thirty-three of the Public Health Act, 1875.	Those contained in sections two hundred and thirty-three, two hundred and thirty-four, and two hundred and thirty-six to two hundred and thirty-nine (both inclusive) of the Public Health Act, 1875.	In the case of boroughs (2), that prescribed by section two hundred and forty-six of the Public Health Act, 1875, and in the case of other urban sanitary authorities that prescribed by section two hundred and forty-seven of the same Act.

NOTES.

(1) "Urban sanitary district," "urban sanitary authority," "rural sanitary district," "rural sanitary authority," and "contributory place," have the meanings respectively assigned to them in the Public Health Act, 1875 (m).

(2) "Borough" means any place for the time being subject to an Act passed in the session holden in the fifth and sixth years of the reign of King William the Fourth, chapter seventy-six, intituled "An Act to provide for the Regulation of Municipal Corporations in England and Wales," and the Acts amending the same (n).

(m) 38 & 39 Vict. c. 55; Chit. Stat. vol. v. tit. "Public Health." See ss. 5—12 of that Act, p. 303, ante.

(n) See Act of 1882, p. 1, ante. The schedule to the Act of 1835 will still have to be referred to for the names of the majority of the boroughs, i. e. of all except those incorporated after the Act of 1835. See list, p. 343, post.

Board of Trade Rules under Sect. 8 of the Electric Lighting Act.

Rule I. No application for a licence or for the renewal of a licence can be entertained unless proof of the consent of the local authority to such application is given to the Board of Trade.

Rule II. When applications for provisional orders authorizing the supply of electricity within the district of any local authority are received by the Board of Trade from such local authority, and also from any other authority, company, or person, the Board of Trade will give a preference to the application of the local authority of the district in every case where, in the opinion of the Board of Trade, no special circumstances exist which render such a preference inexpedient.

Application and Deposit.

Rule III. Every application for a licence or provisional order must be made by memorial signed by, or on behalf of, the applicants, headed with a short title descriptive of the proposed undertaking (corresponding with that at the head of the advertisement hereinafter mentioned), addressed to the Board of Trade, and praying for a licence or provisional order. With the memorial must be deposited six copies of the licence or order, as proposed by the applicants, with the schedule or schedules (if any) referred to therein.

Rule IV. The deposited copies of the proposed licence or order must be in print. They must be printed on one side only of the page of paper, so as to leave the back of the page blank, and each schedule annexed must begin a new page.

The names and addresses of the parliamentary agents or

L.C.   z solicitors for the licence or order must be printed on the outside of the draft.

There must be a notice at the end of the draft, stating that objections are to be made by letter addressed to the Board of Trade, marked on the outside of the cover enclosing it, "Electric Lighting Act," and that this letter is to be sent to the Board of Trade within two months from the date of the newspaper containing the first advertisement of the application. The draft must contain amongst other things—

1. Address and description of the applicants.
2. A description of the proposed area of supply.
3. A statement of the purposes for which a supply is to be given, viz., any or all of the public or private purposes specified in section *three* of the Act.
4. A general description of the proposed works.
5. Provisions concerning the breaking up of streets not repairable by a local authority and concerning interference with railways and tramways, where powers are sought to be obtained by the licence or order for those purposes.
6. Conditions of supply, including price, nature and amount of supply, obligation to supply, &c.
7. Period for which concession is sought.
8. Provisions for securing the safety of the consumer and of the public from injury by shock, fire, or otherwise.
9. Provisions for enforcing the performance by the undertakers of their duties in relation to the supply of electricity, and for the revocation of the licence or order where the undertakers fail to perform such duties.

The applicants are also to deposit a sufficient number of such printed drafts at offices in London and within the proposed area of supply to be specified in the advertisement, such copies to be there furnished to all persons applying for them, at a price of not more than one shilling each.

Rule V. There must also be deposited with the memorial,—

A published map of the district on a scale of not less than one inch to a mile, or if there is no published map, then the best map procurable, showing the boundaries of the proposed area of supply, and the streets and other places in, over or along which it is proposed to place any electric lines or other works.

A copy of the said map is also to be deposited for public inspection—

> In England or Ireland, in the office of the clerk of the peace for every county, riding or division, and of the local authority of every district; in Scotland, in the office of the principal sheriff clerk for every county, district, or division, and of the local authority of every district in which the proposed area of supply or any part thereof is situate.

Rule VI. There must also be deposited with the memorial,—

1. A list of the local authorities in whose districts the area of supply is situate.
2. A list of the streets not repairable by a local authority, and of the railways and tramways (if any) which the applicants propose to take powers to break up.
3. A list of the canals and navigable rivers (if any) which the undertakers will be empowered under the licence or order to cross.
4. A statement of the capital proposed to be expended and employed in connection with the undertaking, and the mode in which such capital is to be provided.
5. If the applicants are a company incorporated under the provisions of the Companies' Acts, a copy of the memorandum and articles of association.
6. A fee of 50l., by cheque payable to an "assistant secretary of the Board of Trade" to cover ordinary expenses. If in consequence of inquiries, or otherwise, additional expense is incurred, the amount will be charged to the applicants, and must be paid by them in addition to the ordinary fee.
7. Where the undertakers under any licence, order, or special act desire the consent of the Board of Trade to enable them to break up any street not repairable by a local authority, or any railway or tramway which they are not empowered to break up under such licence, order, or special act, the memorial must specially request such consent, and must describe accurately the street, railway or tramway which they propose to acquire power to break up.

Rule VII. Where the approval or consent of any local

authority is required to any application for a licence or order, such approval or consent must be given by a resolution passed at a special meeting of the local authority, held after one month's previous notice of the same, and of the purpose thereof, has been given in the manner in which notices of meetings of such local authority are usually given, and the fact that such a resolution was duly passed must be proved by furnishing a certificate signed by the secretary or clerk to such local authority embodying copies of the notice and of the resolution, and certifying that the notice was duly given and the resolution duly passed.

Rule VIII. In any case where a local authority, company, or person is required by the Act* to give notice to the local authority of the district, "in such manner as the Board of Trade may direct or approve," such notice shall be given in writing, and shall be served, either by leaving the same at the offices of the said local authority on or before the appointed day, or by forwarding the same by post in a registered letter, so that the same would in ordinary course of post be delivered on or before the appointed day.

* See s. 13.

Procedure.

Rule IX. Applicants for a licence or Provisional Order must proceed as follows, *subject in the case of a licence to the application having been previously entertained by the Board of Trade, vide Rule I.;*

They shall publish notice by advertisement of their application, or in the case of a Provisional Order, of their intended application, and every such advertisement shall contain the following particulars:—

1. The objects of the application.
2. Address and description of applicants.
3. A general description of the nature of the proposed works.
4. A description of the proposed area of supply.
5. The names of the streets and other places in, over, or along which it is proposed to place any electric lines or other works.
6. A list of the streets not repairable by a local authority, and of the railways and tramways (if any) which the applicants propose to take powers by the licence or order to break up.

7. A list of the canals and navigable rivers which the undertakers will be empowered under the licence or order to cross.

8. An office in London, and another office within the proposed area of supply, at which printed copies of the draft licence or order when applied for, and of the licence or order when made, can be obtained at a price of not more than one shilling each.

The advertisement is to be headed with a short title, descriptive of the undertaking (corresponding with that at the head of the memorial), and it must state that every local or other public authority, company, or person desirous of making any representation to the Board of Trade, or of bringing before them any objection respecting the application, may do so by letter addressed to the Board of Trade, marked on the outside of the cover enclosing it, "Electric Lighting Act," within two months from the date of the newspaper containing the first advertisement.

The advertisement is to be inserted, once at least in each of two successive weeks in one and the same newspaper, published and circulating in the proposed area of supply, or in such other newspaper as the Board of Trade may direct; and once at least in the London, Edinburgh, or Dublin Gazette, accordingly as the proposed area of supply is situate in England, Scotland, or Ireland.

Rule X. In all cases of applications for a licence, renewal of licence, or provisional order to which objection is made by any person locally interested, the Board of Trade will, if either the applicants or the objectors so desire, hold a local inquiry of which due notice will be given.

Rule XI. If any local or other public authority, company, or person desires to have any clauses or other amendments inserted in the licence or order, they must deliver the same to the parliamentary agents or solicitors for the order, and also to the Board of Trade on or before the time limited for bringing objections.

Rule XII. When a licence or provisional order is ready, and before the same is delivered, the applicants must deposit at the office of the Board of Trade a description of the lands (if any) which they propose to purchase for the purposes of the licence or provisional order, and must produce to the Board of Trade the contracts for the purchase of all such lands.

Rule XIII. When a licence or provisional order has been made by the Board of Trade and delivered to the applicants, they shall forthwith deposit printed copies for public inspection in the offices specified in Rule V., and shall supply copies to all persons applying for the same, and shall further publish the same as the Board of Trade may direct.

Special Provisions as to Provisional Orders.

Rule XIV. In the case of provisional orders the following additional regulations must be observed :—

1. The advertisements must be inserted in *October* or *November*.
2. A copy of the advertisement and map must be deposited *on or before the 30th November*, in the offices specified in Rule V., and at the Board of Trade.
3. The memorial must be lodged on or before 21*st December*.
4. The parliamentary agents or solicitors for the order must be prepared to prove compliance with the provisions of the Act and these rules by the 25th January, and all such proofs must be completed on or before the 25th February. Six days' notice will be given of the day and hour at which such agents or solicitors are to attend for the purpose at the Board of Trade, and printed forms of proof will accompany the notice. These forms should be filled up and brought with the requisite documents to the Board of Trade at the time fixed for receiving proof.

T. H. Farrer,

The Board of Trade, Secretary.
        October, 1882.

NOTE.—*These Rules are with the following exceptions the same as those issued in August last.*

Rule V. The words " the lands which the applicants propose to take for the purposes of the licence or order " have been omitted.

Rule IX. The wording of the first few lines of this Rule have been altered in order to make its meaning more clear.

APPENDIX.

TABLE OF PLACES TO WHICH THE MUNICIPAL CORPORATIONS ACT, 1882, APPLIES.

[*The* Figure *on the left-hand side denotes the Year in which the Place became subject to the Act of* 1835.

The Figure *on the right-hand side denotes the number of* Councillors, *a division of which number by* Three *will give the number of* Aldermen. *A* Second Figure, *if any, denotes the number of* Wards, *if any.*

Of the Letters *on the right-hand side,* P. *denotes "Parliamentary Borough" (including in that expression a part Parliamentary Borough),* Q. *that the Borough has a separate Court of Quarter Sessions, and* S. *that the Borough has a separate Commission of the Peace.*]

1862. Aberavon. 12. P. S.
1835. Aberystwith. 12. S.
1835. Abingdon. 12. P. Q. S.
1862. Accrington. 24 ; 4. S.
1835. Andover. 12. P. Q. S.
1835. Arundel. 12.
1847. Ashton-under-Lyne. 24. P.

1882. Bacup.
1835. Banbury. 12. Q. S.
1869. Barnsley. 18 ; 6.
1835. Barnstaple. 18 ; 2. Q. S.
1867. Barrow. 24 ; 8.
1835. Basingstoke. 12.
1835. Bath. 42 ; 7. P. Q. S.
1868. Batley. 18 ; 3.
1835. Beaumaris. 12.
1835. Beccles. 12.
1835. Bedford. 18 ; 2. Q. S.
1835. Berwick - on - Tweed. 18. Q. S.
1835. Beverley. 18. S.
1835. Bewdley. 12. P. Q. S.
1835. Bideford. 12. Q. S.
1877. Birkenhead. 42 ; 8.
1838. Birmingham. 48 ; 16. P. Q. S.
1851. Blackburn. 42 ; 7.
1875. Blackpool. 21 ; 6.
1835. Blandford. 12.
1835. Bodmin. 12.
1838. Bolton. 48 ; 9. P. Q. S.
1868. Bootle. 18 ; 3.
1835. Boston. 18 ; 2. P. S.

1848. Bradford. 48 ; 9. P. Q. S.
1835. Brecon. 12. S.
1835. Bridgnorth. 12. P. Q. S.
1835. Bridgwater. 18 ; 2. S.
1835. Bridport. 18 ; 2. P. S.
1854. Brighton. 39; 7. P. Q. S.
1835. Bristol. 48 ; 13. P. Q. S.
1835. Buckingham. 12. Q. S.
1861. Burnley. 24 ; 8. P.
1878. Burslem 15 ; 3.
1878. Burton. 24 ; 4.
1876. Bury. 18 ; 3. P.
1835. Bury St. Edmunds. 33 ; 5. Q. S.

1835. Calne. 12. P.
1835. Cambridge. 30 ; 5. P. Q. S.
1835. Canterbury. 18 ; 3. P. Q. S.
1835. Cardiff. 30 ; 5. P. S.
1835. Cardigan. 12. P.
1835. Carlisle. 30 ; 5. P. Q. S.
1835. Carmarthen. 18 ; 2. P. Q. S.
1835. Carnarvon. 18. P. S.
1835. Chard. 12.
1876. Cheltenham. 18 ; 6. P.
1835. Chester. 30 ; 5. P. Q. S.
1835. Chesterfield. 12. S.
1835. Chichester. 18 ; 2. P. Q. S.
1835. Chippenham. 12. P.
1835. Chipping Norton. 12.
1835. Chipping Wycombe. 18. P.
1881. Chorley. 24 ; 4.
1835. Clitheroe. 12. P. S.

1835. Colchester. 18; 3. P. Q. S.
1835. Congleton. 18; 3. S.
1876. Conway. 12. P.
1835. Coventry. 30; 5. P. S.
1877. Crewe. 18; 3.

1867. Darlington. 18; 6. P. S.
1835. Dartmouth. 12. Q. S.
1835. Daventry. 12.
1835. Deal. 18; 2. P. Q. S.
1835. Denbigh. 12. P. S.
1835. Derby. 48; 8. P. Q. S.
1835. Devizes. 18; 2. P. Q. S.
1837. Devonport. 36; 6. P. Q. S.
1862. Dewsbury. 18; 3. P.
1835. Doncaster. 18; 3. Q. S.
1835. Dorchester. 12. P. S.
1835. Dover. 18; 3. P. Q. S.
1835. Droitwich. 12. P.
1865. Dudley. 30; 7. P.
1864. Dunstable. 12.
1835. Durham. 18; 3. P. S.

1835. Evesham. 12. P. S.
1835. Exeter. 42; 7. P. Q. S.
1835. Eye. 12. P.

1835. Falmouth. 12. S.
1835. Faversham. 12. Q. S.
1835. Flint. 12. P.
1835. Folkestone. 12; 3. P. Q. S.

1835. Gateshead. 30; 5. P. S.
1835. Glastonbury. 12.
1866. Glossop. 18; 3.
1835. Gloucester. 27; 4. P. Q. S.
1835. Godalming. 12.
1835. Godmanchester. 12. P.
1835. Grantham. 12; 2. P. Q. S.
1835. Gravesend. 18; 2. P. S.
1835. Grimsby. 24; 4. P. S.
1835. Guildford. 12. P. Q. S.

1848. Halifax. 30; 10. P.
1857. Hanley. 18; 3.
1851. Hartlepool. 12. P.
1835. Harwich. 12. P. S.
1835. Hastings. 18; 6. P. Q. S.
1835. Haverfordwest. 12. P. S.
1860. Hedon. 9.
1835. Helston. 12. P. Q. S.
1835. Hereford. 18; 3. P. Q. S.
1835. Hertford. 12. P. S.
1881. Heywood. 18; 3.
1846. Honiton. 18.
1865. Huddersfield. 42; 12. P.
1835. Hull. 42; 7. P. Q. S.
1835. Huntingdon. 12. P.

1881. Hyde. 18; 3.
1835. Hythe. 12; 4. P. Q. S.

1835. Ipswich. 17; 5. P. Q. S.

1875. Jarrow. 18; 4.

1882. Keighley. 18; 6.
1835. Kendal. 18; 3. P. S.
1835. Kidderminster. 18; 2. P. S.
1835. King's Lynn. 18; 3. P. Q. S.
1835. Kingston-upon-Thames. 24; 4. S.

1835. Lancaster. 18. S.
1835. Launceston. 12. P.
1875. Leamington. 18.
1835. Leeds. 48; 16. P. Q. S.
1835. Leicester. 42; 7. P. Q. S.
1835. Leominster. 12. P. S.
1881. Lewes. 18. P.
1835. Lichfield. 18. P. Q. S.
1835. Lincoln. 18; 3. P. Q. S.
1835. Liskeard. 12. P. S.
1835. Liverpool. 48; 16. P. Q. S.
1835. Llandovery. 12.
1835. Llanidloes. 12.
1865. Longton. 18; 3.
1835. Louth. 18. S.
1835. Ludlow. 12. P. Q. S.
1876. Luton. 18; 3.
1835. Lyme Regis. 12.
1835. Lymington. 12. P.

1835. Macclesfield. 36; 6. P.
1835. Maidenhead. 12.
1835. Maidstone. 18; 4. P. Q. S.
1835. Maldon. 12. P. Q. S.
1838. Manchester. 48; 15. P. Q. S.
1857. Margate. 12; 4. Q. S.
1835. Marlborough. 12. P.
1853. Middlesborough. 30. P.
1835. Monmouth. 12.
1835. Morpeth. 12. P.

1835. Neath. 12.
1835. Newark. 18; 3. P. Q. S.
1835. Newbury. 18; 2. Q. S.
1835. Newcastle - under - Lyme. 18; 2. P. Q. S.
1835. Newcastle - upon - Tyne. 48; 9. P. Q. S.
1835. Newport (I. of W.). 18; 2. P. S.
1835. Newport (Mon.). 24; 4.
1835. Northampton. 18; 3. P. Q. S.

1835. Norwich. 48; 8. P. Q. S.
1835. Nottingham. 48; 16. P. Q. S.

1849. Oldham. 24; 8. P.
1835. Oswestry. 18. Q. S.
1878. Over Darwen. 18; 6.
1835. Oxford. 30; 5. P. Q. S.

1835. Pembroke. 18; 2. P. S.
1835. Penryn. 12. P.
1835. Penzance. 18; 2. Q. S.
1874. Peterborough. 18; 3. P.
1835. Plymouth. 36; 6. P. Q. S.
1835. Pontefract. 18. P. Q. S.
1835. Poole. 18; 2. P. Q. S.
1835. Portsmouth. 42; 6. P. Q. S.
1835. Preston. 33; 6. P. S.
1835. Pwllheli. 12. P.

1835. Reading. 18; 3. P. Q. S.
1863. Reigate. 18; 2.
1835. Retford. 18; 3. P. Q. S.
1835. Richmond. 12. P. Q. S.
1835. Ripon. 12. P. S.
1835. Rochester. 18; 3. P. Q. S.
1856. Rochdale. 30; 10. P. S.
1835. Romsey. 12. S.
1871. Rotherham. 18; 6.
1835. Ruthin. 12. P.
1868. Ryde. 18; 2.
1835. Rye. 12. P. Q. S.

1835. Saffron Walden. 12. Q. S.
1835. St. Alban's. 12. S.
1868. St. Helen's. 18; 6.
1835. St. Ives' (Cornwall). 12. P. S.
1874. St. Ives' (Huntingdon). 12.
1844. Salford. 38; 12. P.
1835. Salisbury. 18. P. Q. S.
1835. Sandwich. 12. P. Q. S.
1835. Scarborough. 18; 2. P. Q. S.
1835. Shaftesbury. 12. P.
1843. Sheffield. 48; 9. P.
1835. Shrewsbury. 30; 5. P. Q. S.
1835. South Molton. 12.
1850. South Shields. 24; 3. P.
1835. South Wold. 12.

1835. Southampton. 30; 5. P. Q. S.
1867. Southport. 30; 6.
1835. Stafford. 30; 2. P. S.
1835. Stamford. 18; 2. P. Q. S.
1857. Staylybridge. 24. 4.
1835. Stockport. 39; 6. P. S.
1835. Stockton-on-Tees. 24; 4. P. S.
1874. Stoke-upon-Trent. 18; 3.
1835. Stratford-upon-Avon. 18; 3.
1835. Sudbury. 12. Q. S.
1835. Sunderland. 48; 9. P. S.
1835. Swansea. 18; 4. P. S.

1835. Tamworth. 12. P.
1877. Taunton. 18; 3. P.
1835. Tenby. 12.
1835. Tenterden. 12. Q. S.
1835. Tewkesbury. 12. P. Q. S.
1835. Thetford. 12. Q. S.
1835. Tiverton. 18. P. Q. S.
1835. Torrington. 12.
1835. Totnes. 12.
1835. Truro. 18; 2. P. S.
1849. Tynemouth. 18; 3. P.

1848. Wakefield. 24; 7. P.
1835. Wallingford. 12. P.
1835. Walsall. 18. P. Q. S.
1847. Warrington. 27; 5. P.
1835. Warwick. 18; 2. P. Q. S.
1835. Wells. 12. S.
1835. Welshpool. 12. P. S.
1835. Wenlock. 18; 3. P. S.
1835. Weymouth. 18; 2. P. S.
1835. Wigan. 30; 5. P. Q. S.
1835. Winchester. 18; 3. P. Q. S.
1835. Windsor. 18; 2. P. Q. S.
1835. Wisbech. 18; 2.
1848. Wolverhampton. 36; 8. P. Q. S.
1835. Worcester. 36; 5. P. Q. S.
1857. Wrexham. 12. P.

1835. Yarmouth. 36; 6. Q. S.
1854. Yeovil. 12.
1835. York. 36; 6. Q. S.

TABLE OF STATUTES UNDER WHICH THE TOWN COUNCIL OF A BOROUGH HAS SPECIAL JURISDICTION.

Adulteration—38 & 39 Vict. c. 63 (Sale of Food and Drugs Act, 1875). By sect. 10 of this Act the town council "of every borough, having a separate Court of Quarter Sessions, or having under general or local Act of Parliament, or otherwise a separate police establishment," may, and if required by the Local Government Board, must, appoint one or more persons as analysts of all articles of food and drugs sold within the borough.

Baths and Washhouses—9 & 10 Vict. c. 74; 10 & 11 Vict. c. 61; and 41 Vict. c. 14. By 9 & 10 Vict. c. 74, these Acts may be "adopted" by the town council of any borough for the establishment and management of baths and washhouses therein; the expenses being chargeable on the borough fund.

Burial—17 & 18 Vict. c. 87, ss. 1, 2; 20 & 21 Vict. c. 81, s. 29. By these Acts the town council may be appointed a burial board by Order in Council; and as to expenses, borrowing powers and accounts, see 20 & 21 Vict. c. 81, ss. 22, 29; and 17 & 18 Vict. c. 87.

Cattle Plague—41 & 42 Vict. c. 74 (Contagious Diseases (Animals) Act, 1878). By sect. 9 and sched. 2 of this Act the town council is constituted the local authority for carrying out this Act, the expenses to be chargeable on the borough rate, and the town clerk to be the clerk.

Dogs.—34 & 35 Vict. c. 56 (Dogs Act, 1871). By sect. 3 of this Act the town council may, "if a mad dog or dog suspected of being mad is found within their jurisdiction," make "an order placing such restrictions as they think expedient on all dogs not being under the control of any person."

Education—39 & 40 Vict. c. 79 (Elementary Education Act, 1876). By sect. 7 of this Act the town council is constituted, in school districts not being within the jurisdiction of a school board, the local authority, or "school attendance committee," to "consist of not less than six nor more than twelve members of the council," having the duties of enforcing the Act respecting the employment of children; of complaining to the Education Department of any breach of the regulations of sect. 7 of the Education Act, 1870, as to the conduct of a public elementary school (sect. 7); of complaining to a court of summary jurisdiction of the non-attendance of children (sect. 11); and the power of making bye-laws (sect. 21).

Explosive Substances—38 Vict. c. 17 (Explosives Act, 1875). By sect. 67 of this Act the town council of any borough not being assessed to the county rate (see sect. 150 of the Act of 1882, p. 83, *ante*,) is, and the town council of every other borough may become, by order of a Secretary of State, on the application of the council, the local authority for assenting to or dissenting from the grant of a licence by the Secretary of State for a new factory or magazine for gunpowder or other explosives (sect. 6); for granting a store licence for gunpowder or other explosives (sect. 17); for providing magazines in special cases (sect. 72); and for enforcing a general power of search for explosives (sects. 73, 74), the expenses being chargeable on the borough fund or rate (sect. 70).

Gardens—26 & 27 Vict. c. 13. By this Act enclosed gardens or ornamental ground in any public square, &c., if neglected, may be taken care of by the town council at the expense of the borough.

Labourers' Dwellings—14 & 15 Vict c. 34 (Labouring Classes Lodging-Houses Act, 1851); 29 Vict. c. 28; 30 & 31 Vict. c. 28 (Labouring Classes Dwelling Houses Acts, 1866 and 1867); 31 & 32 Vict. c. 130 (Artizans and Labourers' Dwellings Act, 1868) (amended by 42 & 43 Vict. c. 64, and 45 & 46 Vict. c. 54); 38 & 39 Vict. c. 36 (Artizans and Labourers' Dwellings Improvement Act, 1875) (amended by 42 & 43 Vict. c. 63, and 45 & 46 Vict. c. 54).

The Acts of 1851, 1866 and 1867 may be "adopted" by the town council of any borough as an urban sanitary authority. Upon the adoption of the Act, corporate land may be appropriated and lodging-houses erected thereon, or money may be borrowed for the purposes of the Act.

The Act of 1868 and its amending Acts constitute the town councils, as urban sanitary authorities, local authorities to take down or improve *separate* dwellings unfit for human habitation, and to build and maintain better dwellings in lieu thereof.

The Act of 1875 and its amending Acts, which apply only to boroughs having a population of 25,000 and upwards, empower the town council, as urban sanitary authority, to frame "schemes" for the improvement of a *body of* houses, courts, or alleys within particular areas.

Libraries—18 & 19 Vict. c. 70 ; 29 & 30 Vict. c. 114 ; 40 & 41 Vict. c. 54 (the Public Libraries Acts of 1855, 1866 and 1877). These Acts may be "adopted" in any borough by a majority of two-thirds of the burgesses present at a meeting to be convened by the mayor on the request of the town council or any ten ratepayers. By the Act of 1877 the opinions of the ratepayers may be ascertained by voting papers. Upon the Act being adopted, free libraries may be established and maintained by the town council at the expense of the borough, the rate not to exceed one penny in the pound.

Lunatic Asylums—16 & 17 Vict. c. 97 (Lunatic Asylums Act, 1853); 18 & 19 Vict. c. 105. By sect. 8 of the Act of 1853, a borough may, on resolution of the town council, establish a separate lunatic asylum; and by sect. 129 the duties of visiting justices may be transferred to the town council.

Markets—10 & 11 Vict. c. 14 (the Markets and Fairs Clauses Act, 1847); 38 & 39 Vict. c. 55 (the Public Health Act, 1875), s. 167. Sect. 167 of the Act of 1875 incorporates sects. 12—16 and sects. 21—41 of the Act of 1847, which relate to the holding of the market, weighing goods and carts, and stallages, rents, and tolls.

Nuisances—38 & 39 Vict. c. 55 (Public Health Act, 1875), s. 91.

Sanitary Matters—Public Health Act, 1875.

School Attendance—See **Education**.

Slaughter-Houses—10 & 11 Vict. c. 34 (the Towns Improvement Act, 1847); 38 & 39 Vict. c. 55 (the Public Health Act, 1875). The 169th section of the Act of 1875 incorporates sects. 125—131 with respect to slaughter-houses.

Weights and Measures—41 Vict. c. 49 (Weights and Measures Act, 1878). By sects. 43 and 63 of this Act the town council of a borough having a separate court of quarter sessions, and, by resolution, the town council of any borough, are the local authority for appointing inspectors of weights and measures.

STANDING ORDERS OF THE HOUSE OF COMMONS HAVING SPECIAL REFERENCE TO MUNICIPAL CORPORATIONS (a).

24. . . . . In cases of Bills whereby it is proposed to alter or extend the municipal boundary of any city, borough, or urban sanitary district, a map on a scale of not less then three inches to a mile, and also a duplicate thereof, showing as well the present boundaries of the city, borough, or urban sanitary district as the boundaries of the proposed extension, shall be deposited with the town clerk of such city or borough, or clerk of such urban sanitary district, who shall at all seasonable hours of the day permit any person to view and examine such map, and to make copies thereof.

Map and duplicate to be deposited with town clerk, &c., in case of alteration of municipal boundaries.

134. It shall be competent to the referees on private Bills to admit the petitioners, being the municipal or other authority having the local management of the metropolis, or of any town, or the inhabitants of any town or district alleged to be injuriously affected by a Bill, to be heard against such Bill, if they shall think fit.

Municipal authorities may be allowed locus standi against any bill.

134a. The municipal or other local authority of any town or district alleging in their petition that such town or district may be injuriously affected by the provisions of any Bill relating to the lighting or water supply thereof, or the raising of capital for any such purpose, shall be entitled to be heard against such Bill.

Municipal authorities entitled to locus standi against lighting and water bills.

Tramway Bills.

171. No powers shall be given to any municipal corporation, local board, improvement commissioners, or other local authority, to place or run carriages upon any tramway, and to demand and take tolls and charges in respect of the use of such carriages.

No powers to be given to local authorities to place or run carriages upon tramways.

(a) See also S. O. 22, as to consent to tramway bills, and S. O. 33, as to deposit at Local Government Board Office of bills promoted by municipal corporations.

Local Government.

Estimates of proposed application of money borrowed by local authorities in certain cases to be recited in Bill and proved before select committee.

172. In the case of all Bills whereby any municipal corporation, local board, improvement commissioners, or other local authority in England or Wales, are authorized to borrow money for any purpose to which the several Acts specified in Part I. of the schedule to the Local Government Board Act, 1871, relate, without the sanction of the Local Government Board, estimates showing the proposed application of the money for permanent works within the meaning of the 57th section of the Local Government Act, 1858, or as defined by any subsequent Acts, shall be recited in the Bill as introduced into Parliament and proved before the select committee to which the Bill is referred.

Committee to consider clauses of Bill in reference to various matters affecting local government, &c., and report thereon.

173a. In the case of any Bill promoted by or conferring powers on a municipal corporation or local board, improvement commissioners, town commissioners or other local authority, or public body having powers of local government or rating, the committee on the Bill shall consider the clauses of the Bill with reference to the following matters :—

(a.) Whether the Bill gives powers relating to police or sanitary regulations in conflict with, deviation from, or excess of the provisions or powers of the general law.

(b.) Whether the Bill gives powers which may be obtained by means of bye-laws made subject to the restrictions of general Acts already existing.

(c.) Whether the Bill assigns a period for repayment of any loan under the Bill exceeding the term of sixty years, which term the committee shall not in any case allow to be exceeded, or any period disproportionate to the duration of the works to be executed or other objects of the loan.

(d.) Whether the Bill gives borrowing powers for purposes for which such powers already exist, or may be obtained under general Acts without subjecting the exercise of the powers under the Bill to approval from time to time by the proper Government department.

And the committee shall report specially to the House:—

> In what manner any clauses relating to the several matters aforesaid have been dealt with by the committee; and

> Whether any report from any Government department relative to the Bill has been referred to the committee; and

> If so, in what manner the recommendations in that report have been dealt with by the committee; and

> Any other circumstances of which in the opinion of the committee it is desirable that the House should be informed:

And the report of the committee shall be printed, and shall be circulated with the votes.

INDEX.

———

ABATEMENT of election petition, by death of petitioner, 51.

ABSENCE,
    disqualification of mayor, by two months', 24.
        of councillor, by six months', 24.
    of mayor or deputy mayor at council meeting, 144.
    of recorder or deputy recorder at sessions, 92.

ABSTRACT,
    of annual returns by Local Government Board, 17.
        submission of, to Parliament, 17.
    of accounts, by treasurer, 17.
        may be inspected and copied, 126.

ACCOUNTABILITY of officers, 12.

ACCOUNTS,
    treasurer to make up, half-yearly, 16.
        to submit, for audit, 17.
        to print abstract, 17.
    penalty on officer not delivering, 13.
    may be inspected by council, 126.
        and copied by any councillor, 126.

ACT OF PARLIAMENT,
    local saving for, 134. And see LOCAL ACT.
    schedule of repealed Acts, 139.
        of Acts repealed as to boroughs within Act of 1882..141.

ACTION,
    for penalty on unqualified person acting in office, 25.
    for act done in execution of Act, 121.
        must be commenced in six months, 121.
        tender of amends, 121.
        payment of costs of defendant officer out of borough fund, 122.

ADULTERATION, expenses incurred in detecting, not "general county purposes," 84.

ADVERTISEMENT, newspaper proprietor inserting, for council, not disqualified, 8.

ADVOWSON, obligations and powers of corporation in respect of, 65.

AFFIRMATION in lieu of oath, 128.

L.C.   A A

INITIALS, sufficient description of Christian name by, 129.

INJUNCTION restraining council from declaring a corporate office vacant, 24.

INN, recorder may not grant licence, 92. See INTOXICATING LIQUOR.

INSANITY, exemption for, from obligation to accept office, 22.

INSOLVENCY, avoidance of office by, 24. See BANKRUPTCY.

INSPECTION,
of minutes of proceedings of council, 126.
by any burgess on payment of one shilling, 126.
of treasurer's accounts, 126.
general provisions as to, 126.

INTEREST,
disqualification by, for being elected councillor, 8.
of councillor from voting by, 14.

INTERPRETATION CLAUSE,
of the Act of 1882..2.
of Part IV. as to "Corrupt Practices," 39.

INTOXICATING LIQUORS,
explanation of terms "town corporate," &c., in Licensing Act, 1828..131.
they include boroughs having separate commission of the peace, 131.
recorder may not grant licence to sell, 92.
stipendiary magistrate may, 89.
power of Vice-Chancellor of Cambridge in granting licences, 133.

JURISDICTION,
of borough quarter sessions, 91.
of borough civil court, 99.

JURIES,
every burgess qualified and liable to serve on, 100.
unless by law exempt or disqualified, 100.
summoning of sufficient grand jurors, 100.
of petty jurors, 100.
mode of service of summons, 100.
lists of persons summoned, 100.
no person to be summoned more than once a year, 100.
fine for non-attendance, 101.
levy of fine by distress, 101.
Juries Act, 1870, unaffected, 101.
exemptions and disqualifications, 101.

JUSTICE, administration of, 82—85.

JUSTICES OF THE PEACE,
jurisdiction of county justices, 85. See COUNTY JUSTICES.
separate commission of peace for borough, 86.
Queen may grant on petition of council, 86.
appointment thereupon of borough justices, 86.

LOANS,
  corporation may raise on security of land, 56.
  provisions for repayment of, 59.
    sinking fund, 60.
  council may raise for municipal buildings, 64.
    for sanitary purposes, 310.

LOCAL ACTS,
  transfer of powers under paving, lighting, &c., 74.
    to corporation by trustees under the Acts, 74.
    trustees not bound to make transfer, 74.
    nor council bound to accept it, 74.
  power for council to extend Lighting Act, 75.
  exercise of powers under, generally, 75.
  general saving for effect of, 134.

LOCAL GOVERNMENT BOARD,
  approval of bye-laws against nuisances by, 15.
  of dates up to which accounts to be made by, 16.
  annual returns to, of receipts and expenditure, 17.

LUNACY,
  exemption by, from obligation to serve office, 22.

MAGISTRATE,
  jurisdiction of county, in borough, 85. See COUNTY JUS-
    TICES.
  appointment of borough justices, 86. See JUSTICES OF
    THE PEACE.
  appointment and powers of stipendiary, 88. See STIPEN-
    DIARY MAGISTRATE.

MANDAMUS,
  to mayor, to insert name in burgess list, 28.
    limit of time for application, 28.
    inquiry into title by court, 28.
  notice of, to party affected, 121.
  may be peremptory in first instance, 121.
  to hold election, 37.

MARRIAGE,
  succession to qualifying property by, 21.
  occupancy by predecessor equivalent to occupancy of suc-
    cessor, 21.

MARRIED WOMAN, not entitled to be enrolled as burgess,
  35. See WOMAN.

MAYOR,
  qualification and term of office of, 10.
  salary and precedence of, 10.
  power of, to appoint deputy, 11.
  appointment of auditor by, 16.
  time and mode of election of, 34.
  an ex-officio borough justice, 86.
    unless disqualified to be mayor, 86.

L.C.   B B

QUORUM,
    of councillors, at council meeting, 144.
    of watch committee, 103.

RATE,
    borough rate, 78.
    watch rate, 106.
    county rate, 83. See BOROUGH RATE, &c.
    special, power to continue, 66.
    qualification by, for enrolment as burgess, 4.
        for election as councillor, 7.
    corrupt payment of, punishable as bribery, 269.

RATEPAYERS,
    consent of, to promoting or opposing bill, 301.
        mode of ascertaining consent, 313.

RECORDER,
    Queen may appoint, in quarter sessions borough, 89.
    must be a barrister of five years' standing, 89.
    holds office during good behaviour, 90.
    is a borough justice ex officio, 90.
    must take oaths and make declaration, 90.
        what oaths, 87.
        form of declaration, 158.
    has precedence next after mayor, 90.
    may serve in Parliament, except for the borough, 90.
    may not be councillor or stipendiary magistrate for the
      borough, 90.
    salary of, 90.
        on increase of, no re-appointment necessary, 90.
    may act for two or more boroughs conjointly, 90.
    must hold sessions quarterly, or oftener, 91.
    has jurisdiction of county sessions, 91.
        except as to rates, 91.
        or licences to keep an inn, &c., 91.
    may appoint deputy in case of illness or absence, 92. See
      DEPUTY.
    may form second court, if sessions likely to last more than
      three days, 93. See SECOND COURT.
    is judge of borough civil court, 96.

RELIEF, PAROCHIAL, disqualification for franchise by receipt
    of, 5.

RELIEVING OFFICER, attendance of, before revising bar-
    rister, 179, 186.

REPEAL,
    of Acts in schedule 2.
        schedule of repealed Acts, 139.
        savings from repeal, 137.

RESIDENCE, qualification for franchise by, 5.

RESIGNATION of corporate office on payment of fine, 23.

RESPONDENT,
    to election petition, who may be made, 43.
        two or more to same petition, 45.

SUMMONS,
  service and execution of, outside borough, 120.
  to council meeting, nature and service of, 144.

SUNDAY, exclusion of, in computation of time, 125.

SURGICAL ASSISTANCE from municipal charity, no disfranchisement, 211.

TABLES,
  of boroughs subject to Act of 1882..343.
  of statutes, 346.
  of contents of Act of 1882, xxix.

TIME,
  computation of, 125.
  Greenwich time to be kept, 31, note (a).

TOWN CLERK,
  appointment of, by council, 11.
    may not be member of council, 11.
    may not be treasurer, 12.
  security by, and remuneration of, 12.
  holds office during pleasure of council, 11.
    vacancy to be filled in twenty-one days, 11.
  has charge of charters, deeds, &c., 11.
  must make returns of receipts and expenditure to Local
    Government Board, 17.
    penalty for not making returns, 17.
  examination by, of burgess list, 27.
  countersigning by, of order for payment of money out of
    borough fund, 77.
  where none, or incapable, mayor may appoint person to act
    for him, 26.
  return of fines by, 119.
  posting of fees by, 127.

TOWN COUNCIL, municipal corporation acts by, 6. See
  COUNCIL.

TOWN HALL,
  council may buy land for building, 55.
    may borrow money for, 55.
      may levy rate for, 64.
  mode of fixing notices on, 126.

TRADING, freedom of, notwithstanding custom or bye-law, 131.

TRANSITORY PROVISIONS,
  as to transactions before 1860..68.
    transfer of investments in names of trustees, 68.
    scheme respecting mortgage debts, 69.
    consolidation of debts, 70.
  as to transactions before 1835..70.
    saving for sales, &c. in pursuance of contracts, 70.
      for creditors in respect of tolls or dues, 70.
      for debts contracted before Act of 1835..71.
      against new liability to debts before Act of 1835..71.

WARD,
> where person elected in more than one, 36.
> making up of ward rolls, 27.
> division of borough into wards, 19.
>> on petition of two-thirds of council, 19.
> number of councillors in, divisible by three, 19.
> table showing number of wards in each borough, 343.
> division of, into polling districts, 35.
> at election, alderman returning officer, 30.

WARRANT,
> service or execution of, outside borough, 120.
> may not be removed by certiorari, 118.

WATCH COMMITTEE,
> council to appoint from time to time, 102.
>> not to be more than third of council, 102.
> may act by majority, with a quorum of three, 103.
> to appoint borough constables from time to time, 103.   See
> CONSTABLES.

WATCH RATE,
> power of council to levy, if leviable at commencement of
> Act, 106.
> not to exceed 8*d*. in the pound, 107.
> levy of, where part only of parish liable, 108.
>> appeal from rate, 108.
> warrant for, to be issued by mayor, 109.
> money raised by, to go to borough fund, 109.

WATERWORKS ACT,
> trustees under local, may transfer powers to corporation, 74.
> with consent of council only, 74.

WOMAN,
> right of, to vote, 35.
>> if unmarried, 35.

WORKING MEN'S DWELLINGS, conversion of corporate
land into sites for, 58.

LONDON : C. F. ROWORTH, PRINTER, BREAM'S BUILDINGS—E.C.